DEVELOPING MANAGERIAL SKILLS IN ENGINEERS AND SCIENTISTS

SUCCEEDING AS A TECHNICAL MANAGER

Van Nostrand Reinhold Series
in Managerial Skill Development
in Engineering and Science

DEVELOPING MANAGERIAL SKILLS IN ENGINEERS AND SCIENTISTS

SUCCEEDING AS A TECHNICAL MANAGER

M. K. Badawy, Ph.D.

Professor of Management and
Applied Behavioral Sciences
Cleveland State University

VNR VAN NOSTRAND REINHOLD COMPANY
NEW YORK   CINCINNATI   TORONTO   LONDON   MELBOURNE

Copyright © 1982 by Van Nostrand Reinhold Company Inc.

Library of Congress Catalog Card Number: 81-15921
ISBN: 0-442-20481-7

Manufactured in the United States of America

Published by Van Nostrand Reinhold Company Inc.
135 West 50th Street
New York, New York 10020

Van Nostrand Reinhold Company Limited
Molly Millars Lane
Wokingham, Berkshire RG11 2PY, England

Van Nostrand Reinhold
480 Latrobe Street
Melbourne, Victoria 3000, Australia

Macmillan of Canada
Division of Gage Publishing Limited
164 Commander Boulevard
Agincourt, Ontario MIS 3C7, Canada

15 14 13 12 11 10 9 8 7 6 5 4

Library of Congress Cataloging in Publication Data

Badawy, M. K.
    Developing managerial skills in engineers and
scientists: Succeeding as a Technical Manager

    (Van Nostrand Reinhold series in managerial
skill development in engineering and science)
    Includes index.
    1. Engineering—Management.   2. Research—Manage-
ment.   3. Executives.   I. Title.   II. Series.
TA190.B33   658'.0023'73   81-15921
ISBN 0-442-20481-7   AACR2

To Afaf,
who has made
the past memorable
the present exciting
and the future promising

**Van Nostrand Reinhold Series In
MANAGERIAL SKILL DEVELOPMENT
IN ENGINEERING AND SCIENCE**

M.K. Badawy, Series Editor

Developing Managerial Skills in Engineers and Scientists: Succeeding as a Technical Manager, by M.K. Badawy

Modern Management Techniques in Engineering and R&D, by J. Balderston, P. Birnbaum, R. Goodman, and M. Stahl

Series Introduction

Developing Managerial Skills in Engineers and Scientists: Succeeding as a Technical Manager is the first volume in the Van Nostrand Reinhold Series in Managerial Skills in Engineering and Science. The series will embody concise and practical treatments of specific topics within the broad area of engineering and R&D management. The primary aim of the series is to provide a set of principles, concepts, tools, and practical techniques for those wishing to enhance their managerial skills and potential.

The series will provide both practitioners and students with the information they must know and the skills they must acquire in order to sharpen their managerial performance and advance their careers. Authors contributing to the series are carefully selected for their experience and expertise. While series books will vary in subject matter as well as approach, one major feature will be common to all volumes: a blend of practical applications and hands-on techniques supported by sound research and relevant theory.

The target audience for the series includes engineers and scientists making the transition to management, technical managers and supervisors, upper-level executives and directors of engineering and R&D, corporate technical development managers and executives, continuing management education specialists, and students in technical management programs and related fields.

We hope that this dynamic series will help readers to become better managers and to lead most rewarding professional careers.

Preface

Developing Managerial Skills in Engineers and Scientists: Succeeding as a Technical Manager is addressed to engineers, scientists, technical executives, managers, supervisors, and students of engineering and R&D management who wish to become better managers. It is, for the most part, a book on managing rather than a book about management. It takes a broad view of managing as an occupation, a career, and a major concern for technical professionals and their employers—high-technology organizations.

The book seeks to develop a practical conceptual framework of the process of managing engineering and R&D functions, as well as to point out the avenues and options for developing or improving the managerial skills of technical people. As such, this book is intended not only for new and prospective managers, but also for those who have many years of experience in technical management.

This book has been written with the following objectives in mind:

1. to provide a self-development tool for would-be technical managers and for managers wishing to improve their knowledge and skills.
2. to provide a learning and development guide for technical managers for better career planning, development, and management.
3. to provide corporate planners, human resources development executives, and organization development specialists with a handy tool for effective management of organizational careers of professionals.
4. to provide a text for courses on engineering and R&D management, and career management, among others.

Why this approach? Like engineering and medicine, effective management requires both knowledge and practice. Knowledge without practice breeds a "blue-sky" theorist. Practice without knowledge breeds a trial-and-error layman. Knowledge *and* practice breed a well-grounded, competent practitioner. So one justification for this approach is that managing—like engineering and medicine—is an applied professional discipline in which theory and practice must be closely intertwined.

Most available books on technical management are either philosophical treatises that are out of touch with reality, or oversimplified cookbook-type manuals that are narrow in scope and superficial in treatment. Writing a different kind of book, one dealing with the nitty-gritty of what is encountered in the process of technical managing, was thus my prime objective. As a result, this book provides a relevant framework along with the tools necessary for succeeding in management.

This book is organized into eight parts. Part I, What It Takes to Make It in Management, consists of two chapters. After developing a conceptual framework of the skills and functions of management in Chapter 1, Chapter 2 deals with the nature, causes, and remedies of managerial failure.

The problems involved in the transformation of engineers and scientists into managers are discussed in Part II (Chapter 3). Part III points out ways in which companies, jointly with technologists, can ease the transition from technical to managerial careers (Chapters 4 and 5). The value and role of formal management education in developing management skills is discussed in Chapter 6.

Part IV addresses the technical supervisory functions and the special problems technical managers deal with in the course of doing their jobs (Chapter 7). How to develop administrative skills in the three functional areas of management (organizing, planning, and controlling) is the subject of Parts V, VI, and VII (Chapters 8-11). Finally, Part VIII presents some final thoughts and provides a comprehensive overview of the book (Chapter 12). It also provides you with an extensive list of the most modern and useful books and articles on managerial skill development in engineering and science (Chapter 13).

Writing this book was a complex undertaking in which many efforts and sacrifices were made by many people. First and foremost, my deepest appreciation goes to my wife—to whom this book is dedicated—for her love, contributions, encouragement, and support. Next, many technical managers and executives in a variety of organizations provided ideas, insight, and suggestions that contributed substantially to the development of the book. I am grateful to them all. My thanks also goes to Perry Pascarella and Tom Comella for their helpful suggestions. To Marion Bocian, who capably and patiently administered the word-processing phase of the project, I am most grateful. A special note of thanks and appreciation goes to Debbi Clark for typing most of the manuscript. Margaret Rothacker and Connie Reed, collaborated on parts of the typing chores—to them I am most appreciative.

I sincerely hope that this volume will prove to be a rich source of information for all who read it. While it does not provide pat answers and formulas, it does offer a distillation of principles that have made other managers and organizations successful, along with many examples of how the principles were applied in practice. It will provide you with the proper tools to guide you through the management jungle and to help make you a more effective manager. As a manager (or a potential manager), you must do what you are paid to do—manage. And this book, hopefully, will show you how.

M.K. Badawy
Willoughby, Ohio

Contents

DEVELOPING MANAGERIAL SKILLS IN ENGINEERS AND SCIENTISTS

SUCCEEDING AS A TECHNICAL MANAGER

PART I
WHAT IT TAKES TO
SUCCEED IN
MANAGEMENT

1
The Skills of Management

The need for management is universal. All organizations, large or small, share one thing in common: they need to be managed. This applies equally to the company, the engineering and R&D division or unit, the school, the police department, the church, and even the family, to name only a few. In every one of these institutions, resources must be managed so that organizational goals are achieved, whether these goals are to make a profit or to provide quality education to university students or to put a man on the moon. In short, the manager is the driving force, without his[1] services, resources would stay as they are—they would never become products or services. Managers, therefore, make things happen.

Similarly, engineering and R&D supervisors, managers, and executives are charged with managing the technical operation of a company. The organization, coordination, direction, allocation, and control of the resources at their disposal are their prime responsibilities. How well they perform these tasks will largely determine the firm's efficiency and effectiveness. Their efforts, like those of other functional units within the company, are directed toward the achievement of one thing: results. Thus, their contributions are measured accordingly.

If you are a scientist or an engineer and you spend your time on the job doing technical work, then you are a technologist or a specialist.[2] But if you spend your time supervising or managing engineering or R&D activities, you are a supervisor or a manager. In the former instance, you are doing things yourself, while in the latter you are getting them done through others. There is a world of difference between the two. Newly appointed technical managers are faced with many questions such as:

- What is management?
- What is a manager?

---

[1] Although I fully recognize that managers can be and often are women, for convenience I have used the masculine pronoun throughout the book to refer to both male and female managers.
[2] While there are important differences between engineers, scientists and technologists, the latter term is used here to broadly refer to all of these groups.

- What do managers do?
- How are managers different from nonmanagers?
- How are managers different from supervisors and executives?
- How are line managers different from staff managers?
- Are managers made or born?
- Is management a science or an art? Is it universal or limited to the scope of the organization?
- Are managerial skills learnable? Can they be developed?

Answering these questions, as well as others, and providing an overview of what is involved in the management of technical activities are the prime tasks of this chapter.

WHAT IS MANAGEMENT?

The literature on management is extensive.[3] Management has been viewed by scholars and practitioners as a discipline, an occupation, a profession, a system, and a process. Management is an established academic discipline, and undergraduate and graduate degrees in management are offered by many colleges and universities. Managers have come to be regarded as a class of professionals belonging to the many occupational and professional associations that cater to the needs of managers and promote their professional status. Moreover, management has been viewed as a system of inputs (resources and factors of production), processes (managerial tasks and activities), and outputs (products and services salable at a profit).

There is no scarcity of material on the principles, theories, and concepts of management. Indeed, there are almost as many definitions of management as there are writers in the field. No wonder some have considered the field of management theory a "jungle."[4] The area of engineering and R&D management, as a component of the broader field of management, is certainly no exception.

The confusion has been further compounded by management training and executive development seminars. Their emphasis has been primarily theoretical and has sought to increase managers' knowledge but not their ability to apply it. This book will present specific techniques to be used when you are faced with specific problems, and will show you how to use them.

We can now answer the question, what is management? As used herein, *management* is *the process of getting things done with and through others.* Our view is quite pragmatic: Managing is a task or an activity—a *process*—requiring the

---

[3] For purposes of designating reference material, every effort was made to avoid confusing multiple references. However, references to material mentioned in this book occasionally apply to different sections within the same chapter as well as to more than one chapter.
[4] Koontz, Harold. The Management Theory Jungle Revisited. *The Academy of Management Review,* 5, 2 (April 1980): 175-188.

performance of several *functions* by individuals possessing a specific set of *skills*. The central point is that these functions are performed through other people. So, management is what a manager does to get things done through others.

What, then, does the task of managing entail? Three elements stand out:

1. Management is a process comprised of several activities and tasks to be undertaken or accomplished: planning, organizing, directing and controlling. The essence of managing lies in the practice of these activities. Without undertaking these tasks, you are not a manager—you are a technician, a specialist, an expert, or a consultant serving in an advisory capacity.
2. The ultimate goal of managing is to achieve an objective. The process of management, therefore, is goal-directed. It is a means to an end (i.e., profitability and growth).
3. Managers are responsible for the performance of those working for them. They get paid not for what they do but for what their subordinates do. Technical managers, for example, are responsible for motivating engineers, scientists, and technicians to get the job done and to handle the engineering and R&D functions of the organization. The degree to which managers have to do things for themselves is the degree to which they have failed as managers.

In summary, any organization consisting of more than one individual needs a means of coordinating its efforts toward a common objective. This means is management, the process of getting things done with and through others. It involves the performance of several functions and requires the possession of a set of professional skills. While the term *management* is more commonly used in private enterprises and *administration* in public agencies, both terms will be used in this book interchangeably, reflecting the author's conviction of the universality of management theories and principles.

WHAT IS A MANAGER?

A manager is a person working for an organization who practices management, makes decisions, solves problems, and is responsible for the work of at least one other individual reporting to him. The ultimate goal of the manager of course, is, to help the organization achieve its objectives in a certain functional area, such as engineering, marketing, or manufacturing. Theoretically, three criteria must be met for one to be considered a manager:

1. A manager must practice management by performing a sequence of co-ordinated activities: planning, organizing, directing, and controlling.
2. A manager must get involved with managerial problem-solving and decision-making. Decision situations are choice situations with several available

options. It is the manager's responsibility, then, to evaluate the different options and make a choice.

3. The manager must have at least one individual reporting to him (this includes a secretary), because managing implies managing *someone*. Managers, thus, must guide, coach, and direct others.

According to management theory, if you do not meet these requirements, you are not a manager. Nevertheless, the word *manager* is used loosely in many organizations, and you will often encounter individuals not meeting all three conditions who are still considered managers. This certainly is not the only discrepancy between management practice and management theory. From a practical standpoint, however, the preceding criteria are sound, and they are used here to differentiate managers from nonmanagers.

Since a manager is a person who manages, the words *executive, manager,* or *supervisor* could be used interchangeably. The core difference between the three relates to the scope of the job to be performed.

Executives are those in the highest management level of an organization who are responsible for its overall direction and management. Chief executive officers, presidents, vice-presidents, and general managers are all executives. *Managers* are those usually charged with functional responsibilities but who do not directly supervise other professionals in the conduct of technical work. Middle-management members responsible for the engineering function, the sales function, the R&D function, or any other specific functions are all managers. *Supervisors* are those who directly supervise other professionals doing technical work. They are first-level management, and they work directly with the "troops." Engineering and R&D supervisors, foremen, and first-line supervisors are examples of first-level management. The relationships between these three management levels are shown in Figure 1-1.

WHAT DO MANAGERS DO?

Napoleon is reported to have said that there are no poor soldiers, only poor generals. An analogy can be drawn between generals and managers. If managers have excellent resources, but manage them poorly, they will get nothing but poor results.

What managers do depends partly on what level they are on. High-level executives typically spend more time on planning, goal-setting, and policymaking than do midlevel managers. Midlevel managers spend most of their time translating the plans and policies filtering from top management into departmental and functional goals, and coordinating activities between the various organizational units and divisions. Moreover, they spend less time making operating and technical decisions than do first-line supervisors (first-level management).

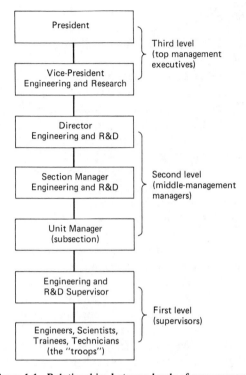

Figure 1-1. Relationships between levels of management.

Next, the nature of the managerial tasks and activities varies depending on the functional responsibility of the manager—for example, sales, engineering, production, or R&D.

Finally, what managers do also depends on whether they are serving in a line or staff capacity. Whereas the line manager has line authority and responsibility for a certain key organizational activity, the staff manager can only suggest, counsel, advise, or recommend certain courses of action to his associates in other divisions, who may accept or reject his recommendations. In a very fundamental sense, then, the staff expert has the right to advise or to provide a service for line managers. For example, the personnel manager has authority vis-à-vis other company divisions regarding employee recruiting and selection decisions.

In summary, your tasks and responsibilities as a manager depend on the management level you are on, the type of function you are in charge of, and the type of authority you have.

The process of managing involves the performance of certain functions. All managers have two types of responsibilities: (1) functional responsibilities and (2) directing people.

Functional Responsibilities

As shown in Figure 1-2, functional responsibilities constitute the administrative aspects of a manager's job. The performance of these tasks is essential to getting the job done. Every manager has three functional responsibilities:

1. *Planning.* Planning is the process of developing a philosophy of managing (i.e., management beliefs, values, and attitudes), setting objectives, establishing goals and devising short- and long-range strategies to achieve these objectives. Decision-making is also an integral part of the planning function which requires the identification of the options available in every functional area (i.e., marketing, engineering, production, R&D, and so on) and choosing between these options. In short, deciding on plans of action to guide the performance of major activities in accordance with company philosophy—"the way we do things around here"—is the essence of planning. It is inherently futuristic.

2. *Organizing.* The organizing function is the process of achieving coordinated effort through the creation of a structure of task and authority relationships. In other words, organizing is the process of dividing up the total organizational activities into tasks or jobs, and the determination of relationships (authority and responsibility network) among these tasks. In this sense, the structure of a division or unit is simply a means toward an end, a vehicle through which organizational and divisional objectives are achieved. In a very real sense, the organizational structure is the "harness" that helps employees pull together in performing according to corporate strategy, philosophy, and policies.

3. *Controlling and monitoring progress.* Controlling is the process of establishing standards of performance, evaluating actual performance against these

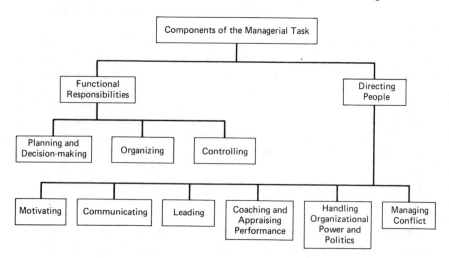

Figure 1-2. Functions and responsibilities of managers.

standards, and correcting deviations from standards and plans. The controlling function is an integral part of the management process and a twin function to the planning process; employing appropriate standards and getting continuous feedback are necessary if an organization's progress toward goal accomplishment is to be monitored.

Directing People

Effective handling of people—subordinates, supervisors, and associates—is the other major function of managers. Managers spend a significant portion of their time directing and coaching the people working for them, which calls for considerable skill in interpersonal relations. As shown in Figure 1-2, managers have six major responsibilities in this area:

1. *Motivating.* Motivating is the process of getting employees to perform the work assigned to them in a manner that meets or surpasses expected standards of performance. Because of the intrinsic nature of motivation, different schemes have to be employed with different groups of employees to stimulate performance and productivity. Fundamental to the success of any motivational plan is the extent to which the intended motivator meets the needs of the employees for whom it is designed.

2. *Communicating.* Communicating can be defined as the process of transmitting meaning to others—the process by which people exchange facts, ideas, and emotions. The key to managerial effectiveness is effective communication to the extent that one can safely say that management is communication. Obviously, the importance of communication goes well beyond management and organizations—it is a factor of enormous importance in every walk of life.

3. *Leading.* Leadership entails influencing a group's activities in order to accomplish certain goals. It involves the behavior of both leader and followers. In managerial leadership, one person exerts social influence over members of a group. While a manager might or might not be a leader, assuming a leadership role and serving as a model for his people to emulate can be quite helpful in accomplishing organizational and divisional objectives. In effect, whereas control focuses on the direction of human behavior, leadership is needed to cause individuals to perform in a desired manner. However, management and leadership are not synonymous. Leadership is simply a managerial style. A manager can be effective—and thus succeed—by adopting other managerial styles as long as they fit the requirements of the situation. Hence, managing is much broader than leading.

4. *Coaching and appraising performance.* Counseling, helping, and coaching employees is an important part of a manager's job. Appraising individual employee performance is also a significant managerial responsibility. These activi-

ties provide the basis for effective performance planning and employee development.

5. *Handling organizational power and politics.* Informal political systems and power structures are typical of organizational life. Learning how to handle organizational power and politics and survive is a crucial interpersonal skill every manager should have.

6. *Managing conflict.* Because of relatively limited resources, authority relationships, internal power struggles, and different individual motivations, conflict is usually a characteristic of interpersonal and interunit relationships within the organization. Resolving conflict, as well as using it constructively to produce new information and to strengthen relationships between individuals and groups, is an important managerial task. Conflict management, thus, is an interpersonal skill of enormous importance for managers at all organizational levels.

All managers perform similar duties in directing the resources for which they are accountable, subject, of course, to the previous qualifications concerning their functions, management level, and the type of authority they have. These duties, known as the functions of management, include planning, organizing, directing, and controlling. To the extent managers are unsuccessful in undertaking these duties, no results will be achieved since management is in the hands of "poor generals." The management process is further illustrated in Figure 1-3.

Figure 1-3. What do managers do?

MANAGERS IN ACTION: A REALISTIC VIEW?

Consider the following view of the function of an executive:

> As nearly everyone knows, an executive has practically nothing to do except to decide what is to be done; to tell somebody to do it; to listen to reasons why it should not be done, why it should be done by someone else, or why it should be done in a different way; to follow up to see if the thing has been done; to discover that it has not; to inquire why; to listen to excuses from the person who should have done it; to follow up again to see if the thing has been done, only to discover that it has been done incorrectly; to point out how it should have been done; to conclude that as long as it has been done it may as well be left where it is; to wonder if it is not time to get rid of a person who cannot do a thing right; to reflect that he probably has a wife and large family and certainly any successor would be just as bad or may be worse; to consider how much simpler and better the thing would have been done if he had done it himself in the first place; to reflect sadly that one could have done it right in twenty minutes, and; as things turned out, he has had to spend two days to find out why it has taken three weeks for somebody else to do it wrong.[5]

Ridiculous? Not at all. This kind of thing is going on in every organization with infinite variations. The sad fact is that there are an awful lot of managers who are utterly incompetent. Worse is the boss who puts up with this nonsense. So, watch out—your managerial performance is the total sum of what your subordinates can do.

MANAGEMENT AS A SCIENCE AND AN ART

Management, like engineering, is an applied art; unlike engineering, it is also a social science. There is a set of management principles, propositions, and foundations constituting the theory or the "science" of management. The field of management certainly offers the manager much less in the way of specific tools and techniques than physics or biology offers the physicist or the biologist. In this sense, management is not a pure science but an applied social science. Because of the nature of its subject matter—dealing with people in organizations—and the diversity of management problems and situations, the field of management just does not lend itself to the application of the scientific method as it would be impossible to develop causal relationships among the variables involved.

Moreover, the field of management has no bounds: It is an interdisciplinary field drawing heavily from social, behavioral, and natural sciences. Contributions to the field of management have come from other such disciplines as eco-

---

[5] Unknown source.

nomics (micro and macro), behavioral sciences (understanding human behavior and interpersonal relations in an organization); engineering (production scheduling, materials handling, methods improvement, research and development); mathematics (operations research and systems design); biology (systems approach); and accounting and statistics (management information systems and models). Perhaps this is why management has been labeled an "unsuccessful" science, as opposed to "successful" sciences like chemistry, physics, and physiology. The point is aptly made in the following quote:

> The unsuccessful sciences do not seem to equip students with a single social skill that is usable in ordinary human situations—no continuous and direct contract with the social facts is contrived for the student. He learns from books, spending endless hours in libraries; he reconsiders ancient formulae, uncontrolled by the steady development of experimental skill, the equivalent of the clinic or indeed of the laboratory.[6]

It follows that while the theory of management can be considered a science in a very limited sense, the practice of management certainly is an art. There is a body of knowledge—a set of principles, propositions and foundations—that constitute the theory of management. The practice of management, on the other hand, requires imagination, creativity, judgment, and experience.

THE UNIVERSALITY OF MANAGEMENT

As you might have guessed by now, while management theory and principles are universal, management practices are not. Although the principles of management are basically the same in different types of organizations and in different countries, managerial practices differ between organizations, between geographical regions in the same country, and certainly across cultures. Marked differences in decision-making, delegation, organizational structure, motivation, and communication have been reported—for example, between American management styles and those adopted by European, Japanese, and Middle Eastern managers.[7] Because the practice of management is an art, not a science, management is culture-bound. The creativity, imagination, judgment, values, and cultural background of managers have a significant impact on their management style. In short, while managerial principles and theories are transferable across organizations and cultures, managerial practices and skills must be tailored to fit certain situations and organizations.

---

[6] Mayo, Elton. "The Social Problems of an Industrial Civilization." Boston: Harvard Business School, 1945, p. 23.
[7] See, for example, Drucker, Peter F. Learning from Foreign Management. *The Wall Street Journal* (June 4, 1980); and Badawy, M. K. Managerial Styles of Mid-Eastern Executives. *California Management Review* (Spring 1980) pp. 51-58.

It is important to remember that management is partly a science and partly an art. *Scientific management,* brought to the scene early in this century by Frederick W. Taylor and his associates, was almost entirely an engineering achievement. Taylor, the father of the scientific management movement, believed that a scientific approach based on observation and experimentation was essential to management. The art of management, on the other hand, has been more highly developed by nonengineers.

Because of the differences in the subject matter, content, orientation, and skills between management on the one hand and engineering and science on the other hand, many technologists find the transition to management troublesome. They find themselves moving from highly objective and exact technical and scientific fields to highly subjective and uncertain environments without objective measures, principles, and guidelines to fall back on. This generates a great deal of anxiety and frustration during the transition period; this topic will be further explored in Chapter 3.

WHY STUDY MANAGEMENT?

The "skills approach" to management taken herein implies that management skills, to a large degree, are developable. Of course, there is no question that some traits of successful managers are innate—for example, aptitudes, ability, talent, and intelligence. Yet, the idea that managers are born is passé. There is considerable evidence that, to a large degree, managers are made and that managerial skills can be developed.[8] This view, obviously, rejects the "traits approach" to management and leadership and adopts a skills-oriented approach.

My argument is based on a strong premise: Since managerial performance depends on fundamental skills rather than on personality traits, the criterion for identifying potentially successful managers should not be what managers are (innate traits and characteristics), but rather what they do (the types of skills they exhibit in performing their jobs). In short, desirable traits do not guarantee good or superior performance—good skills do. The process of developing the right fit or matching the individual's skills with the requirements of the situation is what actually counts.

For engineers and scientists switching to management (and for technical managers in general), the study of management is crucial. Managerial success is largely a function of learnable skills. Research shows that all managers, regardless of their natural abilities, can improve their managerial performance through education, training, and practice. Of course, they must have a strong will to

---

[8] See, for example, Mintzberg, Henry. The Manager's Job: Folklore and Fact. *Harvard Business Review* (July/August 1975): 18-26; and Badawy, M. K. Enhancing Managerial Competence of Engineers and Scientists (IEEE, 1979 Midcon Professional Program Proceedings, Chicago): 24-4/1-8.

manage. Just as it would be difficult for one to learn music or painting or surgery without a strong motivation to do so, the same holds true for management skills. Therefore, if the technologist has a strong desire to manage people, backed up with certain personal and professional qualifications, the capacity to manage—the skills—can be developed.

It is obvious that the study and development of the technologist's management knowledge and skills can be quite satisfying from a personal and professional career standpoint. However, the skills will not be developed by reading a book, or attending a seminar, or taking a course in management. Courses and books develop knowledge, not skills. The only way to develop these skills is by putting the knowledge into action—by practicing it. Hence, learning the principles of management and then practicing them using various techniques is the best way to sharpen managerial competency. This subject will be further explored in Chapter 6.

PREMISES OF THIS BOOK

There are five major premises underlying the presentation in this book:

1. Managers are made, not born.
2. There are no poor engineers or scientists, only poor managers.[9]
3. Management, unlike engineering and science, is an applied social science. It is also an art.
4. Managing is a skill; the only way to learn it is to practice it.
5. The primary problems of engineering and R&D management are not technical—they are human. Many technical managers fail because they were never trained in organization and management skills.

SUMMARY

Management requires the organization, coordination, and direction of all corporate resources in order to achieve predetermined objectives. The manager is the driving force—through his activities, results are achieved. The process of managing requires the performance of several functions through the possession of a set of professional skills. Management skills are learnable, and the best way to develop them is through practice and experimentation. There is a set of ingredients of managerial competence that determines the extent of managerial success or failure. This is the subject of the next chapter.

---

[9] There are, admittedly, variations in abilities and skills among engineers and scientists. However, these variations are probably larger among technical managers than among technologists.

2
Why Managers Fail

Chapter 1 developed a practical framework of the process of managing and the functions and responsibilities of managers. It also established that while management principles are largely universal, managerial practices must be tailored to fit particular situations. In this chapter, the ingredients of managerial competency will be explored. A profile of the managerial skill mix (MSM) appropriate for effective management at different levels will be developed. Some causes of managerial failure as they apply to technical managers will then be discussed, along with some possible remedies.

INGREDIENTS OF MANAGERIAL COMPETENCY

You may recall from Chapter 1 that managing is a task or an activity viewed as a *process* requiring the performance of several *functions* through the possession of a specific set of professional *skills* using certain *techniques*. The relationship between these four components are illustrated in Figure 2-1.

The management process consists of a sequence of activities involving the maximum coordination and allocation of the resources available to an organization in order to achieve its objectives. These activities are the managerial functions of planning, organizing, directing, and controlling. Management skills—the abilities managers exhibit in carrying out their jobs effectively—are needed to perform these functions. Skills, thus, are what managers do—specific types of behavior—that result in effective performance. In undertaking their responsibilities, managers use several tools and techniques. The specific techniques they need depend on their functional responsibilities—i.e., project management, financial tools, marketing, management science models, management information systems, etc. In short, skill is the manager's ability to translate knowledge into action using appropriate management tools and techniques.

What are the ingredients of managerial competency? What are the prerequisites for success in management? Before we answer this question, we should first define what we mean by "success" in management. A good criterion for measuring a manager's performance, I believe, is his or her contributions to the or-

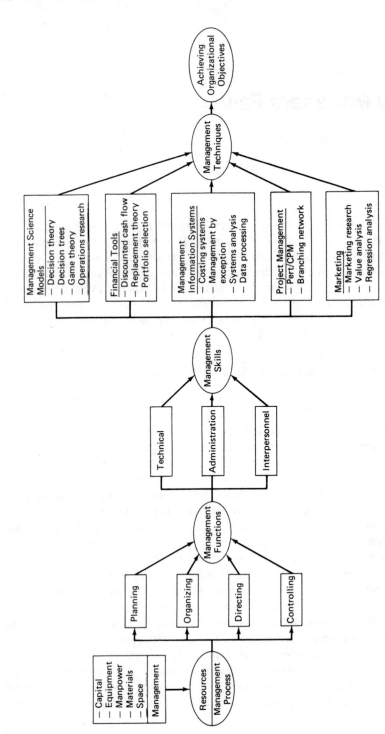

Figure 2-1. The relationship between management process, functions, skills, and techniques.

ganization. Given the difficulties in operationalizing this concept, managers must demonstrate superior performance—to be eligible for corporate rewards—and contribute to the attainment of organizational goals. My practical and consulting experience in a number of organizations clearly demonstrates that organizations usually do not reward people on the basis of effort, but rather only on the basis of results. In short, the name of the game is, What have you achieved?— not How hard have you worked.

As shown in Figure 2-2, managerial competency has three interrelated components: knowledge, skills, and attitudes.[1]

Knowledge

Like medicine and engineering, management requires the practitioner to acquire a specific body of knowledge. Management as a discipline has a body of knowledge, consisting of observations, concepts, principles, hypotheses, foundations, and theories. As noted previously, while management is not a pure science like physics or chemistry, it is an applied social science advancing rapidly toward the status of a profession. The major point here is that sophisticated knowledge in the principles and elements of administration is a prerequisite for managerial

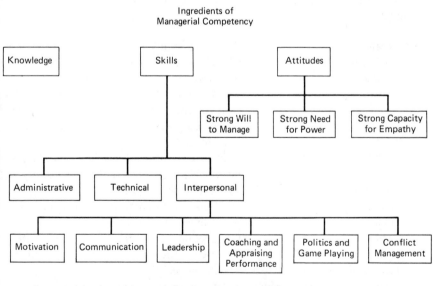

Figure 2-2. Ingredients of managerial competency.

[1] This discussion is based on my article "Easing the Switch from Engineer to Manager," *Machine Design* (May 15, 1975): 66-68.

success. In addition, due to the ever-increasing complexity of the managerial task and the multidimensional managerial environment, today's managers must know much more about administration and its functional processes than their predecessors.

Management knowledge need not necessarily be acquired via "formal" management education, that is, by obtaining a university degree in management. While the question of whether management can be taught is debatable, the question of whether it can be learned is less open to debate. Although we do not know yet what constitutes the ingredients of management education or what its goals should be, there is considerable evidence that management is learnable, that people can learn about it just as they can learn about other fields of human experience such as music and surgery. There is also evidence that people can exceed their potential. In short, management knowledge is crucial for effective practice, and it is learnable via several vehicles including experience, formal and informal training, personal development efforts, and on-the-job training.

Skills

Management knowledge by itself is not enough for managerial competency. As discussed previously, while management theory is a science, management practice is an art. Therefore, to be effective, the manager must develop a set of professional skills.[2] These skills are:

- *Technical.* Technical skills include the ability of the manager to develop and apply certain methods and techniques related to his tasks. The manager's technical skills also encompass a general familiarity with, and understanding of, the technical activities undertaken in his department and their relation to other company divisions. The manager's technical specialization, formal education, experience, and background form a strong foundation for the development of technical skills.
- *Administrative.* Administrative skills relate primarily to the manager's ability to manage. Effective management, of course, reflects the ability to organize, plan, direct, and control. It is the capacity to build a workable group or unit, to plan, to make decisions, to control and evaluate performance, and finally to direct subordinates by motivating, communicating, and leading them into a certain direction that would help the organization achieve its objectives most effectively. The core elements of administrative skills are the ability to search out concepts and catalog events; the capacity to collect, evaluate, and process pertinent information; the ability to distinguish alternatives and make a decision; and resourcefulness in directing others and communicating to them the reasons behind the decisions

---

[2] For more on this point, see Katz, Robert L. Skills of an Effective Administrator. *Harvard Business Review* (January/February 1955): 33-42.

and actions. Superior administrative skill is, of course, related to and based on other skills such as cognitive and conceptual skills.

- *Interpersonal.* Interpersonal skills are probably the most important of all. Since managing is a group effort, managerial competency requires a superior ability to work with people. The manager, to be effective, must interact with, motivate, influence, and communicate with people. People make an organization, and through their activities, organizations either prosper or fail. Managing people effectively is the most critical and most intricate problem for the manager of today.

Attitudes

Attitudes, the third ingredient of managerial competency, are essentially the manager's value system and beliefs toward self, task, and others in the organization. Attitudes include those patterns of thought that enable one to characterize the manager and predict how well he will handle a problem. Attitudes are partly emotional in origin, but they are necessary because they determine two things. First, the acquisition of knowledge and skills is, in part, a function of attitudes, and second, attitudes determine how the manager applies his knowledge and techniques.

Attitudes are also important in determining managerial competency for another reason: They tell us what needs are dominant in an individual at a certain time, and thus we can predict and identify the individual's managerial potential. This identification is crucial for enhancing future managerial effectiveness.

Modern psychological research tells us that effective managers share at least three major attitudinal characteristics: a high need to manage, a high need for power, and a high capacity for empathy.

The need or will to manage has to do with the fact that no individual is likely to learn how to manage unless he really wants to take responsibility for the productivity of others, and enjoys stimulating them to achieve better results. The "way to manage" can usually be found if there is the "will to manage." Many individuals who aspire to high-level managerial positions—including engineers and scientists—are not motivated to manage. They are motivated to earn high salaries and to attain high status, but they are not motivated to get effective results through others. Thus, they will not make competent managers.

The need to manage is a crucial factor, therefore, in determining whether a person will learn and apply what is necessary to get effective results on the job. The key point here is that an outstanding record as an individual performer does not indicate the ability or willingness to get other people to excel at the same tasks. This partly explains, for example, why outstanding scholars often make poor teachers, excellent engineers are often unable to supervise the work of other engineers, and successful salesmen are often ineffective sales managers.

Second, effective managers are characterized by a strong need for the power derived from such sources as job titles, status symbols, and high income. The point is that power seekers can be counted on to strive to reach positions where they can exercise authority over large numbers of people. Modern behavioral science research suggests that individuals who lack this drive are not likely to act in ways that will enable them to advance far up the managerial ladder.[3] Instead, they usually scorn company politics and devote their energies to other types of activities that are more satisfying to them. For many engineers and scientists, power emanates from "professional" sources other than sources of managerial power. While managerial power is based on politics, titles, and organizational status, professional power is based on knowledge and excellence in one's discipline and profession. In short, the power game is part of management, and it is played best by those who enjoy it most.

The third characteristic of effective managers is the capacity for empathy—being able to cope with the emotional reactions that inevitably occur when people work together in an organization. Effective managers cannot be mired in the code of rationality, which explains, in part, the troublesome transition of some engineers and scientists to management. Individuals who are reluctant to accept emotions as part of being human will not make "human" managers, and, in turn, they will not be managerially competent.

To sum up, knowledge, skills, and attitudes are the three interrelated components of managerial competency. To be effective, managers must possess the authority that comes with knowledge and skills, and be able to exercise the charismatic authority that is derived from their own personalities. They also must have an "appropriate" attitude based on a thorough understanding of the nature of the managerial task and a keen will and ability to manage.

THE MANAGERIAL SKILL MIX

How important are the technical, administrative, and interpersonal skills for managerial effectiveness? They are all closely interrelated and can be significant in determining your success in management. However, experience shows that the relative importance of these skills varies with the management level you are on and the type of responsibility you have.

As shown in Figure 2-3, technical skills are inversely related to your management level: They are most important at lower management levels but that importance tends to decrease as you advance to higher levels in the organization. This is only natural because managers usually start as specialists (e.g., teachers, lawyers, doctors, scientists, engineers, accountants). As an engineering or R&D supervisor, you are only involved in a limited amount of managerial activity. You may do some planning, scheduling, or performance appraisal. Most of your time, however, is spent working with the "troops." Thus, your ability to use

---

[3] McClelland, David C., and Burnham, David H. Power-Driven Managers: Good Guys Make Bum Bosses. *Psychology Today* (December, 1975): 69-70.

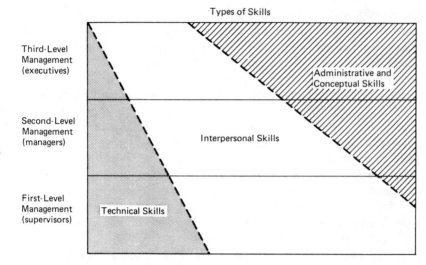

Figure 2-3. The managerial skill mix (MSM).

methods, techniques, and equipment—technical skills—is of critical importance. You are on the firing line. You are expected to direct your subordinates in technical areas to get the job done.

As you advance to middle management, and certainly to upper management, you will find that while technical skills decrease in relative importance, the importance of administrative skills increases. Moving up the ladder means moving away from the technical end of the operation and moving closer to general management. You must divorce yourself from technical details and become accustomed to seeing the "big picture." Your administrative and conceptual skills will become far more important. You will need the ability to see the organization from a macro—not micro—perspective as a total system of many interacting components, with engineering and R&D as subsystems within a highly dynamic environment.

Managerial success on upper management levels, then, is determined by your vision and ability to understand how the entire system works (the conceptual skill), as well as your capacity for organization and coordination between various divisions (the administrative skill). How much you know about the technical details of the operation becomes considerably less important. In fact, beyond middle management, "special knowledge" can actually be a detriment to the individual. Indeed, the need for specialized knowledge for those in upper management is greatly overrated.

Handling people effectively is the most important skill at all levels of management. Since managing is a group activity or a team effort, your most valuable asset is people. As you climb the management ladder, your problems will change from technical problems to people problems. Knowing how to handle them effectively, I believe, is the art of the arts. If a manager has considerable technical and administrative skills, but his interpersonal skills are wanting, he is a likely candidate for managerial failure. Conversely, problems that occur because technical or administrative skills are not up to par will be more easily surmounted.

It is important to remember that success in management is largely determined by the manager's ability to understand, interact with, communicate with, coach, and direct subordinates. This statement should not be taken to undermine the importance of technical and administrative skills in managerial effectiveness, but rather to underscore the ability to get along with people as a prerequisite for success in management. (Technical skills on the other hand, are of enormous importance for success in engineering or science.) Do not regard both types of skills as opposite poles, but rather as specific points on a continuum.

While interpersonal skills are presumably important at all levels of management, they are perhaps most important at the lower and middle levels, where managers interact with subordinates, supervisors, and associates. At upper management levels, where the frequence of these interactions tends to decrease, the importance of interpersonal skills decreases as conceptual and administrative skills become more important. It is also possible that with the increased degree of power and influence upper-level managers typically have, they can afford to pay less attention to interpersonal relations, and hence they become less sensitive to human needs and individual satisfaction.

Some technical managers and supervisors find it difficult to get away from "the bench" and do what they are paid for—namely managing. But everything in life has a price. Perhaps this is one of the prices managers must pay—the price of management! I have seen quite a few technologists in management who were not willing to pay this price, so they tried to do technical and managerial tasks simultaneously—with the incompatible requirements of two different roles. I have seen others enter management without realizing what they were getting into. The paths taken by both groups turned out to be very costly—they failed! The lesson is quite clear: The "right" mix of the three skill types at different management levels must be properly maintained.

MANAGERIAL FAILURE

Organizations fail because managers fail. Managers fail because they perform poorly. Performance is one of the prime criteria that an organization uses in evaluating employee contributions. While many managers deny it in public, performance is hardly the sole basis for appraising employees. Managerial jobs are no exception. Given the difficulty of measuring managerial performance accurately and objectively, organizations consider the manager's contributions to the accomplishment of the company's goal to be the most concrete basis for distributing rewards and making salary adjustments and promotion decisions. Thus, managerial failure can be defined as the inability of the manager to meet certain performance standards imposed by his superiors. It can also be defined in terms of organizational policies. A manager has failed if his performance is considered unsatisfactory or unacceptable by virtue of some preestablished criteria. Managerial success, on the other hand, is reflected in added responsibility, promotion, title change, and increased salary. Managerial "failure" is not intended to imply that the manager is demoted because he totally failed to get the job done but rather that he failed to accomplish results that he is capable of achieving.

Causes of Managerial Failure

Why do managers fail? Causes of managerial failure can be numerous. Since managerial performance is a product of the interaction of many factors inside the individual and in the surrounding environment, managerial success or failure will be determined by factors in both areas. Bear in mind that failures in management are rarely due to a single cause. Typically, aspects of the individual interact with aspects of the environment to create the problem.

Research has shown as many as 35 types of factors as potential causes of unsatisfactory managerial performance.[4] Any one of these factors can contribute to the failure of a manager. Some of these factors are more likely to operate than others because of the nature of managerial work. As shown in Table 2-1, there are three groups of factors containing nine categories representing possible causes of performance failures. The first four categories refer to aspects of the individual. The remaining five categories refer to different aspects of the environment: categories five to eight refer to the various groups of which the individual is a member, while the ninth category is contextual, referring to nonhuman aspects of the environment and the work itself which may be strategic to performance failure.

Note the relative importance of the different factors. As shown in the table, the most dominant causes of performance failure are deficiencies of an intellectual nature, frustrated motivations, membership in and relations with different groups, and economic and geographic factors.

Discussing all possible causes of managerial failure in detail would be impractical. Thus, for our purposes here, I shall focus on the forces relating to the individual manager himself or to his job.

Individual Factors

The development of management skills and the ability to convert them into effective actions are crucial to managerial competency. The lack of ingredients necessary for effective managerial performance will lead to poor results. Lack of knowledge of management principles and concepts, for example, will hamper a

---

[4] Miner, John. The Challenge of Managing. Phildelphia: Saunders, 1975, pp. 215-216.

Table 2-1. Causes of Managerial Failure.[a]

CATEGORY	HIGH	LOW	RA
A. Individual Factors			
I. Problems of Intelligence and Job Knowledge	X		
1. Insufficient verbal ability			
2. Insufficient special ability			
3. Insufficient job knowledge			
4. Defect of judgment or memory			
II. Emotional Problems	X		
5. Frequent disruptive emotion (anxiety, depression, guilt, etc.)			
6. Neurosis (anger, jealousy, and so on, predominating)			
7. Psychosis			
8. Alcohol and drug problems			
III. Motivational Problems			
9. Strong motives frustrated at work (fear of failure, dominance, need for attention, and so on)	X		
10. Unintegrated means used to satisfy strong motives	X		
11. Excessively low personal work standards			X
12. Generalized low work motivation			X
IV. Physical Problems	X		
13. Physical illness or handicap including brain disorders			
14. Physical disorders of emotional origin			
15. Inappropriate physical characteristics			
16. Insufficient muscular or sensory ability or skill			
B. Group Factors			
V. Family-Related Factors	X		
17. Family crises			
18. Separation from the family and isolation			
19. Predominance of family considerations over work demands			
VI. Problems Caused in the Work Group	X		
20. Negative consequences associated with group cohesion			
21. Ineffective management			
22. Inappropriate managerial standards or criteria			
VII. Problems Originating in Company Policies	X		
23. Insufficient organizational action			
24. Placement error			
25. Organizational overpermissiveness			
26. Excessive spans of control			
27. Inappropriate organizational standards and criteria			
VIII. Problems Stemming from Society and Its Values			X
28. Application of legal sanctions			
29. Enforcement of societal values by means other than the law			
30. Conflict between job demands and cultural values (equity, freedom, religious values, and so on)			
IX. Contextual Factors			
C. Factors in the Work Context and the Job Itself			
31. Negative consequences of economic forces	X		
32. Negative consequences of geographic location	X		
33. Detrimental conditions in the work setting			
34. Excessive danger			
35. Problems in the work itself			

[a] From Miner, John B. "The Challenge of Managing." Philadelphia: Saunders, 1975, pp. 330-3.

24

manager's performance. In addition, developing managerial skills is difficult when management knowledge is insufficient or lacking. Managerial failure could also be caused by a deficiency in one or more of the three skills necessary for managerial competency, as discussed previously. Managerial failure is rarely caused by technical incompetence. Technologists chosen for management positions have usually proven their technical skills, which weigh heavily in their selection. While most technical managers are improving their managerial skills, they are also losing some of their technical skills, but probably not to the extent that they become incompetent managers. In short, although some managers may fail because they have become incompetent technologists, this is not a typical cause for failure.

Many technical managers get fired, not because they lack technical competence, but because they lack managerial competence (another common practice, sadly, is to transfer incompetent managers back into a heavy technical role!) Managerial failure can thus result from inadequate management and administrative skills. Establishing a well-functioning unit or division with a sound structure and clear authority and responsibility relationships is crucial for achieving divisional objectives. In addition, developing policies and procedures consistent with objectives and goals, allocating resources, and monitoring progress toward goal achievement are key managerial tasks. These activities call for considerable administrative skill on the manager's part.

The major cause of managerial failure among engineers and scientists is poor interpersonal skills. Many technologists are more comfortable dealing with matters in the laboratory than they are dealing with people. Because most of them are loners, they are used to doing things for themselves. Once promoted to management, however, they have to delegate responsibility to others. They often find this extremely difficult, especially if they have less than complete confidence in their subordinates' abilities. As a result, many technologists find that their advancement—and their managerial careers—are limited more by human factors than by technical ability.

Managerial failure also occurs when an individual becomes a manager for the wrong reasons. This happens when a person seeks the attractive rewards (e.g., economic) associated with a managerial position, yet has no strong will to manage. Such managers do so poorly that they become "retired on the job." This situation will be discussed in greater detail in Chapter 3.

Job-Related Factors

The causes of managerial failure relating to the manager's job itself are numerous. A more detailed discussion is presented in Chapter 3. However, a brief account of some of the job-related factors causing managerial failure follows.

Some managers, especially new managers, are unwilling to pay the price of being a manager, i.e., loneliness. They seem to be unaware that the higher one climbs on the managerial ladder, the more lonesome it becomes, the fewer peers one has to talk to, and the more restraint one must exercise over what one says. As a result, while they may enjoy the new challenges and the greater opportunity to make unilateral decisions, they find themselves nostalgic for the "good old days" when it was not so lonely. They therefore try to act like "one of the boys."[5] In doing so, they often lose the respect of the people they manage. Employees want to look up to the boss. They want to feel that they can turn to him for necessary decisions. The genesis of this managerial failure is the desire to be liked rather than respected! It is interesting that managers who are found to be most effective are usually categorized by their subordinates as "fair but firm."

In addition, new managers sometimes fail to adjust to the demands of their role. Managerial positions are usually characterized by a high degree of power over other people, some standards for controlling human behavior in work settings, large amounts of visibility and influence, and a keen understanding of how corporate power and politics work. These characteristics require that managers play multiple roles. If managers are uncomfortable with these factors, they could develop a strong fear of failure. This situation might very well lead to poor managerial performance.

Managers are members of many groups, such as families, professional organizations, departmental and corporate committees, and community clubs and organizational bodies. Each of these groups expects them to play a specific role. Managers often find that they cannot fulfill each of these roles, and role conflict results. For example, long work hours and a hectic travel schedule mean less time spent on family responsibilities.

Other job-related causes of managerial failure include the following:

1. The manager's failure to let go of his last job. This is especially true in the case of engineers and scientists and results in the lack of delegation. This, in turn, deprives the subordinates of valuable learning opportunities and overburdens the manager.

2. The manager's natural preoccupation with his former areas of interest, such as engineering, research, manufacturing, or finance. The manager's failure to overcome the tendency to give disproportionate attention to the old function will result in conflicting loyalties. Forgetting that one is a manager first and a technologist second can cause poor time management and marginal performance of managerial duties.

3. Failure to maintain a balance between different objectives and priorities. An appropriate balance must be maintained among divisional, organizational, and employee objectives. There must also be a balance between job performance objectives and personal development objectives (upgraded knowledge and skills).

---

[5] This discussion is partly based on McCarthy, John F. "Why Managers Fail," Second Edition. New York: McGraw-Hill, 1978, pp. 3-34.

4. The tendency of some managers to farm out their responsibilities. Some managers do not recognize their responsibility for on-the-job training and coaching. They are all too eager to send their subordinates to courses conducted by staff agencies and outside trainers and consultants. While there are many occasions when it is wise to use these outside resources, the manager must make certain that such training is utilized by the subordinates when they return to the job. Without a standing policy of what training should cover and who should be trained and by whom, the manager runs the risk of abdicating coaching and training responsibilities. Poor development of subordinates' hinders their professional growth, and the manager becomes indispensable. When a manager's responsibilities and salary remain the same over a long period of time, this stagnation is sometimes an indication of managerial failure. Upward movement on the managerial ladder, if based on one's managerial capability, is the ultimate reward of success.

SUMMARY

In the absence of concrete figures on managerial "malpractice," it is difficult to estimate the number of ineffective or unsuccessful managers in organizations. However, experience shows that there are a lot of incompetent managers around. As discussed herein, managerial failure is caused by an individual or job-related factors, or both.

The best way to deal with performance failure, I believe, is to prevent it. Unfortunately, managers are willing enough to put out the fires but they take little interest in fire prevention. Dealing with ineffective performance requires diagnosing the causes and then coming up with appropriate remedies. The possible causes of managerial failure have been analyzed in this chapter. However, the scrutiny of your own performance and the development of a personal plan of action must remain your responsibility. Some guidelines to help you are provided in Chapters 4 and 5.

Success in management is hardly an accident. It is a function of several factors. By the same token, managerial incompetence emanates from a variety of sources. In the case of engineers and scientists, to what extent do both sets of forces operate? This question will be explored in Chapter 3.

PART II
TRANSFORMATION OF
ENGINEERS AND
SCIENTISTS
INTO MANAGERS

3
Problems in Career Transition

If you are an engineer or a scientist, the odds are good that either you are a technical manager or you will become one. I suspect that many questions go through your mind in the course of evaluating your career choices. For example, What is the nature of management as a career path for engineers and scientists? Why do technologists switch to management? What is in management for me? What frustrations (and thrills) can I expect during the transition period? What adjustments must I make to deal with them? What can be done to ease this transition? These questions will be discussed in this chapter.

STATISTICS ON SCIENTISTS AND ENGINEERS IN MANAGEMENT

In 1978 the total population of scientists and engineers in the United States was estimated to be 2.7 million: 1.3 million scientists and 1.4 million engineers.[1] Business and industry continued to be the largest employer of engineers and scientists (62%) and showed a growth rate of 7% between 1976 and 1978. Research and development continues to be the major primary work activity of 27% of the employed scientists and engineers, followed by management and administration, and then teaching. Research and development and management or administration both grew about 9% between 1976 and 1978, while teaching showed a 7% growth rate. This point is crucial for our purposes in this book because next to R&D, management is the primary work activity for the largest number of engineers and scientists.

As shown in Figure 3-1, the distribution of primary work activities in 1978 differed between scientists and engineers. Of the 543,000 industrially employed scientists, 37% were primarily engaged in R&D activities (including management). Over 60% of these were involved with applied research or development. Of the 1.3 million employed engineers, about 75% were engaged in development, managerial activities, or production/inspection.

---

[1] National Science Foundation. Science Resources Studies Highlights (NSF80-305). March 19, 1980, pp. 1-7.

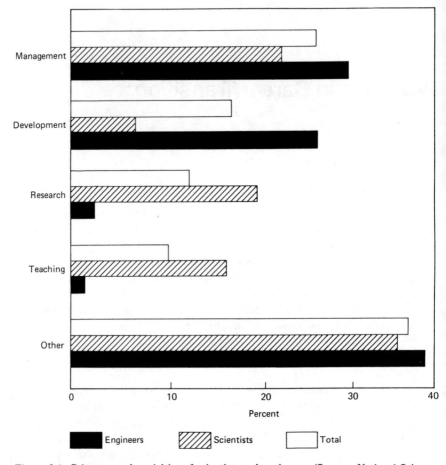

Figure 3-1. Primary work activities of scientists and engineers. (Source: National Science Foundation. Science Resources Studies Highlights. March 19, 1980, p. 4.)

It is noteworthy that over 40% of the industrially employed engineers were engaged in R&D work, including management, with an overwhelming proportion active in development work. Note also that while the difference between the percentage of the industrially employed engineers and scientists engaged in R&D and its management is not that large (40% vs. 37%), Figure 3-1 shows engineers to lead scientists in the management category. The reverse is true in the case of basic research.

The preceding figures are consistent with the results of recent studies showing that more and more technologists, particularly engineers, are assuming supervisory and managerial responsibilities at some point in their careers. A recent study by the Engineering Manpower Commission shows that 68% of the engineers in the United States are employed as managers by age 65. Furthermore, while only 37% have more than nominal managerial duties during the first five years of employment, 73% of engineers between the ages of 45 and 50 have significant managerial responsibilities. The extent of these responsibilities ranges from minor supervisory duties to full executive assignments. Similarly, many technologists start out with positions in engineering or R&D management and then end up in general management.

It has been estimated that in the 1980s more than 50% of American corporations will be headed by individuals with an engineering background; it is thus reasonable to conclude that engineers will have a great impact on the quality of life. The place of engineering and R&D functions in corporate strategy is also bound to become more significant because of the trend toward greater R&D spending in the years ahead. In 1981, R&D expenditures are expected to increase by 13.7% over 1980 levels to $68.6 billion, with the largest increase in expenditures—over $48 billion anticipated in the industrial sector.[2] Corporate R&D managers see the impressive gains in spending by many industries as a sign that top management is placing new emphasis on R&D.[3] In fact, some say that the driving force behind increased spending is the fear that United States industry is losing its ability to innovate.

MANAGEMENT AS A CAREER PATH
FOR ENGINEERS AND SCIENTISTS

A technical supervisor or manager is primarily concerned with the planning, organizing, directing, and controlling of the activites of engineers, scientists, designers, draftsmen, and other technical and nontechnical personnel to achieve desired goals in R&D, design, manufacture, construction, operation, or maintenance of a product, device, structure, or machine. Because of the increasing complexity of technology, industry, and modern life in general, the effective management of technology requires a technical approach accompanied by an understanding of modern complex organizations as sociotechnical systems. At no other time in history was the need for good technical managers greater than it is today. Yet, they are in short supply.

As a natural reaction to the demand for technical managers, it would be normal and appropriate for a large number of engineers and scientists to encounter managerial responsibilities at some stage in their careers. Given that not all technologists need become managers and not all of them will, engineers seem to be particularly suited for managerial positions. In fact, according to one estimate, one out of every three engineers ends up in management. Why? First, the engineer's familiarity with analytical skills, optimization of complex systems, and use of quantitative and simulation techniques is all-important in managerial

---

[2] Research Management, Vol. XXIV, No. 2 (March 1981), p. 2.
[3] "More Speed Behind R&D Spending," Business Week (July 7, 1980), p. 47.

problem-solving and decision-making. Thus, the engineer's respect for basic facts and analytical mind should give the engineer a premium. Although a technical background has by no means come to supersede other essential qualifications for managerial competence, (as discussed in Chapter 2), it should be a "helping" factor depending on the scope and level of the management position in question.

Second, the engineer, as an applied scientist, has much in common with the manager. Both have strong pragmatic orientations and fairly similar career objectives. Indeed, the research available suggests that the average engineer has an organization orientation that manifests itself in a lesser commitment to the profession, in greater concern with the goals and approval of the organization, and in focusing on an organization career. The goals of engineers have been found to be in much better accord with the aims of business than with the scientific aims of publication, knowledge for itself, or independence from the practical affairs of the company. In short, the typical engineer is actually a manager or an "organization man." This is why many engineers tend to see management as a natural path for career advancement.

While the engineer has a lot more in common with the manager than does the scientist, many scientists have also ended up in supervisory and managerial positions. Differences between engineers and scientists in terms of their adaptation to managerial environments are not so much determined by their occupational status as they are by personality characteristics, management styles, value systems, type of position, and management level involved. At the risk of generalizing, my observations and experience suggest that, on the average, scientists find the transition to management more difficult than do engineers. I would also contend that this is perhaps due to fundamental differences between both groups in work goals, need orientations, and career objectives. In short, the management "culture" is much more compatible with the engineering "culture." The values of management (i.e., profitmaking, efficiency, and growth) are much more in line with those of engineering than with those of science (i.e., the scientific method, finding out the truth, basic research as an end by itself). While it is "knowledge for knowledge" in science, it is "knowledge for money" in business.

Whether you are an engineer or a scientist, your administrative responsibilities will become increasingly important as your career advances. Remember that because of the nature of technical project organization, interdisciplinary teamwork, and specialization, supervisory responsibilities in a project, team, or divisional context will become an integral part of your job—regardless of your career goals.

CAREER CHOICES AND THE TRANSITION TO MANAGEMENT

What career choices do you have? Management, obviously, is not the best career for everyone. In making the transition to management, you have three career choices. The determining factors in each choice are career goals and your perceptions of the reward system operating in your organization. As shown in Table 3-1, these choices are:

1. You are switching to management because you have a strong motivation to manage, backed by a demonstrated or potential capacity to manage. Your motivational pattern is essentially that of a manager, moving into management would enable you to satisfy your career goals. As shown in Table 3-1, you are a technologist in transition to management, to whom this book is entirely addressed. It has been estimated that over half of the engineers at midcareer fall into this category.

2. Although you enjoy work in your field of specialty, a career in management is appealing to you, but you are somewhat reluctant to make a move. You are not at all sure whether you can swim in the new waters of management. This is the state of the undecided technologist. Your final decision will largely depend on how strong your ties are to your specialty relative to how attractive a move into management is. Your immediate and long-range career objectives, your present situation at your company, and your general assessment of personal and professional life-style will enter into your decision. While your motivation to go into management is not as strong as in the first career choice, it might nevertheless be of sufficient strength that you will opt for a management career. Granted you are not totally sure that this is what you really want to do, the rewards and satisfactions drawn after making the transition might surpass your expectations. About 25% to 35% of engineers at midcareer fall into this category. This book is equally addressed to this group.

3. A management career is unattractive to you, and you stay in your profession or specialty. You are the professionally loyal technologist. Practicing your specialty is of prime importance to you, and hence, the motivational patterns of a manager have a decidely negative appeal. If you should ever decide to make

Table 3-1. Career Choices and the Transition to Management,

	EXTENT OF MANAGERIAL COMPETENCE (OR POTENTIAL)		
CAREER STATE	KNOWLEDGE OF MANAGEMENT FUNCTIONS	MANAGEMENT SKILLS AND CAPABILITIES	MANAGEMENT MOTIVATION
Technologist in Transition to Management	High	High	High
Undecided Technologist	Moderate	Moderate	Moderate
Professionally Loyal Technologist	Low	Low	Low

the transition to management—for example, to improve your financial status— the experience would prove to be quite frustrating.

Although some have estimated that only 10% to 20% of the engineers at mid-career fall into this third group, my experience happens to be quite different. As a consultant conducting career goal interviews and counseling for technologists in a number of high-technology organizations, I have seen far more incompetent engineering managers and supervisors at midcareer. Their performance is marginal, and they have no clear sense of career direction or of how (or why) they got into management in the first place. Technologists in this group would do better to stay "at the bench," as this is where they can make the greatest contributions to the organization. If it is at all possible—in view of our imperfect employee recruiting and selection techniques—these individuals should be identified and screened as they certainly constitute poor risks as potential management candidates. For the professionally loyal group, this book will explain what it takes to succeed in management, describe the critical differences between technical and managerial careers, and offer some "safeguards" against being drawn into management.

Although the three choices were presented as distinct career states in Table 3-1, this is rarely the case in real-life situations. It is not uncommon to find technologists who are equally loyal to their organization (state 1) and their profession (state 3). So it is not really an "either-or" situation. Rather, a technologist might be high on both orientations, or low on both, or high on one and low on the other. In addition, it is rare for a technologist to rank the same way (high, moderate, or low) on the three ingredients of managerial competence. The probability is higher for variations among these ingredients within the same individual. It is even more so in the case of management skills and capabilities, one of these ingredients, as the individual's degree of competence will vary among his technical, administrative, and interpersonal skills. In short, both career choices and the extent of managerial competence shown in Table 3-1 are somewhat over-simplified just for purposes of the discussion. However, you should look at each of these matters as a continuum with relative tendencies to lean more one way or the other within the same individual.

Management is frequently viewed as the road to advancement within an organization. But for many scientists and engineers, the transition to management is a hard one and in fact may not even be desirable.[4] My experience shows that neither the technologist nor those responsible for his progress fully understand the nature of the managerial task itself—or the peculiar stresses of the transition from technology to management. Many scientists and engineers switch to management for the wrong reasons; thus, the wrong individuals often are promoted to management. They set themselves up for failure. Before we deal with the possible problems associated with the transition from the technologist to manager,

---

[4] Badawy, M. K. Prescription for Success. *Industrial Research* (June 1976): 100-103.

let us take a look at the reasons why technologists switch to management in the first place.

WHY TECHNOLOGISTS SWITCH TO MANAGEMENT

Human beings are limited in their ability to understand the causes of their behavior, which is primarily based on their perceptions of themselves and the world around them. This is precisely why they tend to see what they want to see and hear what they want to hear. Clearly, perceptions and reality are not the same. It follows that asking engineers or scientists why they want to switch to management is a futile exercise. Being human, technologists will respond with what they *think* the reasons for the contemplated transition are. However, the real reasons could be different, indeed.

Given the personalized nature of the situation—different technologists switch to management for different reasons—and the "soft" nature of the data available—subjective responses based on their perceptions in the research studies reported—I am afraid that the information available, as in all other social science disciplines, can only point out stereotypical patterns of technologists' motivations for the transition to management. This is an important point and should be kept in mind throughout this discussion.

In career goal interviews for engineers and scientists that I have conducted over the years, about 80% of them have indicated that their career goal is to become a supervisor or a manager within five years. My interviews with new engineering graduates have revealed that many of them see management as "where to fly." Their response is usually some variation of the theme, "I want to be in middle management." Many of them are living in the illusion that they either are ready for management or will be once they get an M.B.A. Nothing could be farther from the truth. Rarely did any of them say, "I want to be the company's best systems analyst (or process engineer or mathematician)."

Why do technologists want to go into, or switch to, management in the first place? This question has been dealt with in several research studies.[5] A composite of the responses by the engineers and scientists who were subjects of these studies appears in Table 3-2. The 14 terms given in the table representing the reasons why technologists switch to management can be combined into six major cateogries: financial advancement; authority, responsibility, and leadership; power, influence, status, and prestige; advancement, achievement, and recognition; fear of technological obsolescence; and random circumstances.

---

[5] See, for example, Bayton, James A. and Chapman, Richard L. "Transformation of Scientists and Engineers into Managers." Washington, D.C.: National Aeronautics and Space Administration, 1972; Balderston, Jack. Do You Really Want to Be A Manager? *Journal of the Society of Research Administrators,* IX, 4 (Spring 1978); and Badawy, M. K. Understanding Role Orientations of Scientists and Engineers. *The Personnel Journal,* 50, 6 (June 1971): 449-455.

Table 3-2. Reasons Why Technologists Switch to Management.

1. To advance in position.
2. To work on a broader scope.
3. To do more interesting work; technical work is too routine.
4. To contribute to the organization's goals.
5. To have more prestige and status.
6. To have more opportunities for achievement and recognition.
7. To make more money.
8. To have more opportunities for risk-taking in decisions.
9. To be a leader.
10. To have more influence and power.
11. To exercise more authority.
12. To have a great degree of responsibility.
13. To have opportunities to initiate or influence policies, programs, and methods.
14. Because management is the ultimate level of advancement possible for a technical person.

Financial Advancement

Many technologists believe that the only way to improve one's financial status is to move into management. It is true that the reward system in most organizations is geared toward managerial advancement as an index of success. My observations in many organizations simply support this point. Accumulated evidence also suggests that even where the dual-ladder system, which provides for parallel technical and managerial paths of advancement, exists, the managerial path still provides much more attractive rewards in terms of pay, power, prestige, and status symbols. The unwritten message is, "If you want a bigger share of the organization's goodies, go to management."

Authority, Responsibility, and Leadership

Technologists sometimes switch to management in reaction to being the underdog. They believe that being a manager is the only way to make the right things happen, to straighten out the chaos and inefficiency around them, and to show other people the right way to do a job. They see in management an opportunity to assume a leadership role with far more authority and responsibility than what their technical positions have ever enabled them to have.

Power, Influence, Status, and Prestige

As discussed in Chapter 2, a strong need for power is a characteristic of effective managers. While not too many technologists are willing to admit it, power has been found to be a strong motivation among those opting for a management career. The implication is that a strong need for power could be a desirable motivation to go into management—provided it is used wisely. The point you should keep in mind, however, is that the motive for power, influence, and status is difficult to identify. Technologists usually say things like, "I've always wondered what it would be like to be in charge and push the group into the right direction," or "I've had these good ideas all along but I've never had the influence or ability to test them," or "I've always wanted to make these contributions to the company's goals but I've never had the opportunity."

But what they are really saying is "I want to be the boss." Power, influence, status, and prestige are usually part of the reward package associated with managerial positions. In a sense, power is like money or sex; people shy away from talking about them and seeking them in public.

Advancement, Achievement, and Recognition

For many scientists and engineers, getting into management is the ultimate advancement. An explicit symbol of achievement and success is to be the boss. Indeed, it is part of the American work ethic. The frills that go with a management position—which can include high salary, an office with elegant furnishings, a private secretary, and the other trimmings—are all elements in the index of success. They fulfill the technologist's need for achievement, advancement, and recognition—the need for success. They also have a positive phsychological effect on the individual, who feels like a valued member of the organization. Indeed they constitute a tangible measure of the individual's worth to the company.

Frequently, personnel managers spend an inordinate amount of time designing policies regarding organizational status symbols. These are intended to equalize the material office possessions of individuals on the same level and to differentiate between individuals at different technical (i.e., junior versus senior engineers or scientists) or management levels (supervisors versus managers, and so on). Unfortunately, this common practice creates an organizational "culture," which reinforces the need for differentiation on the part of organizational members.

If this practice goes unchecked or if it allows the material gap between technical specialists and technical managers to widen, it could be a strong motivation for many technologists to go into management in order to get a larger share of the pie. My experience indicates that this situation is the norm in many companies. It is dangerous because in a sense it forces many technologists to abandon their professions and go into management. They switch because they have to, not because they want to! This might partly explain the high rate of incompetence and managerial attrition among technical supervisors and managers in some organizations.

Fear of Technological Obsolescence

Because of the complexity and rate of technological change, some engineers and scientists find it extremely difficult to keep up with developments in their fields and to stay alive professionally. Obsolescence can be a personal or an organizational phenomenon, or both. It occurs when a previously utilized person can no longer be used by the organization. It is usually caused by the individual's inadequate knowledge and inadequate skills, and the failure to develop an appropriate fit between the technologist's skills and the organization's needs. Threatened by technical obsolescence, the technologist might see management as the only alternative. At companies where the dual-ladder system—technical and administrative ladders—exists, special care should be taken so that the managerial ladder is not used as a face-saving dumping ground for technologists who have failed as professional specialists. On the other hand, neither should the technical ladder be allowed to become a dumping ground for incompetent technical managers. In the former case, the result is second-rate managers who are considered by many to be second-class citizens managing the engineering and R&D functions. In the latter situation, technical activities will be performed by second-class professionals. Both courses are, in my judgment, equally undesirable, and, indeed, represent some of the problems of the dual-ladder reward system. Such problems have occurred in several engineering and R&D laboratories including Amoco Research Center, American Cyanamid Company, Air Products and Chemicals, Inc., and Philip Morris, U.S.A.

While I have seen examples of both types of incidents in high technology organizations, the frequency of technologist's using management as an "escape" due to the fear of technological obsolescence is higher than the frequency of technical managers returning to the technical specialty in response to the fear of managerial failure. I contend that there are at least two reasons for this situation:

1. With the ever-increasing technological complexity, it is difficult for an engineer or a scientists to go back to "the trade" after a few years in management. This problem will become even more acute in the future. This point is significant when you consider that the average technical age of the technologist is down to 3 to 5 years.

2. The technologist's move from management back to the technical ladder usually has a negative connotation. "What are they going to think of me if I go back? that I couldn't make it?" the technologist wonders. Comprehensive career assessment and employee development programs, like those at IBM, alleviate such fears by allowing technologists to switch to management for a trial or a testing period with the well-publicized option of returning to the bench if things don't work out.

This problem of switching to management is compounded because, in general, technologists value the rewards associated with managerial positions.[6] Engineers, in particular, consider moving into management a landmark of career advancement. If they have to return to their technical fields because of marginal managerial performance, they have a deep sense of failure, resentment, and disappointment, and a poor self-image. To many engineers, it is only hierarchical advancement that brings increased authority, power, and prestige.

Random Circumstances

"Random circumstances" is the sixth category of reasons why technologists switch to management. It is not unusual to find engineers and scientists making an unplanned move into management. This move could be in response to an offer initiated by management to the technologist and presented as a "promotion". It could also be due to the sudden transfer, replacement, or advancement of the individual's immediate superior. The move (and I have witnessed many of these incidents) could also be totally political or made purely for survival purposes. Examples include promotions based on friendships or visibility considerations, and not on managerial competence or potential.

A more serious situation occurs when a technologist wants to become the boss simply to keep someone else from getting the position (usually a co-worker in the same division with whom he never got along). These incidents, which unfortunately happen in most organizations, are usually considered to be hidden or unmentionable motivations for going into management. Sadly, the costs could be prohibitive to both the individual and the organization.

It should now be clear that a technologist's move into management could be reinforced by a variety of reasons (or stimuli) depending on the individual's career goals and values, and the reward system operating within the organization. It is obvious that those factors are some motivations for technologists to

---

[6] See my Industrial Engineers and Scientists: Motivational Style Differences. *California Management Review*, 14, 1 (Fall 1971): 11-16; and Organizational Designs for Scientists and Engineers: Some Research Findings and their Implications for Managers. *IEEE Transactions on Engineering Management* (November 1975): 134-138.

switch to management only as one possible career choice for them (becoming line managers). Two other career paths, as discussed previously, are available: (1) remaining as a professional specialist or (2) becoming a staff specialist so that one can use knowledge and analytical ability to advise higher levels of line management without having to direct and control people.

I contend that the motivations of those in each of the three career states are quite different and require different sets of qualifications to match the role requirements of each career option. I also maintain that, although our discussion so far has not attempted to differentiate between engineers and scientists as two separate occupational groups, important differences do exist between (and within) these groups regarding their motivation to move into management. Furthermore, my research studies along with those of others have reported substantial differences between engineers and scientists regarding their work goals, need orientation, values, and job attitudes.

THE TROUBLESOME TRANSITION

Many engineers and scientists have made, or will make, the transition to management smoothly and successfully. However, the record is less than promising. While there is no law of nature that says good technical practicioners cannot be good managers, it is unlikely that they will be. Although they are well qualified for management by virture of their analytical skills and backgrounds, many technologists switch to management for the wrong reasons and to satisfy the wrong needs. Hence, they do not make competent managers. There is substantial evidence derived from my own research studies and those of others that the transition to management has been troublesome for many technologists, and that many of them have failed because they were generally ill-equipped for such a career.

Why? As shown in Table 3-3, there are three groups of factors causing this problem:

1. The nature of technical education.
2. The nature of the organization's management systems and policies.
3. The nature of scientists and engineers as a group.

Technical Education

The problems facing many technologists in switching to management can be traced back, in part, to the type of education they received in the engineering or science college. A comprehensive review of a number of technical undergraduate curricula has revealed that they focus entirely on technical subjects with a major concentration on conditioning and equipping the students with

Table 3-3. Causes of the Troublesome Transition
from Technologist to Manager.

1. The nature of technical education
2. The nature of the organization's management systems and policies
   a. Technical competence as a criterion for promotion
   b. The dual-ladder system
   c. The nature of the management task
3. The nature of scientists and engineers as a group
   a. Bias toward objective measurement
   b. Paralysis by analysis
   c. Fear of loss of intimate contact with their fields
   d. Technologists as introverts
   e. Poor delegators
   f. Inadequate interpersonal skills

the basic methods and attitudes of science. Minimal, if any, attention is given to preparing them for careers in management, which is a high aspiration of many technologists.[7] The present educational system erroneously overdevelops their analytical skills (as model builders), while their managerial skills (as decision-makers) remain highly underdeveloped. Thus, as far as management is concerned, this system equips technologists with the wrong skills.

In addition, the criteria for success in science and engineering on the one hand, and in management on the other hand, are not the same. The training of engineers and scientists typically emphasizes the reduction of all problems to terms that can be dealt with by objective measurement and established formulas based on predictable regularities; the world of management is far less exact and less predictable than the world of science or engineering. Just because technologists can skillfully use the scientific method, manipulate a slide rule, read blueprints, and build complex mathematical models does not at all mean that they can be managers—let alone good ones. The point to bear in mind, then, is that the concise techniques and solutions to engineering and scientific problems are vastly different from the complex ill-structured and tentative techniques and solutions to business and management problems.

This situation leads to the inescapable conclusion that, because of the inadequate preparation of engineers and scientists for careers in management, many competent technologists may not become competent managers.

[7] Gilmour, Alexander S. Engineering Investment: An Approach to Management Education for Undergraduate Engineers. *IEEE Transactions on Engineering Management,* **23,** **4** (November 1976): 157-162; and Goldberg, Edward, and Gray, Irwin. Management Development For the Practicing Engineer. *Engineering Education* (November 1973): 105-107.

The Organization's Management Systems and Policies

Some of the problems faced by engineers and scientists in making the transition to management are related to the management systems and policies adopted by the organization. Three major items stand out in this respect:

1. The use of technical competence as a criterion for promotion to a managerial position.
2. The dual-ladder system.
3. The nature of the managerial task itself.

Technical Competence. In many companies, the most qualified professionals are considered the best candidates for promotion to management.[8] Nevertheless, research suggests that these individuals make the poorest managers.[9] Research also shows that there is a great deal of dissatisfaction among engineers and scientists working for individuals they consider to be incompetent technical managers.[10] They demand that managers be as competent at managing as the professionals are in their technical fields.

However, many technical managers are former technical professionals who, promoted without any additional training, are vastly less competent at managing than their subordinates are at technical work. Attracted by what a management position offers, but without the will or the skills to manage, they are good candidates for managerial failure. This phenomenon is not unique to science and engineering professionals.[11] It is also common among other groups of professionals—doctors, lawyers, professors, and so on—in which the "Peter principle"— that each person is promoted to his own level of incompetence—is indeed working.

Should a company, then, look for less competent professionals to promote to management? This, of course, is hardly the answer. It is essential that the technical supervisor be technically competent, if for no other reason than to command the respect of his subordinates. However, the individual does not have to be the expert in the group. Indeed, the expert's need for professional excellence might stand in the way of competent management. Rather, management should look well beyond a candidate's technical ability to his motivation for switching to management, knowledge of the basic principles of the field, administrative skills, decision-making ability, ability to work with and handle people, leadership style, and capacity to operate within the organizational system. All of these elements are important in determining a technologist's managerial potential.

---

[8] Badawy, M. K. One More Time: How to Motivate Your Engineers. *IEEE Transactions on Engineering Management*, **25**, 2 (May 1978): 37-42.
[9] Hughes, E. Preserving Individualism on the R&D Team. *Harvard Business Review* (January-February 1968).
[10] Rosica, G. Organized Professionals: A Management Dilemma. *Business Horizons* (June 1972): 59-65.
[11] Drucker, Peter F. Managing the Knowledge Worker. *The Wall Street Journal* (November 7, 1975).

The balance between technical and managerial competency is a delicate one, and those technologists who are equally capable in both areas are rare indeed. Technical capability by itself is hardly a sufficient prerequisite for success in management. The practice of promoting the most technically competent to administrative positions can have many dysfunctional consequences and should therefore be abandoned. The prime criterion in the identification of managerial potential should be the technologist's demonstrated ability (or potential) to bridge the gap from a technical orientation to a management orientation. Until this criterion is sufficiently recognized and adopted, many newly appointed technical managers will have a lot of problems handling their new managerial tasks.

Dual-Ladder System. The concept of the dual-ladder is familiar to many engineers and scientists. For the last two decades, the dual-ladder system has been widely adopted by many engineering and research organizations including Bell Laboratories, General Mills, Westinghouse, Imperial Chemical Industries, Union Carbide, Mobil Oil, General Electric, and IBM. The dual ladder is a system by which two paths (the administrative and the technical or professional paths) for promotion and advancement are created within an organization.[12] Technical people can choose either path according to their personal goals, values, and career choices. The system was initiated to give scientists and engineers flexibility in choosing between a technical or a management career while ending up with equally attractive reward packages from the company.

For the dual-ladder system to work efficiently, it must meet a number of criteria:

1. The technical and administrative ladders must be equally attractive to technologists in terms of salary scales and status symbols and other noneconomic rewards.
2. Neither ladder should be used as a dumping ground for individuals who are unsuccessful on the other ladder.
3. Criteria for promotion on the technical ladder must be rigorous and based on high technical competence and achievement.
4. Both ladders must have the full support of management.
5. The system must be fully accepted by the technical staff.

As elegant as the criteria might be, research shows that the dual ladder is not without its problems.[13] Since exploring this issue in detail is beyond the scope of this chapter, it will suffice here to say that these criteria represent a

---

[12] See, for example, Emmons, W. D. The Pioneering Research Approach. *Research Management,* **XX,** 4 (July 1977): 27-29; and Meisel, S. L. The Rungs and Promotion Criteria. *Research Management,* **XX,** 4 (July 1977): 24-26.
[13] Wolff, Michael F. Revamping the Dual Ladder at General Mills. *Research Management,* **XXII,** 6 (November 1979): 8-11; and Moore, D. C., and Davies, D. S. The Dual Ladder: Establishing and Operating It. *Research Management,* **20,** 4 (July 1977): 14-19.

good theory. In practice, every one of these criteria has been violated consciously or unconsciously in many organizations. The dual-ladder system, in fact, represents two different "cultures." Status, role expectations, job responsibilities, and task assignments are much more well defined on the rungs of the managerial ladder than the technical ladder. This results in career anxiety and frustration for technical professionals.

A second related problem is that the administrative ladder is more consistent with the workings of the business "culture" in terms of criteria for promotion, titles, and so on. Everyone knows, for example, what the title "manager" implies, but few people outside of the specialist's peer group know what a "research associate" or "group leader" is. This poses some difficulties with the professional's need for recognition. A third problem is the inherent condition that the technical ladder runs counter to the business psychology of success being associated with becoming the "boss." In addition, the technical ladder is more compressed: The professional can go only so far, whereas the promotional path for managers is wide open. Finally, many technical people feel—contrary to what management usually claims—that technologists generally do not get ahead as fast as managers. Given the career goal orientation of many professionals, especially engineers, to go into management, those working under the dual-ladder system may come to think that they are second best. As discussed earlier, they see the "goodies" associated with management positions to be lacking (at least in a relative sense) in technical and research positions.

Aside from these factors, the single most important factor hampering the effectiveness of the dual-ladder system is the fact that the rewards for both ladders are usually not equally attractive. Managerial practices at many organizations clearly show that the rewards for the managerial path are usually more appealing than those for the technical path—contrary to management's claims about equality. This situation forces many engineers and scientists into taking managerial positions for which they are poorly prepared and toward which they are not positively motivated.

In short, the system itself has had some undesirable consequences. While it is probably true that this situation has not directly made the transition to management troublesome, it is equally true—based on the evidence available—that it has reinforced and intensified the problem. It should be kept in mind, however, that the dual-ladder system is good in concept, and the problems have arisen primarily from the difficulty of its implementation.

Nature of the Managerial Task. There are vast differences between the world of science and engineering and the world of management, and there are no systematic rules and laws governing the behavior of the people with and through whom the technical manager must operate.

The newly appointed supervisor is expected to play a complex dual role.[14] He is expected to speak two languages. As a manager he worries about such things as efficiency, return on the engineering and R&D dollar, and channeling R&D efforts and gearing the pressure to achieve economic ends (company goals). On the other hand, as a professional technologist he is expected to have the professional skills and attitudes to keep up with developments in his field, to work with his colleague-subordinates with diverse orientations and research interests, and to create the "proper" climate conducive to their creativity, imagination, and satisfaction.

The newly appointed manager is troubled by the loss of his "nice guy" image—he does not want to hurt anyone and he does not want to stop being one of the boys. As discussed in Chapter 2, this hurdle is particularly difficult if he has not completely identified with the company. He still associates "management" with hurting rather than helping people. He does not yet realize that his prime function as a manager is to help his company grow through encouraging the professional growth and maturity of his people.

The newly appointed manager has little or no time to spend on the things he really enjoys doing. Having to abandon his professional interests is particularly difficult for the technologist; it has been precisely these predilections that have accounted thus far for his success. In their place he is expected to devote himself to activities that until now have ranked low in his scale of values—the skills of management. Just how unfavorably the technologist is likely to regard these skills is shown in the following statement: "By and large, the scientist-engineer sees the manager as a bureaucrat, paper-shuffler, and parasite, an uncreative and unoriginal hack who serves as an obstacle in the way of creative people trying to do a good job, and a person more interested in dollars and power than in knowledge and innovation."[15]

Finally, having opted for the management route simply because it seems to be the only way he can substantially raise his income and achieve greater prestige in the company, the technologist feels trapped: He has sold his birthright for a mess of pottage. Obviously, he must attempt to understand the nature of organization and managerial activities and drastically revise his scale of values to become a good manager.

---

[14] Badawy, N. K. Prescription for Success, op. cit.
[15] From a speech made by Harvey Sherman, past president of the American Society for Public Administration (1963).

Scientists and Engineers as a Group

So far I have discussed two major sources of problems facing technologists in their transition to management: the nature of technical education, and the nature of the organization's management systems and policies. The third and last sources is related to some of the special characteristics of technologists (Table 3-3). These characteristics are not necessarily typical in every situation, but they can be considered general stereotypes.

Bias Toward Objective Measurement. Having been trained in "hard" sciences, where exact measurement is one of the natural beauties of the scientific method, engineers and scientists are more comfortable working with things that they can objectively control and measure. Managers, on the other hand, must rely on intuition and judgment in dealing with attitudes, biases, perceptions, emotions, and feelings. The fact that these intangible variables are hardly measurable—let alone controllable—makes the technical manager's job thoroughly frustrating. To be sure, one of the things that technologists must learn in order to succeed in management is to stop insisting on using a yardstick to measure everything. The nature of management—contrary to engineering and science—defies objective and tangible measurement.

Paralysis by Analysis. Engineers and scientists, more than others, suffer from this disease: the tendency to wait for all information to be in before they make a decision. I can think of no worse cause of managerial failure—it is a clear case of how the professional's technical training can hamper rather than enhance his chances for success. In management, you will never have all the facts, nor will there ever be riskless decisions. All decision-making involves risk taking. An adaptation of Pareto's principle would be that 20% of the facts are critical to 80% of the outcome. Being slow to decide, waiting for more facts, is known as "paralysis by analysis."

The inability of engineering or R&D supervisors to adjust to making managerial decisions on the basis of incomplete data and in areas where they lack first-hand experience (since the information is usually provided by other people and divisions) results in managerial anxiety.[16] The fact that they must function within a highly ambiguous and unpredictable environment makes them unsure about the data available, thereby reinforcing a neurotic demand for more data in an attempt to make riskless decisions. If this cycle is not somehow broken and appropriate adjustments made, it can be a deadly time waster and a complicating factor in the transition to management.

---

[16] For more on this point see Steele, Lowell W. Innovation in Big Business, New York: Elsevier, 1975, p. 186; and Thompson, Paul, and Dalton, Gene. Are R&D Organizations Obsolete? *Harvard Business Review* (November-December 1976).

Fear of Loss of Intimate Contact with Their Fields. Effective managers always focus on what needs to be done, when it should be done, and how much it should cost, rather than on how to do it. Since managers must get things done through other people, the question of "how" should always be left to them. Technologists usually find this difficult to understand, and in their zeal to stay professionally competent, they try to keep intimate contact with their specialties. As a result, they fail to delegate and they tend to handle the technical details as well. As noted in Chapter 2, they try to do two jobs in the time of one! The manager, to be sure, is paid to get things done—not to do them himself; this is the job of his subordinates. Sacrificing some of their technical competence—in a relative sense—is the price technical managers must pay for staying managerially competent.

Technologists as Introverts. Many engineers and scientists are "introverts" rather than "extroverts." Research shows that introversion is usually associated with creativity. The problem is that while creating is an individual (introvert) activity, managing is a team (extrovert) activity. The ability to work with others and to be a good team player is one of the distinctive skills of successful and competent managers. The "lone wolf" nature of many technologists could, therefore, make it doubly difficult for them to function effectively as technical managers.

Poor Delegators. One of the most valuable skills a manager can possess is the ability to delegate. You should never undertake what you can delegate. You cannot grow as a technical manager unless you delegate, and your subordinates expect you to. However, technical managers have been found to be very poor in learning to achieve things through others: They are poor delegators. As discussed in Chapter 2, technologists are doers rather than delegators because they believe, rightly or wrongly, that they perform a task better than anyone on their staff can. Developing the will to delegate requires a change in the technologist's attitudes, behavior, and assumptions about people working for him. He might even have to force himself to delegate tasks to his subordinates. At any rate, whatever it takes, delegation is one of the prime skills technical supervisors must acquire to enhance their managerial competence.

Inadequate Interpersonal Skills. Since this point was already discussed in Chapter 2, few more comments are in order here. A major source of problems and headaches for managers is "people" problems. Yet, poor interpersonal skills have been found to be a major factor in managerial failure among technical managers. Management requires dominance of personality traits and characteristics which are alien to most engineers and scientists. Managers must deal with the diffuse, the intangible, and the intractable, and with insufficient information.

Perhaps what is needed are managers who analyze like technologists but act like people!

In short, while the special analytical skills possessed by scientists and engineers make them attractive candidates for management, some of their personality characteristics and behavioral patterns might make the requirements for managerial competence alien to them. This mismatch could make the transition to management most troublesome and result, ultimately, in a tragic waste of a valuable resource.

SUMMARY

Management as a career path is attractive to many engineers and scientists. This assertion is supported by the statistical data available as well as by my own observations and experience. Yet, the transition to management has been difficult because of several complicating factors. Examination of these factors clearly shows that both employing organizations and technologists share the responsibility for these difficulties.

Through its policies and practices, management has, in a sense, encouraged technologists to switch to managerial careers without their having adequate skills or even a strong interest in pursuing this career path. The problem is intensified by some characteristics of technologists which run counter to requirements for success in management. These characteristics include a preoccupation with managerial problem-solving rather than problem-finding, a preference for well-defined problems that can be solved by specific techniques rather than the unstructured situations typical of management problems, an overspecialization in a narrow field instead of a focus on interdisciplinary issues, and an intolerance for ambiguous situations and insufficient decision-making data.

For a smooth transition to management, a joint partnership between employing organizations and technologists (and possibly other parties such as educational institutions) must be established. The roles to be played by each party to ease the technologist's move into management will be the subject of the three chapters in Part III.

PART III
EASING THE TRANSITION
TO MANAGEMENT

4
What Management Can Do

The possible problems facing engineers and scientists in transition to management were explored in Chapter 3. For the transition process to be smooth and successful, it must be effectively managed. What management and technologists can do to ease this process is the subject of this and the following chapter. Whether you are a technologist in transition or a technical manager (or an upper-level executive), this discussion is developed with you in mind.

The question this chapter addresses itself to is: What can management do to help the technologist make the transition from the technical to the managerial role successfully? The term "management" here refers to those who are responsible for the organization, planning, and direction of career planning and employee development activities of professional engineers and scientists. In a broad sense, these include technical managers, directors, and technical executives in charge of the corporate engineering and R&D functions, as well as technical development program managers and executives. In a more specific sense, you—as a technical manager or supervisor—represent "management" to the technologist.

While specific solutions would have to be tailored to fit particular situations, this discussion will provide some broad guidelines and answers to deal with the issues and questions involved. Facing the issue from the organization's or management's standpoint, the first part of the chapter will provide several guidelines to help technologists with the transition process. The balance of the discussion will present a comprehensive career planning and development program that management can adopt for effective career management of professionals.

GUIDELINES FOR MANAGEMENT

Easing the transition from technical positions to the management of technical activities is a joint responsibility. While it is management's responsibility to provide the organizational climate, support, and development programs that ease the transition problems, it is your responsibility—as a technologist—to develop your managerial knowledge and skills and seek the necessary support for a successful and smooth transition.

I would like you to remember two things at this point. First, it was your decision (normally) to move into management and it is thus your responsibility to make the move successfully. The second thing to remember is that there is no road back from an unsuccessful venture to management for a technical specialist; the only recourse is to find another job.

There are seven mechanisms, or tools, that management can employ to ease the transition from a technical to a managerial role. These mechanisms, shown in Table 4-1, are discussed in detail in the following sections.

Identify Managerial Potential

Managerial skills are manifested in performance, not merely in potential. However, potential must be identified, since management cannot afford an ad hoc approach to staffing managerial positions because of the high cost of executive failure. A random approach usually results in poor selection decisions.

To identify the managerial potential of technologists we must separate the variables leading to high potential from those leading to poor potential. The fact of the matter, however, is that there is no single "ideal" style of managing—rather there is more than one effective style. It follows that we need to focus on results as criteria, for quite different managers using different behavioral avenues can achieve similar results. What needs to be identified, then, is not a set of personal traits—rather it is a sample of behaviors.

This suggests that in the identification of the potential of management candidates, the critical variable is not what a manager is—his traits—but rather what he does—his behavior and the way he handles certain situations. Given the contextual nature of management (being situation-oriented), this approach is realistic because it shifts the focus away from the individual traits and puts it on individual behavioral patterns.[1] Less effort is made to look under the skin and more to sample job-typical behaviors expected of successful managers.

Table 4-1. Mechanisms for Easing the Transition to Management.

1. Identify managerial potential.
2. Employ better selection methods.
3. Make the dual ladder work.
4. Provide appropriate support, orientation, and coaching.
5. Reward managers for subordinates' development.
6. Provide training in the functions and skills of management.
7. Provide opportunities for management internships.

[1] Fitzgerald, T. H., and Carlson, H. C. Management Potential: Early Recognition and Development. *California Management Review* (Summer 1972): 22-30.

Can Managerial Potential Be Identified? There is no single uniform pattern for identification of managerial potential, training, selection, or development of managers. Selection and assessment processes are imprecise, at best. There are a great many scales, measures, inventories, instruments, indicators, and projective materials available, ranging from the trivial and superficial to the solemnly clinical. Descriptions of these techniques have dominated large space in textbooks by industrial psychologists elaborating on the measurements of personal traits correlated to managerial success.

In my judgment, most of these yardsticks have serious weaknesses and, as predictors of managerial potential, have not really been worth their salt. The state of the art does not allow us to identify managerial potential in an exact manner because the predictive validity and reliability of the available instruments is not high.

Measures of Managerial Potential. In view of the current state of the art, what are the tools at the manager's disposal? There are four major tools for assessing the potential of management candidates:

1. Personal interview.
2. Performance evaluation.
3. Evaluation of experience and seniority.
4. Assessment center.

Research shows that the personal interview is the most widely used. The available evidence, however, shows interviews generally to be ineffective, serving to fill the needs of the interviewer more than serving as a reliable selection device.[2]

Both performance evaluation (i.e., how well the candidate is doing on his present job) and assessment of experience tend to be unsystematic. Supervisors' ratings can be highly biased.

Perhaps one of the most promising aids in the identification of managerial potential is the assessment center. Because of the high potential value of this technique, let us see what it is, how it works, and how it compares to other techniques.

What Is the Assessment Center and How Does It Work? In an assessment center, management situations are presented to candidates and their reactions are observed. A panel of observers—assessors—makes an aggregate assessment, identifying the candidate's strengths and weaknesses. The candidate—the assessee—undertakes a series of tests and exercises (both group and individual) designed

---

[2]Campbell, John P., Dunnette, Marvin D., Lawler, Edward E. III, and Weick, Jr., Karl E. "Management Behavior, Performance and Effectiveness." New York: McGraw-Hill, 1970. 1970.

to elicit key forms of behavior that serve as indications of managerial success. The dimensions to be assessed include: leadership, organizing and planning, decision-making, oral and written communication skills, initiative, energy, resistance to stress, delegation, self-direction, and overall potential.

Tests and exercises used to tap these dimensions include the in-basket exercise (simulated accumulation of memos, reports, notes of incoming telephone calls, letters, and other material. The candidate is asked to dispose of these materials in the most appropriate manner by writing letters, notes, self-reminders, agenda for meetings, etc.), leaderless group discussions, management games, individual presentations, interviews, and projective tests.

The assessment center technique has been used successfully and with some enthusiasm by such organizations as the American Telephone and Telegraph Company, General Electric, J. C. Penney, International Business Machines, Standard Oil of Ohio, Sears Roebuck, and the Internal Revenue Service. The general technique was developed for the Strategic Services in World War II.

How Does the Assessment Center Technique Compare with Other Techniques? There is some evidence that the assessment center method is almost certainly more valid than any other means of identifying and analyzing a candidate's management potential.[3] While the effectiveness of an assessment center has not been proved beyond a shadow of a doubt, it seems that use of an assessment center for identifying management potential is a sounder and fairer method than those traditionally used by management. Studies also show that assessment center evaluations seem sufficiently high to support their further use. In general, assessment centers have been found to be effective and to contribute to the selection process.

The strengths of the assessment center technique over other traditional methods of identifying managerial potential can be summarized as follows:

1. The use of several assessors is superior to the single boss's appraisal in typical performance evaluation systems.

2. Several yardsticks are used in evaluating potential, and they are common to all assessors.

3. The training assessors receive helps to sharpen their observation and interviewing skills.

4. Candidates participating in assessment centers receive training exercises—in-basket, group presentation, and problem-solving exercises—that will eventually pay off as management training experiences.

5. The assessment center experience has a positive influence on morale and job expectations of candidates. It provides them with the opportunity to show

---

[3] Bytham, William C. Assessment Centers for Spotting Future Managers. *Harvard Business Review* (July–August 1970): 150-160 and 162-163; and Howard, Ann. An Assessment of Assessment Centers. *Academy of Management Journal,* 17, 1 (March 1974): 115-134.

their management abilities in fairly realistic situations and also to understand the requirements for the positions for which they are considered.

Like all other techniques, the assessment center has some problems. The weaknesses or limitations of this technique can be summed up as follows:

1. Those who do well in assessment centers may become "crown princes" and their future success may become a self-fulfilling prophecy. Those without this royal status may develop a morale problem.

2. Candidates who do poorly in assessment centers may feel that they have received the kiss of death as far as their future with the company is concerned. This may cause some undesirable job turnover.

3. Individuals who have not been nominated for participation might develop an unwarranted high degree of anxiety.

4. The nomination procedure for assessment centers might create the organization man syndrome in that supervisors might nominate those higher on conformity and lower on independence—thus eliminating the unusual or imaginative candidates for management. To get around this, however, supervisory nominations could be supplemented by self-nominations, peer nominations, or assessment of everyone at a job level for possible selection to management positions.

5. The whole mechanism of assessment centers generates stressful situations for the candidate since his entire career might depend on superb "stage" performance for a few days at the assessment center. While stress is, indeed, part of the manager's world and one of the forces he deals with, he might be subjected to a more intensive dose knowing that he does not yet have the job and he is being tested for it.

6. The cost of running these centers could range from the price of a few meals to several thousand dollars per candidate. These include installation costs, assessors' fees, psychologists' time, travel, materials, meals, and accommodations. No matter how high the cost, however, it should be compared with the cost of executive failure resulting from a poor selection decision. Also the importance of the position for which the candidate is selected should be kept in mind.

Based on the above discussion, I believe the assessment center is a promising concept. Given that it is far from perfect, it is superior to other traditional approaches to identification of managerial potential. There is no reason why this technique could not be used in identifying engineers' and scientists' potential for management. Some organizations—such as IBM—have, in fact, gone one step further and employed the technique in a more elaborate form as a career development center. In this sense, the techniques become an ongoing assessment procedure for potential of many management candidates including technologists.

It is clear from the above discussion that one way you—as a technical manager—can help ease the transition of some of your technologists to management would be through the proper identification and assessment of their potential. Since the best way of appraising and developing managerial capability is in the context of the job, candidates should be given the kind of responsibility that will help identify their potential and contribute to its development.[4] Actually, the first supervisory job should be a testing period during which the new manager is offered the opportunity to try out the role before committing himself to management because he does not have the first idea what management is all about.

Your technologists must somehow be helped to appreciate the rewards that can follow from training themselves to overcome the problems of transition and making a definite commitment to becoming managers. First, there is the reward of seeing one's people grow in professional capability and in general maturity. Second, there is the sense of accomplishment in seeing a complex project—which no one individual could have completed on his own—grow to fulfillment under one's direction. Third is the satisfaction of guiding the course of technological advancement in the direction one believes it should follow. Finally, management also has its brighter side. Although people sometimes are unpredictable, managing them in today's complex organizations can be both challenging and rewarding.

Employ Better Selection Methods

More often than not, unfortunately, the wrong technologists are "promoted" into management without having been adequately prepared to overcome the difficulties involved in this troublesome transition. Teaching the wrong candidates the right skills will not make them competent managers. A second way to ease the transition from technologist to manager, then, is via better selection.

There are several problems that will face you as a technical manager in selecting the "right" people for management positions. One problem is that technical competence—perhaps the most visible aspect of the technologist's performance—is hardly a sufficient prerequisite for effective managerial performance. As discussed in Chapter 3, just as academic performance in school is a poor predictor of potential managerial performance, competent technologists will not necessarily make competent managers.[5] Yet, you will find that technical competence is, erroneously, the most widely used criterion in selecting technologists for supervisory or managerial positions. This "best-salesman syndrome"—the assumption that the individual who is best at doing the work will be best at supervising it— is clearly inappropriate.

Another problem relates to the fact that you will probably attempt to select people with the "right" motivations for management. This would be a commend-

---

[4] Badawy, M. K. Enhancing Managerial Competence of Engineers and Scientists, in Developing Managerial Skills in Engineers and Scientists (*IEEE MidCon Professional Program Proceedings,* Chicago), **24,** 4 (1979): 1-8.

[5] See, for example, Badawy, M. K. Design and Content of Management Education: American Style. *Management International Review,* **18** (1978): 75-81; and Livington, J. Sterling. Myth of Well-Educated Manager. *Harvard Business Review,* **49,** 1 (1971): 79-89.

able way to do the task as long as your perceptions of the "right motivations" and those of your subordinates aspiring to management are the same. The fact of the matter is that they are not. Motivation is considered the most critical problem in selecting scientists and engineers to become managers.[6] Research clearly shows that superiors differ with their subordinates over the degree of satisfaction to be obtained in their subordinates' jobs as potential managers. These differences may arise from the difference in hierarchical perspectives and expectations, or they may reflect a lack of understanding by the superior about the motivational problems facing the subordinate in transition. In short, because of the differences in importance attached to selection criteria by technologists and their superiors, the wrong individuals might often be selected for managerial positions. Therefore, the transition to management might turn out to be quite problematic for a technologist—chosen by his superior—with a superb technical competence simply because managerial motivation has little appeal for him.

A third problem facing you in the selection process relates to the underdeveloped state of psychological selection technology. All the available measuring devices—interviews, tests, and so on—are far from perfect, as discussed above. There is no perfect model available as a substitute for the subjective judgment of the superior.

Finally, there is the criterion problem: what you will be looking for in the technologist as a basis for "promoting" him to management. As discussed earlier in this chapter, selection of managers on the basis of a set of identifiable traits, such as empathy and intelligence, would be inappropriate and has, therefore, been rejected. This is because success in management can be achieved through the possession of different sets of traits—not a unitary set—but only as long as they happen to fit the demands or requirements of a particular situation. A more realistic approach, therefore, is what is known in the applied behavioral science literature as the situational or "contingency" approach to management. In practical terms, the essence of this approach is, "it all depends." That is, the effectiveness of a particular set of skills or managerial style will simply depend on the nature and characteristics of the situation. A managerial style could be effective only if it "fits" the requirements of the situation.

Practical Tips for better Selection. The above analysis has several implications for you as aids in managerial selection. These can be summarized as follows:

1. As a technical manager, do not get trapped in traits or attributes of the individual as they are intangible variables difficult to operationalize and link to managerial behavior.

2. Use behavior as a basis for measurement by seeking to identify managerial skills which are actively specific behaviors that result in effective performance.

---

[6] Bayton, James A., and Chapman, Richard L. "Transformation of Scientists and Engineers into Managers." Washington, D.C.: NASA, 1972, p. 106.

3. Use the conceptual scheme—developed in Chapter 2—of ingredients of managerial competency as a basis for assessing the candidate's knowledge, skills, and attitudes. In order to help you with the managerial selection process, a checklist is shown in Table 4-2. Study it, and use it as a guide for identifying the major dimensions and the strengths and weaknesses of management candidates. Remember that this checklist is a flexible tool and should be adapted to fit you own situation.

It is obvious from Table 4-2 that managers choosing other managers should dig deeper and look beyond the candidate's technical background and ability. Your central concern—as a manager—should be with the extent to which the ingredients of managerial competence are present in the candidate translated in the form of identifiable skills. The question you should never lose sight of in assessing the technologist's managerial potential is: Does he have what it takes to succeed in management? This question will revolve around his knowledge, his attitudes, and most important, his skills.

Make the Dual Ladder Work

The third mechanism that management can adopt for easing the transition from technologist to manager is the establishment of equally attractive reward systems for both technical and managerial career paths. This measure will indirectly help with the transition process by encouraging technologists to choose their career directions more on the basis of their backgrounds, interests, and skills, and less on the basis of economic and noneconomic rewards. This approach will pay off for both the individual—better use and development of one's professional assets—and the organization—better management and technical capabilities.

As discussed in Chapter 3, the key to making the dual ladder work is effective implementation. This system has been revamped recently at General Mills, for example, with several modifications undertaken to make it more functional. By way of building a viable duel-ladder system, here are some suggestions for your consideration:[7]

1. Establish an ongoing committee that will not only devise the appropriate ladder to meet your organization's particular needs, but will administer it as well.
2. Make certain the technical ladder goes as high as the management ladder, with salary parity at each level.
3. Design the ladder so that people can move freely between engineering support groups and R&D. This avoids the all-too-common isolation of

---

[7] Wolff, Michael F. Revamping the Dual Ladder at General Mills. *Research Management,* **XXII**, 6 (November 1979): 8-11.

Table 4-2. A Checklist for Managerial Selection.

I. *Knowledge*
1. How much management knowledge does he have? Experience?
2. Does he have enough respect for managerial work? How much value does he attach to managerial as opposed to technical work?
3. Would he be willing and able to upgrade his management knowledge through education and training?

II. *Skills*

A. *Administrative*
1. Does he have any administrative experience? What kind?
2. To what extent has he been involved with management of projects and task forces?
3. To what extent does he understand the way the organization operates and how the administrative system really works?
4. Has he been doing and carrying out his share of administrative duties and responsibilities?
5. Does he like to make decisions? Solve problems? And how much risk would he be willing to take?
6. How does he relate to authority, power, and responsibility?
7. What type of skills, if any, does he have in the area of organizational structure and design?
8. Does he have any skills in the area of planning and resource allocation?
9. Is he effective in appraising others' performance?
10. Would he be comfortable working against deadlines?
11. Is he good in administrative details?
12. Is he good at getting things done through others? At follow up and feedback?
13. Would he delegate authority to others?

B. *Interpersonal*
1. Is he good in working with people?
2. Is he a team player? Or a loner?
3. Would he be effective in motivating and inducing others to work hard?
4. Is he good at "sizing up" people?
5. Is he a good communicator?
6. Does he maintain healthy relations with his associates and superiors?
7. Does he take initiative and exhibit leadership qualities in working with others?
8. How does he handle conflict? How would he go about resolving it?
9. How does he relate to power? Would he use it wisely?
10. How do "people" fare on his scale of values?
11. Would he be willing to learn to appreciate subjective things like emotions, feelings, and values, and their place in management?

C. *Technical*
1. Does he have the professional respect of his peers?
2. Where do his loyalties lie? To the field? Or the organization? Or both?
3. Can he identify with the big picture—the organization—even if this means less time spent on his specialty?
4. Can he play the dual role of professional administrators (as a professional and also a manager of technical activities)?

III. *Personality and Career Orientation*
1. What are his personal motives?
2. Why is he interested in moving to administration and becoming a technical manager?
3. Why is he working for this particular organization?
4. What needs is he trying to fulfill through his job?
5. What are his career objectives? What does he have planned for himself for the next five, ten, fifteen years?
6. Would he be preoccupied with getting the job done—as a potential manager—or with maintaining the "nice guy" image?
7. How strong (or dominant) are his needs for achievement and power? Is he power or achievement-oriented? Is he power-driven?
8. Is he capable of interacting, relating, and empathizing with others?

the two groups and is an important aid to the career development of young technical people.

4. Be flexible. Permit bypassing rungs, and allow technical people to report to managers on the same level where necessary to form project teams.

5. Give nondegreed people opportunities for advancement by providing rungs on the ladder for them as well.

Appropriate implementation of the above guidelines help easing the transition from technologist to manager by ensuring that engineers and scientists, in their move into management, are responding to motives and career objectives other than just economic incentives. Although you—as a technical manager—can never be sure whether or not this was the case, the odds are very much in your favor.

Provide Appropriate Support, Orientation, and Coaching

The newly appointed manager needs training to cover both the immediate and the long-range aspects of his job. On taking up his duties, the new supervisor finds himself confronted with a mountain of paper work. Suddenly, he is beset by a swarm of administrative problems: How do I get a raise from someone? What rights do I have regarding discipline in this case? Where do I sign this time card? And so on.

Steps should be taken to see that he is given adequate instruction and coaching in handling these purely administrative aspects of his job. But he needs more than this kind of stop-gap first aid. He needs an intelligent insight into company policies, management systems, and procedures, because supervision involves more than the mechanical application of rules and regulations. He needs insights also into the difficulties he will encounter in making the transition from technical man to manager and requires help and guidance in overcoming them. Above all, he should be helped to answer the question, "What does it mean for me to be a manager?"

But how can this be done? Well, the time to start this kind of orientation is as soon as possible after the supervisor has grasped the administrative details of his new job. There are various ways in which this aid might be provided. Naturally, the prospective manager's superior should be in the best position to give him the necessary counsel. Unfortunately, the superior himself may be little wiser in these matters than the subordinate. If this should be the case, the counseling might be undertaken by a personnel specialist. Other possibilities are some form of in-company training program conducted by either the training department or an outside consultant, or attendance at outside seminars where the prospective manager can meet with people from other specialities who nevertheless have the same needs as his own. My own preference is for the training to be done within the plant and, better still, within the organization unit to which the man is assigned in collaboration with an outside management consultant. A management consultant with a solid background in applied behavioral sciences could be very helpful in designing and implementing the necessary training for those prospective managers—and possibly their new superiors—which would enhance their managerial orientation and skills and also help them to make a smoother transition from technology to administration.

Reward Managers for Subordinates' Development

Technical managers are busy people. The many responsibilities they have, the emphasis on short-range results, immediate payoffs, and the continuing pressures to "look good" in the eyes of their superiors focus their attention, out of necessity, on functional activities that will enhance divisional efficiency. This means spending most of their time doing the activities that will actually appear on the balance sheet or the profit/loss statement—in the short run. The bottom line, again in the short run, is all that counts!

Although developing your subordinates might be a high priority item to you personally, it will probably be at the bottom of your daily agenda because of the other more compelling pressures competing for your time. One way to help your subordinates in the transition to management would, then, be through supervisory counseling, coaching, and support.[8] To achieve this end, four avenues must be pursued:

1. Subordinates' development must become a viable criterion in evaluating supervisory performance.
2. Appropriate rewards and incentives should be employed to induce supervisors to meet subordinates' development needs.
3. Supervisors should be provided with appropriate means (including education and training) to develop subordinates' skills in transition to management.
4. Upper-level managers should take a long-range view toward human resources development rather than expecting a short-range and quick payoff. Developing competent managers is, after all, one of the organization's best investments.

Provide Training in the Functions and Skills of Management

The sixth mechanism for easing the transition to management is via appropriate management training and development. Training and development for technologists in transition will be needed in three areas:

1. The management functions to be performed.
2. Personal skills needed for performance of these functions.
3. Motivational-value patterns to be satisfied.

---

[8] For more on this point see Bayton, James A., and Chapman, Richard L. Making Managers of Scientists and Engineers. *Research Management* (November 1973): 33-36; and Hall, Douglas T. "Careers in Organizations." Pacific Palisades (California): Goodyear Publishing Company, 1976, p. 157.

Training in the management functions would include basic grounding in the principles and techniques of supervising, planning, organizing, evaluating, and program assessing. Research shows that technologists do not experience a great deal of difficulty in learning and handling these functions.

The second area where training and development are needed relates to the personal skills of the newly appointed manager. As you will recall from our discussion in Chapter 2, three types of skills are necessary for managerial competency: technical, administrative, and interpersonal. Table 4-3 presents some examples of topics that should be covered in each of the three skill training areas. Research generally shows that the skills area has the greatest potential as a source of tensions and frustrations for the technologist in transition. It also shows that the administrative and interpersonal skills are usually the most problematic in the transition to management. The technical skills, however, will not cause major problems. This is, of course, in line with our previous discussion in Chapter 2 and 3.

Training and development needs in the third area—motivation and rewards—will depend on the type of orientation, values, and career objectives your technologists have. You will recall from our discussion in Chapter 3 that three types of orientations and career choices could exist:

1. "The technologist in transition to management," with a strong loyalty to the organization, strong managerial motivation orientation.

Table 4-3. Training and Development Needs in Management Skills.

ADMINISTRATIVE	INTERPERSONAL	TECHNICAL
Job descriptions	Handling people	Knowledge of fundamental technology
Understanding the organizational system	Coordination	Application of technology
Organizational relationships	Leadership	State of the art
Problem-solving techniques	Motivation techniques	
Managerial decision-making	Effective communication	
Program evaluation	Forming and managing effective teams	
Coping with organizational constraints (budgets, resource allocation, personnel policies, etc.)	Managing innovation and creativity	
Coping with environmental factors		

2. "The undecided technologist," who enjoys working in his field but finds a career in management appealing, yet is somewhat reluctant to move into management.
3. "The professionally loyal technologist," with a strong loyalty to his profession, for whom managerial motivation definitely has a negative appeal.

There is considerable research evidence that the type 1 orientation will be more typical among engineers than scientists. Conversely, the type 3 orientation will be more typical among scientists than engineers. Managerial motivations would clearly have a negative appeal to more scientists than engineers. As discussed in Chapter 3, it is entirely possible, of course, that the three types of orientations could be found, to varying degrees, within both engineering and science populations.

It follows that training and development needs would depend on the type of orientation the technologist has during the transition. The stronger the managerial orientation (type 1), the easier and less intensive the training would be. Individuals with a strong "specialist motivation" (type 3) would experience the most frustration in the transition. In the case of the "undecided technologist" (type 2), the intensity of the training and the extent of frustrations experienced through the transition period would largely depend on how attractive a management career is to the technologist, his degree of loyalty to both the profession and the organization, and his long-range career objectives.

Provide Opportunities for Management Internships

This is the seventh, and last, mechanism that can be employed for easing the transition from technologist to manager. Training and development programs based upon intellectualized and cognitive approaches (lectures, discussions, cases, and readings) will not be sufficient. Therefore, another approach to ease the transition to management is by providing opportunities for technologists to test management waters before making a final commitment to management as a career. Given the nature of your subordinates' management knowledge and background, it would be quite beneficial to give them "hands on" opportunities not merely to learn about management but to do some actual managing.

Project assignments with significant managerial responsibilities, venture teams, rotational assignments, and task leadership groups are a few examples of "learning by doing" in actual management situations. These opportunities, handled effectively, could provide significant insights for you and your would-be managers in the process of managerial selection and transition.

A closely related practice is to have management candidates go through an internship program as a testing period as discussed in Chapter 3. This would be an excellent arrangement for them to learn, practice the skills of their "new" possible position, and undertake some personal assessment; and for their managers to see and evaluate them in action. As noted earlier in this chapter, this testing period approach is already part of a comprehensive career development program at some organizations including IBM. As discussed in Chapter 3, two criteria must be met for this procedure to work effectively: The internship arrangement must be "bought" by both technologists and management so it becomes part of the internal "culture" of the organization; and both the technologist and management must retain the right to "call it off" should things not work out. This way, there will be no stigma implying managerial failure.

As you can see, these "preentry" or management internship programs in some form or another would provide technologists with the opportunity to assess the type of satisfactions, if any, they will obtain through performing the managerial role. This point relates closely to the question of their motivation. The amount of satisfaction derived will, of course, depend on several variables including their career objectives, their values, and the degrees of their professional and organizational orientations at that point.

In summary, what I have discussed so far in this chapter are the mechanisms and programs that management can adopt in an effort to help technologists with the transition to managerial careers. As you will note, the transition is a multiphase evolutionary process over time. It is a difficult process for the technologist, and for easing it a well-thought-out and intensive strategy would have to be developed by management (the role of the technologist in this connection will be the subject of Chapter 5). The components of this strategy are the seven items discussed so far in this chapter. For a comprehensive list of these items, please return to Table 4-1. What management can do for effective career management of professionals will be discussed in the balance of this chapter.

CAREER PLANNING AND EMPLOYEE DEVELOPMENT (CPED): AN ACTION PLAN

The above discussion clearly points out that as a technical manager you have definite responsibility for helping your subordinate scientists and engineers who are aspiring to management to make a smooth transition to management. This effort, however, is not done in a vacuum. Nor could the need for it be fulfilled through the establishment of some isolated hodgepodge management development activities for your engineers and scientists. In fact, the effectiveness of such efforts has been seriously questioned.

What Career Planning and Employee Development (CPED) Is

What is needed is a total system of career planning and employee development for technical people. What is CPED? It is a well-defined systematic set of activities and strategies involving a careful planning, directing, and monitoring of the careers of scientists and engineers in such a way as to enhance their skills and potential for their own self-development and career growth as well as for maximum utilization of their contributions to the organization. These efforts, to be successful, must be carefully managed by the organization as well as the individual technologist. It must, therefore, be a joint effort of organization career planning and individual career planning. Managing organizational careers (organization career planning) will be dealt with in this chapter, whereas managing individuals' careers (individual career planning) will be discussed in Chapter 5.

Components of a CPED System

The system I am proposing here is highly integrated and comprehensive. It is directed toward the maximum utilization of professional technical resources in a manner that will enhance both individual development and growth as well as total organizational effectiveness. Whether these resources will continue in their professional careers or develop managerial careers is simply immaterial. Since a detailed discussion of all system dimensions involved would probably require a separate volume, I shall focus on those relevant elements of the system only in so far as they relate to management efforts in easing the technologist's transition to management.

The manner in which the system is designed and implemented depends—among other things—on the organization's human resources development philosophy, backgrounds and orientations of technical executives and directors, needs and makeup of technologists, and overall top management goals and priorities. The proposed system, as it applies to technologists in transition to management, consists of four interrelated elements or components:

1. Subordinates' development and career counseling.
2. Career assessment and development programs.
3. Career coping programs.
4. Management development program.

A flowchart describing the four elements of the system and their interrelationships is shown in Figure 4-1.

Subordinates' Development and Career Counseling. You will recall from our previous discussion in this chapter that providing appropriate support, orientation, and coaching is one of the seven mechanisms employed by management to help the technologist in transition. Similarly, career counseling is a continuing process. As shown in Figure 4-1, it involves constant interaction with your subordinates, performance appraisal and feedback, identification of areas of professional strengths and weaknesses, and overall career direction.

The decision to go to management would involve a major change in the career direction of the technologist. Different forms of career counseling long before the technologist reaches "the moment of truth" will be necessary.

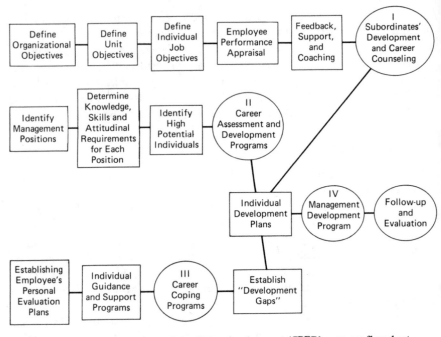

Figure 4-1. Career planning and employee development (CPED) program flowchart.

How can you provide the proper orientation and counseling for your subordinates by way of preparing them for the management transition? Here are some guidelines:

1. Establish good rapport and provide a supportive atmosphere for the group.
2. Establish two-way communication.
3. Provide feedback on day-to-day performance.
4. Do regular and thorough performance appraisal and coaching.
5. Show tolerance of occasional mistakes as part of the learning process.
6. Assign jobs that involve added responsibilities and a variety of experiences.
7. Keep an eye on promising management candidates and learn as much as possible about their career orientation and interests.
8. Level with those technologists aspiring to management for the wrong reasons or without the proper qualifications.

As noted earlier, subordinates' counseling and development, to be done effectively, must be given high priority by top management, and managers must be provided with appropriate means and rewards to induce them to undertake such efforts. Yet, my experience and observations at many organizations suggest that managers usually get bogged down in the day-to-day "fire fighting," and an organization can hinder managerial development by supervisory pressures exerted on subordinates for immediate results. This point is well made in the following quote:

Daily pressures are stressed to the exclusion of any ability to concentrate on what may be required for tomorrow. Competence is defined with respect to the present, not the future, so that little if any support is given to self-development efforts beyond the employees' presently defined technical specialty. Many organizations base rewards on short-term results, which seem to imply that personal development efforts should occur before joining or at least not on company time.[9]

The implications for you are clear. Subordinates' development and career counseling constitutes a significant component of a CPED system. If done properly—with the above guidelines in mind—the payoffs for both the organization and technologists in terms of better career planning efforts will very much be worth the effort.

Career Assessment and Development Programs. A program for career assessment and development for scientists and engineers is the second component of a CPED system (Figure 4-1). The career assessment program is essentially a personal evaluation approach designed to help managers and potential managers discover the intricacies, subtleties, and difficulties associated with interpersonal relations, leadership skills, and administrative complexities. It provides participants with an evaluation of their strengths and weaknesses in these areas, thereby stimulating a desire on their part for training and development activities suited to their individual needs.

The career assessment and development program has been implemented, in different forms, at 3M Company, Kodak, Xerox, International Business Machines, Travellers Insurance, AT&T, and other organizations with favorable results. You should note here that the career assessment concept is different from the assessment center concept discussed earlier in this chapter. The primary objective of the career assessment program is to provide a personal development opportunity, not to identify managerial talent for selection and promotion.[10] Therefore, no records would be maintained except those controlled by the participants themselves. Development is intended not only for the participants but for the staff as well, as most of the staff or observers are selected from upper management.

---

[9] Dalton, Gene, and Thompson, Paul H. Accelerating Obsolescence of Older Engineers. *Harvard Business Review*, 49, 8 (September-October 1971): 57-67.
[10] This discussion is based primarily on Hart, G. L. A Workshop Approach to Improving Managerial Performance. *Research Management*, **XX**, 5 (September 1977): 16-20.

Employees who are viewed by management as having high growth potential for leadership positions or who might otherwise benefit from this personal development opportunity are nominated by their management to attend the career assessment program. These programs vary in length from three to five days and are usually staffed jointly by experienced line executives, management development specialists, and outside consultants. The level of tension, anxiety, and apprehension tends to subside among participants over time. This tension reduction phenomenon is another major difference between these programs and assessment centers, which tend to increase anxiety, purposefully or not. Tension reduction occurs at the career assessment program because participants are aware that their performance results will not be included in their personnel files, nor will they be used formally by management for selection purposes.

Participants become involved in a variety of experiences designed to reveal their interpersonal and leadership skills, while the staff makes an effort—through interviews, reports, and other structured experiences—to develop reports covering predetermined personal and interpersonal skills and describing participants' behavioral characteristics. Only one copy of the report is made and is retained by the participants. Reports, typically, cover observations of the individual's strengths and limitations as perceived by the staff. Also included are a number of development recommendations should the participant desire to work toward improvement in his areas of deficiency.

The career assessment program is a very sound concept. Research demonstrates that this technique has had remarkable results when used as a personal evaluation technique employed primarily as a tool for personal development. It has led to improved managerial behavior, attitudes, and managerial performance of technical managers and supervisors. The strength of this technique emanates primarily from the fact that the evaluation results were fed back to the participants themselves for their own career development planning.

This technique would provide you with the opportunity to identify skill strengths and limitations in your subordinates aspiring to management. It would also give scientists and engineers the opportunity for systematic evaluation of their leadership and interpersonal skills with valuable career development recommendations.

Career Coping Programs. The third phase of an integrated CPED system is for you to provide the technologist in transition to management with the necessary direction and support to cope with the prospective career change and "career anxiety" (Figure 4-1). Technologists should be encouraged to maintain personal vitality through taking control of their own career and life management. Career and life goals are often idealized and fail to change over time with the changes brought on by personal and career pressures. The result is career anxiety, which manifests itself in undesirable side effects such as the loss of personal vitality accompanied by increasingly mechanistic performance.

If you are like most managers, you usually assume that you have rewarded a technologist for an outstanding job by "promoting" him to supervisor. He is expected to be grateful because you have taken him from among the "troops" and made him a part of the "management team." When he does not act accordingly, you are disappointed and tend to analyze failure in terms of his shortcomings. You do not analyze the failure from the standpoint of how you, as management, have created it from the beginning by making loose promises about being a part of management or about future personal development. You do not think of what effects the promotion has on the status and ego of the promoted individual. Have you really done him a favor? Is he really on the "management team"? Have you elevated or lowered his status? What kind of ego state will he be in now? These questions, among others, tend to generate tensions, anxiety, and frustration for the newly appointed supervisor.

A significant source of this anxiety is that the technologist is being taken off the top of the heap and put on the bottom of another heap.[11] Instead of being the superstar technologist, he now is the newest supervisor who does not know the ropes. The whole heap is now piled on top of him. This dilemma is known as "the heap reversal theory" and is illustrated in Figure 4-2. It creates feelings of alienation, loneliness, and uncertainty about whether switching to management was a wise decision in the first place. As a newly appointed manager, he

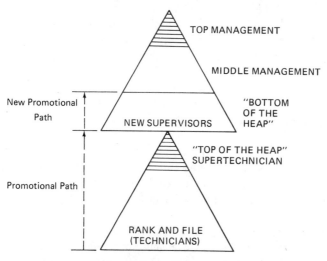

Figure 4-2. Heap reversal theory diagram. (From Benson, Carl A. New Supervisors: From the Top of the Heap to the Bottom of the Heap. *Personnel Journal* (April, 1976): 71.)

---

[11] Benson, Carl A. New Supervisors: From the Top of the Heap to the Bottom of the Heap. *Personnel Journal* (April 1976): 176-178.

is no longer "one of the boys," misses his field of specialty, and has a magnetic attraction to return to the good old days when things are not going well.

As you can see, the heap reversal syndrome is not atypical. It has dramatic psychological impacts on many technologists throughout the transition process. Through well-designed career coping programs, individual guidance, support, and coaching activities, the psychological problems involved in this transition can be alleviated. Furthermore, through the joint assessment of the individual's strengths and weaknesses, areas of deficiency and development gaps can be identified upon which training and development plans will be based.

Management Development Program. The management development program is the fourth and final component of a CPED system. Providing appropriate means for engineers and scientists to acquire management training both prior to and during management assignments is an integral component of a sound CPED program (Figure 4-1). The nature, orientation, and content of the management development program will, of course, depend on the specific management requirements of the company and the development needs of technologists. It is important to note here that management development is essentially self-development and that technologists, as noted above, will generally need to be trained in the functions, skills, and motivations of management.

Program Phases. There are four phases or stages in establishing a management development program: preparation, design, implementation, and evaluation. Program preparation concerns the process of training "needs analysis," collecting data about the organization and trainees and their jobs for background to form a basis for developing program objectives and strategy. Program design covers all activities involved with the actual development of program content, media and training approaches, and orientation. As you will note in Figure 4-1, the management development program is based on individual development plans which, in turn, are based on the outputs of the three other components of a CPED system: career counseling, career assessment, and career coping programs. In other words, these components constitute the major inputs to the management development program. The execution of the program constitutes the implementation phase, followed by program follow-up, assessment and evaluation.

Requirements for Program Effectiveness. All training efforts are change efforts. They are primarily directed toward changing, upgrading, and developing the knowledge and skills of the "learner." As noted earlier, while some characteristics that managers must have to be successful in specific jobs are not trainable, most managerial skills can be developed through training, experimentation, and practice.

For establishing and implementing an effective management development program for technologists, the following requirements and criteria must be met:

1. There must be a perceived need for the program by both management and technologists. It must be created to fill a void or a gap.

2. The value, objectives, and expectations of training should be clear. What are we looking for? What objectives do we expect to achieve by going through this program? What kinds of changes can we expect?

3. The program must be relevant. It must be tied closely to the needed changes in the technologist's knowledge, skills, and attitudes.

4. There must be a close relationship between what is taught in this program and what is actually done later on the job. The focus and thrust of training must be not only knowledge development but also skill development. The program content, therefore, must be tailored to fit the actual job content for which the training is undertaken.

5. The program should not be viewed as a spare-time activity. High-caliber, qualified instructors, modern training facilities, and relevant and strong management support will help create a favorable image and incentive for program participation.

6. The inputs into the management development program—as noted above—must be closely intertwined with the other phases of the CPED system, namely: career counseling, career assessment, and career coping.

7. The program must not be developed in a vacuum. It should rather be carefully integrated into the total management system. An appropriate organizational climate—management policies, task orientations, organizational rewards, and so on—must be provided to give the "new" supervisor the opportunity to practice what he was taught (or trained for) and, thus, reinforce his learning experience.

8. The program must become a top corporate concern, receiving a strong management commitment through supportive relationships and structured programs in human resources development.

Program Content. As mentioned above, the general orientation and content of a management development program depend on its objectives, the nature and backgrounds of trainees, their development needs, and the organization's policies and requirements. These programs usually consist of a variety of courses, workshops, and discussion groups using several learning media including lectures, cases, management games, films, small team discussions, role plays, and simulations.

What are the general areas to be emphasized in management development programs for engineers and scientists in transition to management? Again, it is difficult to give a specific answer to this question as this really depends on the many variables mentioned above. By the same token, development programs should be "tailored to fit" since canned packages and ready-made solutions are clearly worthless. Development programs are most effective when they are developed with the needs of the organization and the trainees in mind. Since these needs differ from one organization to another, then the actual content of a specific program must remain "unknown" until the variables determining program content are identified.

By way of helping you define the training areas appropriate for your technologists in transition (among others), an extensive—though not exclusive—list of management development curriculum is shown in Table 4-4. This list presents a variety of courses and training areas revolving around the management functions, skills, and motivations of technologists. The training areas are also clustered around the dimensions of managerial competency and the individual's three developmental needs: self-management, job management, and career management.

As you will note from Table 4-4, there are over sixty areas (and perhaps a lot more) where technologists' knowledge and managerial skills can be developed. You should also keep in mind that managerial development is a continuing process as job and individual needs for training and development will continually change. Your management development program should also reflect the forces operating within the organization and the needs of both the job and job occupants, as well as the external forces in the organization's environment. This is precisely why training and development will be needed in both the micro and macro aspects of engineering and R&D management (Table 4-4).

Your in-house management development programs for engineers and scientists could be staffed internally by setting up a training and development unit. One alternative is using outside resources such as consultants, professional associations, and specialized management training outfits. A combination of both approaches is your third possibility. While there is no scarcity of training and development packages available, including management courses, workshops, seminars, cassette tapes, and other self-instruction aids offered by a variety of national and international outfits, your major concern should be with knowing what you are buying. You must insist on getting the training package that will fit your needs and the best-quality product possible.

To sum up: The above discussion has identified the nature and purpose of a career planning and employee development system (CPED) and described how it works. This system is composed of four types of programs: career counseling, career assessment, career coping, and management development. The nature and orientation of each one of these components has been analyzed. It has become clear that these programs are highly interrelated, and to be effective, they must be approached as integral units of a broader system. The entire system represents a well-coordinated effort for effective career planning and development of professionals.

Table 4-4. Management Development Curriculum for Engineers and Scientists.

DIMENSIONS OF MANAGEMENT COMPETENCE	EXAMPLES OF MANAGEMENT DEVELOPMENT AREAS AND COURSES

Micro Aspects of Engineering and R&D Management
Self-Management
    1. Values clarification and assertiveness training
    2. Self-development
    3. Professionalism and self-awareness
    4. Time management

Job Management
1. *Management Functions*
    1. Fundamentals of management
    2. Principles of organization
    3. The organizational system and how it works
    4. Fundamentals of engineering and R&D management

2. *Management Skills*
  a. Administrative skills
    1. *Organizational Structure Skills*
      a. Organizational designs for professionals
      b. Project management
      c. The organization and its environment
      d. Laboratory management
      e. Personnel administration techniques
      f. Administration of R&D support functions

    2. *Planning and Decision-Making Skills (Management Tools and Technology)*
      a. Managerial decision-making
      b. Quantitative and nonquantitative aspects of decision-making
      c. Managerial accounting
      d. Managerial economics
      e. Computer science and management information systems (MIS)
      f. Budgeting, reporting, and financial analysis
      g. Principles of marketing and marketing research techniques
      h. Management by objectives (MBO) for engineers and scientists
      i. R&D planning
      j. Technological forecasting
      k. Organizational policy planning and strategic goal setting
      l. Value engineering and value analysis

    3. *Managerial Control and Performance Appraisal Skills*
      a. Essentials of performance appraisal
      b. Evaluation and measurement of engineering and R&D
      c. How to evaluate performance of professionals
      d. Techniques of performance appraisal
      e. Interviewing, counseling, and coaching skills
      f. MBO and performance evaluation systems
      g. Development of performance appraisal and program evaluation skills of technical supervisors and managers

Table 4-4. Continued.

DIMENSIONS OF MANAGEMENT COMPETENCE	EXAMPLES OF MANAGEMENT DEVELOPMENT AREAS AND COURSES
b. Technical skills	Courses on state of the art of technology and its app tion (in the technologist's area of interest)
c. Interpersonal skills	1. Human behavior in organizations 2. Development of leadership and interpersonal ski of technical supervisors and managers 3. Group problem-solving and group dynamics 4. Team building and team management 5. Research and engineering personnel administra 6. Effective communication skills 7. Verbal and written communication skills 8. Technical report writing 9. Understanding body language of engineers and scientists 10. Understanding the informal organization systen how it works 11. How to handle corporate power, games and po 12. Winning at office politics 13. Techniques of power and conflict managemen 14. Effective interviewing, coaching, and counselin techniques
C. Career Management	1. Techniques for effective career management 2. Career planning and career winging 3. How to manage your most important investme your career 4. Managing career anxiety and executive stress 5. Self-development and career growth for professionals
II. *Macro Aspects of Engineering and R&D Management* A. Engineering and R&D Interface within the Organization	1. Venture management 2. R&D engineering and marketing interface 3. R&D and top management 4. Product development, assurance and reliability 5. Managing R&D relationships with other corpo divisions
B. Engineering and R&D Interface with the External Environment	1. Technology transfer 2. Social, economic, and political environment o business 3. Licensing and patents 4. Technology assessment and forecasting 5. Venture management (refers to outside projec 6. Managing contract R&D 7. Dealing with external R&D funding clients (age foundations, etc.) 8. Dealing with the government 9. Legal considerations in engineering and R&D

SUMMARY

The role of management in easing the transition consists of developing appropriate mechanisms to provide technologists with the necessary guidance and support; and setting up a system for effective career management of professionals. Seven mechanisms for managing career transition for technologists have been discussed above along with four major phases of a career planning and employee development system (CPED).

It is important to remember that while some characteristics of successful managers in certain situations might not be trainable, the fact remains that most prerequisites for managerial success are learnable skills. A good manager is analogous to a good athlete who was born with some natural endowment, but who through consistent practice, learning, and experience develops the initial endowment into a set of mature skills. Given that the ideal manager is a myth, your task as a technical manager is to determine the nature and characteristics of the situation (the task), and attempt to identify the most promising individual possessing the skills and qualifications for this position using the concepts, tips, and techniques discussed in this chapter—with a good dose of luck! Just in case you miss, charge it to experience, and learn from it the next time around!

Managing career transition for technologists is a joint responsibility of both the organization and the individual technologist. If you happen to be an executive or a manager of technical activities, the dimensions of your task for easing the transition have been analyzed and discussed in this chapter. But if you are a technologist considering a move into management, or if you are already in the transition process, your responsibilities in this respect are the subject of Chapter 5.

5
What Technologists Can Do

In Chapter 3, three sets of reasons were identified as possible causes of the difficulties accompanying the transition from technologist to manager. These reasons relate to the nature of technologists' education, the characteristics of scientists and engineers as a group, and the nature of the organization's management systems and policies. For easing the transition, the notion of a joint partnership between the employing organization, technologists, and educational institutions has been introduced. The role of management in managing career transition for technologists was discussed in Chapter 4. What technologists can do to ease this transition is the subject of this chapter. What the university—engineering, science, and management educators—can do to help develop managerial skills of technologists will be explored in Chapter 6.

A detailed discussion of all aspects of your career planning and the multiple issues involved in effective career management is, obviously, beyond the scope of this book. However, a discussion of the possible problems facing you in the course of your transition to management and how to deal with them in isolation would be quite superficial. This chapter, therefore, will examine the issues involved in career planning as part of a broader system involving your life planning and life-style management. Keep in mind, however, that these issues will be explored only insofar as they relate to the transition problem, leaving detailed information and learning about effective career and life planning to your personal reading. Please consult Chapter 13 of this book for an extensive reading list. This chapter will also provide you with a model that can serve as a useful device for effective planning and career management.

CAREER PLANNING AND CAREER "WINGING"

Management practitioners and scholars are very much divided on the merits of career planning. For a balanced presentation, let us examine both the case for and the case against career planning. Starting out with the negative view, some managers brand career planning as a "useless exercise."[1] They think that it will merely serve as a frustrating reminder of unachieved objectives and that you will be better off "winging it," letting the chips fall freely.

Wingers usually advocate "hanging loose," not setting a lot of goals, and "bending with the wind." Their rationale is that many persons who are constantly asking themselves how they are going to be president of the company are not likely to become presidents. Wingers are also convinced that those who plan their careers do not retain enough flexibility.

Another argument supporting career winging is that career planning is counterproductive. Since our system typically chains people to money and, in many organizations, to a ladder of progression, that kind of planning comes down to "how to bump the next guy up and up, until you get where you want to be."

As you can see from the above analysis, the arguments for career winging can easily be challenged. These arguments, however, are not against career planning as such, but the manner in which it is done. Of course, any type of planning would be faulty if it was based on too many unrealistic goals, inflexible and tight plans, and simple daydreaming without knowing your professional assets and liabilities. This, obviously, would be the wrong prescription regardless of whether you are a career planner or winger. In short, the objections raised against career planning are too simplistic and are focused on the manner of planning (the how) rather than on the concept as such (the what).

THE CASE FOR CAREER PLANNING

Let us now turn to the merits of career planning. Your career can be defined as a set of successive stages relating to your work experiences and activities which are associated with a multitude of perceptions, attitudes, and behaviors over your life span. You might think, then, that your career is a private matter and therefore of concern only to you. This is a partly accurate statement. Indeed, the study and planning of your career should be important to you for several reasons. First of all, your career should be of utmost importance not only to you but to your employees, your family, and many other parties you are dealing with. Your career is a substantial portion of your life. Yet, while your most precious commodity is career time, chances are that neither you nor your employer is spending enough time planning and managing it. Sadly, very few organizations have concrete, meaningful career planning programs for their employees. So, what is most valuable to the individual as far as his professional life is concerned—his career—is receiving the least attention and concern by the organization.

---

[1] This section is partly based on Johnson, Michael L. Plan Your Career or Wing It. *Industry Week* (September 30, 1974): 32-37.

Another reason you should plan and manage your career is that without some fairly defined mission or goal to strive for, it does not matter which way you go. In short, without knowing where you want to go, any route will get you there. Yet technologists (among others) do not spend as much as one full day per year studying and planning their own careers!

A third reason is that while it is your organization's responsibility to provide you with the environment, support, and incentives necessary for effective career planning, the prime responsibility for planning, implementing, and monitoring your career progress is definitely yours. Your career, in short, is your most valuable and expensive investment, as work clearly plays a key role in shaping your life.

Fourth, since management is an important career path for many engineers and scientists, the lack of career awareness on the part of technologists and their managers can be very damaging. As noted in Chapter 3, research shows that technical managers get fired not mostly for lack of technical competence but for lack of managerial and interpersonal competence. This suggests that without effective career planning (including whether to make the transition to management) you might end up as part of this statistic.

Another benefit of career planning is that it will help you recognize your strengths and professional skills so you can play to your strengths and develop deficient areas. Self-appraisal and self-analysis are—as will be seen later—an integral part of an effective individual's career plan.

Finally, planning your career will provide you with some yardsticks against which you can measure career opportunities and assess how they fit your professional goals and personal life-style. These tools and measuring devices—subjective as they might be—would, in fact, be far superior to the "sink or swim" approach.

I believe that individual lives and careers are so precious that they must be managed effectively. Career planning, in my judgment, is an excellent tool for achieving this objective. This is, of course, not to say that your career should be planned rigidly down to the year and month. This not only would be a ridiculous exercise but is also useless and unrealistic. Flexibility in career planning is particularly important in the case of engineers and scientists who, by nature, are masters in developing detailed and overengineered plans. Considerable flexibility in career planning is also called for to accommodate life contingencies—let alone other factors over which you have very little or no control—which can immensely shape your career.

In short, the view taken here in favor of career planning over career winging does not intend to deny the role of chance, luck, and being in the right place at the right time in shaping your career. Rather, career planning is seen as a viable attempt to reduce—not eliminate—the role played by these variables. The alternative is simply a random walk through life.

THE TRANSITION TO MANAGEMENT: CAREER PLANNING AND LIFE PLANNING

As noted in Chapter 4, there are two types of career planning: organization career planning and individual career planning. Organization career planning involves the creation of career ladders (paths) and the process of matching the talents of organizational members with the requirements of available positions.[2] The process of managing organizational careers of technologists through the creation of a career planning and employee development (CPED) system was discussed in Chapter 4.

The other type of career planning—individual career planning—is different. It requires the individual taking full responsibility for the planning, development, and effective management of his career in a manner that will be personally satisfying to him and potentially contributing to his self-development, psychological success, and growth. The point you should keep in mind is that both types of career planning, though different philosophically and procedurally, are interrelated and must be effectively managed. How you can manage your career transition to management will be dealt with in the remainder of this chapter.

The relationship between the individual's decision to switch to management, career planning, and life planning is illustrated in Figure 5-1. As you will note, the decision to switch to management must be viewed in terms of individual, organization, and life planning perspectives. It must mesh well with the individual career and life planning. Put another way, effective career management must focus on the total life span of the individual. Moreover, career planning

Figure 5-1. Relationship between work, career planning, and life planning.

---

[2] Burack, Elmer H. Why All of the Confusion About Career Planning. *Human Resource Management* (Summer 1977): 21-33.

(including management career transition) should include a continuing appraisal of one's personal and professional life.

Individual career planning is only one aspect of life planning. Thus, it is not really a one-shot deal, but rather a continuous lifelong process of personal growth and development of which work is only one part. Your decision to switch to management (a career transition decision) should never be made on a random basis. To help you with making an informed decision whether to go into management, and to ease the possibly troublesome transition, let us now turn to a discussion of some practical techniques.

A CAREER ACTION PLANNING MODEL (CAPM)

Figure 5-2 presents a career action planning model (CAPM), which is a very handy device to guide you through the process of planning and managing your career. This model is universal and is equally applicable, with slight modifications, to your technical career should you decide to stay in your professional field or specialty. Our focus in this discussion, however, will be on managerial career planning and development.

This model consists of the following seven consecutive phases:

1. Life planning and career awareness.
2. Career option analysis and choice-making.
3. Self-appraisal and risk analysis.
4. Preparation for management.
5. Building up your managerial qualifications and skills.
6. Career growth strategies.
7. Follow-up and management career reassessment.

Let us now turn to a discussion of this model, drawing heavily on the previous two chapters. In understanding this model, it is important to remember that your career is actually a movement line consisting of several behavioral patterns with numerous choice points.

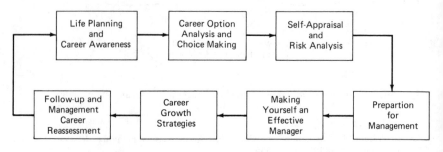

Figure 5-2. Phases of a career action planning model (CAPM).

Life Planning and Career Awareness

By now you know that career awareness is an integral part of a total system of life planning. Your objective in this preliminary phase of the model is, therefore, simply to explore your career and life goals. Naturally, this is not the only time this exploration will be done. While this is probably the first time it is done, your career and life goals should be examined periodically at different stages of life to make sure that your achievements are "in tune" with your expectations. Appropriate modifications in achievements and expectations can, of course, be made accordingly.

What kind of questions do you need to ask yourself at this point of your career? Here is a selected list:

- What am I going to do with my life?
- What are my life goals?
- What are my career work goals?
- Where am I headed? And where do I want to be?
- How consistent are my career goals with my life goals? Are they closely related?

These, admittedly, are not easy questions to answer. However, the answers to these questions will provide you with a good understanding and awareness of your life and career objectives. They will give you a sense of direction and mission. Perhaps more important, completing this phase of the CAPM will help you identify a set of career goals and will therefore help create a commitment. Without committing yourself to some goal and making some effort to achieve it, you are taking a random walk through life and almost any route will get you there. However, the problem is you do not know where "there" is; what a way to manage one's life or career!

But how do you go about your life and career planning? What tools can you use? And what type of technology is available to help you learn about your self-interests and goals? There are many good books and manuals on the subject; references can be found in the last chapter of this book. Life planning and career planning exercises are also becoming popular ways to learn about one's self-interests and career objectives.

What are some of the sources for help in this area? Some informal sources include performance appraisal and feedbacks received from your superiors, friends, family, and associates. There are formal sources, too. Developing self-awareness and effective career plans might require consultation with career counselors and career management specialists. As discussed in the previous chapter, if services such as career assessment, assessment centers, employee counseling, and career development activities are offered by your organization, take advantage of them. Furthermore, other sources of help include professional societies, technical associations, universities, professional specialists, and consultants in your local area.

How you can use the CAPM is presented in Table 5-1. It describes the objective (the what) of each phase of the CAPM, the career planning technology for that phase (the how), and the relationship between that phase and the transition to management decision. As you can see from the table, the objective of career and life planning (the first phase of the model) is to gain knowledge about yourself, your career direction, and its place in the scheme of life through the use of formal and informal career planning technology.

Career Option Analysis and Choice-making

Career option analysis and choice-making constitutes the second phase of CAPM. Having identified some career goals you would like to strive for, you are now ready to undertake a career option alaysis and make some choices (decisions! decisions! decisions!). Fortunately or unfortunately, there is no way to get around this one as choices have to be made at this point.

As you will recall, career choices open to the technologist along with ways for evaluating them were discussed in Chapter 3. Technologists will basically fall into three categories:

1. The technologist in transition to management.
2. The undecided technologist.
3. The professionally loyal technologist.

For a discussion of career orientations of each type, please refer to Chapter 3. The balance of this section will expand, rather than duplicate, on my previous discussion.

In the course of appraising the career options open to you and making choices, you should keep in mind the following critical factors:

1. Ask yourself the right questions: Here is a selected list:
   a. What are my career options?
   b. What are the role requirements for different career paths?
   c. Which role would I be most comfortable with: technical specialty or technical management?
2. Identify your career choices. You have basically two: to stay in your specialty or to go to management. Return to Chapter 3 for a detailed discussion and evaluation of the motivations technologists have for each career path.
3. Understand fully the role requirements for each career path. It would be foolish to make an uninformed decision without understanding the different requirements for each career option. As you will note in Table 5-2, there are fundamental differences between the roles of "technical management" and "tech-

Table 5-1. A Typology of Career Action Planning and Its Relationship to the Transition to Management.

PHASE	OBJECTIVE (WHAT)	CAREER PLANNING TECHNOLOGY (HOW)	RELATIONSHIP TO THE TRANSITION TO MANAGEMENT
I. Life planning and career awareness	To explore career and life objectives.	Formal and informal career planning techniques.	Better understanding of life goals and career direction.
II. Career option analysis and choices making	To identify alternate career paths and evaluate each choice.	Career appraisal guidelines and pertinent occupational information.	Better understanding of career options and the roles associated with the technical specialty vs. technical management.
III. Self-appraisal and risk analysis	To develop a good fit between one's interests and career requirements.	Self-appraisal instruments (i.e., self-directed search).	Increased self-knowledge and understanding of sources of career behavior.
IV. Preparation for management	To explore the alternate routes to the executive suite.	Evaluation of alternative management career paths, and establishment of superior performance record.	Better insights into one's qualifications and ability to match them with the requirements of alternate paths to management.
V. Making yourself an effective manager: an action plan	To build one's management competence and develop his qualifications and skills.	Managerial skill assessment techniques.	Recognition of one's managerial strengths and weaknesses and development of a plan to enhance his competence.
VI. Strategies for career growth	To identify avenues for career advancement and design mechanisms for executive survival.	Techniques for establishing oneself as a manager; techniques for executive survival and for handling the boss.	Increased control over one's destiny and ability to manage one's career for advancement and growth.
VII. Follow-up and management career assessment	To assess career performance and life goals.	Evaluation of internal career notions and external career realities.	Obtaining of feedback so career cycle is either concluded or repeated.

Table 5-2. The Alternate Administrative Career Paths:
Some Role Differences.[a]

TECHNICAL MANAGEMENT	TECHNICAL SPECIALIST
Counsels, guides, directs people	Is consulted by people
Is sensitive to feelings, attitudes	Is intuitive, creative
Evaluates people's performance	Evaluates data systems or methods
Forecasts, analyzes, controls costs	Technical performance outranks cost
High verbal skill required	High analytical skill required
Transmits and enforces policy	Logic outranks conformity
Directs what methods to use	Determines operational methods
Makes decisions from insufficient data	Seeks additional data
Accepts organizational hierarchy	Accepts hierarchy of truth
Seeks relationships to business goals	Seeks relationships among technical facts

IN WHICH COLUMN DOES AN INDIVIDUAL'S PREDILECTION
GENERALLY FALL?

[a]Source: Balderston, Jack L. Do You Really Want to Be a Manager? *Journal of the Society of Research Administrators,* IX, 4 (Spring 1978).

nical specialist." Exploring and understanding these role differences is impera-tive so you can determine where your predilection generally falls. This under-standing will also help you in another way: to see which role requirements will fit best with your career goals (the first phase of the CAPM), and your self-appraisal (the third phase of the model, discussed later in this chapter).

4. Determine, tentatively, which role is best for you. Your determination has to be tentative at this stage of the model and will not, of course, be final until a self-appraisal is undertaken (the next phase of CAPM). However, a pre-liminary exploration of the reasons why you want (or do not want) to go to management would be quite helpful for your career planning at this point. Here are five practical tips:

a. Management is not the best career for everyone, nor is it necessarily the best path for career success. It is, indeed, one of the routes and if you do not have what it takes to succeed in management (see Chapters 1-3), then managerial work is not for you and you should stay away from it.

b. A move into management is typically a one-way street and, thus, is usually irreversible. As pointed out in Chapters 3 and 4, this move must be carefully planned after considerable soul searching and motive exploration. I cannot em-phasize the importance of this point enough. My consulting and career counseling experience in a number of organizations clearly suggests that the supply of once-happy technologists turned unhappy and ineffective managers is limitless. In a substantial number of these cases, the primary cause was that the type of career planning we are undertaking now was never done.

c. Never—under any circumstances—choose a career option because your spouse, family, friends, associates, or the world at large looks more favorably upon one choice of action than another. It is your career, and you are the one who must be comfortable with it personally and professionally. Granted that all these parties will be considered in the career planning process, in the final analysis only two things really matter: Whether this is what *you* want to do for the foreseeable future; and whether *you* have the qualifications and skills for succeeding in doing it. If the answer to either or both questions is no, and yet you somehow end up in this particular career, you will only be opting for misery and you had better get busy teaming up with other poor souls since—as you, of course, know—misery loves company!

d. Do not get carried away with or hung up on the glamor, prestige, and power typically characteristic of most management positions as opposed to technical positions. Always evaluate these attractions in view of the expensive price you pay should you fail (also the payoffs should you succeed). While some of these attractions exist in all of us, it will never hurt you to be realistic in planning your career.

e. Regardless of what your friends, associates, superiors, subordinates, or even society at large say or impress upon you, it all boils down to one—and only one—thing: you are what you do! Therefore, choosing a career path, no matter what that is, involves choosing an identity. You will find out, if you have not already, that the impact of what you do—contrary to other claims—will be ingrained not only in your career potential but literally on your life.

5. Consider your spouse. Whether you are a member of a one- or two-career family, your spouse must be considered in your career planning. Your wife or husband is (or should be) actually your closest career partner. Assuming that the spouse will automatically go along with your career plan would be a mistake. Joint career planning could even be more of a problem in the case of the two-career family simply because you will have more parameters or constraints that must be considered in the career planning decision. Both partners must also discuss and understand the problems, sacrifices, frustrations, and mutual support they can give to each other's career.

The role of the spouse in building or hindering the other partner's career is more significant nowadays than ever before due to the increasing complexity of managerial jobs and the uncertain and fuzzy environment within which the organization operates. These strains are usually translated into long hours at the office, a heavy travel schedule, and a total commitment to one's own career. This will, in turn, require understanding, sacrifices, and support from the spouse.

From the standpoint of career planning, the spouse is also important for a third reason. The way the "corporate spouse" will handle herself or himself in matters relating to the other partner's job, such as socializing, entertainment, interpersonal relations, and corporate politics and "gossip," will have a significant impact on the partner's career success. This is why most organizations today usually look at the spouse's interests, career, and qualifications particularly for those individuals at higher and executive management levels.

To sum up: As shown in Table 5-1, the objective of the second phase of CAPM is to identify alternate career paths and evaluate each choice. Use of the above career appraisal guidelines and other occupational information will provide you with a solid understanding of your career options and the different roles associated with each. This information will be the basis for making career choices.

Self-Appraisal and Risk Analysis

Self-appraisal and risk analysis is the third phase of CAPM. So far you have developed some awareness of your career and your life goals. You have also analyzed your alternate career paths and the options associated with each. In doing all this, you have, undoubtedly, been finding out things about yourself that will help you in career planning and also in smoothing the transition to management should you decide to follow this route.

The objective of this phase of CAPM is to help you discover more about yourself through a rigorous self-appraisal. The ultimate outcome of this phase is to develop a good fit between your interests, objectives, abilities, and experience on the one hand and the requirements, rewards, and opportunities of your career path on the other (the outcome of the first two phases).

In undertaking this personal evaluation or self-appraisal exercise, several questions need to be asked here such as:

- Who am I?
- Why do I want what I want as a career? In other words, why do I want to stay in my field or switch to management (depending on your career orientation and interests)?
- What are my "real" motives?
- Do I have what it takes to succeed in my specialty or in management or in both? What are my strengths and weaknesses?
- Do I have what it takes to make it in other career lines?
- What if I fail in career X? What will my options be then? What are the risks involved to me?

Understanding oneself has never been easy, and answering these questions certainly is not an exception. Philosophers have been wrestling for centuries with the question: Why do people behave as they do? While their answers are far from conclusive, we now have enough information to guide us through the self-appraisal phase of CAPM. Here are some practical tips and guidelines:

1. Get to know yourself better. As you may recall from our discussion of the first phase of CAPM, some formal and informal sources of help in understanding oneself and increasing one's career awareness are available. These include career assessment, assessment centers, interest inventories, and other self-analysis instruments to help you identify your strengths and weaknesses. Another self-administered career planning exercise is Holland's self-directed search.[3] It is a clear and easy-to-use instrument which attempts to match your abilities and interests with the characteristics and requirements of specific occupations.

2. Understand your motivations. The motivations to stay in your technical specialty or to go into management are not the same. These motivations were discussed in considerable detail in Chapter 3 and thus will not be repeated here. The primary questions you will be attempting to answer here are: What are my real motives, for example, to go into management? Is it in search of power, status, achievement? Or is it a political tactic to block someone else's move into management? Is my choice a response to financial incentives or to frustration in technical assignments? Does it relate and fit with my own career plans? Am I responding to my basic needs, or to external pressures? What is the influence of my immediate company environment on my career decision?

Answers to the above questions, among others, would be very helpful in understanding your motivations. Although you will still be dealing with perceived but not necessarily real motivations, your answers will give you some insights into the possible causes behind your anticipated career move.

3. Find out whether you are executive material. As you know by now, the view taken in this book is that traits do not make good managers, but combinations of appropriate behavioral patterns and requirements of managerial situations do. Nor are you expected to be a born manager, because managers are made—for the most part. It follows that if you opt for a management career, you must do a lot of learning and develop many new skills.

In addition to what has already been discussed in previous chapters, there are a number of things successful managers do and certain norms they share and believe in. A selected sample of these norms and behavioral patterns is shown in a checklist in Table 5-3. An important aspect of the self-appraisal phase of CAPM, then, is to check this list—based on research, observations, and experience—to see to what extent you are "executive material."

As you can see from Table 5-3, the world of management is quite different from the world of engineering and science. Proving yourself by superior job

---

[3] Holland, John L. "Making Vocational Choices: A Theory of Careers." Englewood Cliffs, N.J.: Prentice-Hall, 1973.

Table 5-3. Are You Executive Material: A Selected Checklist.

EXECUTIVE BEHAVIORAL CHARACTERISTICS	YOUR RESPONSE	
Here are some characteristics of executive behavior shared by many successful managers. To what extent can you accept the "fact" that:	YES	NO
1. Job proficiency is only a partial requirement for promotion and advancement (your promotions depend on the good will of your superiors).	☐	☐
2. Your promotion is based, to a large extent, upon compatibility with your superior. You must understand him and then tune yourself in to what the boss expects.	☐	☐
3. Team play—not independence—and playing the corporate game are fundamental prerequisites for career progress; and you must follow the rules of the game.	☐	☐
4. You need to develop coping skills to deal with everyday frustrations.	☐	☐
5. You must continually prepare for the future and never let yesterday hold you back.	☐	☐
6. You must have a good sense of vocation—a deep-rooted unsentimental desire to do good.	☐	☐
7. Getting to be a key subordinate to your boss can increase his effectiveness and can open many doors for you.	☐	☐
8. By making yourself indispensable, you will move up, but by acting as though you are indispensable, you will move out.	☐	☐
9. Being a lone wolf is alien to management and could destroy your career (also see item 3 above).	☐	☐
10. Broadening your knowledge and management skills away from your vocationalism is a fundamental requirement for executive career advancement.	☐	☐
11. Your performance will be judged more on the basis of your leadership and administrative skills and less—much less—on the basis of technical skills.	☐	☐
12. Continuing education and other self-development efforts will become a way of life for you.	☐	☐
13. Your management career will not only be controlled by you but partly (if not largely) by the organization and the people you work with.	☐	☐
14. You must learn to delegate and take pride in your subordinates' achievements.	☐	☐
15. Your task as a manager is not to do the work yourself but to get it done through others.	☐	☐
16. You will not be able to spend enough time with your family. If you want a full family life, you had better be satisfied with a lesser job.	☐	☐
17. Your appearance, what you wear, and your mannerisms will have a lot to do with your "executive image" and career direction and advancement.	☐	☐
18. Acceptance of organizational policies and willingness to conform are important criteria for managerial career success. The organization must come first.	☐	☐
19. You are expected to be an individualist privately and a conformist publicly.	☐	☐
20. You will need a mentor or a sponsor "upstairs."	☐	☐

performance is, of course, quite important, as discussed in previous chapters. However, you, as a manager, are on the stage—the organization forum. Your performance, I am afraid, will be judged against many other criteria, many of which are alien to your technical and professional values (also see Table 5-2). So, do not try to evaluate the values of management as some of them might not even be rational. This is the way things are, and if you cannot accept and live with most of the items on the checklist (Table 5-3), perhaps you should have serious second thoughts about going into management in the first place.

Some of the items on this checklist might be shocking to some technologists, but this is not unexpected. These items, however, represent some truths about how organizations operate for the most part. If you can relate to these stereotypes, then they have reaffirmed your age-long beliefs; but if you cannot, just look around in your organization more carefully. If you still cannot relate to them, this is indeed unfortunate!

4. Understand sources of career behavior. Perhaps the most critical question you should attempt to answer at this phase of CAPM is: Why do I want what I want (technical specialty or technical management) as a career? In order to get some insights into answering this question, you must understand sources of career behavior, that is, why people behave as they do. Without getting too technical, let us now explore this question.

Figure 5-3 presents sources of our career behavior. As you can see from this figure, three major variables affect the individual's life and career movement.[4]

1. Heredity.
2. Shaping factors (the environment in which one is born and raised).
3. Maturation issues (ages/stages factors).

In the process of growing up, we gain first a hint of our limitations and potentials. Then, later in life, we develop a resonably strong impression of these plus/minus capabilities. The shaping factors can be "good" or "bad" depending upon how well these social impacts prepare us for life and work. The ages/stages factors account for the variability and changing nature of people over time. In adolescence and early adulthood, our interests, attitudes, and values are frequently borrowed or spliced on by the interventions of others and/or their reactions to us. In later life, some or much of this excess baggage is shed and a clearer perception of who we are and where we want to go results.

You will note in Figure 5-3 that important components are the internal career notions and the external career realities. The internal career notions relate to our self-esteem and career self-concept, which grow together throughout life. That is, there is a dynamic interrelationship between the two which takes form

---

[4] This section is primarily based on Leach, John L. The Notion and Nature of Careers. *The Personnel Administrator* (September 1977): 49-55.

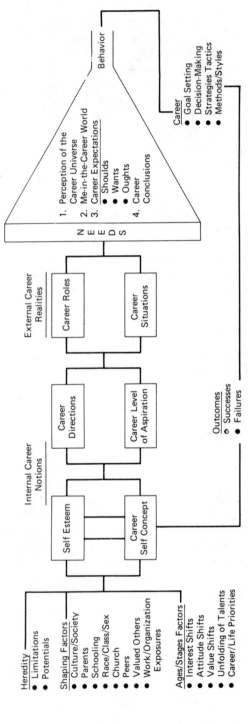

Figure 5-3. Sources of our career behavior. (From Leach, John. The Notion and Nature of Careers. *The Personnel Administrator* (September 1977), p. 53.)

in the career directions that we set for ourselves and the career level of aspiration toward which we mobilize our energy and effort.

While the internal career notions are formed quite early in life, the external career realities do not really exist until later. The fact is that we have not had sufficient time to reality-test these self-perceptions. But when the career begins later in life, it is not until then that we have the first opportunity to experiment with actual career roles and career situations—reality checking.

The feedback we receive from the real world is filtered through the needs-of-the-moment or current-life stage. Depending upon the person and career examined, either a blurred or a clear perception of the career universe emerges. The person-in-the-career world (where he fits and does not fit) also emerges in general fashion early in the career and more specifically later in the career.

When the individual is planning the career, consciously or otherwise, early shapings continue to play a role, and these are referred to as career expectations. Here the person is constantly grappling with what he wants to do versus the "shoulds" and the "oughts." The resolution finally decided upon by the person represents the career conclusions or the basis for the career plan. All career goal setting, decision-making, strategies/tactics, and methods/styles yield an outcome— either success or failure. Depending upon the outcome, this feeds back upon internal career notions (self-esteem and career self-concept).

It is obvious from Figure 5-3 that an understanding of the sources of your career behavior is crucial for effective career and life planning. It is also interesting to note that you will typically be checking the external career realities (roles and situations) against your internal career notions (self-esteem, career self-concept, career directions, and career level of aspiration).

To sum up: Your objective in the self-appraisal phase of CAPM (Table 5-1) is to evaluate your strengths and limitations so an appropriate fit can be developed between your level of aspiration and career self-concept on the one hand and your career situations and career roles on the other hand. You should always remember, however, that quite a bit of psychological material has already been processed before career behavior is actually produced (see Figure 5-3). A thorough self-appraisal, therefore, would be quite helpful in career and life planning.

What I have discussed so far are the first three phases of CAPM, namely: life planning and career awareness, career option analysis and choice-making, and self-appraisal and risk analysis. In order to proceed with a discussion of the rest of the model, we would have to assume—based on your exploration of the first three stages—that you will opt for management as a career path. Let us now turn to a discussion of the other phases of the model.

Preparation For Management

So, you want to be a manager! The next phase of CAPM, then, is to prepare for the job. While there is not a single "best" route or a prescribed formula to get into management, some practical recommendations can be made.

1. Explore the routes to the executive suite. It would be wise to simply describe for you the alternate avenues that can get you into management without passing value judgments on them. Since there is no one best method, a good approach would be to use your own judgment and pick up the route or routes that will fit your particular situation. Some of these routes are:[5]

a. Display a superior technical competence. Regardless of the real merit of this approach, most appointed managers were former technologists. Your superior technical competence will actually make you stand out and get "promoted" to management. It will, then, pay to establish an excellent technical performance record.

b. Show good organizational and management skills. This could be done through learning people-handling skills, making effective presentations, working well with deadlines, and showing an ability for coordination of work activities such as in task forces and project management assignments.

c. Demonstrate appropriate leadership qualities. If you can display a superior capacity for leading teams of people, influencing the direction these teams take, an ability to sell your ideas and persuade others to buy them, these will be considered valuable management assets.

d. Sharpen your communication skills. Superior communication skills—verbal, written, and body language—along with sharp technical skills will make you uniquely qualified for management.

e. Always favor more visibility and exposure. Belonging to the boss's club or professional organization, chairing committees, getting important assignments, and participating in community activities and fund raising activities are some good ways to get more visibility and exposure. Those individuals simply stand out as good management prospects. The point you should keep in mind is that these activities should be done in subtle ways and in good taste.

f. Develop sponsor-protegé arrangements. Having a close relationship with a superior based on solid performance achievements and demonstrated competence could be very helpful. As a superior moves up, he likes to get competent subordinates promoted so they can continue working for him. A similar arrangement is to have a mentor at a higher management level. This individual empathizes with your achievements, is impressed with your skills and qualifications, and could be an instrumental factor in your career progress.

---

[5] Few of the points discussed in this section are based on Karger, Delmar W. and Murdick, Robert G. "Managing Engineering and Research," Second Edition. New York: Industrial Press, 1969, pp. 512-516.

g. Consider executive mobility. If planned well, job changes could help broaden your experience, improve your skills in new fields, broaden your connections and contacts, and increase your visibility and exposure. This, ultimately, could help you spot some good management opportunities and, of course, improve your financial status.

h. Earn a management degree. A combination of a technical background and an M.B.A. (Master of Business Administration) has been and still is very attractive. Individuals with this background are perceived by employers to be more "fit" for high-level managerial positions. Whether or not this is really the case is debatable and will be explored in Chapter 6. What is important here, however, is that getting an M.B.A. degree will certainly open many management doors for you. Moreover, assuming that the present trend will continue, it will pay handsomely in terms of the reward package you will get from your employer.

2. Establish an excellent performance record. In addition to exploring the routes to the executive suite, another approach to preparation for management is to establish a solid performance record. Your performance record, of course, carries considerable weight in your preparation for a move into management. Here are some tips:

a. For every assignment, know what is expected of you, and how your performance will be measured.

b. Seek help and advice from your boss as needed.

c. Keep your relationship with your boss on the highest professional level and empathize with his professional needs.

d. Take initiative in creating new work assignments and complete them to the best of your professional capacity.

e. Seek committee assignments and participate actively in professional societies and associations.

f. Establish a reputation of being prompt in meeting deadlines and honor all your commitments.

g. Develop a viable program for self-development.

h. Make every attempt to relate job performance to career planning.

To sum up: As shown in Table 5-1, the objective of this phase of CAPM is to explore the possible routes to management, assess each one of these paths in terms of your own situation, and select the right route or routes for you. Establishing a superior performance record is also an effective way to prepare for management. This brings us to the next phase in the model: how to build up your management skills.

Making Yourself an Effective Manager: An Action Plan

So you are now a supervisor or a manager! The purpose of this phase of CAPM is to help you develop your management competence and build up your qualifications and managerial skills. This section will present an action plan to help you enhance your managerial effectiveness.

1. Assess your management skills. A logical starting point for managerial self-development is evaluation of your current management skills. Your objective here is to identify your strong skills as well as areas of deficiency.

An easy instrument to use is the skills rating chart in Figure 5-4. Read the instructions at the end of the chart, then use the chart to rate your own skills. Compare your ratings with the average skills profile in Figure 5-5. Based on this comparison, identify a profile of your "needs analysis," which should serve as a basis for developing a managerial skill development program for you.

2. Learn how to learn. Perhaps the most important component of managerial effectiveness is the development of the skills necessary for anticipating, recognizing, and coping with change. Since the forces of change are continually at work and will further intensify during the 1980s and 1990s, managing change in our jobs, careers, and organizations will become crucial for effective management.

3. Learn how to manage your time. Everything we do requires time. Time is totally unelastic and totally irreplaceable. Your managerial effectiveness is largely a function of how you use your time. We are all controlled by our habits to some degree. Recognizing your bad habits and doing something about them is essential for effective time management. There are several references on time management included in the last chapter of this book for further reading.

How can you make the most of your time? Table 5-4 provides you with some mechanisms on how to beat time wasters and manage your time effectively.

4. Develop contingency plans. In the course of your management career (or any type of career for that matter), problems will often arise and conflicts at work and at home might occur. You should anticipate what conditions might arise and develop contingency plans for them. You should also prepare yourself to take advantage of opportunities when they come along.

It is clear from the above discussion that the objective of this phase of CAPM is to employ appropriate techniques to build your management competence and develop your skills. Four mechanisms were emphasized: assessing your management skills, learning how to learn, effectively managing your time, and developing contingency plans. Several other strategies should, of course, be explored for enhancing your managerial effectiveness depending on your present background and qualifications and your development needs.

	LOW	MEDIUM	HIGH
. Using the experts—getting information, opinions, ideas from well-informed people inside or outside your company.	•	•	•
. Building a reputation—making yourself known; developing a favorable name for yourself in the company.	•	•	•
. Activating—getting people to understand and follow your instructions.	•	•	•
. Imparting information—making yourself understood by subordinates and superiors.	•	•	•
. Judging people—gauging individuals so as to be able to establish good relations and mutually increase job satisfaction.	•	•	•
. Working with subordinates—establish cordial and effective relationships with those who work for you.	•	•	•
. Interviewing—talking with people face to face.	•	•	•
. Listening—learning from the words of others how they think and feel.	•	•	•
. Getting cooperation—motivating people to join you in accomplishing departmental goals.	•	•	•
. Maintaining good relations with your superior—being both friendly and businesslike in your dealings up the line.	•	•	•
. Using working time effectively—being able to get 60 minutes of work out of every hour.	•	•	•
. Decision-making—arriving at a logical conclusion and sticking to it.	•	•	•
. Planning—developing a course of action to accomplish a definite objective.	•	•	•
. Controlling paper work—maintaining the flow of interoffice communications and reports, and maintaining communication with business associates outside your company.	•	•	•
. Getting information—uncovering the facts you need to advance your work.	•	•	•
. Delegation—making subordinates responsible for some of your activities, while retaining control.	•	•	•
. Problem solving—licking the tough situations that interfere with efficiency.	•	•	•
. Pacing your energy expenditures—conserving your energy so you can complete the day without undue fatigue.	•	•	•
. Concentration—being able to stick with a complex or difficult task until you reach completion or find a workable solution.	•	•	•
. Memory—remembering events, incidents, ideas, plans, and promises.	•	•	•
. Budgeting your time—accomplishing the objectives of your job by efficient allotment of your time.	•	•	•

structions: Simply circle the dot corresponding to your estimate of your level of ability in each skill *ea. Try to be as objective as possible in rating your different skills as "low," "medium," or "high." you are too lenient or too harsh in estimating your skills, your assessment will be too subjective and ill not be a good basis for analysis and improvement. After completing the chart, draw lines connecting the dots you circled. The resulting profile will be your estimated abilities in several key management areas. If your skills profile resembles a straight line continuing the length of the chart, you have probably not judged yourself honestly. Experts at the Research Institute of America tell us that a ood balance between "high," "medium," and "low" is an indication that the rater has been fair in estimating his skills. Compare your profile with Figure 5-5, an "average" ranking. How do you compare? ased on this comparison, identify your areas of strength and weakness and develop a plan to improve em. Remember, your goal is not to compare favorably with an "average manager" but rather to evelop above-average—or even better—managerial skills.

'igure 5-4. Skills rating chart. (Based on a discussion of this instrument in Fulmer, Robert M. "Supervision: Principles of Professional Management." Beverly Hills: Glencoe Press, 1976, p. 24.)

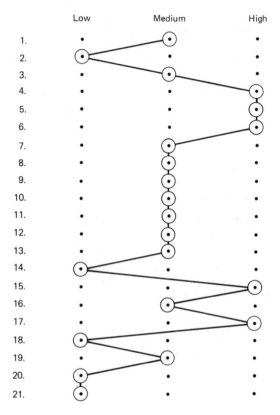

Figure 5-5. Average skills profile. (From Fulmer, Robert M. "Supervision: Principles of Professional Management." Beverly Hills, Glencoe Press, 1976, p. 27.)

Career Growth Strategies

In the fourth phase of the CAPM, career growth strategies, your objective is to grow and advance in your management career. Of course, advising you on how to manage your career for advancement and growth is a risky proposition, because it really depends on your objectives developed in earlier stages of this model and your definition of success: climbing to the top? getting rich? leading a happy and satisfying professional and personal life? maintaining honesty and integrity? The point you should keep in mind is that while these goals are not necessarily mutually exclusive, they can compete with each other.

The following strategies for career growth—which are not, of course, inclusive—are offered for those whose objectives include climbing the executive ladder.

Table 5-4. How to Manage Your Time.[a]

1. Get an early start.

2. Anticipate your needs (e.g., tokens, change for tolls, stamps, writing pads, clothes you will wear the next day).

3. Concentrate on the essentials (list the "Must Do" jobs in order or priority).

4. Discourage interruptions (tactfully!)

5. Be precise in your goals (pinpoint your destination at the beginning).

6. Create deadlines.

7. Listen effectively.

8. Seek shortcuts (review work patterns, delegate, depend on office machines such as dictating and copying equipment).

9. Use idle time (travel time and waiting time can be used in thinking about problems, catching up on your readings, or recording drafts of a speech or paper).

10. Learn from mistakes (jot down your mistakes and other ways in which you wasted time so you can avoid making the same mistake twice).

[a]From Kasner, Eric. How to Manage Your Time. *Chemical Engineering* (July 8, 1974): 99-100.

1. Establish yourself as a manager. In order to establish yourself as a manager, you need to answer the following questions:

a. What is my role in management? You need to determine your managerial role: whether you want to stay in the engineering and R&D management activities or you want to move to nontechnical management areas. The latter areas include functions such as marketing and production management activities. A prime concern here would be your desired focus of technical expertise in both areas as well as the extent of your willingness to learn about nontechnical management functions.

b. Do I want to eventually move to general management? This is another choice you would have to make between staying in functional management (i.e., production, R&D, engineering) or moving into general management.

c. Do I want to have a line-management position or a staff position reporting to management? Because the concepts of line and staff management are discussed in Chapter 8, I shall not go into these concepts in detail here. It is important, however, to mention that both line and staff managers make valuable contributions to their organizations. The central point is that while the line manager has the functions, jurisdiction, and authority and power that are typical of managerial positions, the staff manager is really a specialist, an advisor, and a consultant. Experience and observations show that while staff managers could be very powerful and important people in the organization, this, quite frankly, is not the norm—it is the exception.

I do not want this point to be misunderstood. The choice between staff and line positions has to be yours. There are two things you should understand, however:

1. If you allow yourself to be dominated by others' desires, to become over-committed to a fairly narrow specialty, and remain in a staff position too long, it will be increasingly difficult for you to switch to line management.
2. Looking at your organization as a cone, staff management tends to be on the outer surface, while line management is closer to the central power axis.

2. Master organizational survival techniques. Given that all human organizations are political, you will need to learn some techniques in order to survive in the organization jungle. Executive survival is really a field in its own right. From the standpoint of your career growth and advancement, here are seven techniques as an "executive survival kit."

a. Identify "career secrets". Your task here is to search for the techniques and shortcuts tested and proven to work in your organization for quick advancement. These represent "dues-paying" behavior (e.g. special projects or career assignments). While these secrets, obviously, are unwritten, finding out about them by decoding the organization and uncovering these techniques will prove to be invaluable for your career progress.

b. Search for a mentor. If you do not have one yet, this is the time for intensive search. Refer to my previous discussion in this chapter (fourth phase of CAPM) about getting visibility and exposure. The mentor, naturally, might or might not be your boss. It all depends!

c. Do not overidentify with the organization. A certain amount of loyalty is expected and even required. But an overdose is not! Experience shows that those who overidentify with the organization might, ultimately, get burned. This point will be further explored later in this section.

d. Learn how to handle your boss. Peter F. Drucker, my former teacher (and mentor) at New York University, is absolutely correct. People—including you and your boss—do not come in the proper sizes, shapes, and character, and with the proven characteristics needed to accomplish the tasks posed by an organization.[6] Neither can people be machined down or recast for the accomplishment of required tasks. People are always "almost misfits, at best."

---

[6] Drucker, Peter F. "The Effective Executive." New York: Harper & Row, 1967.

Getting back to your boss, how should you handle him? The answer is very simple: carefully and with tact! Here are some techniques for your "tool kit."

1. Always remember that you are being evaluated by your supervisors, and the evaluation of your immediate supervisor is always the strongest and most important. Troublemakers' chances for advancement are practically zero.
2. Your performance is being evaluated in terms of what satisfies the superior. This means you should do the job the way the superior would do it, and when you deviate be sure you can justify it.
3. Needling the superior is a pleasure a climbing executive can not afford. It never helps at evaluation time.
4. Do not bypass the immediate superior and work around him with the one above. While this may be encouraged by upper-echelon executives, unless the immediate superior is kept well informed of all activities, sooner or later there will be roadblocks.
5. Keep the boss informed of matters for which he is held responsible. You must be willing to support and enforce decisions rendered by your superiors.
6. When the boss makes a mistake, do not hesitate to rescue him.
7. When he delegates authority, maintain it completely—within reasonable limits—with no further delegation.
8. Accept the role as a subordinate.
9. All of your actions, whether large or small, must reflect some loyalty to the organization (see item c above). You will never become a member of top management unless you are considered loyal to the company.
10. You must be a good team player. "Fitting" with people at higher levels is very crucial as top-level executives are constantly looking for individuals of their "type."

e. Do not question executive norms and understand the politics of promotion.

1. As you climb the ladder, be invariably ready to leave behind a lot of intimate friends. If you want to maintain old friendships, you had better not take the promotion—you are exepcted to cut them off. This seems to be one of the prices for promotion—to mingle, dine, travel, and socialize with the "right" people! (this point was also elaborated in Chapter 2, Why Managers Fail).
2. Your spouse is expected to do the same—to abandon old friends unquestioningly! An executive's wife, for example, can be downright dangerous to her husband's career if she insists on keeping close friendships with the wives of her husband's subordinates.

3. You are expected to accept every required move without question. To turn it down, without an extraordinary reason, practically seals you to that level.

f. Recognize the dilemmas of career growth and deal with them. At least three dilemmas exist. Since several of these points were already made above, a brief treatment will be made here.[7]

1. Political insensitivity and passivity: If you become insensitive to the political environment around you and passive about finding out how the organization really works, you can easily hinder your career. If you do not know, for instance, that a central rule for managerial success is to "please the boss," you will not know how to handle him, will you? That is, if you do not know the *true* criteria by which your performance is being evaluated, it is unlikely that you will pass the test.
2. Loyalty dilemmas: There are at least five different commands implicit in the notion of loyalty: (1) Obey me. (2) Protect me and do not let me look bad. (3) Work hard. (4) Be successful. (5) Tell me the truth.

Clearly, some manifestations of loyalty are in conflict with others. Do you "happen" to know what version of loyalty is expected by your organization? Does your boss expect strict obedience but will he be angry if obedience leads to poor performance? Does he interpret mistakes as disloyalty but still expect advance warning of impending failure?

Do you get a sense of disappointment and frustration when loyalty demands may violate your values, as when the organization brooks no excuse for failure and demands that the hierarchy be protected at all costs? Do you also know that overly candid communication with outsiders is considered one of the most heinous organizational crimes because it threatens the security of the hierarchical system? If you do, the only comfort I can provide you with here is simply to say that most organizations are like that and that there are many others out there in the same boat with you!

3. Personal anxiety: The third and last of career dilemma, personal anxiety over one's career, can result from several sources, including: (1) Integrity: Am I losing my values? (2) Commitment: Am I doing something valuable? (3) Dependence: Am I losing control of my life?

g. Follow career commandments. This is the seventh and last technique in your "executive survival kit." The following 13 career commandments are based

---

[7] This section is primarily based on Webber, Ross A. Three Dilemmas of Career Growth. *M.B.A. Magazine* (May, 1975): 41-44, 47, and 48.

on the experience and observations of managers in many organizations.[8] They
are so true that they can probably be considered "golden rules." They include
some points that have already been made in this chapter.

1. Good performance that pleases your superiors is the basic foundation of
success. Recognize, however, that not all good performance is easily measured.
Determine the real criteria by which you are evaluated and be rigorously honest
in evaluating your own performance against these criteria.

2. Manage your career; be active in influencing decisions about you. Good
effort is not necessarily rewarded.

3. Strive for positions that have high visibility and exposure where your heroic
deeds can be observed by higher officials. Check to see that the organization has
a formal system of keeping track of young people. Remember that high-risk line
jobs tend to offer more visibility than staff positions such as corporate planning
or personnel, but also that visibility can sometimes be achieved through community activities.

4. Develop relations with a senior executive who can be your sponsor. Become a complementary, crucial subordinate with different skills from your superior.

5. Learn your job as quickly as possible and train a replacement so you can
be available to move and broaden your background in different functions.

6. Nominate yourself for other positions; modesty is not necessarily a virtue. However, change jobs for more power and influence, not primarily status
or pay. The latter could be a substitute for real opportunity.

7. Before taking a position, rigorously assess your strengths and weaknesses,
what you like and do not like. Do not accept a promotion if it draws on your
weaknesses and entails mainly activities that you do not like.

8. Leave at your convenience, but on good terms, without parting criticism
of the organization. Do not remain under a superior who is not promoted in
three to five years.

9. Do not be trapped by formal, narrow job descriptions. Move outside
them and probe the limits of your influence.

10. Accept the fact that responsibility will always somewhat exceed authority and that organizational politics are inevitable. Establish alliances and fight
necessary battles, and minimize battles with superiors to very important issues.

11. Get out of management if you cannot stand being dependent on others
and having them dependent on you.

12. Recognize that you will face ethical dilemmas no matter how moral you
try to be. No evidence exists that unethical managers are more successful than
ethical ones, but it may well be that those who move faster are less socially con-
scious. Therefore, from time to time you must examine your personal values
and question how much you will sacrifice for the organization.

---

[8] Ibid.

13. Do not automatically accept all tales of managerial perversity. Attributing others' success to unethical behavior is often an excuse for one's personal inadequacies. Most of all, do not commit an act that you know to be wrong in the hope that your superior will see it as loyalty and reward you for it. Sometimes he will, but he may also sacrifice you when the organization is criticized.

In summary, the objective of this phase of CAPM has been to identify some avenues for your career advancement as well as provide you with some mechanisms as an "executive tool kit" for organizational survival. Several strategies have been identified to help you establish yourself as a manager. In addition, a handy package of techniques has been described that can enable you to get more control over your destiny and to achieve career advancement and growth.

The picture painted in this section is quite realistic and is typical of most organizations of today. Sound a bit gloomy? Your boss will probably swear on a stack of bibles that he could not relate to it and he might deny it exists (he might deny this even to himself). One thing I would like you to keep in mind, however: These "facts" are part of the "unmentionables" in organizations, and you probably will not find them anywhere else besides this book!

Follow-Up and Management Career Reassessment

Throughout this model, we have been looking forward. You are now at the final phase of CAPM; time for follow-up and assessment. It is also time for looking backward! You will go right back to the early phases of this model, especially to the first (life planning and career assessment) and the third (self-appraisal and risk analysis) phases. As mentioned earlier, the self and career appraisal processes go on continually.

At this point of your career, you might be reaching a plateau—a "hold pattern" is encountered in this phase.[9] As you will recall in the third phase of CAPM (self-appraisal and risk analysis), your internal career notions and external career realities will probably clash unless the plateau is perceived as a satisfying career option (Figure 5-3): The first glimmer of the second career intrudes. If concern begins to mount with this plateau, career ambivalence sets in. Life goals are now more seriously examined. Depending upon the solution selected, the career cycle is either concluded or repeated. If the latter occurs, typically the person returns to the first phase, life planning and career awareness and exploration.

There is no rigid timetable for reassessing your career and life objectives. To assess the opportunities that arise more objectively, you should always keep your goals in mind.

---

[9] Leach, op. cit., p. 52.

To sum up: Discussion of the seven phases of CAPM is now complete. You should be able to use the tools and techniques presented in the above analysis for planning and developing your managerial career. Needless to say, you should make appropriate modifications at different stages of the model to accommodate your own circumstances and situations.

SUMMARY

Your career is your most precious commodity and represents a substantial portion of your life. While it is the organization's responsibility to provide you with the environment, support, and incentives necessary for effective career planning, the ultimate responsibility for planning, implementing, and monitoring your career progress is only yours. There are two types of career planning: organization career planning and individual career planning. As you will recall, the role of management in managing career transition for technologists was explored in Chapter 4, where a career planning and employee development (CPED) model was also presented.

This chapter has looked at the other side of the issue: the role of the technologist in managing his own career. The view taken has been that individual career planning is only one aspect of life planning. The decision to switch to management must be answered in terms of individual, organization, and life planning perspectives. A career action planning model (CAPM) consisting of seven consecutive phases has also been developed. These phases must be thoroughly understood for effective managerial career planning and development.

The last dimension of this subject—the role of management education in developing your managerial skills—will be explored in Chapter 6.

6
Should You Go For An M.B.A.?
Role of Management Education in
Developing Management Skills

One of the routes to the executive suite explored in Chapter 5 was to get a graduate degree in management—a Master's in Business Administration (M.B.A.). The rationale was that because of the inadequate preparation of engineers and scientists for careers in management in the undergraduate school, they tend to experience several difficulties in their new careers, which often makes the transition to management far from smooth (Chapter 3). Getting an M.B.A. degree was thought to be the cure. It has, therefore, become a popular degree for many organizations to encourage their technologists to go for; and many management schools and management educators—naturally—applaud the trend.

The task of this chapter is to explore the value of academic management education, as it stands today, from the standpoint of you, the technologist. What is being done in academic management programs? Does the M.B.A. really prepare you for a management career? Does it provide you with the skills necessary for effective management (Chapter 1)? In short, is the M.B.A. really worth it for technologists? Are there other options? And what are the implications of this exploration for university educators in both engineering and business administration?

Throughout the discussion, the role of the university in easing the transition from technologist to management will be examined. But remember that our focus in this chapter is on the M.B.A. and its value from the point of view of engineers and scientists—not necessarily from that of the university. Let us first approach the subject from a broader perspective. I shall start out with a brief discussion of the alternate mechanisms for developing your management skills, then eventually channel the discussion toward academic management education.

HOW TO BUILD YOUR MANAGEMENT SKILLS

A detailed discussion of formal and informal approaches for developing your management knowledge and skills was already undertaken in Chapters 2, 3, and

4 of this book. To refresh your memory, please refer to the discussion of training technologists in the functions and skills of management, management internships, management development programs, and management development needs for engineers and scientists in Chapter 4.

What I would like to add here is that formal approaches to developing managerial skills of technologists usually include:

- Management workshops or seminars sponsored by management groups, consulting firms, or professional societies.
- In-house training programs.
- University degree programs.
- University continuing education programs.
- Corporate management education and development centers.
- Job assignments and job rotation.
- On-the-job training.
- Temporary assignments to other areas.
- Any other types of programs formally sponsored by the organization or outside agencies.

Informal approaches to management development include self-instruction programs, private study and reading, sabbaticals, attendance of professional meetings, participation in professional conferences (papers, discussion groups, etc.), symposia, membership in professional organizations, and other types of self-initiated management development efforts.

How do technologists and their employers feel about these management development efforts? While there is a general agreement among employers that individual development and continuing education activities are so vital for combating obsolescence, there are considerable variations in philosophies, practices, and programs directed toward this objective. Technologists, on the other hand, have certain preferences of learning experiences and learning situations. Table 6-1 presents the results of 1500 respondents to a recent IEEE survey.

To sum up, there are basically three approaches to developing managerial competence of technologists:

1. Degree-oriented development efforts.
2. Nondegree-oriented development efforts.
3. On-the-job training and development efforts.

The two latter types can be initiated by either the individual or his employer and can be presented as an in-house or off-house training effort. These management development activities can also be provided by many sources including professional associations, universities, consultants, and training departments. The first type—development through acquiring an academic degree—is basically the domain

Table 6-1. Technologists' Preferences of Learning
Experiences and Learning Situations.[a]

PREFERENCES OF LEARNING EXPERIENCES	PREFERENCES OF LEARNING SITUATIONS
1. Reading	1. Books
2. Problem-solving	2. Evening program
3. Experimentation	3. Home-study correspondence courses
4. One-to-one dialogue with expert	4. Periodical literature
5. Observation	5. One-day program
6. Small-group discussion	6. Audio-cassettes
7. Listening	7. On-the-job training
8. Preparing a presentation on the subject	8. Two-day live program
9. Gaming	9. Audio cassette and slide package
10. Emulating an expert	10. Live television
11. Response to a deadline	11. Motion pictures
	12. Five-day live program
	13. Videotape and video cassette
	14. Computer-aided instruction
	15. Telephone contact
	16. Two-week live program

[a]From IEEE survey.

of the university. This will be the focus of our discussion in the balance of this chapter.

CAN MANAGEMENT BE TAUGHT?

The view taken in this book is that managing is a skill. This means that it is learnable. As you will recall from our discussion in Chapters 1 and 2, three ingredients of managerial competence were singled out: knowledge, skills, and attitudes. Three types of skills were also identified: technical, administrative, and interpersonal. The point you should keep in mind, however, is that the three components of managerial competence are not equally learnable in a university or classroom setting. Nor are the three types of skills developable to the same degree in the same setting. In short, knowledge is much easier to learn than skills and attitudes; technical and administrative skills are much easier to develop than interpersonal skills on a classroom bench.

In other words, all the university business school can do in a classroom setting is teach *about* management; it cannot teach management. It can teach an individual what a manager does without enabling him to do it; a person can learn to manage, but not necessarily be taught to manage.

In summary, managing is a skill, and the only way to acquire this skill is by practicing it—by putting it to use. It follows that while management concepts, theories, and principles (management knowledge) are learnable in an academic setting, managerial practices are not unless the learner is permitted to put the learning into action (learning by doing). No amount of education or training will really develop the manager's skills.[1] Only he can develop these skills through practice, experience, and application.

THE VALUE OF THE M.B.A. FOR TECHNOLOGISTS

The M.B.A. is perceived as a valuable degree that will open many doors for graduates. Most employers consider it a "union card" or a "passport" to higher levels of management along with such associated "goodies" as higher salaries, status, prestige, and of course, executive power. There is considerable evidence supporting this point. One 1979 Harvard Business School graduate, who had some work experience, commanded $53,000 to start. Employers conducting on-campus interviews at the University of Chicago's Graduate School of Business have increased from 200 in 1976-77 to 290 in 1979. In recruiting M.B.A.s, some organizations feel they are screening into their operations a high-potential fast-track manager who is best prepared to give long-term value.

This favorable image of the M.B.A. degree perceived by employers has intensified the demand for M.B.A.s. Graduate schools of business and management have swiftly and cheerfully reacted to the challenge. The situation has been ideal for the proliferation of large numbers of M.B.A. programs, including many of marginal quality. Combined with the strong demand for the M.B.A., another factor contributing to the growth—unprecedented in the history of American higher education—in the number of colleges offering the degree has been the ease with which universities can make money on them. Setting up an M.B.A. program does not require many changes in the physical facilities and faculty resources. Many schools, as a result, have jumped on the bandwagon, offering marginal M.B.A. programs—which at this point makes a shakeout inevitable. In fact, just 134, or 27%, of graduate-level business schools are accredited by the American Association of Collegiate Schools of Business (AACSB).[2]

The picture, in terms of demand and supply, has been changing very fast, however. Many educators are concerned about a glut of M.B.A.s as early as 1980s.

---

[1] While most of the discussion in this chapter applies to the M.B.A., some comments apply to undergraduate programs as well.
[2] *The Wall Street Journal* (November 2, 1979), p. 40.

In 1950, only six universities offered the degree. Today almost 600 schools grant the M.B.A. In 1964, 6000 students were graduated with the degree. The proliferation of new M.B.A. programs in the 1970s, at the rate of more than 30 a year, has vastly expanded the supply of M.B.A.s; in 1980, the number of such degrees awarded was 52,000, compared with only 21,235 in 1970.

So, in spite of the expected glut of M.B.A.s, the perceived image of M.B.A.s is generally favorable. What more do we want? What about the real value of the degree? I suppose that for effective planning of your career and enhancing of your management skills, you will want something with real substance—with more than just a favorable image.

Is there some intrinsic value to the M.B.A.? Looking at the M.B.A. in general, and from the standpoint of the technologist in particular, there is not—or should not be—an intrinsic value to the degree. Contrary to the popular beliefs, quite frankly, the perceived value of the M.B.A. is simply not true in reality. Whether a graduate degree in management has anything to do with skill development and potential managerial performance is open to serious question, to say the least. Except for testimonial observations, there is no concrete evidence whatsoever suggesting that those with an M.B.A. perform better as managers than those without it. Management education, in fact, has been viewed by some as a myth!

Now, don't get me wrong. I am not really quarreling with the M.B.A. in concept. As an M.B.A. educator, I think the concept, in fact, is good—but the implementation is poor! Perhaps getting a degree in management is the right answer to the wrong problem. The question becomes, then, where has the management school gone wrong? Before answering this question, let me conclude this section by saying that as a technologist interested in developing his managerial competence, you do not need an M.B.A. because it will not provide you with what you are looking for: management skills. This, of course, does not mean that the M.B.A. training will not provide you with valuable knowledge. But how good is that knowledge to you if it is not backed up with tangible and concrete skills? In short, the M.B.A. simply is not the answer to this problem you are trying to solve.

This argument becomes even more compelling when you consider the following statement:

> Our schools of administration and management have designed their curricula to do other things. At one time most concentrated on teaching by the case-study method, presumably in the belief that managers-to-be would benefit from practice in unstructured decision-making ... but our study gives us reason to believe that this kind of instruction does not develop the wide array of talents managers need. In the 1960s many schools of management turned away from the case-study philosophy, devoting their attention instead to the teaching of theory. It is interesting to note that much of this theory deals, not with the job of managing per se, but with the underlying disciplines—

economics, psychology, and mathematics . . . . All of this knowledge will be useful to the manager-to-be, but almost none of it relates directly to those things he will be called upon to do in the job of the manager . . . . We must recognize that although the management school gives students M.B.A. degrees, it does not in fact teach them how to manage. Hence these degrees can hardly be considered prerequisites for managing, and the world is full of highly competent managers who have never spent one day in a management course.[3]

WHY THE M.B.A. IS THE WRONG DEGREE FOR YOU

As you can see, the accumulated evidence suggests that management education is in trouble. Based on this evidence, our current approaches to education and career development are obsolete. They are incapable of preparing and developing the managerial know-how, skills, and attitudes required to effectively manage and cope with the accelerating rate of social and technological changes in society and its institutions. Both the universities and the world of work have allowed themselves to become so absorbed in their own particular concerns that they have tended to overlook their essential interdependence.[4]

The M.B.A. curriculum is too theoretical and too academic, and does not, in fact, provide technologists with the proper training and skills they are going to need to function effectively as managers. The M.B.A. program clearly reflects the growing divergence between management education and management practice. A diagnostic view of the basis for this judgment follows.

Management Education is too Rational

Management education is largely based on theoretical, neat, and unrealistic models of administrative behavior. It does not deal with the realities of organizational life. Management graduates, as a result, are mired in the code of rationality. The argument here is not to rather have graduates mired in the code of irrationality, but simply to propose that rationality in the classroom and in the real world could very well be (and they sure are!) two different things. The point is that value systems, which partly constitute the basis of rationality, in the management school and in the real world are simply not the same. They represent two different cultures. In fact, management, according to one writer, requires more "operant behavior" and the development of nonrational skills.[5] Indeed, organizations are not interested in utopianism but rather in pragmatism—of which, however, very little is characteristic of management education today.

---

[3] Mintzberg, Henry. "The Nature of Managerial Work." New York: Harper & Row, 1973, p. 186.

[4] For more information on this point see, Drucker, Peter F. Is Business Letting Young People Down? *Harvard Business Review* (November-December 1965): 53; and Toffler, Alvin. "The Future Shock." New York: Random House, 1970, pp. 357-367.

[5] Handy, Charles. Exploding the Management Education Myth. *European Business* (Spring, 1971).

To give an example, students are frequently taught in management and organizational behavior courses the importance of individual competency and hard work as prerequisites for advancement and successful career development in organizations. Is this really the way organizations and their members operate? What happened to politics, personal contacts, survival mechanisms, "win-lose" strategies, ways to "beat the system," and "games people play"? These tactics, of course, are not necessarily healthy, nor are they necessarily the best, and yet they are highly representative of how many—if not most—organizations function. At some point, the individual in most organizations is expected to be a political animal, not only to acquaint himself with the rules of the game, but to play it, too. Any management educator with even a second-hand consulting experience can easily attest to this. Is it not fair, then, to make students at least aware of the realities of organizational life instead of presenting a "normative utopianism" which will do nothing for them but get them more confused? As educators in a professional school—I believe—we not only are expected to do this, we also owe it to our "clients."

There Is A Gap between Management Science and Management Technology

The manager lacks the body of technology with which to apply science. Although economics, behavioral sciences, and mathematics offer knowledge relevant to the practice of management, little technology exists to transfer scientific knowledge into prescriptions for practice.[6] There is heavy emphasis in management curricula upon the basic disciplines and the tools of management with very little consideration given to the functional areas, or to business. Another reason for the gap between management science and management technology is that there is no other discipline in which practice seems so unaffected by its own principles.[7] There is, for instance, no other intellectual area in which the practitioners contribute less to knowledge than management. The point here is certainly not to put the blame on academicians when practitioners do not contribute much to the body of knowledge or vice versa. Rather, it is to suggest that just as the theory of management is probably deprived of valuable contributions by practitioners, the practice of management is probably deprived of valuable contributions by academicians. This is an unhealthy sign that the gap between the theory and the practice of management is widening—hardly a condition for a professional discipline to mature and grow.

Management Education is Based on the Wrong Assumptions

Examples of wrong assumptions in management education include those concerning the mission of schools of management (knowledge vs skill development);

---

[6] Filley, A., and House, R. Management and the Future. *Business Horizons* (April 1970): 10.
[7] Drucker, Peter F. op. cit.

the general orientation and structure of curricula (discipline or product orientation vs market or end use); admission criteria (academic grades are poor predictors of potential managerial performance); and student-faculty relationships (the student is presumed to be passive in the learning process). These assumptions appear to be faulty and should be reexamined.

Management Education has not Yet made the Transition From Folklore to Science

Management educational programs have largely failed partly because management is one of the few academic areas that does not have an "internal" foundation. That is, in business there is no common internal base, and we build upon the foundations constructed in other disciplines, unlike, for instance, medicine or chemistry. While it is generally true that the management discipline—after relatively short concentrated study—is probably in an improved position compared with medical science—after several thousand years of study—the fact remains that medicine and other established disciplines have all along had a common internal base, strong internal foundations, and well-recognized boundaries. Yet, this has not been the case in management. I maintain that the proper study for managers is management itself, and that focusing on the core field of management is a fundamental prerequisite for the field to grow and mature; otherwise, how will management education—compared with medical education—ever make the transition from folklore to science? McGuire makes the point well:

> Unless we can determine the nature of management, and then begin to probe into it deeply and sensibly, we shall never satisfactorily create a discipline of administration. . . . Rarely has there been a concerted effort to get to the heart of our purpose of existence. . . . If we are to gain respectability as an integrated field of study, we shall eventually have to make administration and management as central and common to our teaching and research as it is to the names of our schools and colleges.[8]

Management Education has Little Management in it

A thorough examination of typical management curricula reveals that considerable coverage has been given to subjects such as financial analysis, operations research, marketing, and management information systems, while the heart of the manager's job—the actual management processes—receives very little attention. This point was well made in this statement:

> The emergence of organizational behavior in the past two decades as a full fledged discipline in colleges and schools of business administration has had

---

[8] McGuire, Joseph. "The Collegiate Business School Today: Whatever Happened to the World We Know? Collegiate News and Views (Spring 1972): 5.

both salutary and questionable consequences on management education. . . . There appears to be a trend to synonymize organizational behavior with the practice of management, a movement that seriously neglects the teaching of concrete managerial skills in such areas as planning, controlling, and decision-making. The major cause of this phenomenon can be traced to the infusion of "behavioral scientists" into management faculties and the tranformation of doctoral programs in management into doctoral programs in organizational behavior.[9]

Departments of management at university business schools are beginning to look very similar to psychology departments at arts and sciences colleges in terms of faculty structure and, to a lesser degree, curriculum offering. This trend is not only inappropriate, it is quite serious. It looks like the modern university has two psychology departments instead of a department for psychology and another for management. In order to appreciate the seriousness of this trend, consider the following:

In short, the behavioral contributions to the study of management are becoming (have become?) the principles of management. I believe, as a behavioral scientist, that this approach short changes students who require a broader exposure to management in general and/or a deeper exposure to organizational behavior in particular. Management departments, by and large, now produce not potential business leaders, but rather, mediocre applied behavioral scientists. . . . We are teaching management rather than managing. Management is a fine subject for Ph.D. candidates who go on into research and study organizations. But it is not a very good subject for those undergraduates and M.B.A. students who intend to go out and make organizations work.[10]

Management Education Fails Partly because It Equips Students With the Wrong Skills

First of all, management education, as discussed above, is knowledge-oriented but not skills-oriented. Secondly, it overdevelops the individual's analytical skills but underdevelops his administrative and interpersonal skills. While there is no question about the importance of quantitative, behavioral, and computer techniques for the manager, most of these valuable techniques will remain largely unused because the student has not been taught how to use these tools in practice

---

[9] Muczyk, Jan. Management vs Organizational Behavior (talk given at a session on "Redefining the Parameters of Management and the Domain of Management Education," The Academy of Management Conference, Kissimmee, Florida, 1977).
[10] Aronoff, Craig E. The Parameters of Management or What Business Are We In? (talk given at a session on "Redefining the Parameters of Management and the Domain of Management Education," The Academy of Management Conference, Kissimmee, Florida, 1977).

in the first place. In addition, the problems that the textbooks solve are often not the important ones.[11] Would it not, then, make more sense to teach these techniques with a view to their applications in functional areas, and to design tool courses that are problems-oriented, not techniques-oriented? Thirdly, despite various attempts made in the classroom to develop the student's problem-finding skills through role playing, simulation techniques, the case method, and so on, the student's diagnostic skill remains highly underdeveloped, simply because the data and problems were given to him, not found. Finally, graduate management education mistakenly provides students with a top-management skill orientation, so by the time they graduate they are all set to be presidents. To me, these simply are the wrong values, for the new M.B.A. will hardly start at the top, and furthermore, different types of skills are required at different managerial levels (Chapter 2). All in all, this type of educational socialization is not only dangerous, but can have disturbing effects on both graduates—due to their superficial orientation—and their employers—due to their disillusionment with the management schools' programs.

The Learning Process Itself it at Fault

The learning process is faulty for several reasons. For one thing, gaining knowledge is not equivalent to learning how to apply knowledge profitably. Business schools for years have used cases, exercises, role playings, simulations, and management games as surrogates for managerial problem-solving on the job. The assumption underlying these pedagogical methods is that experience is the best teacher. This assumption is highly questionable. As discussed earlier, to acquire managerial skills there is no substitute for the opportunity to relate learning to actual experience via actual application. This is, in fact, why the value of these experience-centered educational techniques is highly limited. Secondly, the most common model in the management school is "learning by modeling" rather than "learning by discovery." In "modeling," the student mirrors the attitudes, knowledge, and skills of a model, who is the teacher or authority figure. In "discovery," the student learns through deduction and induction by formulating the problems, concepts, and assumptions for himself rather than accepting them from his models; thus, he is active in the learning process. Thirdly, instruction is faculty-oriented not student-oriented. The learning experience is highly structured, and the student, as the recipient of knowledge, has no choice about what to learn, or how, when, and where. The point is that the system does not encourage or provide adequate opportunity for exploration of individual interests and identification of one's own needs, capabilities, and potential. The student, hence, plays a very passive role in the learning process.

Fourthly, while some management skills are cognitive (finance, accounting, marketing, administrative planning, organizational design, and so on), others are

---

[11] Webber, Ross. The Three Dilemmas of Career Growth. *MBA* 9, 5 (May 1975): 255.

noncognitive (leadership, interpersonal dynamics, stress coping, and so on). Yet both types of skills are assumed to be teachable by the same methods (lectures, simulations, etc.) in academic settings. Noncognitive skills, however, can be developed only on the job where the action is.

Fifthly, although the behavioral processes found in all types of organizations are similar, the content, the contexts, and constraints upon these processes are different and should be treated as such.[12] Yet, the approaches taken to teaching these subjects at different organizational settings have been designed as though these differences do not make a difference. This is preposterous.

Finally, management schools are training mediocre behavioral scientists to take their places as managers in large bureaucratic organizations.[13] They have also failed by overemphasizing processes and underemphasizing content, for managers must understand not only how decisions, for instance, are made, but what information and materials are relevant to various kinds of decisions in various contexts.

Preparation of Management Faculty is Faulty

Management faculty preparation is faulty for several reasons. For one thing, faculty have been taught only management, not managing. Thus, this is the only thing they can teach. Secondly, they have never been required in typical doctoral programs in management to demonstrate skills in teaching methods. Their teaching methods—if developed—have resulted from a sink-or-swim approach. Thirdly, most management faculty have never had a single day's experience practicing management. How can someone teach management without having had any experience as a manager? Second-hand consulting experience, if available, is not the same as actual managing. No wonder some professors of management cannot even manage a school picnic!

Finally, by virtue of their academic training, many management professors feel uncomfortable with management practitioners. Understandably, they cannot relate to each other and they do not speak the same language. Both groups, therefore, tend to develop negative stereotypes about each other—they are, indeed, members of two different breeds!

Values and Cultures Differ between Professors and Practitioners

As discussed above, differences in value systems and cultures between the schools and the business community are enormous. There is a lamentable tendency in all of academia—and business schools are no exception—to be concerned primarily with publishing, and that concern keeps management professors out of touch with the practical business world. Another facet of these differences in cultural values is highlighted by the conflicts between academicians and busi-

---

[12] Aronoff, op. cit.
[13] Ibid.

nessmen on what business schools should teach. In a longitudinal study of graduate business students at MIT, Schein found that the attitudes of the senior executives and those of the business school faculty were quite different, showing that their environments represent two quite different worlds.[14] This gap is seen by the critics of business schools as evidence that management education is hopelessly irrelevant to the training needs of business firms. Supporters, however, see this discrepancy as a measure of the innovation that business schools create by introducing new attitudes and values into business, through the newly hired M.B.A.

According to the responses to a recent AACSB survey on how some business school courses rank in importance, academic respondents placed their main emphasis on economics, while the business groups put economics third in importance and accounting first.[15] Management of human resources ranked seventh on the corporate list but ninth among academics. And quantitative analysis was placed fourth by academics, while business ranked it a poor tenth.

Finally, learning has to take place in one environment and be put to work in another, and it is left to the student to make the transition. For example, the student has to realize that, trained in analysis, he must spend his time on data collection, and adjust from a world where analysis is highly regarded to a world where that sort of perfection is far too costly and thus is justly condemned. After lengthy instruction in problem-solving, he must turn problem finder. One cannot help but wonder: If the two cultures must be different, how can the student be helped in changing from one to another? Is this really the "normal" relationship between a professional school and its "clients"?

In short, the above analysis clearly points out that while the M.B.A. degree might provide you with some knowledge, concepts, and techniques necessary for effective management, most of management education is too academic and, in fact, has little management in it. Worse yet, it will not help you learn the skills necessary for managerial competence. Management education and management practice are, sadly, so far apart that the accumulated learning experience in school is largely irrelevant to effective day-to-day management practice. A set of nine significant reasons have been identified in the above discussion as causing this unfortunate situation.

ALTERNATIVE SOURCES OF GRADUATE MANAGEMENT TRAINING FOR TECHNOLOGISTS

From the previous discussion, it is obvious that current university approaches to management education will not really prepare you adequately for a future

---

[14] Schein, Edgar H. Attitude Change During Management Education: A Study of Organizational Influences on Student Attitudes. *Administrative Science Quarterly,* 11, (1967): 601-628.
[15] *Business Week,* "A Plan to Rate Business Schools" (November 9, 1979), p. 174.

management career. In most engineering schools, management subjects are not even taught.[16] In schools of management where these subjects are taught, you merely learn about management—not how to manage.

For building up your management skills, there are, of course, several nonacademic paths which have already been outlined in the first section of this chapter. Development efforts, naturally, do not have to be through getting academic degrees. Development can, in fact, be undertaken without management development.[17] Any combination of the above approaches along with on-the-job training opportunities should be sufficient as long as they fit your professional needs.

IMPLICATIONS FOR UNIVERSITY PROGRAMS ON ENGINEERING AND R&D MANAGEMENT

As discussed earlier in this chapter, a strong partnership between students, the university, and industry is needed if management education is to be effective. The above discussion of the current status of management education reveals that the alliance between the three parties is shaky, and its basic foundations need to be reexamined. It also clearly demonstrates that there are several problem areas that warrant the concern of management educators and practitioners and call for reexaming the assumptions, methods, and approaches employed by the school of management in doing its task.

How can the university help better prepare technologists for careers in management? Two strategies are proposed here:

1. Infusion of management training in technical curricula.
2. A graduate program on engineering and R&D management.

It would be wise to take a second look at technical engineering and science curricula with an eye toward giving the student a sufficient grounding in management disciplines, applied behavioral sciences, and the actual workings of the business enterprise. Given that this "one-shot deal" type of training will not make managers out of technologists, it might help them in their transition to management and smooth their career adjustment process.

The other proposed strategy is for university educators to consider offering a graduate program on engineering and R&D management for engineers and scientists desiring to go for an academic degree in management. While the proposed program might overlap with some of the programs already available under a variety of names, it should be different from both those and M.B.A. programs.

---

[16] Gilmour, Jr. Alexander, Engineering Investments: An Approach to Management Education for Undergraduate Engineers. *IEEE Transactions on Engineering Management,* **23,** 4 (November 1976): 157-162.
[17] Gellerman, Saul W. Developing Managers Without Management Development. *The Conference Board Record* (July 1973): 32-37.

The philosophy, requirements, and content of the proposed program would, naturally, have to be left for the faculty of the concerned schools and would largely depend on their backgrounds, program objectives, and "market needs." Whether this program will be offered by the school of management or engineering or undertaken as a joint venture by both partners is again a matter to be worked out by the respective schools.

The proposed program would be superior to M.B.A. programs for preparing technologists for careers in management in that:

1. It takes an action-learning strategy with a strong skill-development orientation.
2. It has a balanced content combining learning by doing with cognitive learning through breadth in scope and depth in analysis.
3. It adopts a clinical positive—as opposed to normative—approach to management education incorporating appropriate strategies for adult learning.
4. It recognizes crucial foundations of managerial skill development as essentially a self-development process.

SUMMARY

This chapter has explored alternative sources of training for managerial skill development. It has become clear that the M.B.A. degree might not provide you with the skills necessary for managerial competence. The M.B.A. does, however, provide valuable knowledge of management concepts and principles. Practical strategies have been proposed for the university to better prepare technologists for careers in management. As you will note, I have stopped short of answering the question of whether you should go for an M.B.A. degree—since this question can be answered only by you. After all, it is your career!

Now that you are a supervisor or a manager, what do technical supervisors really do? This is the subject of Chapter 7.

PART IV
TECHNICAL SUPERVISORY
FUNCTIONS

7
Functions and Responsibilities of Technical Managers

In the previous parts of this book, you have been thoroughly exposed to a detailed analysis and discussion of the skills of management, the possible causes of managerial failure, and the possible problems facing technologists in the course of transformation into managers. What technologists, management, and educational institutions can do to ease the transition process has also been explored. Having become a supervisor or a manager, you are now on the stage!

This chapter will serve as a stepping stone between the earlier parts and the remaining portion of the book; it will help you understand the functional and administrative aspects of your managerial position. Whether you are a newly appointed or an experienced manager, you will find the discussion equally relevant and practical. For the novice supervisor, this analysis will provide a valuable practical framework for understanding the problems of technical organization and management. For the experienced technical manager, this framework will help him sort things out and gain the knowledge necessary for improving his present performance.

SUPERVISORS VERSUS MANAGERS:
THE CRITICAL DIFFERENCE

As you will recall from our previous discussion in Chapters 1 and 2, all managers perform essentially the same basic functions: planning organizing, directing, and controlling. Their prime task is to get the job done with and through others. The scope of their responsibilities, however, varies by virtue of the management level they are on, their functional unit or activity, and the type of authority they have.

Supervisors are managers on the first level of management. However, the term *supervision* applies to managers at all levels of management who direct the work and activities of others. As you will note in Figure 7-1, the supervisor, in a very real sense, plays a keystone role, and his position lies at the critical stress area

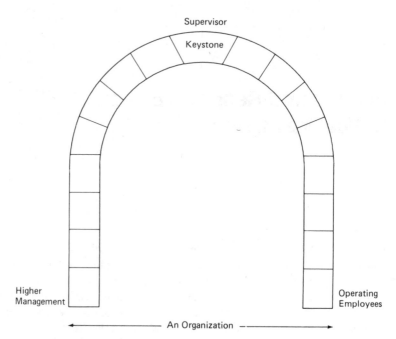

Figure 7-1. The supervisor as keystone. (From Kavis, Keith. "Human Relations at Work: The Dynamics Of Organizational Behavior." New York: McGraw-Hill, 1967.)

between management and employees. The stress between the two legs of the arch culminates at the keystone block. If the block were removed, the arch would fall.

The supervisor's position differs from positions at higher levels of management in many respects. First of all, he is the only one whose subordinates are nonmanagers. They are professional specialists in technical fields. All other managers at higher levels supervise employees who are identified with management. Secondly, the supervisor often finds himself attempting to serve two masters equally well: management at higher levels and subordinate technologists (the troops), usually with two different sets of expectations. This does not only put him in a uniquely difficult situation but also calls for different relationships and approaches to deal with these issues.

Another difference between supervisors and upper-level managers is that because the supervisor deals directly with the "troops" performing the technical function, his technical skills must be up to par for effective planning and direction of the technical activities of his subordinates. The supervisor might also end up doing some detailed technical work himself. As discussed in Chapter 2, the importance of technical skills, however, tends to decrease at higher levels of management, where managers are expected to be more concerned with the broad co-ordination of narrow specialized functions (R&D, engineering, marketing, and so on) than with the latest technical details in a specialized area. It would be accurate, then, to view supervisors as having a "vertical orientation"—they are more technically specialized—and upper-level managers as having a "horizontal orientation"—they are more generalistic.

The fourth difference between supervisors and upper-level managers is that the number of individuals reporting directly to a supervisor, commonly known as the span of control, is much broader than the number reporting to managers at higher levels. In addition, while higher-level managers can supervise employees directly or indirectly through their subordinate managers, supervisors are limited to direct face-to-face management of subordinates. Supervisors work directly with technologists on a face-to-face and day-to-day basis.

In sum, it is clear that there are a number of critical differences between supervisors and upper-level managers. While all managers have supervisory responsibilities, the first-level supervisor is a manager who works on the firing line with the troops and, in many respects, represents management to them. Therefore, as an engineering or R&D supervisor, you are a manager; you are also the keystone block between the two legs of the arch—without your services the arch would fall.

THE NATURE OF MANAGERIAL WORK

Just what does a manager do? Although this question has been answered in Chapter 1, it needs o be further elaborated and expanded on here. You might be surprised to know that of all the tons of information, books, and journal articles on management, very little has been written on the actual job of managing and the activities managers spend their time doing. In fact, most of what has been written is the "wisdom" type of material preaching on what a manager should do—but not focusing on what he actually does. Most of the available material, therefore, has very little value.

Most management writings characterize the manager as someone who plans, organizes, directs, and controls resources for achieving departmental and organizational objectives. While the list of management functions varies from one author to another, the essence and content of these functions stay the same. Likewise, definitions of the tasks of engineering and R&D managers, or any others for that matter, revolve basically around the same principles. While these writings, indeed, provide us with a normative view of the managerial task, they do not really go deeply into the actual job of managing and what it entails. They also erroneously give the impression that the manager's task can be neatly analyzed and his time systematically scheduled so he will be "planning" for most of the morning, and "organizing" and "controlling" most of the afternoon.

These descriptions of the managerial task, in short, are too simplistic, too idealistic, and lifeless. They also represent common misunderstandings and misconceptions of what managers actually do. Experience and observation clearly show that crisis management, fire fighting, flying by the seat of the pants, intuition, and even luck are characteristic of what many managers do and how they operate. Indeed, these managerial styles are the norm, not the exception.

It is important to note here, then, that the management process approach described in this book (also known as the functional approach, referring to the manager's tasks of planning, organizing, directing, and controlling)provides you with a broad practical framework of the manager's job. This scheme, while in the back of the manager's mind, covers a wide range of scattered and fragmented activities the manager handles on a daily basis using the mechanisms described above. It follows that the approach taken in this book describes what managers actually do in practice—how they manage in action. Discussion in this and previous chapters is not, of course, inconsistent. A schematic representation of the management process appears in Figure 7-2.

Let us now get back to the question of what a manager does. Any manager is primarily charged with the responsibility of getting the right things done through others by employing the resources at his command—money, people, facilities, and equipment—to achieve the organization's objectives. Managers in such diverse organizations as businesses, government agencies, or churches do very much the

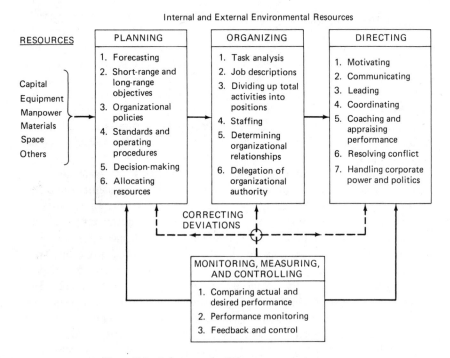

Figure 7-2. A framework of the management process.

same work, see very much the same world, share very much the same perceptions.[1] In its most rigid interpretation, "doing the right things" means doing exactly what the manager's boss tells him to do.

As you will note in Figure 7-2, managers are usually given the objectives (the what), the resources (the how much), and the time schedule (the when) for achieving these objectives. The methods, procedures, and arrangements for getting the job done (the how) are, and indeed should be, usually left up to the individual manager. Managers and supervisors are, incidentally, expected to follow the same pattern in delegating work to their subordinates.

In addition to goals and resources given to the manager, another "given" variable is his environment. This includes the internal environment consisting of the organization's policy, structure, technology, and the people with whom the manager will have to work in order to get the "right" job done. It also includes the external environment composed of competitors, legal and political framework, suppliers, vendors, economic conditions, the international situation, and the cultural conditions within which the organization operates.

A manager's job, then, can be perceived as a system composed of inputs, processes, and outputs. Using these inputs—goals, resources, and environment—the manager must perform certain managerial processes and activities in order to transfer these inputs into outputs. His objectives will ultimately have to be achieved through others. This means that the job of the manager is composed of the following: (1) communication, (2) analysis, (3) commitment, (4) communication, (5) planning, (6) commitment, (7) communication, and (8) achievement.

To sum up: the managerial process includes such component functions as planning, organizing, staffing, directing, controlling, coordinating, communicating, decision-making, representing, investigating, and motivating. The final output of the managerial task is the achievement of the ultimate objectives of the organization through producing a product or offering a service to satisfy customers' or clients' needs. A system diagram of the functions of a manager appears in Figure 7-3.

MANAGERS IN ACTION: FOLKLORE AND FACT

In line with the systems approach to the functions of a manager described above, it is clear that the manager is part of an open network of relationships, constraints, and internal and external sources of pressure on his time and the ways he allocates organizational resources at his disposal. It would, therefore, be helpful for you here to look at managers in action and see the kinds of roles they play in undertaking their daily activities.

---

[1] Drucker, Peter F. Memo to Managers: Find Outside Pleasure. *Research Management* (July 1977): 8.

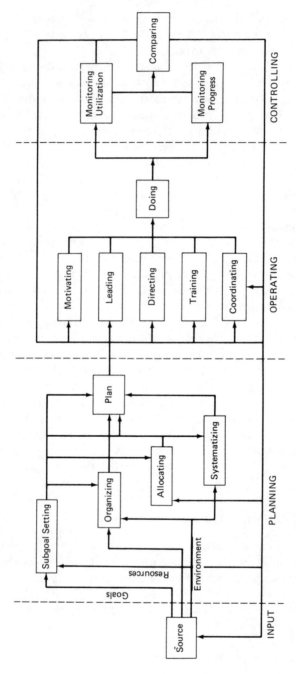

Figure 7-3. A system diagram of the functions of a manager. (From Goodman, Richard A. A System Diagram of the Functions of the Functions of a Manager. *California Management Review* (Summer, 1968): p. 32.)

What do managers really do in practice or in action? Sadly, the common descriptions of neat and systematic activities in management textbooks (folklore) simply do not match what managers actually do in practice (facts). As you will note in Table 7-1, the managerial task can factually be described as follows:[2]

1. Not only do managers want to encourage the flow of current information, but they also are conditioned by their own work loads. No matter what the manager is doing, he is plagued by the possibilities of what he might do and what he must do.

2. When managers must plan things, they generally do so implicitly within the context of their daily actions; their plans are not usually the result of two weeks of meetings held at the organization's mountain retreat.

Table 7-1. Some Folklore And Facts About Managerial Work[a]

FOLKLORE	FACTS
1. The manager is a reflective, systematic planner.	1. Managers work at an unrelenting pace; their activities are characterized by brevity, variety, and discontinuity; and they are strongly oriented to action and dislike reflective activities.
2. The effective manager has no regular duties to perform, and he should spend more time planning and delegating and less time seeing customers and negotiating.	2. Managerial work involves performing a number of regular duties, including ritual and ceremony, negotiations, and processing of soft information that links the organization with its environment.
3. The manager needs aggregated information, which a formal management information system provides.	3. Managers strongly favor the verbal media, namely, telephone calls and meetings. They also use documents and observational tours.
4. Management is, or at least is quickly becoming, a science and a profession.	4. Managers' programs—to schedule time, process information, make decisions, and so on—remain locked deep inside their brains. These programs are usually described as the use of judgment and intuition.

[a]Adapted from Mintzberg, Henry. The Manager's Job: Folklore and Fact. *Harvard Business Review* (July-August 1975): 18-26.

[2] This section is based primarily on Mintzberg, Henry. The Manager's Job: Folklore and Fact. *Harvard Business Review* (July-August 1975); and Burke, Richard. Management by Intuition or Flying by the Seat of Your Pants. *Bell Telephone Magazine,* 56, 2 (March-April 1977): 12, 14, and 15.

3. The job of managing does not breed reflective planners, and managers are geared to action.

4. Managerial plans exist only in managers' heads—as flexible, but often specific, intentions. The manager is a real-time responder to stimuli, an individual who is conditioned by his job to prefer live to delayed action.

5. Managers have a variety of regular duties including performing ritual and ceremony, negotiating and securing "soft" external information and passing it along to their subordinates.

6. The controlled disorder in which many managers operate is more typical than the cool unharried environment described in many management textbooks.

7. Managers seem to cherish "soft" information especially gossip, hearsay, and speculation for its timeliness. Managers identify decision situations and build models not with the aggregated abstractions an MIS (management information system) provides, but with specific tidbits of data.

8. A considerable amount of managerial communication is verbal in nature. Since managers rarely write down much of what they hear, the strategic data bank of an organization is not in the memory of its computers, but in the minds of its managers.

9. Because of the extensive use of verbal media, managers are reluctant to delegate tasks. Delegating a task might take so long that the manager may find it easier to do the task himself. This situation can lead either to overloaded executives or to delegation to subordinates with inadequate briefing.

10. The manager's prime medium of sending or receiving information is word of mouth. In this respect, the modern manager is virtually indistinguishable from his counterparts a thousand years ago making key decisions concerning sophisticated technology based on intuition and judgment. Only his work pressures have intensified.

11. In making managerial decisions, managers, like pilots flying by the seat of their pants, rely heavily on their know-how based on past experience. But instead of being "off instruments," as an aviator might say, they are "off theories."

12. Good managers, like good pilots, have a certain feel about situations and can generally make pragmatic, time-saving, and accurate leaps into problem-solving. They thrive on grayness; after all, they get paid for making sound decisions before a situation gets to the black or white phase. On the other hand, less intuitive bosses often delay decisions until the grayness of a problem falls into discernible black or white patterns, but, then, almost anyone can comfortably handle an either/or situation.

13. Managers do not have a by-the-numbers book to work from, nor do they have a pat formula or system. Their success depends on more intuitive skills reflecting the essential role of subconscious and extrarational processes in decision-making and policy-making.

14. The manager, typically, is overburdened with obligations, yet he cannot easily delegate his tasks. He therefore is driven to overwork and is forced to do

many tasks superficially. Brevity, fragmentation, and verbal communication characterize his work.

HOW MANAGERS SPEND THEIR TIME

To complement the above portrait of the characteristics of managerial tasks described in the previous section, let us take a look at how managers really spend their time. Research clearly deomonstrates several surprising findings about how managers' time is spent. These findings can be summarized as follows:[3]

1. There is no discernible pattern in the way managers spend their time. They simply bounce from issue to issue, continuously responding to the needs of the moment.

2. Managers respond to the pressures of their jobs with considerable portions of their time consumed in answering mail, returning telephone calls, and attending endless meetings.

3. A manager's environment is usually marked by creative chaos, filled with streams of visitors to the office, phone calls, and other distractions. It is not unusual for middle and top managers to spend 30 minutes or more without interruption only once every two days.

4. Half of the activities engaged in by chief executives, in one study, lasted less than nine minutes, and only 10% exceeded one hour. The foreman, in another study, averaged one activity every 48 seconds. The work pace for both groups was unrelenting.

5. Managers spend more than half their time engaged in verbal communication with peers, outsiders, and subordinates. Surprisingly, they spend little time with their own superiors. The exchange of information, often multidimensional in scope, usually stems from telephone conversations and meetings.

6. Because of their emphasis on verbal or "soft" information, many managers skim written reports, rarely initiate letters, and have little time to browse through trade publications and the like.

7. Unscheduled meetings of 10 minutes or less punctuate high-level managers' workdays, while ceremonial duties—for instance speeches, field trips, and protocol appearances—often take large chunks out of their schedules.

8. Policymakers rarely have time for esoterica such as the five-year plan especially that organizations are not operating in stable static environments.

---

[3] See, for example, Mintzberg, Henry. "The Nature of Managerial Work." New York: Harper & Row, 1973; Stewart, Rosemary. "Managers and Their Jobs." London: McMillan, 1967; Sayles, Leonard R. "Managerial Behavior." New York: McGraw-Hill, 1964; Whitely, William, "Nature of Managerial Work Revisited", Academy of Management Proceedings (38th Annual Meeting, 1978) pp. 195-199; and Weick, K.E., Review Essay: Mintzberg, Henry, "The Nature of Managerial Work", Administrative Science Quarterly (1974) Vol 19, pp. 111-118.

9. Managers, in general, spend little of their contact time in making decisions. The search for ideas and their discussion and evaluation far surpass choice as consumers of time.

While the above analysis is highly representative of how managers spend their time, not all managers will necessarily fit this somewhat frazzled profile. In addition to the fragmented nature of the managerial task itself, perhaps another rationale of why crisis management and fire-fighting, among others, are popular managerial styles is the fact that there is a considerable amount of pressure, frustration, and strain built into managerial positions.

As shown in Figure 7-4, there are multiple sources of pressure on the professional manager. These arise out of his own personality (including his needs, family background, education, and culture) as well as other environmental pressures (including small groups, peers, and reference groups). Pressures also ema-

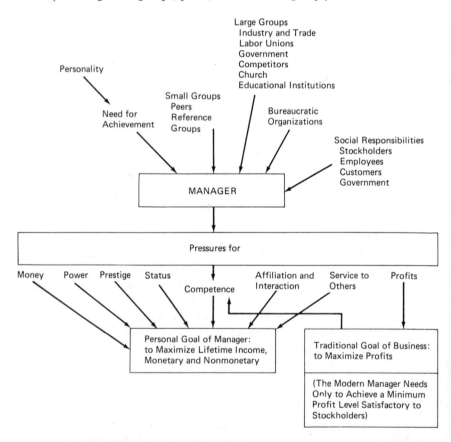

Figure 7-4. Sources of pressure on the professional manager. (From Monsen, R. J., Saxberg, B. O., and Sutermeister, R. A. The Modern Manager—What Makes Him Run? *Business Horizons* (Fall, 1966): 31.

nate from external groups including the government, competitors, and so on. The amount of pressure is further intensified through bureaucratic demands (by the organization itself) for conformity and for positive contributions to further the organization's economic goals and to meet its social responsibility.

ROLES MANAGERS PLAY: CONTENT OF THE MANAGERIAL TASK

What managers do in action and how they actually spend their time should be clear to you by now. The picture will be even clearer when we concentrate on the job content, the goals, and the actions of a manager, that is, the roles managers play. Let me remind you, however, that looking at the manager's various roles is merely an extension of the "process view" of management taken in this book—not a substitute for it. Put another way, viewing managing as a process associated with playing multiple roles will provide you with the most viable, dynamic, and operational framework to understand your job and what it really entails.

The relationship between management functions, roles managers play, and managerial skills is depicted in Table 7-2. It is clear from this table that every managerial process gives rise to specific roles and requires certain types of management skills. Essentially, there are six role sets requiring 22 separate roles to be played by managers. These role sets are:

Decisional roles
Judicial roles
Interpersonal roles
Informational roles
Educational roles
Survival roles

Decisional Roles

Decisional roles relate directly to the managerial functions of planning and organizing and thus partly represent the administrative skills of the manager. As the major decision-maker in his unit or division, the manager acts, for example, as an entrepreneur and a resource allocator, seeking to identify positive and negative forces in his environment so he can adapt to or change these forces. Note that decisional roles also relate to the organizing function of the manager, and include such activities as disturbance handling, negotiation, and the resolution of conflicts over resources and organizational means and ends.

Judicial Roles

Judicial roles relate to the managerial functions of performance appraisal and control which represent part of the manager's administrative and interpersonal

Table 7-2. Nature of Managerial Roles and Managerial Skills.

MANAGEMENT FUNCTION OR PROCESS	ROLE ORIENTATION	ROLE SET	MANAGERIAL ACTIVITIES AND TOOLS	TYPE OF MANAGERIAL SKILL
Planning and Decision-making	1. Forecaster of future trends 2. Entrepreneur 3. Resource allocation	Decisional Roles	1. Decision-making 2. Problem-solving 3. Allocation of resources	Administrative
Organizing	1. Negotiator 2. Disturbance handler 3. Guardian	Decisional Roles	1. Carrying out negotiations 2. Resolving conflicts 3. The organization's anchorman	Administrative
Controlling and Directing	1. Evaluator 2. Assessor 3. Appraiser	Judicial Roles	Performance appraisal and development	Administrative and Interpersonal
Directing	1. Figurehead 2. Leader 3. Liaison	Interpersonal Roles	1. Motivation 2. Leading	
	4. Monitor 5. Disseminator 6. Spokesman 7. Translator	Informational Roles	1. Communication 2. Representation 3. Acting 4. Translation	Interpersonal
Developing and Coaching	The Playing Coach	Educational Roles	Teaching	Technical and Interpersonal
Coexisting and Surviving	1. Person 2. Friend 3. Catalyst 4. Gamesman 5. Politician	Survival Roles	1. Modeling 2. Moderating 3. Politicizing 4. Initiating change	Interpersonal

skills. Here the manager—consciously or unconsciously—plays the role of the "judge," passing judgment on his subordinates' performance and making decisions regarding their promotability and salary adjustment. It should be kept in mind, however, that in addition to the "evaluative" type of performance appraisal, is the "developmental" type where the manager does not play the role of the judge but rather the role of the "coach." Effective performance appraisal systems, in fact, consist of both types.

Interpersonal Roles

In order to get things done with and through people, the manager plays a number of interpersonal roles including performing duties of ceremonial nature (figurehead), influencing and initiating action in his unit or department (leader), and making contacts with his associates and peers (liaison). These roles are part of the manager's direction function, which consists of activities such as motivating, leading, and communicating.

It is noteworthy here that the interpersonal role of the manager is one of managing relationships: The manager has to satisfy the requirements of each relationship by keeping some balance between his relationship with superiors, subordinates, and peers and associates. In this sense, he wears three hats (one for each group). In the process of satisfying the requirements of one set of relationships, he may run to conflict because of inconsistency with the requirements of another set of relationships. In short, the manager must maintain some type of balance between the instructions and directives received from his supervisors, the expectations of his subordinates, and the assistance and cooperation required by his peers.

Informational Roles

Informational roles are closely related to decisional roles. Since information is the basis for decision-making, collecting, retrieving, and disseminating information, informational roles of the manager are crucial for personal and unit effectiveness. Note that informational roles are also interpersonal in nature since they involve the effective receiving and transmitting of information.

An important part of the manager's informational role is that of the translator. A manager, to be effective, should be "bilingual." He usually receives abstract guidelines from his superiors in the form of goals that must be translated into concrete action.[4] The buck stops at the manager, who must assume the bilingual role of translating the strategic language of his superiors into the operational language of his subordinates in order to get results. The language of

---

[4] Uyterhoeven, Hugo. General Managers in the Middle, in Stress, Success and Survival. *Harvard Business Review* Collection, p. 72.

management is business-oriented and company-oriented, whereas the language of those who must solve the technical problems is technical and discipline-oriented. In short, top management knows the results it wants to see, has no idea how to achieve them, and assigns the middle manager the twofold duty of figuring out how to perform the task and then getting it done (i.e., the boss tells what he wants, not how he wants it accomplished.)

Educational Roles

Educational roles relate to the manager's function as a coach or a teacher, helping subordinates develop their technical skills. This specific technical function is particularly important at lower levels of management where technical operations and performance must be supervised and directed by the manager. Some technical operations might also have to be performed by the manager. In a very real sense, then, he is a delegator and a doer—both a coach and a player. Other types of subordinates' coaching and development are, of course, undertaken at other management levels.

Survival Roles

Survival roles constitute another type of the manager's interpersonal skills and relate primarily to the process of socialization and understanding how the system works by learning the "rules of the game." Since all organizations are political entities, survival considerations will impose certain requirements upon the manager, resulting in political and gamesmanlike tactics for advancing, coexisting, and "making it" within the system.

To sum up: The manager's job, as you can see, is an enormously difficult and complex one consisting of six role sets involving 22 individual roles and endless tactics for these roles to be played effectively (although educational and survival roles can be combined as part of the manager's direction function). It is important to realize here that beyond all these roles, the manager is a total person—every manager is a unique human being with his own traits, values, and personal goals. Also remember that while these multiple roles were separated for discussion purposes, they are highly interdependent and are probably played simultaneously.

TECHNICAL SUPERVISORY FUNCTIONS

So far I have been discussing tasks, responsibilities, and roles of supervisors and managers, without a special reference to the engineering and R&D functions, in order to make one point: All supervisors and managers perform the same tasks, undertake the same responsibilities, and play the same roles. You should be careful not to misunderstand this point, however. The point is simply that all managers operate within the same framework as far as the principles and managerial functions are concerned. The practices, the modes of operation, and the managerial styles adapted by individual managers are, of course, different.

An effective manager is someone who commits himself to doing the right thing and does it when he said he would do it within the limits of resources commensurate with the results. This "someone" could be a president of a large corporation, a technical manager, a marketing supervisor, or a machine shop foreman. As discussed earlier in this book, while the nature of the managerial job is the same for all positions, the practices, the manner, the style, and the tools necessary for getting the job done are contingent upon the nature of the managerial assignment, the job objectives, the type of subordinates, the type of technology, the management level, and the scope of your job.

It follows that, contrary to the popular view, the engineering manager or R&D manager is no different from any other manager in terms of his managerial roles and functions (see Table 7-2).[5] Individual differences in talents, skills, and competence obviously exist not only between managers but among all human beings. In fact, there are some differences in the nature and activities of engineering and R&D management positions as such in spite of their being occasionally combined in the book to avoid superficial treatment.[6] The fact remains, however, that there are definitely major differences in managing engineering versus R&D as well as in managing the "R" versus the "D." Furthermore, managerial practices for managing technical professionals in engineering and R&D are different from practices adapted for managing the more traditional business functions such as marketing or manufacturing. Only in this sense is engineering and R&D management different from other types of management functions.

Roles Technical Managers Play

It is clear from the above analysis that technical managers—like all other managers—are responsible for contributing to the objectives of the organization by getting the engineering and R&D activities done through other people. This involves defining objectives, analyzing problems, making decisions, building viable organization structures, evaluating risks, seeking optima, appraising performance, coordinating, and following up.

---

[5] For a different view, see Babcock, Daniel L. Is the Engineering Manager Different? *Machine Design* (March 9, 1978): 82-85.
[6] Badawy, M. K. What Is Wrong with R&D Management? *Industry Week* (June 10, 1974): 41-43; also my Organizational Designs for Scientists and Engineers: Some Research Findings and Their Implications for Managers. *IEEE Transactions on Engineering Management* (November 1975): 134-138.

In undertaking their responsibilities, technical managers play multiple roles. For an integrated treatment of this subject, let us examine these roles from three different perspectives:

1. As seen by the manager himself (through his own eyes).
2. As seen by the manager's subordinates.
3. As required by the organization (through the eyes of peers and supervisors).

Table 7-3 presents a comparative profile of how the technical manager's job is perceived by different parties. You may note that the table was arranged in such a way that similar roles are listed side by side.

How the Technical Manager Sees His Job.   Research[7] shows that technical managers perform several functions and, thus, play multiple roles.[8]

Technical professional: Technical managers see themselves as providing technical direction for their unit and making technical decisions. These activities would, naturally, require a certain amount of technical knowledge and skills. While this point does not mean that the manager needs to be a technical expert, it is, indeed, consistent with the previous discussion that some technical proficiency is crucial for a proper handling of his job as well as for maintaining his subordinates' respect.

**Table 7-3.   A Comparative Profile of Perceived Roles
of Technical Managers.**

BY THE MANAGER HIMSELF[a]	BY THE MANAGER'S SUBORDINATES[b]	BY THE ORGANIZATION[b]
Technical professional	Critic	Achiever
Salesman	Agent	Advocate/salesman
Director/controller	Producer	Resource allocator
Administrator	Stagehand	
Forecaster/planner		Goal setter
Trainer/developer		

[a]Adapted from Steger, Joseph A.; Manners, George; Bernstein, A. J.; and Day, Richard. The Three Dimensions of the R&D Manager's Job. *Research Management* (May 1975): 33-34.
[b]Adapted from Steele, Lowell W. "Innovation in Big Business." New York: Elsevier, 1975, pp. 175-188.

---

[7]This section is partly based on Steger, Joseph A.; Manners, George; Bernstein, A. J.; and Day, Richard. The Three Dimensions of the R&D Manager's Job. *Research Management* (Many 1975): 33-34.
[8]This discussion applies equally to engineering and R&D managers with minor modifications to fit the nature of their respective functions.

Salesman: The technical manager sees himself as the spokesman for his group. This role is one of communication and salesmanship. He must sell his group on various projects and ideas. He sells the group (in terms of capabilities and qualifications) to upper management or to his peers in other divisions. He also may sell an outsider on a project, product, or idea. Excellent communication and persuasion skills are important requisites for effective salesmanship.

Director/controller: The technical manager sees the use of power—acquired by virtue of his position—to direct and control the actions of others as one of his legitimate roles. Since the manager is responsible for getting things done with and through others, it is his prerogative to use his authority and influence to see to it that goals are set, resources are allocated, and results are achieved in the desired manner. Direction and control are, then, parts of the managerial task.

Administrator: Rules, regulations, policies, schedules, deadlines, and procedures are seen, understandably, as part of the manager's job. Administrative activities take a fairly large portion of the manager's time, and the performance of such activities is important for having a smoothly functioning operation.

Forecaster/planner: The planning function is seen as one of the important managerial functions. The technical manager views his role in this area as one requiring setting goals, identifying trends, forecasting future resources, and defining future needs and opportunities.

Trainer and developer: Finally, the technical manager considers training and developing subordinates' skills to be one of his functions. In this capacity, the technical manager plays the role of the coach, helping the subordinate develop his skills in certain areas by actually teaching him or by pointing out to him alternative sources and avenues for knowledge and skill development.

The Technical Manager's Role as Seen by His Subordinates. Let us now look at your job as a technical manager from a different perspective—through the eyes of your subordinates.

What is the boss for? As shown in Table 7-3, technologists see their bosses as playing four different roles. Using the performing arts terminology, these roles are those of the critic, agent, producer, and stagehand.[9] Since the boss's self-image as profiled in the previous section and as seen by his subordinates will naturally overlap to some extent, I shall focus on the striking differences—rather than the similarities—to avoid redundancy. From a comparison of how the boss sees himself to how his subordinates see him, the following profile emerges:

1. While the technical manager sees providing technical leadership and direction for his group as one of his vital roles, his subordinates view him only as a "critic" capable of evaluating and judging their technical activities after the fact.

---

[9] This section is primarily based on Steele, Lowell W. "Innovation in Big Business." New York: Elsevier, 1975, pp. 175-188.

This is a striking difference in perception since the criterion for a "good" technical manager, and thus, what he strives to do—attain technical competence—is not at all consistent with what his subordinates expect him to do—namely to draw forth the talents of his technical people into a competent pool available to the entire operation. These differing perceptions, if accurate, can be a significant source of potential conflict between the two parties. In short, it is the conflict between one who sees himself as a technical leader and others who see him only as a facilitator. The point is that while both parties consider technical skill important for technical managers, they disagree on how it is to be used.

2. Technologists' view of their boss as an "agent" is very similar to the salesman image he projects for himself, as discussed above. The boss is viewed as the representative and spokesman for the group, especially with outside clients such as contractors and funding agencies.

3. Subordinates' view of the boss as a "producer" is much broader than his own perception of the "director/controller" role (Table 7-3). Engineers and scientists consider their producer-boss's skills in bargaining, negotiating, and political in-fighting to be far more important than his professional technical skills. The boss's ability to play (and win) the political game is considered crucial for getting the appropriate share of budgets, space, and other resources. It is also important for getting political support from other divisions in the organization (such as the marketing division) for engineering and R&D policies and programs.

4. The manager's view of his role as an "administrator" is quite similar to the "stagehand" view by subordinates. This essentially refers to the administrative details, including answering letters, joining meetings, maintaining schedules, meeting deadlines, securing contracts, and so on. This represents the technologists' view of the boss as a "paper shuffler" or "pencil pusher."

5. Technologists—to continue the analogies to the performing arts—consider themselves the stars of the show, while they see the boss as being off stage in the wings. It is clear that what managers think of themselves—as the stars of the show—and what technologists think of their bosses are two different things. To many, if not most, engineers and scientists, the work of management is, indeed, subordinated to the technical tasks of professionals. Yet management is now a popular career path to more of them than ever before!

The Technical Manager's Role as Viewed by the Organization. So far I have looked at the technical manager's role through his own eyes as well as through the eyes of his subordinates. The last angle in this triangle is the manager's roles as seen by his superiors and peers. Put differently, these are the roles imposed on him by the institution. Several observations can be made here.

Achiever: The technical manager is expected, by virtue of his position, to be an achiever. This is understandable since the technical manager, like any other manager, is responsible for getting things done through others working for him. He is, therefore, expected to have the drive and the ability to mobilize and direct resources to achieve the best possible results in handling the technical function of his organization.

Advocate/salesman: The second institutional role of the technical manager relates to salesmanship. As you may recall, the same role was perceived by the manager himself and also by his subordinates—as discussed above. It is interesting to note here that "salesmanship" is, in fact, a distinct feature of many, if not most, managerial positions. "Selling" the capabilities and resources of his group to other divisions, to upper management, and to external parties is thus a dominant feature of all technical management positions, especially on the first level (perhaps even more so in R&D). First-level supervisors work directly with engineers and scientists, are naturally more involved with technical decisions and projects, and, perhaps more importantly, work with "given" amounts of resources, usually under severe time pressures.

Resource allocator: A third role the technical manager is expected to play is that of the resource allocator. Again, this role is similar to the "director/controller" and "producer" roles perceived by the technical manager and his subordinates, respectively—as discussed above. This role, obviously, does require collecting information, studying situations, analyzing risks, making choices, and assuming responsibility for these choices.

Goal setter: This is the last of the roles the technical manager is expected to play. It corresponds to the manager's own perception of himself as a "forecaster/planner"—as discussed above. As viewed by the organization, the technical manager is expected to identify objectives, direct resources, and make sure that technical objectives and plans are always in accord with top management goals and priorities.

To sum up: The foregoing analysis paints a portrait of the technical manager's role as seen by himself, his subordinates, and the organization he works for. It is clear from this discussion that these three sets of perceptions are by no means unrelated. In fact, all these roles are intertwined. On the other hand, which role (or roles) you assume will depend on the organizational level you are on and the problems facing your unit or division at that time.

It is equally important for you to remember here the high complexity of these multiple roles and the enormous demands imposed on you for playing them. The fact remains, however, that each role requires a distinctive set of skills (i.e., "salesman" vs "resource allocator") that might be inconsistent with the requirements for playing another role. Perhaps it would be unlikely (indeed unrealistic) to assume that one would be equally competent in all of them. A good rule of thumb would be to concentrate on playing the roles you are most comfortable with—that is, to exploit your strengths while trying to improve on the others. Your most appropriate role (or roles) will, of course, depend on factors such as your managerial capacity and skills, your management level and type of responsibilities, your subordinates, and the expectations placed upon you by your organization (including those imposed by your boss).

One final point: You should often refer to Figure 7-5 looking at your role from different angles. As you can see, it is always possible to take a unidimensional view—looking at just "your" side of the "box"—and to forget how your superiors and subordinates (the other sides of the box) see you. Your perspective, then, will be out of balance. An effective manager will always take a multidimensional view—keeping the three "images" in focus and in the right perspective.

WHAT DO ENGINEERING AND R&D MANAGERS DO?

Having explored the roles of managers in general, and the nature of technical supervisory functions in particular, let us now look into the functions and climate within which engineering and R&D managers and supervisors operate. This section will sharpen the focus and help you develop a feel and appreciation of their complex organizational environment.

The engineering manager has responsibilities to his people, to his management, and to society.[10]   This role is one of many contradictions:

1. He must provide exact answers with inexact and incomplete input.
2. He must do this on a schedule and within a budget, both of which are usually too restrictive.

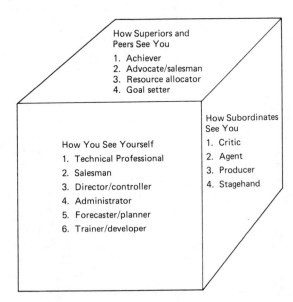

How Superiors and
Peers See You

1. Achiever
2. Advocate/salesman
3. Resource allocator
4. Goal setter

How Subordinates
See You

1. Critic
2. Agent
3. Producer
4. Stagehand

How You See Yourself

1. Technical Professional
2. Salesman
3. Director/controller
4. Administrator
5. Forecaster/planner
6. Trainer/developer

Figure 7-5. Managerial roles of technical managers.

[10] This discussion is based on Holley, C. H. What Is an Engineering Manager? *Electrical World* (Part I, February 15, 1976): 91-94; and (Part II, March 1, 1976): 48-51.

3. He must do this in a world of detail with broad understanding of the overall problem. Too little attention to detail can lead to incompletion, frustration, and lack of recognition of the overall objectives.
4. He must work with people, who are primarily his only resource, and they need to take the natural sciences and materials and translate them economically into a useful product.
5. He must provide proper planning, organization, standards, controls of results, and measurement systems while creating an atmosphere conducive to high creativity and innovation.
6. He must balance short-range goals against long-range viability.
7. He must develop and maintain competence in specialized technical skills and, at the same time, develop broad-gauged products of systems engineers and integrate their combined contributions.
8. He must provide technical growth and continuity for the parent organization while meeting the needs of the development of individuals.
9. He must constantly strive for synergism of all the interrelationships and related technologies with his activity.
10. He must be constantly feeding back experience of his predecessors, competitors, and the results produced by his organization into this engineering process.

The engineering manager, with all this, has to be continuously aware of the requirements of his business and the competition both in the form of other suppliers and in the form of other technologies. He needs to be continuously exchanging information throughout the organization and within the industry, within the restraints of his organization's proprietary interest, so that he can anticipate and take timely actions. In other words, he must be knowledgeable and stay flexible and be prepared for adapting to and influencing change. Therefore, managing an engineering organization is like designing a technical product—it is a compromise.

Let us now turn to the nature and functions of R&D supervision. There are enormous variations in the activities, responsibilities, and titles of first-line supervisors in R&D laboratories. In fact, experience shows that there are no two laboratories in which the first-line supervisors have identical jobs. Responsibilities of first-line supervisors in R&D will vary depending on the nature and characteristics of the laboratory including the following:

1. The range from product development to basic research.
2. The range from government contract to commercial support.
3. The range from a project type of organization to a functional type of organization.
4. The range from a very formal to a very informal organization.

Managing the R&D function consists of several tasks. These tasks can be translated into responsibilities of R&D supervisors including the following:[11]

1. To participate in the selection of creative individuals (appropriate for the organization's interest).
2. To manage his team to provide maximum freedom of action within existing boundary conditions.
3. To participate in the formulation, interpretation, and acceptance of realistic research objectives (a major communications problem).
4. To maintain appropriate and realistic pressure toward accomplishment.
5. To assure appropriate recognition of contributions made by the individual members of his team.
6. To maintain communication between his group and the other parts of the laboratory and the company to provide knowledge of stimulating activities and to provide association of stimulating individuals.
7. To play an appropriate role in the provision of adequate facilities and technical assistance.
8. To understand and stabilize personnel problems involving creative individuals.

Like that of the engineering manager, the R&D manager's job is one of many relationships. In the course of a single day he may have to wear five hats: scientific, administrative, marketing, financial, and personnel.[12] There are times when he is required to wear all five hats simultaneously. Remember that the concept of "hats" corresponds to the concept of roles used earlier in analyzing the technical manager's supervisory functions. For each role the R&D supervisor plays he has to wear a different hat.

COMMON PROBLEMS FACING ENGINEERING AND R&D SUPERVISORS

The problems facing you in the normal day-to-day operations will certainly depend on the nature of your management responsibilities, the organizational level you are on, and the functional specialization of your unit. Research shows, however, that there are some major problems shared by technical managers and supervisors. Table 7-4 presents a list of these problems ranked in order of importance based on empirical data collected from a large sample of technical managers and supervisors.[13]

---

[11] Hillier, James. The Responsibilities of the First Line of Supervision in Research. *Research Management*, 2, 4 (Winter 1958): 233.
[12] Hillier, James. The R&D Manager Wears Five Hats. *Research Management* (July 1972): 33-41.
[13] Hitchcock, Lauren B. Problems of First-Line Supervisors. *Research Management*, X, 6 (1967): 385-397.

Table 7-4. Major Problems Encountered by First-Line RD&E Supervisors and Managers.[a]

1. Insufficient definition of policy from top downward.

2. How to define the goal of a problem, interpret to the researcher its importance to the company, and potential rewards for a solution, in order to motivate.

3. Budgeting manpower and assignments; determining priorities.

4. How to encourage creativity.

5. Doing things myself that I could delegate.

6. Putting out brush fires.

7. Determining optimum degree of help to give to individuals.

8. Excessive secondary demands on my time; paper work; inconclusive meetings.

9. Manpower shortages.

10. Maintaining my own knowledge in fields supervised.

11. Gaining time to properly test a product before it is sold.

12. Marketing analyst's intelligence data—too little/too late.

13. How to provide recognition for and to reward individual accomplishment.

14. Poorly written reports from group members.

15. Getting details cleaned up after a solution.

16. Restrictive salary policy handicapping employment of able personnel.

17. Evaluating applicants.

18. Interpreting results of RD&E work.

[a]From Hitchcock, Lauren B. Problems of First-Line Supervisors. *Research Management,* X, 6 (1967): 392.

It appears from this table that the major problems facing technical managers and supervisors can be grouped into six categories:

1. Technical supervision.
2. Budgeting time and effort.
3. Communications.
4. Personnel.
5. Excessive diversion of R&D and engineering effort.
6. Keeping current in fields supervised.

It is also noteworthy that the two most important problems perceived by the managers in this study were communication problems. Problems relating to technical supervision and the nature of creative technical resources were considered to be quite important. Although it would, of course, be naive to argue that technical supervisors and managers would necessarily have the same problems, the above list would seem to be highly representative.

A MANAGERIAL SKILL DEVELOPMENT MODEL

A discussion of the nature of supervisory and managerial work was the leading section in this chapter. It seems appropriate to conclude it with a short note on the levels of your managerial skill development. Let me remind you that the continuing development of your skills and management capabilities is your own responsibility—as discussed in earlier chapters. Your organization is merely responsible for providing you with the opportunities and environment for fostering this development.

Three Types of Development

As you will note in Figure 7-6, there are three levels (or types) of managerial skills that can be developed in connection with your managerial task (these were also briefly mentioned in Chapter 4):

Self-management: This includes self-development efforts such as handling yourself in a professional manner, learning to be assertive in interpersonal relations, raising your consciousness and self-confidence, and effectively managing your time.

Job management: This relates to developing your managerial skills. As you will recall, three types of skills are required for managerial competence. Administrative skills are those capabilities necessary for performing the functional managerial aspects of your job. These are concrete and thus "hard" types of skills relating to activities such as planning and decision-making, organizational structure, and managerial control. Interpersonal skills relate to the management of people and include such things as motivation, communication, and conflict resolution skills. These skills are behavioral in nature and thus are inconcrete or "soft." Technical skills are those required for effective handling of the professional and technical aspects of your job. They relate, basically, to one's specialty or field of expertise and thus are "hard" or concrete types of skills. As discussed in Chapter 2, acquiring these skills, and combining them—in the right mix—will result in effective job management.

Career management: In addition to self-management and job management, the third level of development concerns your career management skills. This includes such things as career planning—as opposed to career winging—self-development and growth efforts, and dealing with obsolescense.

HOW ARE YOU DOING SO FAR?
GUIDELINES FOR SELF-EVALUATION

Helping you develop your functional management skills is one of the major objectives of this volume. It is also a continuing process. The ability to critically evaluate your own performance is a valuable skill. To help you develop and

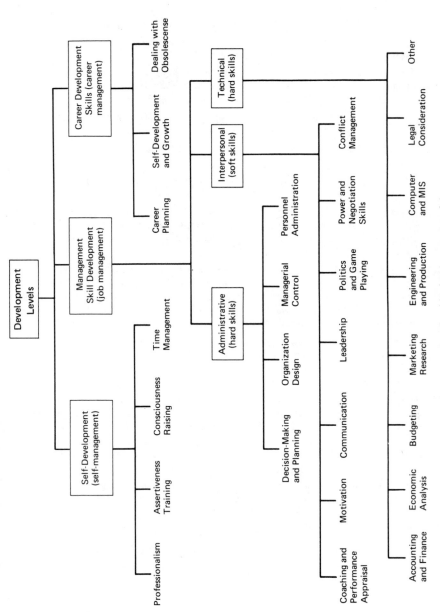

Figure 7-6. A managerial skill development model.

Table 7-5. How Not to Succeed as an R&D Manager.

1. Always pretend to know more than anybody around you.

2. Police your employees by every procedural means that you and your management consultants can devise (time cards, returning late from lunch, drinking coffee at their desks, etc.).

3. Never omit a daily check on the progress of everyone's work (jovial remarks about programs and experiments at regular time schedules every day).

4. Make it a point to have professionally trained employees do technicians' work for long periods of time.

5. Funnel employees into narrowly structured assignments just because they are good at it.

6. Erect the highest possible barrier between commercial decision makers and your technical staff. Overlook the fact that the commercial side of the enterprise has the dual responsibility of identifying commercially viable needs and of reducing technical findings to a marketable state.

7. Provide training for your employees, but only in areas in which they are already knowledgeable. In other words, send engineers to engineering courses, accountants to accounting courses, etc. Persistent narrow channeling of training activities for those individuals who have broader abilities will effectively prevent them from exercising these abilities. Everyone, ultimately, will end up knowing more and more about less and less.

8. Be certain not to speak to employees on a personal level except when announcing a raise to them. Such policy will make it plain that they are considered only as a mere unit of labor to which a certain cost is attached, and that their personal problems, expectations, and concerns do not matter much.

9. To preserve pristine purity of technical and scientific thinking, make certain to separate workers from their budgets. Make it difficult and, better yet, impossible, for your employees to recognize that the dollars that support them must be earned by somebody else in the marketplace. Such a policy will be effective in formulating cascading demands for lavish facilities ranging from electron microscopes to reserved parking places, not to mention technicians without number.

10. Try at all times to be the exclusive spokesman for everything for which you are responsible (a golden tip, however, is never to forget the fact that you are, in a very real way, the creation of the people who work for you and that fairness alone recognizes that they be given credit. And, whatever you do, give credit in public, but apportion blame in private).

[a] Adapted from Fraenkel, Stephen J. How Not to Succeed as an R&D Manager. *Research Management*, **XXIII**, 3 (May 1980): 35-37.

sharpen this skill, here are some guidelines for self-evaluation. Table 7-5 provides some advice on how not to succeed without hardly trying. Indeed, Table 7-5 presents ten "uncommandments" of management.

SUMMARY

This chapter has focused on developing a practical framework of what technical managers do, how they spend their time, and the common problems facing engineering and R&D managers. The roles managers play have been analyzed, with a special emphasis on the actual content of managerial work. Roles of technical managers as seen by themselves, their subordinates, and their peers and superiors have been explored. A model for evaluating your performance and enhancing your managerial skills has also been presented.

As you will recall, the three administrative skills necessary for effective managerial performance are: building an effective organizational structure, planning and decision-making, and measuring and controlling performance. An in-depth exploration of these aspects of your managerial task will be undertaken in the balance of this book.

V
THE ORGANIZING
FUNCTION

8
Let's Get Organized

As you will recall from our previous discussion, effective handling of your responsibilities as a manager or supervisor requires skills in three distinct functions: building a viable organizational structure for your unit or department; managerial problem-solving, planning, and decision-making; and controlling, measuring, and evaluating your subordinates' and divisional performance. These three areas constitute the focus of the balance of this volume.

The purpose of this chapter is to introduce you to the function of organizing as an integral part of your management task. It will provide you with sound principles and guidelines that can help you in designing the structure of the engineering and R&D operations and activities. Naturally, no step-by-step prescriptions will be provided simply because they do not work.

THE MEANING AND PROCESS OF ORGANIZING

A group of individuals with clearly assigned tasks directed toward the achievement of a common goal constitutes an organization. An organization chart is simply a portrait of an organizational structure. In a very fundamental sense, the organizational chart is a normative document showing how the organization should function—not necessarily how it is actually functioning. It follows that the organizational structure is simply a prescribed set of relationships among the different positions and levels in an organization. Organizing, then, could be defined as the process of dividing up total organizational activities into tasks, and determining the relationships between these tasks.

As a manager, your task in the organizing function requires answering several questions such as:

1. Who is going to do what (specialization)?
2. Who is going to report to whom (authority relationship)?
3. How are people and activities are going to be related (grouping)?

4. How can superior-subordinate relationships be defined through task assignments and authority delegation (formal communication and reporting relationships)?

As shown in Figure 8-1, organizing involves four basic steps:

1. Define the organizational objective and the subobjective for each division or department. The organizational structure is simply a mean toward an end. A clear statement of the objective(s) is necessary before a sound organizational structure can be designed. Each manager must translate broad corporate objectives into more specific objectives for his department or unit. This specific statement will be the basis for designing an appropriate organizational structure. Do not start out with a ready-made structure, then ask yourself, "What can I do with it?" Rather, start with the "what"—the objective—followed by the "how"—the structure.

2. Determine the activities necessary to achieve organizational goals. This involves determining the activities and tasks in each functional area necessary for effective performance. A sound approach to do this is by relating the desired goals of your division to the overall purpose of the organization. For example, in a manufacturing firm the primary purpose of the engineering group is the design and supervision of the manufacturing of products that can be sold at a profit. Once the objective is concretely defined, the activities necessary to accomplish it can be determined. The sequence and timing of these activities should also be defined.

3. Arrange the activities into logical groupings: Since the activities have already been logically defined and broken down, the next step is to group the work to be done into work units. These work units represent jobs that can be performed by people. The grouping should be done according to a logical system. For instance, work groups should insofar as possible be composed of activities that are basically similar. Small groups can then be combined into larger groups. This will result in establishing different levels in the organizational hierarchy, and the structural hierarchy of the organization will, then, start shaping up.

4. Assign authority and responsibility for each grouping to someone to assure that the job gets done: The final step is to establish a clear authority-responsibility network. A clear definition of basic relationships between positions and

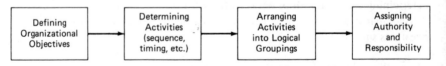

Figure 8-1. Organizing place in the management process.

individuals at different organizational or divisional levels is crucial for smooth organizational functioning. This, accompanied with overall coordination of the activities of all groups, will minimize friction and enhance coordination and cooperation.

To sum up: The result of organizing is an organizational structure—a system of activity-authority relationships. As you can see in Figure 8-2, an organizational structure is a system of activity groupings tied together with authority. It follows that organizing is essentially a two-part process: grouping activities into jobs and delegating authority.

THE IMPORTANCE OF ORGANIZING

As you can see, when you set up relationships between people, resources, and work, you organize. Your responsibility as a manager or supervisor is to make sure that the goals of your division are accomplished and that everyone of your employees understands what to do and why. When you organize effectively, the goal will be achieved efficiently. The central point is that whenever all components such as goals, people, technology, and other resources are tied together in some order, organization exists, but only when these subsystems are arranged in their most sound and productive relationships do efficiency and effectiveness result. It follows that the organization in itself is neither good nor bad. It is merely a tool that, if properly used, enables you to accomplish goals more efficiently and effectively.

Pursuing this discussion one step further, an organizational structure is not a requisite for good management. A sound organizational structure cannot guarantee good management. For good technical management of the engineering and R&D functions, the organization must employ good managers. In this sense, an organizational structure only provides the framework. What you should keep in mind, then, is that while there is no organization without some degree of structure, the structure alone does not make an organization. Structure, however, is absolutely basic to all organizations simply because they are created by people to achieve goals and perform tasks that are too large or too complex for any one individual to accomplish. The structure, then, is a significant helping factor which, combined with capable management ingenuity and talent, will enhance organizational performance and achieve good results.

Figure 8-2. The organizing process.

Thus, a significant part of your managerial job is to organize and define relationships between objectives, activities, processes, and people at different positions. This task is crucial for the following reasons:

1. It helps to divide the total work to be done into specified activities.
2. It defines everyone's duties and responsibilities.
3. It spells out formal authority-responsibility relationships.
4. It enhances cooperation and coordination.
5. It improves efficiency by avoiding duplication of activities.
6. It links the planning and doing aspects of the management process.
7. It serves as a solid basis for the managerial functions of direction and control.
8. It sharpens the focus on organizational strategy and objectives, using the structure as a vehicle for carrying them out.

It should be obvious by now that organizing is a key managerial function. Your task in undertaking this function is very similar to that of the architect in designing a building. Just as he must have specific sets of objectives and constraints before carrying out his design, you must have your organizational strategy and structure closely intertwined into a viable system of formal relationships between people, materials, money, machines, management, and methods for the objectives of your organization to be attained.

THE RESPONSIBILITY FOR ORGANIZING

There are four points I would like you to keep in mind concerning the responsibility for organizing: First, organizing is every manager's responsibility: Since organizing is absolutely basic to all organizations, then the process of organizing must be done to some degree by managers at all levels. The extent and scope of this responsibility will, of course, vary with the management level you are on. While a major reorganization plan is naturally the sole prerogative of top management, middle and first-level managers are responsible for the implementation of organizational plans in their immediate departments or divisions.

Second, no manager, at any level, is free to organize the activities below him in any way that he chooses. The essence of this point is simply that you are not a free agent to design the structure of your unit in any way you want. No one, in fact, is. An organization operates within a set of internal and external constraints or parameters such as budgets, technology, internal technical strengths; capabilities; weaknesses, controls, checks and procedures, management goals, philosophy; priorities, market and economic forces, political and government regulations; and so on. These forces create demands and impose constraints upon the organization's ability to function effectively.

No manager, at any level, can ignore the impacts of these forces on the organization. In other words, you cannot ignore the parameters imposed upon the organization by both its internal and external environments. While top management usually has some discretion in shaping and even controlling the internal constraints, it has either minimal or no control over the outside forces—which are, by the way, usually taken as "givens." The organization, as you can see, is indeed an open system operating within a constantly changing environment.

Another significant implication of this point is that managers at the first and even middle levels have very little to do with the way the organization is formally structured. Furthermore, while initiating and effecting changes in an existing organizational structure are the responsibility of top management, these organizational plans cannot be implemented without the approval of the board of directors and the stockholders—major constraints. The amount of discretion you have in organizing the activities in your division or department does, however, depend on your particular situation including the amount of authority you have, your boss's style of leadership and management philosophy, the nature of tasks done by your subordinates and their qualifications, and general management policies and procedures. It is clear why no manager is really a free agent and also why many utopian textbook prescriptions for structuring organizations are too academic and usually do not work.

Third, one of the final products of organizing is the creation of positions or jobs. The ultimate outcome of the process of organizing is a formal organizational structure with administrative levels, divisions, relationships, and an authority-responsibility system. In a very real sense, then, the core product of the organizing process is the grouping of activities in some fashion and thus the creation of positions to be staffed by potential members of the organization.

Fourth, organizing is not a one-time process. It is an ongoing process because structures are tools with which to implement plans to achieve particular objectives. Since structures are largely determined by the organization's objectives, which are constantly changing in response to changes in the internal and external constraints mentioned above, then the organizing process is actually a continuing one.

This point becomes more significant when you consider the fact that organizational structures at various levels are usually inherited. Rarely do you have the opportunity to develop a completely new organizational structure. This means that changing or making major modifications in the inherited structure might be enormously difficult. Yet, organizing and reorganizing are activities that you are expected to undertake continually as tools in assuming your managerial responsibilities and achieving results.

TYPES OF ORGANIZATIONAL STRUCTURES

Characteristic of all organizations is having two types of organizational structures: formal and informal. The formal structure of an organization is a network and a framework of officially established relationships between divisions (horizontal level) and various management levels (vertical). It is a direct outcome of the organizing process undertaken by the manager and is clearly reflected in a formal organization chart.

The informal structure of an organization, on the other hand, is a set of voluntary and unplanned (as opposed to officially and consciously developed) network of interpersonal realtionships, methods, and procedures that emerge and are developed among members of an organization. Because of the spontaneous nature of the informal structure, it does not appear on the organization chart. Informal leadership and communication channels, lunch and coffee break conversations, small group interactions, cliques, friendships, group gossip, and grapevines are all powerful components of the informal structure of an organization. Compared to the formal structure, the informal organization is loosely developed and unconsciously maintained, and is usually out of line with the formal, neatly developed organization chart. In a very real sense, the informal organization truly describes how things actually get done in an organization.

Thus, it is crucial that you not only recognize the existence of the two patterns of organizational structures but also understand how they function. Let us, then, turn to a discussion of the nature and characteristics of both structures.

Nature of Formal and Informal Organizations

As noted above, the formal organization is the prescribed mechanism through which the objectives of the organization are ultimately achieved. It is also the broad framework of official relationships between individuals, positions, and management levels within which the spontaneous voluntary forces of the informal organization operate. It would, indeed, be a mistake for you to ignore the informal organization or to attempt to use it as a total substitute for the formal hierarchy. Both strategies could be highly dysfunctional. In short, you need to understand and work within both types of organization. The principles of formal organization will be discussed later in this chapter.

Why do informal organizations emerge? You can look at your organization—like any other—as a social system of relationships, roles, and formal and informal groups. Since man is a social animal, employees satisfy their social and security needs by joining groups and creating informal entities independent from the formal structure. Employees also join different groups to fulfill their identification needs and for a sense of protection and belonging.

Research shows that informal groups satisfy employees' needs that are not usually satisfied—indeed, should not be expected to—through the formal structure. In short, social, security, and identification needs are usually largely satisfied through the informal organization system. Employees may also consider the informal groups to which they belong as valuable means for protecting their interest against "management." It goes without saying that the informal organization can either support or impede the formal organization, depending on the goals of the informal network. Some guidlines and tips for handling the formal and informal organization will follow later in this chapter.

Some Characteristics of Formal and Informal Organizations

Table 8-1 presents a comparative profile of the major characteristics of formal and informal organizations. As you will note, formal organizations are distinctively different from informal structures. These differences lie in several areas including the nature of each system, its objectives, organizational norms, leadership, authority, power and control, reward systems, status and symbols, communications, and discipline.

Let me remind you that wherever people work together, informal groups will be formed, friendships, cliques, and gossip groups will emerge, and thus, the informal organization network will come into being. There is nothing you or anybody else can do to prevent this. A smart manager will never fight the informal organization. Not only will he attempt to recognize it and understand it, he will also try to use it to his own advantage. Remember, your subordinates can do wonders for you, giving you support when you need it, acting as good will ambassadors to other divisions, and serving as excellent sources of information for you on what is happening elsewhere in the organization.

THE ORGANIZATION CHART: WHAT YOU SHOULD KNOW ABOUT IT

What the Chart Can Tell You

Your organizing activities will result in a formal organizational structure that is reflected in the organization chart. The chart, thus, is a graphic representation of how the organization should function. It delineates a system of formal lines of authority, responsibility, communication, and chain of command that must be maintained as if the organization were to function "by the book." As will be seen below, the organization actually cannot and does not. It follows that the organization chart, in the final analysis, shows what should be rather than what is. It is the skeleton of the organization's structure.

Why is a formal organizational chart necessary? As shown in Table 8-2, there are several good reasons for the chart to exist including the following:

1. It defines the formal structure of the organization and the various administrative layers.
2. It shows the major reporting relationships, the flow of work, and the areas of responsibility.

Table 8-1. Characteristics of Formal and Informal Organizations.

CHARACTERISTIC	FORMAL ORGANIZATION	INFORMAL ORGANIZATION
1. Nature of System	Static—organizations without people.	Dynamic—organizations in action, with people.
2. Objective	Achieving overall organizational goals.	Possible combination, such as knowing what is going on, getting even with the boss, resisting changes and protecting group members.
3. Leadership	Authority and responsibility are given or assigned to managers as a function of their formal positions.	The informal leader emerges as the representative or the spokesman for the group.
4. Authority	Based on principles of sound organization including specialization and division of labor; basically bureaucratic in nature.	Peer interaction and respect are important: "If you really want to know what's happening see John, he always knows"; "Max is the expert on that subject, he'll be glad to help."
5. Power and Control	Directly related to one's position on the organization chart, and job description.	A function of one's clout, influence, connections, and informal impressions made on individuals "upstairs."
6. Reward System	Prescribed packages for sharing or withholding organizational "goodies" depending on loyalty and contribution—or lack of it—to the organization.	Reflected in terms of more or less status in the group.
7. Status and Symbols	Prescribed to fit the organization's "image"; sharply differentiate between employees at different levels.	Behavior and dress codes are sharply enforced; higher-status individuals are informally recognized in various ways by the group.
8. Communications	A formal communication system is designed to follow the chain of command.	The grapevine is a powerful source of information which might reinforce or detract from formal communications.
9. Organizational Norms	Formal rules, policies and procedures strictly guide individual group behavior; a system of formal standards of behavior and expectations is developed.	A strong desire to be accepted by the group, to be "in," to "fit," to be "one of the boys"; a strong tendency to conform to group expectations.
10. Discipline	Enforced based on organizational formal policies and procedures.	Imposed by the group on individuals who do not conform to the group's norms and standards; Group acceptance and satisfaction of the social need are more valued than material rewards earned by the "rate buster."

Table 8-2. How Much Should You Expect from the Organization Chart?

WHAT THE CHART CAN TELL YOU	WHAT THE CHART CANNOT TELL YOU
1. The formal structure	1. Nature of various managerial roles and how they relate to different functions.
2. Departments, divisions, and their components	
3. Basic levels and layers of management and the chain of command	2. How the organization is functioning in reality
4. Major reporting relationships including who is (supposed to be) whose superior	3. Variations in people's authority, influence, and responsibility
5. Framework for budgeting and resource allocation	4. The informal lines of communication within the organization
6. Procedures, directives, and other related matters	5. Vast differences between line and staff concepts
7. Nature of activities to be performed by different organizational units	6. The informal organization structure
8. Bases for grouping activities (i.e., functional, regional, project, or product basis)	

3. It identifies the basic relationships between different departments and divisions as well as the basic levels of authority and the chain of command throughout the organization.

4. It provides a convenient framework for scheduling, budgeting, and resource allocation.

5. It serves as a handy tool and a basis for establishing procedures, issuing directives, and designing management information systems (formal communication networks).

6. It provides outsiders (clients, contractors, funding agencies, bankers, and other interested parties) with a "working" map of the formal structure of the organization.

A sample organization chart is shown in Figure 8-3.

What the Chart Cannot Tell You

It is clear that while the formal organization chart performs several useful functions for you, it does have some major drawbacks. What is wrong with it? In principle, there is nothing wrong with the chart as such. However, as you will note in Table 8-2, there are many important things that the chart cannot tell you.

First of all, while the chart shows basic divisions of work and authority-responsibility relationships, it does not identify organizational functions and show

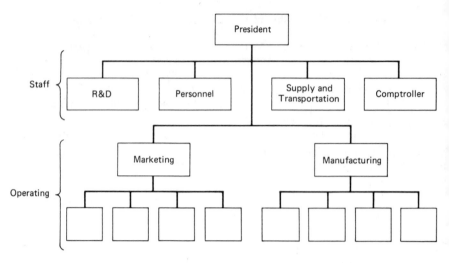

Figure 8-3. Sample organization chart.

how individuals relate to these functions. The roles managers play in relation to their work groups and to the organization stay undefined. Therefore, the chart does not show how the organization actually works.

Second, the chart is simply a symbolic representation providing a framework of company functions and showing how they operate. Because the chart provides a simplistic arrangement of the organizational blocks (functions), it does not present any background about the role occupants—the people. In a very fundamental sense, then, the chart is lifeless. It is a stage without actors—static. Only if the players and the roles they assume were considered would the chart represent a real organization in action.

Third, the chart does not show the variations in the degree of authority, responsibility, and influence of people within the organization. The impression given is that two individuals on the same level on the organizational chart assume the same degree of authority and responsibility. Nothing could be further from the truth! Differences in authority and influence do exist not only between people on the same management level but also between levels. That is, an individual at a lower level might well have considerably more influence and clout in the organization than his counterparts at higher levels. This is largely determined by variations in individuals' personalities, needs, styles, connections, contacts, and ways of manipulating the system. Yet, these variables are literally unknowns on the organization chart.

Fourth, although the chart provides prescribed communication routes in the organization, it does not usually show the informal lines of communication and the shortcuts necessary to avoid the routine and the red tape of the formal communication networks. Because of the intricate nature of the informal communication network, it is impossible to have it appear on the chart. Yet, managing is a group activity where team effort is crucial for effective organizational functioning.

Fifth, the chart does not truly distinguish between line and staff relationships. In principle, the line manager takes orders from above and passes them on to subordinates below. The staff manager does not actually have a command relationship since he is not really involved in the chain of command. This means that—as will be further discussed below—while the line manager tells others what to do, the staff manager must sell his ideas. However, in spite of this "neat and pure" distinction between line and staff relationships, the staff authority may take any one of several forms ranging from couseling and advising to the functional type of authority (authority over operating departments by virtue of the staff manager's specialized knowledge and expertise in a certain field). Note that the typical organization chart says nothing regarding the type of authority the staff has with respect to different areas, and thus, no one really knows—from the chart alone—how the organization actually operates.

Finally, because the chart reflects only the formally sanctioned structure, it does not show the informal organization that emerges in all formal organizations. As discussed above, the informal organization describes the way things actually get done in an organization in spite of the formal structure. Yet, the chart says nothing about informal connections, norms, organizational symbols and rituals, informal influences, power centers, politics, likes and dislikes, and the organization's codes for "appropriate" behavior and "prescriptions" for getting a fair shake and getting ahead. Since descriptions of how "the game is being played around here" typically stay off the record and go unwritten, it becomes exceedingly difficult for the manager—or anyone else for that matter—to discover the rules of the game without appropriate socialization and grounding in how the informal structure works. This understanding would definitely give you an edge in that you can probably cut through the "red tape" and, thus, get better results in terms of higher efficiency and effectiveness. This advantage can be compounded when you consider that the organizational formal chart (and the informal structure) is ever-changing with newcomers, transfers, promotions, job changes, and reorganization efforts. Without constant updating of the chart, it will simply become obsolete.

Based on the foregoing analysis, you can see, I trust, the benefits and also the risks of reading too much into the formal organization chart. It is a useful document but is an insufficient source of information about who, indeed, is running the show and how the organization is actually managed. This point was aptly made in the following statement: "Organization charts come in various sizes, colors and even textures. Most are black and white and printed on paper. Some are affixed to office walls and made of materials that are easily changed. Some charts are highly detailed; some are very sketchy. Some are stamped confidential and locked in the desks of a chosen few; others are broadly distributed and easily available. Despite these and other variations that might be noted, all organization charts have at least one thing in common: They don't always show how the organization works. Or, as some people say, they don't show the real organizations."[1]

FUNDAMENTAL PRINCIPLES OF ORGANIZATIONAL STRUCTURE

Nature of Principles of Organization

By now we know that every organization has two types of organizational structures: one formal, reflected on the organization chart, and the other informal, representing relationships between people, likes and dislikes, cliques, power centers, organizational politics, and so on. We also know the major characteristics of each organizational form. Naturally you will relatively have much more control over the formal than the informal structure. This is simply because the general objectives of the organization (including your division), the type of technology used, characteristics of the tasks to be done, and your subordinates' backgrounds and qualifications are some of the variables determining the shape and character of the formal structure. However, remember that the extent of your involvement and how much say you will have about the nature and design of the organizational structure will largely depend on the management level you are on. The higher the level, the more authority you will have—within the limits discussed earlier in this chapter.

Focusing on the formal structure, are there some principles and guidelines to follow in designing the organization? While there certainly are some principles that can be considered useful guidelines for designing an efficient and effective organizational structure, they must be used with caution. Experience shows that while these principles constitute the basis of good organization and management, they should never be taken as "givens." Contrary to science and engineering fields, there are no "givens" in management since everything depends on a host of other things. The contingency approach referred to earlier in this book is definitely characteristic of management actions and practices.

A second reason you should not use these principles across the board is the fact that hardly a management system exists in any organization that does not occasionally violate some of these principles—sometimes with sound justifications. In project-type organizations, to give you an example, the "two bosses" for functional managers and the responsibility far exceeding the project manager's authority are certainly familiar problems. These are clear violations of the conventional principles of "unity of command" and "parity of authority and responsibility."

Furthermore, there are as many organizational structures as there are organizations, for each type of organization is unique and has its own special structure

---

[1] Unknown source.

of people, resources, and goals to be achieved, as discussed above. In addition, not only is there no one best method to design an organization, there are also no two organizations that are exactly alike in their structure.

Finally, the structure appropriate for an organization at a specific time may be totally inappropriate at another under a different set of conditions. It is not unusual, then, to see different structures for two departments within the same company with apparently similar problems. Also, it is common to find one type of organizational structure (i.e., functional or product type) being adopted by one division while it has just been abandoned by another division within the same company.

Organizational Principles Every Manager Should Know

With the above major considerations and qualifications in mind, let us now turn to a discussion of some of the conventional and fundamental principles of organization. For discussion purposes, these principles will be clustered into three major categories:

1. Authority and power principles.
2. Division of labor and specialization principles.
3. Coordination and communication principles.

Please bear in mind that this is a practical classification, and certainly is not intended to be exhaustive. However, it will give you the necessary integrated framework that you will be able to use in day-to-day operations. Other principles can, of course, be added or deleted as needed. Importance, practicality, and relevance—rather than exhaustive academic exploration—were my criteria for offering you this framework. A summary of these principles appears in Figure 8-4 and will be discussed below.

Authority and Power Principles. The first category of fundamental principles of organization concerns the authority and power system in the organization. As shown in Figure 8-4, this system consists of four major principles:

1. *Scalar Principle.* This principle establishes that authority and responsibility flow smoothly in a hierarchy of formal relationships from the chief executive to the lowest level in the organization. The scalar chain is an important principle since it not only defines authority and responsibility relationships between superiors and subordinates, but it also establishes the lines of formal communication and decision-making.

2. *Unity of Command.* This principle requires that no subordinate report to more than one boss on any given aspect of his job. The essence of this principle is that since no man can serve two masters well, a subordinate should receive as-

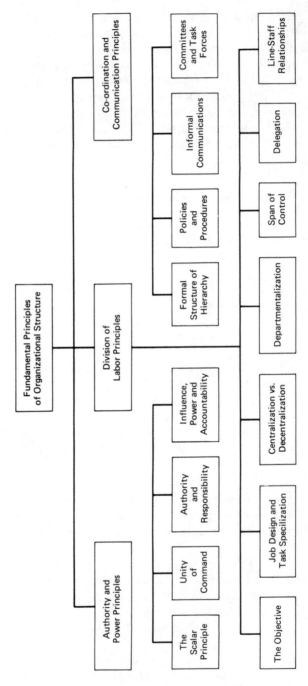

Figure 8-4. Fundamental principles of organizational structure.

signed duties and authority from one superior and be accountable only to that superior.

There are several justifications for the concept of unity of command:

a. It minimizes duplication and conflict in instruction down the line.
b. It decreases confusion and buck-passing since every one is accountable to only one boss.
c. It prevents diffusion of responsibility since the boss is ultimately accountable for getting the job done.
d. It helps improve communication and promote mutual understanding between the boss and his subordinates.

Unfortunately, there are several instances where the principle of unity of command is frequently violated. These include situations where bypassing one or more levels of intermediate supervision (in either direction) occurs. In either case, this seriously undermines the direct boss-subordinate authority relationship. While bypassing might be justified in certain situations (i.e., urgent information needed that will take longer to get by going through the formal chain of command), it should generally be discouraged since it creates resentment and confusion. Another example of violations to the principle of unity of command concerns the relationship between functional staff authority and the line manager. When the supervisor of quality control at the plant level receives instructions to establish acceptable levels of quality from his functional superior, the division manager of quality control, these instructions may conflict with those standards established by the plant manager who is his direct line superior. Now, which instructions is he supposed to follow?

As will be discussed in further detail later, the problems resulting from the dual authority sources of line and staff are minimized when the functional authority of staff is clearly defined to the extent that instructions given by the staff manager within a given functional area should be issued only by the immediate line superior. This arrangement reduces confusion for the subordinate and strengthens the unity of command concept.

3. Authority and Responsibility.

Nature of managerial authority. The formal relationship between superiors and subordinates in an organization is one of authority and responsibility. Managerial authority can be defined as the right to act or to direct the actions of others in the attainment of organizational goals. If you closely examine this definition of authority, you will note three characteristics (two explicit and one implicit):

a. Authority is a right.
b. As a result of possessing this right, you are entitled to act, either directly through your own actions or indirectly through the actions of your subordinates.
c. The power to use penalities or rewards so that the desired action is completed is implied in this definition. Power remains implicit since there are great variations in the amount of power associated with different types of managerial authority, as will be discussed later in this chapter. There is, in fact, one type of authority—staff authority—that is purely advisory in nature with no power whatsoever.

Sources of authority. Managerial authority may emanate from several sources. These include:

a. *Institutional:* your managerial authority refers to your formal right to issue orders or directives by virtue of your position in the organizational structure; it is thus granted to (or withdrawn from) you strictly within the organizational environment. In short, the source of your authority in this situation is your association with your particular institution which granted you authority by virtue of your position on the organizational ladder. In a broad sense, authority is actually derived from the laws of our society.

b. *Subordinates:* for your authority to be effective, it must be accepted by your subordinates. It follows that the related concept of subordinates' acceptance is crucial since there is not authority, according to this view, unless the person who is the object of that authority accepts the order or directive as authoritative. Thus, it is subordinates' acceptance, not the laws of society, that is the source of authority.

How can we reconcile the above two sources of authority? To avoid confusion, let me establish that managerial authority, as stated above, carries with it rewards and penalities that may be used to encourage compliance. Furthermore, while occasions may arise when subordinates refuse to accept the direction of authority, this is not the norm. It follows that your managerial authority will be granted by the organization, and that using the power you have by employing the rewards or penalties as needed will produce the desired result. Subordinates' disobedience, then, does not really cancel authority, since authority still exists; it does, however, render authority ineffective because "managing by force"—authoritarian management—is not always the best management style.

An important point you should keep in mind, however, is that managerial authority, as discussed above, is not absolute. Factors that limit the effectiveness of authority include restrictions imposed by higher-level executives (i.e., you might be required to get prior approvals for expenditures exceeding certain amounts), power conflicts arising from overlapping and dual authority, and subordinates' acceptance. The key point you should remember is that subordinates' disobedience does not negate or cancel managerial authority; it merely limits its effectiveness.

Parity of authority and responsibility. Responsibility means the duty to perform assigned tasks. When you delegate authority to your subordinates, you must delegate responsibility along with it. It is the responsibility of the subordinate, then, to perform the assigned duties and functions of his position satisfactorily. An important theoretical concept is the principle of parity of authority and responsibility. The essence of this principle is that for effective delegation, the authority granted to a subordinate must be equal to the responsibility assigned to him. This principle recognizes the need for delegated authority and emphasizes that delegated authority should be of sufficient scope so that the assigned responsibility may be accomplished.

While there might be sound theoretical justification for the principle of parity of authority and responsibility, it is often violated in practice, and employees end up with a great deal of imbalance between authority and responsibility. As unfortunate as this might sound, for most managers and subordinates responsibility will always be greater than their authority for one or more of the following reasons:

a. Managerial responsibility seldom carries with it the power necessary for the literal achievement of assigned responsibilities. A sales engineer, for example, cannot force customers to buy, and yet he is "responsible" for the sales in his territory. So, there may be too little authority granted for the task at hand.

b. Since authority is not absolute, as mentioned above, it is always circumscribed by statements of company policy and procedures which define the limits of authority for each organizational level. In short, there are situations in which the manager has little or no power to direct the actions of others.

c. Since the principle of unity of command is frequently violated in practice through bypassing downward (i.e., the manager's superior goes directly to the manager' subordinates for information), this can mean that the manager in the middle is relieved of part of this authority and left only with the responsibility. This results in a clear violation of the principle of parity of authority and responsibility.

As you can see, the principle of parity of authority and responsibility is a sound theory. But in practice, it has been grossly violated to the extent that one wonders whether this organizational principle is really practical. And if it is, why do people always end up with more responsibility than authority? The answer to this question lies squarely in human nature.

How much authority and responsibility can your boss give you? Regardless of the beauty of the concept that authority should be commensurate with responsibility for effective delegation, experience clearly shows that this is a most violated concept in practice: Things just do not work out this way.

To start with, responsibility is something one assumes—it cannot be granted. You are either responsible and you will act responsibly, or you are not and never will be. Many managers do not desire responsibility, yet they will not admit it! Such candor, especially in business, is rare.

While responsibility is a character trait, authority is not. We all yearn for power in one form or another. Organizational authority is merely an expression of that deep need, and peers and subordinates know it. We resist someone else's authority because, if it is unchecked, our own power will diminish.

So, the answer to the question of how much authority and responsibility your boss can give you is a simple one: none. Responsibility is either assumed by you or is not, and your authority (and power) is as extensive as what you can extract from your peers and subordinates. If you cannot relate to this candid way of putting it, just take a look at things around you at the office. I could not help in this discussion but to expose you to the "elegant theories" first, then qualify them with a reasonable dose of practical realities.

4. *Influence, Power, and Accountability.*

Nature of influence and power. Influence describes the ability of the manager to control others by suggestion or example rather than by direct command. It exists not by virtue of the formal supervisor-employee relationship, but by the unconscious choice of one person to emulate a behavioral pattern suggested or manifested by another.

Power can be defined in different ways. It is the ability to control the behavior of someone else, or the capacity to deprive another individual of some satisfactions or to inflict certain costs on him for noncompliance. In either case, there is a negative connotation in the definition.

Power versus authority. Unfortunately, many managers tend to confuse power with authority. There are at least two major differences between the concepts. First of all, while authority is a right, as discussed above, power is simply an ability. The essence of this point is that one can have authority but not power, if he is not able to use his authority effectively. The weak manager or the "Mr. Nice-Guy"—who is never able to issue an order or to discipline or fire someone—is a familiar case in point.

The other major difference between the concepts is that while authority is always based on power, power can exist without authority. Normally, managers have the authority which is based on power, and they are able to use this power in order to get things done. On the other hand, a manager can have and use power but not have the authority—the right to act. Power in this case could emanate from sources other than the bureaucratic or institutional right, such as the individual's expertise or charisma, as will be discussed below.

How much power do you have over your subordinates? What determines the amount of power you have over your subordinates? This amount is a function of at least two factors: the degree of dependency and the amount of choice. The degree of your subordinates' dependency on you partly determines the amount of power you have over them. The more dependent they are upon you, the more power you have over them. For example, the degree of power you have over a certain subordinate will increase significantly when he perceives you as controlling his job advancement, destiny, and life. The opposite is true when the employee keeps his options open, develops his skills, and manages to stay marketable. This is a very smart tactic on the part of the employee since it reduces his dependency on the organization and, hence, the organizations's power over him.

The other factor determining the amount of power you have over a subordinate is the degree of choice he has in fulfilling his objectives (and needs) without having to go through you. The more choice the individual has, the less power you have over him and vice versa. For example, many engineers and scientists nowadays are undertaking a variety of personal development efforts and elaborate career development plans for several reasons, including increasing their career choices and profeesional options and avoiding getting "stuck" or becoming overdependent on the organization for fulfilling their personal and professional goals.

Bases of power. You will recall a previous point about authority being always based on power. Power, in turn, is derived from one or more of the following sources:

a. Coercive power is based on the subordinate's perception of the superior having the ability to punish him.
b. Reward power is based on the subordinate's perception of the boss having the capacity to reward him.
c. Legitimate power is based upon the subordinate's conviction that the boss has a legitimate right—to do what it takes to get the job done—which the subordinate should accept. This type is also called "institutional power" since it is derived from the manager's position in the organization.
d. Referent power is based on the subordinate's desire to identify with a charismatic leader, whom he follows out of blind faith.
e. Expert power is based on the subordinate's perception that the boss has special knowledge or expertise which can be useful in satisfying one of his needs.

A close examination of the bases of power listed above reveals two important points you should always keep in mind: The first point is that what determines the power relationship with your subordinates is not necessarily your real power but rather your perceived or image power. While your real power is largely a function of your position, your title, and the organizational level you are on, your perceived power is totally a function of the image your subordinates have of you. The way you handle yourself, their interactions with you, your managerial style, and many other subjective things are the bases for their image and impressions of you.

Obviously, managers vary in their skills and ability to convey the "right" image. Whether or not the perceived image coincides with reality—"the real you"—is immaterial here. The important point is that you project the image you want your subordinates to have of you through effective "impression management." It follows that your perceived power, then, can be greater or lesser than your real power, and this image serves largely as the basis for your relationships with your subordinates.

The other point you should keep in mind here is that there are two major types of power: positional and personal. Positional power is, obviously, related to your job with the organization. It stems from the fact that your managerial authority is based on power which is, in turn, derived from your position, title, and other similar bureaucratic sources. Since most people resent the use of raw power of position, and since using it can impede your efficiency and effectiveness, you should rarely resort to the use of your positional power. The frequent use of positional power as the only major way to get things done is, in fact, characteristic of weak managers. This does not mean that positional power should never be used; rather it should be used with discretion.

Personal power is the power the manager has or acquires because of his personal qualities and leadership capabilities. It is based on mutual understanding and respect between the superior and his subordinates. This way the manager can induce subordinates to perform work effectively without having to fall back on the use of his positional power.

Accountability. Accountability is the liability created for the use of authority. It is an obligation to report to one's superior for the achievement of objectives. While the subordinate is responsible for an assigned task or activity, the manager is always accountable to his superiors for results. The crucial point is that although responsibility and authority may be delgated to subordinates, accountability to one's superior can never be delegated. Although the engineering and research vice-president delegates authority and responsibility to engineering and R&D division managers, he remains accountable to his superior, the president, for the successful discharge of the engineering and research function.

Does this mean that you will be accountable to your boss for your subordinate's performance? Absolutely! Even though you delegate authority to a subordinate who is responsible to you, you are always answerable to your own superior for your actions and for the actions of your subordinate. This means that when an employee is given a task, every superior in the line above him is accountable to his superior for the performance.

It is important for you to remember here that in the delegation process—as will be discussed below—while responsibility is assigned downward, accountability actually flows upward in an organization. Your obligation to your boss for getting the work done can never be delegated to anyone else. This concept is known as the "principle of absoluteness of accountability."

To sum up: So far in this discussion, I have focused on the first category of fundamental principles of organization: authority and power principles. Four principles were discussed: scalar principle; unity of command; authority and responsibility; and influence, power, and accountability. Let us now turn to a discussion of the second group of principles: division of labor and specialization.

Division of Labor Principles. As shown in Figure 8-4, there are seven major principles relating to how the overall work of an organization is divided and allocated. These principles are:

1. The objectives.
2. Job design and task specialization.
3. Departmentalization.
4. Span of control.
5. Decentralization versus centralization.
6. Delegation.
7. Line-staff relationships.

1. *The Objectives.* Since the organizational structure is primarily a mean towards an end, the formulation of a set of objectives must precede the development of the organizational structure. Clearly stated objectives give the organization a sense of direction, guide performance, and facilitate the overall management process. Without objectives—as discussed earlier—not only will the organization drift aimlessly, but it will also lose its reason for existence.

2. *Job Design and Task Specialization.* The extent to which the overall task of the organization (or any of its departments) is divided into specialities is an important organizational principle. The degree of task specialization or generalization depends, of course, on such factors as the nature of activities to be performed, technology, staff's backgrounds, and cost considerations.

Task specialization is a significant form of division of labor. Since specialization is characteristic of this day and age, organizations will become even more dependent on technology and staff experts with specialized skills for achieving their future functions. This is nowhere more apparent than in the case of science and technology. Task specialization is an important organizational principle especially in the case of engineering and R&D operations. This is so because your managerial task requires that you become a generalist—who knows less and less about more and more—while at the same time you are responsible for the organization and management of specialists—who know more and more about less and less. An appropriate balance between these two extremes on the continuum would, therefore, be a major organizational consideration.

3. *Departmentalization.* Essentially departmentalization deals with how the organization (or division) is broken down into distinct administrative units and how employees and activities are divided up both horizontally and vertically. It is based on the process of grouping activities into organizational units, and single units into groups of units. While there is no optimal way to departmentalize, there are some major bases for departmentalization which, because if its nature, will be further discussed in Chapter 9.

4. *Span of Control.* By definition, span of control (sometimes called span of management) is the number of people reporting directly to a manager. The size of managers' spans of control clearly influences the number of organizational units or departments, their arrangement, and the number of administrative layers in the organization. Departmental structure, in turn, influences the length of lines of communication in the organization in terms of the number of levels through which information must pass, up or down, along the chain of command.

In a given organization, the wider the span of control of individual managers, the fewer the administrative layers and the shorter the lines of communication. Conversely, the narrower the span, the larger the number of administrative layers and the longer the lines of communication. Because the manager possesses only so much knowledge, energy, and time, the number of people he can supervise effectively will reach a point beyond which the quality of supervision—among other things—will start declining.

However, this does not necessarily mean that there is an "ideal" span of control. Contrary to common beliefs, there is not. What, then, determines the size of the span of control? Experience clearly shows that managers vary considerably in terms of the number of people they can supervise effectively. Some managers can supervise 10 to 15 (or more) people; others only 5 to 8; still a third group can supervise none—they barely manage themselves!

To give you some guidelines, Table 8-3 presents some of the major determinants of the size of the span of control. These are largely self-explanatory. It is obvious that either wide or narrow spans would be desirable in certain situations depending on the factors in Table 8-3. Thus, arguments over the desirability of either span size as such are pointless. Although narrow spans result in a taller organizational structure (with several layers), they are believed to encourage faster and more effective problem-solving and group performance. With close supervision, however, the employee tends to become "boss oriented." On the other hand, wide spans result in a flatter organizational structure. This type of structure encourages individual initiative and assumption of responsibility for one's own work.

Table 8-3. Factors Determining Size of the Manager's Span of Control.

1. Supervisory ability (competence).

2. Subordinate ability (competence and skills).

3. Complexity of activity supervised (the more complex the activity, the narrower the span).

4. Degree to which the activities are integrated.

5. Extent to which the manager must perform nonmanagerial duties.

6. Demands on personal time from other people and units.

7. Adequacy of performance standards.

8. Amount of authority delegated.

9. Availability of staff assistance.

10. Degree of standardized procedure within the organization.

11. Organizational level the manager is on (spans are narrower the higher the level of one's position in the organization).

12. Financial capability of the organization (narrower spans mean more managers and are more costly).

At any rate, those who try to sell you on ready-made formulas computing the "optimal" size of span of control are doing you a disservice. Stay away from the formulas—they do not work in management!

5. *Decentralization versus Centralization.* Decentralization is the degree to which the decision-making authority is dispersed throughout the organization. In centralized organizations, all decisions are made at the highest possible level. In decentralized structures, the authority to make decisions is delegated to the managers at lower-echelon organizational units. The criterion, then, is the locus of the decision-making authority, that is, the level on which decisions are actually made. The advantages and disadvantages of decentralization are shown in Table 8-4.

It is noteworthy here that there are degrees of centralization and decentralization in all organizations. So it is not really an either-or situation. It follows that the concept of decentralization of authority is relative in its nature; an organization is never completely centralized nor is it completely decentralized. The extent to which authority is delegated within an organization is a measure of the degree of decentralization of authority within that organization. Also the extent of centralization or decentralization in an organization depends on the nature of the functions and activities involved. The advantages and disadvantages of centralization are simply the opposite of those presented in Table 8-4. Making a choice between both systems (or the extent of each) would certainly require weighting and assessing the merits of them both.

Table 8-4. Advantages and Disadvantages of Decentralization.

ADVANTAGES	DISADVANTAGES
1. Rapid response to changes in work situations and local conditions.	1. Could result in overlapping and duplicated activities.
2. Decisions are made by those most familiar with local situations.	2. Diffused decision-making power might discourage the adoption of innovations.
3. Frees top management from day-to-day supervisory responsibility so executives can focus on planning and policy-making.	3. Loss of control.
	4. Cost considerations.
4. Gives managers at lower levels and their subordinates the opportunity to develop their skills and capabilities through participating in problem-solving and decision-making.	5. Could encourage interdepartmental competition and reinforce conflict.
5. Encourages individual initiative and responsibility, thus resulting in greater satisfaction and motivation.	6. Preoccupation with performance and results might lead to an overemphasis on short-range profitability while losing sight of long-range corporate objectives.

Managers must be careful not to confuse decentralization with departmentalization. As discussed above, the latter requires the grouping of work and people into manageable units; however, the mere creation of separate departmental units does not constitute decentralization. For example, the vice-president of engineering and research who appoints ten engineering managers, each in charge of a different product, is further departmentalizing the engineering function along product lines, but he is not necessarily decentralizing the engineering function.

Some managers mistakenly confuse decentralization with geographic dispersion. One of the bases of departmentalization is grouping activities and people into separate divisions serving different geographical areas such as the East Coast, the Midwest, and the western region of the United States. For example, the division of one large manufacturing plant into five widely separated smaller plants certainly results in geographic dispersion, but not necessarily in decentralization.

In the above examples, the key to whether the appointment of product engineering managers or the building of geographically separate plants is decentralization, or merely further departmentalization, is the effect of such changes upon the decision-making process within the organization.

6. *Delegation.*

Nature and importance. As you will recall from our previous discussion, your task as a manager is not to do things yourself. Rather, it is to get them done through other people. Perhaps you can accomplish any one or two activities better than anyone under your command; but can you possibly do all things as well?

Even if you could, this is not what you are getting paid for; you are getting paid to manage others and get them to do things—not to do them yourself. In short, delegation is one of the most useful tools at your disposal. It is also a sound organization and management principle. To the extent that you are not delegating, you are not getting things done through others, and consequently, you are not managing.

Delegation can be defined as an organizational process that permits the transfer of authority from superior to subordinate. There are many good reasons for delegation, including:

a. Delegating important tasks to subordinates gives them opportunities for valuable training and skill growth and development.

b. Delegating enhances effective communication with subordinates.

c. Delegating gives subordinates the opportunity to participate in decision-making and thus creates a commitment toward putting these decisions into action.

d. Delegating gives the manager the opportunity to do what he was hired to do: managing.

How to delegate. As you can see, a strong case can be made for the necessity and importance of delegation as a management tool. How should you go about delegating tasks to your subordinates? There are three steps or aspects of delegation:

1. Assigning responsibility: This involes three steps:

a. Determining the activities and tasks the subordinate is responsible for performing, using his job description and all other tools available to you in defining the exact scope of the subordinate's duties.

b. Specifying the results he is responsible for achieving in each area of activity. This is a crucial element in the delegation process and if it is not done well can cause unneeded tension and problems in your relationship with your subordinates. The difficulty of defining expected results in some engineering and particularly R&D operations should not deter you from discussing them and agreeing on them with your subordinates. Rather, it calls for flexibility in the process of defining expected results—not for avoiding it.

c. Agreeing with the subordinate on how performance will be measured. This activity is often neglected by many managers, but it is, in fact, the crux of the delegation process. If the expected results and how they will be measured are not clearly understood by the subordinate, he may well confuse effort with performance. He might expect to be rewarded on the basis of how hard he has been working (effort, number of hours, etc.), whereas the normal criterion in evaluating his performance is what he has accomplished. In short, it is results, not effort, that count.

The first phase of the delegation process, then, requires a clear definition of all the duties that must be performed in order to complete a given task. Assigning responsibility involves defining the activities to be performed, specifying the expected results, and agreeing on the yardsticks to be used in measuring performance.

2. Delegating authority: Assigning responsibility to your subordinates for performing certain duties requires that they either act on your behalf or direct others to act in the performance of those duties. Hence, authority must be delegated to them to empower such action. The point you should remember here is that in this situation, you still retain complete control over the delegated authority as you still remain ultimately responsible and accountable for the accomplished duties.

Delegating authority to subordinates is not a one-shot deal. In addition to agreeing with the subordinate on how the desired results are to be achieved, providing guidance, support, and coaching is an important part of the delegation process.

3. Creating accountability: When a subordinate accepts responsibility for the performance of certain duties delegated to him and the authority granted to him, he incurs an obligation. This obligation is his accountability for the proper use of authority on behalf of his superior and the performance of assigned responsibilities. Remember that a subordinate's accountability is the end product of delegation, and without this accountability, there is no true delegation.

How is accountability different from responsibility? Many management students and practitioners equate both concepts and, in fact, use them synonymously. However, I view them as being different. A practical way to differentiate between them is to remember that a subordinate is responsible for the performance of duties assigned to him and is accountable to his superior for the satisfactory performance of those duties.

Three requirements for effective delegation. The above analysis clearly describes the three integral phases of the delegation process: the assignment of responsibility, the delegation of authority, and the creation of accountability. For the process of delegation to be most effective, three fundamental principles must be observed. Since these principles were already discussed above, they will briefly be mentioned here:

a. Principle of parity of authority and responsibility.
b. Principle of absoluteness of accountability.
c. Principle of unity of command.

For a detailed analysis of these principles, the reader is referred to the previous discussion in this chapter.

How much do technical managers delegate? It is obvious from the foregoing discussion that delegation, done well, can ehance communications between you and your subordinates, give them the opportunity to develop their skills and make a meaningful contribution to the organization, and—perhaps most important—enable you to spend your time managing rather than doing. To achieve these results, you must follow the principles of effective delegation discussed above. An excellent management rule, then, is: *Never undertake what you can delegate.* The assumption, of course, is that it is delegatable to someone who can do it competently.

Yet, experience and observation show that managers generally tend to underdelegate (a few managers tend to overdelegate, however). In fact, my experience in counseling managers at a number of organizations clearly suggests that managerial failure is more frequently caused by the inability of otherwise potentially successful and capable managers to delegate than by any other single reason. This is, indeed, a very sad situation that results in many dysfunctional consequences including the problems of the continually overburdened boss and the underutilized subordinate. While there can be many reasons for lack of sufficient delegation among managers, I believe that it is, in the final analysis, a matter of attitude (the will to delegate). I have found that characteristic of those managers are attitudes such as, "My way is the best way," or "If you want a job done well, do it yourself." Since this is not the proper place to get into the variety of possible causes of lack of sufficient delegation among managers as they are discussed elsewhere,[2] it will suffice here to mention that delegation is a must for effective management, and that managers do not change their attitudes for or against delegation overnight. Just as with smoking, most people do not stop simply by listening to a good lecture on the possible hazards of the habit. Whatever they are going to do, it must come from inside—it must spring from within based on a firm conviction that this is what they want to do.

The problems of insufficient delegation among managers is even further compounded in the case of technical engineering and R&D managers and supervisors. As former engineers and scientists, technical managers have been socialized throughout their education and technical training to respect and thrive on detailed analysis, scientific explorations, detailed meticulous work activities, and exactness expressed in the form of numbers to the third decimal place. It is largely by virtue of their superb technical skills that many of those individuals (mistakenly, as discussed in earlier chapters of this book) get "promoted" to management.

The very skills that have earned them a promotion can turn out to be a severe liability, however. Most of those newly appointed—and many senior—managers find it exceedingly difficult to let go of the detailed technical part of their jobs and turn it over to others. Put differently, they destroy the fruits of delegation by oversupervision. Tragically, these managers might not even admit this

---

[2] See my book, "Improving Leadership Skills of Engineering and R&D Managers and Supervisors." New York: Van Nostrand Reinhold, in press; also Uris, Auren "The Executive Deskbook." New York: Van Nostrand Reinhold, 2nd Edition, 1976, Chapter 5.

to themselves, and they become quite innovative in seeking false excuses and scapegoats for insufficient delegation (or lack of it).

7. Line-Staff Relationships.

Meaning and importance. The last principle in the division of labor category of the fundamental principles of organizational structure is the line-staff concept. The line organization describes the superior-subordinate relationship in the vertical chain of command running from the top to the bottom throughout the organization. This type of direct authority is in line with the scalar principle characterizing the line structure. The staff organization, on the other hand, consists of the functions that are not in the line function chain of command, and provides advice, service, and counsel to the line organization. Figure 8-5 shows the line-staff organizational relationships.

Functions of line authority. An important concept is that there are two aspects to the definition of line authority:

a. Line authority is a command relationship entitling the superior to direct the work of his subordinates. In this sense, it is the right to issue instructions to others to carry out organizational goals. The manager, therefore, is part of the line organization and, in turn, is subject to the direction of his superior. As shown in Figure 8-5, the directors of engineering, manufacturing, and marketing are part of the line organization, are line managers with the authority to direct their subordinates, and are, in turn, responsible (and accountable) to the vice-president.

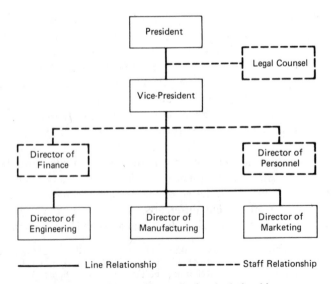

Figure 8-5. Line-staff organizational relationships.

b. The other aspect of the definition of line authority focuses on the type of organizational function. The criterion here for distinguishing between line and staff is the degree to which the function in question contributes directly to achieving organizational objectives. It follows that line functions are those which are directly concerned with achieving the objectives of the organization. Any function that is not directly concerned with achieving the primary objectives of the organization is, then, a staff function.

A crucial factor in determining the nature of a specific function, then, is the nature of the business or industrial activity of the organization. Production and sales, for example, are usually considered line functions, whereas purchasing is classified as staff in a manufacturing organization. Yet, the purchasing activity (and sales) is a line function in a department store. Another example is that while finance is usually classified as a staff function in most firms, it is part of the line organization in a loan company. You should also remember that line authority should not be equated solely with line units. A staff department head also has line authority over those who report to him in the staff department.

Functions of staff authority. As mentioned above, staff positions do not bear direct responsibility for accomplishing the primary objectives of the organization. Staff positions are created to provide line managers with data and information based on specialized knowledge, expertise, and familiarity with sound and sophisticated techniques. This information is valuable in decision-making and control of line operations. The important point to remember here is that the function of the staff specialist is to suggest, counsel, advise, and recommend courses of action to line managers. But he is characterized by his lack of authority over line managers.

Two forms of staff. There are two forms of staff authority:

a. Personal staff: Here you should understand the important differences between an "assistant to" a manager and an "assistant manager." As shown in Figure 8-6, the "assistant to" is simply a personal assistant to his boss. He usually has no specific function to perform but receives a wide variety of assignments from his boss, with authority granted only for each individual assignment; and he acts as a personal representative of his superior.

Note that the assistant general manager in Figure 8-6 is not a staff specialist. He is part of the line organization. The operating executives report to the general manager through the assistant general manager. The general manager can assign specific activities to the assistant manager. An example would be to have all staff services (such as purchasing, plant engineering, personnel, quality control, and accounting) report directly to the assistant manager, while the general manager oversees the line functions of the organization. The point you should keep in mind here is that subordinates, as designated, report directly to the assistant manager; that he has well-defined responsibilities assigned to him; and that he assumes the full authority of the general manager in his absence.

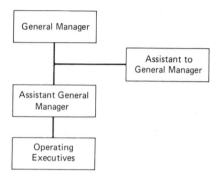

Figure 8-6. Organizational position of the personal staff.

b. Specialized staff: The need for a specialized staff has resulted from the increasing size and complexity of organizations, the rapid change in technology, and the intensive specialized knowledge requirements in certain technical fields. Because of the constant pressures on line managers and the fact that they might not have the specialized skills needed, the task is usually assigned to specialized staff personnel.

While there is considerable overlap in the functions and the forms of staff authority exercised by specialized staff personnel, three forms of staff authority can be identified as shown in Figures 8-7 and 8-8.

a. Service authority: This is a situation where a staff specialist may have the authority to provide a specific service for the line organization.[3] As shown in Figure 8-7, examples include the services rendered by production planning, purchasing, and plant engineering supervisors to the plant manager. Their responsibilities cover planning and controlling the flow of production, procuring, and maintaining the physical facilities, respectively. These units exercise service authority in providing these services for the line organization.

b. Advisory authority: This is a situation where the staff organization provides advice and counsel for the line organization concerning special sets of problems. This is also called the authority of ideas. As you will note in Figure 8-7, examples include the advice and counseling offered by the personnel, industrial engineering, quality control, and accounting units to the line organization. While there is a strong element of service in the activities handled by each of these staff units, it would be appropriate to regard their authority as advisory in nature. Remember that the three forms of staff authority are not really clear cut, nor are the functions to be performed by specialized staff personnel.

---

[3] This section is based partly on Sisk, Henry L. "Principles of Management: A Systems Approach to the Management Process." Cincinnati: South Western, 1969, pp. 298-301.

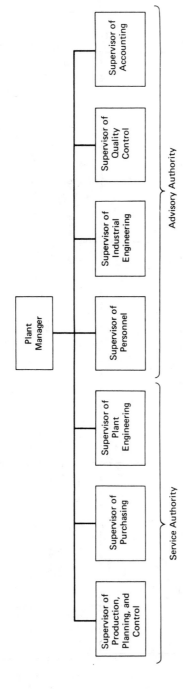

Figure 8-7. Typical staff organization at the plant level. (Adapted from Sisk, Henry L. "Principles of Management: A Systems Approach to the Management Process," Cincinnati: South Western, 1969, p. 300.)

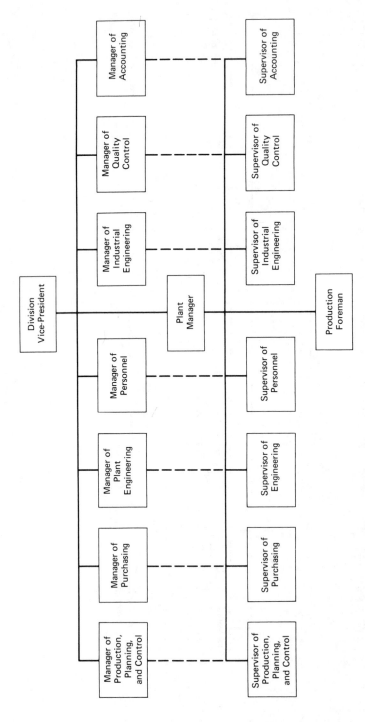

Figure 8-8. The exercise of functional authority. (Adapted from Sisk, Henry L. "Principles of Management: A Systems Approach to the Management Process." Cincinnati: South Western, 1969, p. 301.)

c. Functional authority: This type of authority provides the staff specialist with considerable latitude to make decisions in his own functional area, thus regulating and constraining the activities of the line organization. As shown in Figure 8-8, there are two ways of exercising functional authority. First, staff managers may be granted functional authority over their counterparts who are in lower levels of the organization; and second, the particular functional speciality in question may be separated from the line manager's job and assigned to the appropriate staff specialist. Note that the plant supervisor of each staff function reports functionally (usually indicated by a dotted line) to his staff counterpart at the next higher level. In large organizations this next higher level may be a geographic division, and the managers at the divisonal level report to their counterparts on the corporate staff. In addition, the plant staff supervisor performs that portion of the production foreman's job which falls within his specialty.

In functional authority situations, as a general principle the staff manager is given limited line authority over a certain phase of a line manager's operation. He also exercises this authority along lines other than those established by the formal organizational structure. For example, the cost accounting supervisor may be given functional authority over the cost accounting specialists in the production unit regarding all production costs. In case of problems, the cost accounting supervisor may go directly to the cost specialists, bypassing the immediate supervisor—the production foreman. Another example is when the legal department in an R&D organization is given authority to reject patent applications approved by line departments. A third example is the authority of the safety specialist to have chemical departments closed when he feels that fumes in the work area reach an unsafe level.

It should be clear from the above discussion that this type of functional staff authority should be limited to exceptional situations; otherwise it could completely restrict the line manager's authority and effectiveness.

Problems in line-staff relationships. The line-staff concept creates the problem of duality of authorities, functions, and organizations. Two authorities exist within an organization—line authority with its right to command, and staff authority with its right to advise. You will also note that there is a duality of function—the line function is associated with the achievement of primary company objectives while the staff function supports the line. This complex situation results in referring to an organization as though it were two separate units: the line organization and the staff organization.

This leads, in the final analysis, to serious conflicts and misunderstandings in the line-staff relationship. The resulting problems and tensions in the relationship can be even further compounded by the perceptions and stereotypes both line and staff managers form about each other. A sample of these stereotypes appears in Table 8-5.

It is clear from Table 8-5 that these problems are basically attitudinal in nature and reflect difficulties in communications and proper understanding of each other's role. In fact, the origins of the problems and distorted images line and staff managers have of each other can be attributed to some or all of the following reasons:

a. Neither side understands or appreciates the reason for, role, and function of the other.

b. Staff people lack or have insufficient authority that in their view should go hand in hand with an advisory position.

c. There mere existence of the functional authority along with the need for limiting the authority of staff managers complicates organizational relationships and creates coordination and communication problems.

d. Typically, neither line nor staff knows where the authority and responsibility of one department ends and another begins, or where responsibilities overlap. Departmental or functional lines of responsibility, accountability, and authority are not clearly established.

e. Each department often sees the entire organization in terms of its own interest—a narrow and short sighted view—failing to see that other departments' interests are just as important for achieving organizational objectives.

Table 8-5. Stereotypes of Line and Staff Managers As Seen by Each Other.

LINE	STAFF
1. Staff people do not know or understand what is going on at the operating level.	1. Line managers are not cooperative in helping implementing pet staff ideas.
2. They lack responsibility because they are not on the "firing line."	2. They are unimaginative bureaucrats who enjoy the power but do not appreciate informed advice and counsel.
3. They are overeducated specialists whom no one can understand (this creates resentment).	3. They often resist staff assistance.
4. They could be viewed as organizational glut; are carried as overhead without contributing their share of direct costs.	4. They have more authority than they should, while staff has less authority in their areas of expertise.
5. They offer advice and recommendations—which are uncalled for—and, thus, interfere with line operations.	5. The real problem lies in how the line managers go about implementing programs and procedures designed by the staff.
6. They usually have direct lines of communication with upper management, thus creating envy and frustration to lower line managers.	
7. They often try to overstep the authority given them.	

f. Staff managers may, mistakenly, get beyond their area of responsibility and end up passing out direct orders to line personnel (i.e., industrial engineering, production control, and quality control in their close work relationships with line managers).

g. The overuse (or underuse) of highly paid staff people can cause problems in the "appropriate" utilization of staff talents and, thus, upset the balance needed in the line-staff relationship.

h. The difficulty in classifying line-staff roles by profession creates confusion since what might be a line function in one organization may be a staff function in another. A good example would be the research department carrying line authority in an R&D organization, but being a limited staff function in a highly product-oriented organization.

i. Frequently, some managers may exercise line, staff, and functional authorities interchangeably in carrying out their daily responsibilities. What the manager is doing at a specific time will determine the type of role and authority he has then.

Because of the above factors, some conflict and tension in the line-staff relationship is not uncommon or unusual, but an excessive amount is. These problems could be alleviated to a large degree through mutual line-staff understanding, communication, and perhaps more important, clear definition of authority, responsibility, and accountability relationships between individuals and departments. Let us also not forget that, no matter what, some conflict is natural, inevitable, and even healthy. But the amount of conflict should be managed or kept under control so it will not seriously disrupt the organization and hamper the achievement of its objectives.

To sum up: Seven principles have been discussed in this section constituting the second major category of fundamental principles of organization. These principles were: the objective of the organization, job design and task specialization, departmentalization, span of control, decentralization versus centralization, delegation, and line-staff relationships.

Coordination and Communication Principles. The objective of the third group of organizational principles is to enable the manager, in the organizing process, to achieve good coordination among departments, groups, and individuals. As shown in Figure 8-4, there are several ways to achieve coordinations and enhance communication in the organization, including the following major mechanisms:

1. Formal structure or hierarchy.
2. Policies and procedures.
3. Informal communications.
4. Committees and task forces.

1. *Formal Structure or Hierarchy*. As discussed earlier in this chapter, the formal organizational structure is the skeleton and framework of official relationships between individuals, positions, and management levels on the hierarchy. This formal hierarchy is the most basic means of organizational coordination and is therefore a central element in any bureaucratic organization. Since all organizations, to varying degrees, contain bureaucratic elements, the formal structure is seen as a system composed of divisions, subunits, administrative layers, and rules and procedures designed to minimize duplication in activities and enhance efficiency and coordination.

Needless to say, an integral part of this structure is the routine and the red tape and the checks and balances built into the system which most likely create frustration and tension for members of the organization. Since discussing the dysfunctional aspects of bureaucratic structures is beyond the scope of our objectives here, it will suffice to say that for engineering and R&D operations other forms of structure have been adopted by many organizations, and will be discussed in Chapter 9.

In short, what you should keep in mind here is that your managerial position in the organizational structure is actually the linking element between subordinates and higher levels of management. Coordination is an important aspect of your job. In this sense, the formal structure provides a means for coordinating tasks, communication flows, and decision-making up, down, and across the organization. Indeed, the coordinating role of first-level managers or supervisors is the one and only link between their work groups and the rest of the organization. The significance and magnitude of this role should, therefore, be quite evident.

2. *Policies and Procedures*. Another important coordination mechanism is the establishment of a set of policies and procedures. The distinction between policy and procedure is often ambiguous. A policy is a set of guidelines developed by higher management to assist lower level managers in handling anticipated problems in various areas (i.e., product quality, product engineering design, etc.). A procedure is a prescribed specific behavior for managers to follow in certain situations. It tells the manager (or his subordinate) exactly what to do in the described situation.

Remember that rules, policies, and procedures are part of the organizational system and are designed to improve communication, standardize action in similar situations, and enhance efficiency and coordination. However, you should avoid creating too many rules and procedures as they may intensify the red tape and routine, and cause confusion and ambiguity. A good rule of thumb is to understand the reason behind rules and procedures before enforcing them, and to make sure they are not getting in the way instead of helping out.

3. *Informal Communications*. The importance of the informal communication network in getting things done faster by cutting through the red tap and taking shortcuts has already been discussed above. It should be added here that the informal network of relationships, including the grapevine, is an excellent

medium for organizational coordination. Through informal contacts, friendships, and harmonious relationships with people in his and other divisions or on other levels of management, the manager can get faster action and handle more problems and situations without burdening the formal hierarchy with an excessive number of rules and procedures.

You should be cautious about two things in using the informal network. First, always keep your boss in the picture. Let him know that you are dealing with coordination problems through the informal network without an established policy or procedure. This is an important tactic for keeping him informed, getting his support, and making sure that similar problems are being handled in a uniform way. Second, be sure that the solutions adopted in dealing with specific problem situations do not contradict the established formal rules, policies, and procedures.

4. *Committees and Task Forces.* Committees and task forces are found in all organizations. There are many good reasons for the creation of a committee, including:

a. Group judgment can be better than individual judgment—"two heads are better than one." While we all know that this is not necessarily so, the judgment of a group tends to be better than that of a single individual in certain situations.

b. Cooperation is assured in the execution of plans developed by the committee. Members of the committee feel strongly about implementing and "selling" the recommendations they participated in formulating. Their commitment to these actions and plans helps in the execution process.

c. Coordination between various activities and functions can be improved. Executive committees, for example, are usually formed at the upper levels of an organization of managers of key functional areas. This arrangement permits exchanging information and improving understanding and communications.

Numerous objections to using committees have been raised. The most important disadvantages include:

a. Committees can be costly in terms of the effort and time taken by employees in committee meetings and also in terms of the possible losses incurred when timeliness is a factor in determining the worth of the decision. Committees are very time consuming, which can be dysfunctional if timeliness of the decision is a major factor.

b. Committee actions and recommendations must represent a thinking or a decision process that is common to all members; hence, it must be representative of the lowest common denominator. Thus, the value of group judgment as an advantage can be seriously reduced or even lost.

c. The diffusion of responsibility and the inability to clearly determine accountability of individual members make committees particularly ineffective as organizational structures.

A task force, like a temporary committee, is set up to accomplish a specific task, after which it disbands. Unlike a temporary committee, a task force usually draws members from the various departments concerned with the accomplishment of a certain task. The creation of a task force emphasizes the mission and forces action. Members also tend to focus more on the mission or job to be done, and responsibility is more specific than in the case of committees.

In short, achieving a high degree of coordination and communication between departments, groups, and individuals is a crucial managerial task. For this purpose, four mechanisms were introduced in this section. These include the formal structure or hierarchy, organizational policies and procedures, informal communications, and committees and task forces.

SUMMARY

This chapter has, among other things, introduced you to the fundamental principles of organizational structure. These principles constitute important guidelines for management to use in answering three major questions relating to the design of an organization. These questions are:

1. How can we define the lines of formal communication, decision-making authority, and power in the organization?
2. How can we divide up the work that must be done?
3. How can we achieve coordination among departments, groups, and individuals in the organization?

Answering these questions, through the application of the principles discussed in this chapter, results in a formal structure or a hierarchical pyramid usually known as *bureaucracy*. All modern organizations are to some degree bureaucratic in nature. They also are designed to be impersonal, rational, and efficient with primarily economic—not human—orientations. No wonder the bureaucratic model of organizations is viewed as a "machine" type of model that causes conflicts, tensions, and frustrations for organizational members.

Bureaucratic climates are also considered unhealthy and conducive to apathy, distrust, and lack of initiative on the part of the employees. This is because the bureaucratic system is characterized by official and rigid authority relationships, bureaucratic power, tight controls, and long decision-making chains of command. It would not be an exaggeration, then, to expect the bureaucratic form of organization to be highly dysfunctional, creating tensions and conflicts for engineering and particularly R&D personnel—highly educated and creative groups.[4] It

---

[4] For a detailed statement of sources of conflicts for engineers and scientists see Badawy, M. K. Bureaucracy in Research: A Study of Role Conflict of Scientists. *Human Organization*, 32, 3 (Summer 1973): 123-133.

should be kept in mind, however, that the bureaucratic model of organization has generally proved to be quite efficient, and in spite of its weaknesses, no better substitute for it is available at this time.

Now that you have developed an understanding of the organizing process and the fundamental principles of organizational structure, an application of these principles to the organization of engineering and R&D operations will be undertaken in Chapter 9.

9
Developing Your Organizational Design Skills

As discussed in Chapter 8, building an organizational structure involves four major steps:

1. Defining the organizational objectives.
2. Determining the activities to be performed to achieve these objectives.
3. Arranging these activities into logical groupings.
4. Assigning authority and responsibility for each grouping to someone in such a way as to provide coordination and get the job done.

The task of this chapter is to analyze and describe the process of developing organizational structures in engineering and R&D, to compare and contrast alternative designs of technical organizations, to identify the variables you must consider in designing an organizational structure, and finally, to pinpoint some practical mechanisms for developing your managerial skills in this area. Naturally, discussion in this chapter will draw heavily on the concepts and principles discussed in Chapter 8.

ORGANIZING ENGINEERING AND R&D OPERATIONS: SOME CONSIDERATIONS

The task of developing a new organizational structure or modifying an existing one requires two major considerations. First, the activities and the type of work to be performed to achieve the engineering and R&D objectives must be determined. These activities will depend, among other things, on the type and number of products, the resources and facilities available, and the size of departmental budgets. Possible areas of engineering work might be:[1]

---

[1] This section is partly based on Karger, Delmar and Murdick, Robert. Managing Engineering and Research. New York: Industrial Press, 2nd Edition, (1969), Chapter 3.

1. Research
2. Advance engineering development
3. Engineering systems design
4. Engineering component design
5. Engineering development and proof testing
6. Technical supporting services
7. Package and style design
8. Application engineering
9. Field engineering

Secondly, after identifying key positions in the engineering or R&D organization, you must combine elements of work into positions to be filled by individuals with the proper qualifications for such positions. Position descriptions or guides must be developed. Each position guide provides a statement describing the activities to be performed by the job occupant and the principal functions for which this individual is responsible. An example of a position guide for a manager appears in Figure 9-1.

As you can see, building an organizational structure or modifying an existing one is an involved task. Assuming that objectives have been identified and activities to be performed have been determined, the remaining task relates to arranging activities into logical groupings and assigning authority and responsibility relationships to provide the necessary efficiency and coordination. How this can be done in engineering and R&D will be the focus of the balance of this chapter.

PATTERNS OF ENGINEERING AND R&D ORGANIZATIONS

You will recall from our previous discussion that departmentalization is a major form of specialization and division of labor. It requires the grouping of activities into organizational units, and the single units into groups of units. There is no specific pattern or ideal way to organize engineering and R&D operations. However, there are several bases for departmentalization, as will be discussed below. The specific organizational form or pattern will depend on the particular company situation, the type of product, management philosophy, the nature of technology, and the skills and qualifications of its particular personnel.

Four major types or forms of organization of engineering and R&D activities will be discussed:

1. Functional organization.
2. Product organization.
3. Project organization.
4. Matrix organization.

Date _____

POSITION TITLE:
Manager–Thermal Design

ACCOUNTABLE TO:
Manager–Engineering & Research

BROAD FUNCTION

The Manager–Thermal Design has managerial and functional responsibilities for heat transfer and fluid flow characteristics of all designed equipment.

PRINCIPAL RESPONSIBILITIES

Managerial Objectives

1. Plan, organize, initiate, and measure the activities associated with technical aspects, engineering design, development, construction, and operation of equipment as assigned to his component.

2. Recommend to the Manager–Engineering & Research programs and budgets within the policies and objectives of the Engineering & Research organization.

3. Promote the growth, enthusiasm, and effort of all personnel assigned to him by means of technical and general guidance, selection of assignments, and personal contact.

Functional Objectives

1. Perform detailed heat transfer and fluid flow studies.

2. Assist in the preparation of test specifications for heat transfer and fluid flow tests.

3. Furnish surveillance over the design, manufacture, and installation of equipment to ensure compliance with thermal specifications.

4. Prepare progress reports and design-substantiating reports proving compliance of design with hydrothermal specifications.

Figure 9-1. Position guide for a manager. (Adapted from Karger, Delmar W., and Murdick, Robert G. "Managing Engineering and Research," Second Edition. New York: Industrial Press, 1969, p. 49.)

Functional Organization

In a functional organization, the structure is divided into units by functional specialty or scientific and technological discipline. The structure in this case centers around the primary organizational functions, and key activities are grouped into units such as manufacturing, engineering, marketing, and finance.

In an engineering organization, the functional structure would require having sections or units such as product engineering, electrical design, and mechanical design. In a functional R&D organization, activities would be grouped by scientific disciplines such as departments of physics, biology, and chemistry, following the university model of organization. Figure 9-2 presents a functional engineering and R&D organization.

The advantages and disadvantages of different forms of engineering and R&D organizations are shown in Table 9-1. As you will note, the functional form of organization has several strengths including permitting technical specialization, bringing technical specialists from the same discipline together, and reducing overlapping and duplication of activities. Functional organization is often desirable in small companies, and is even common within engineering and R&D operations of large companies.

The drawbacks of functional organization include multiple supervision, slower flow of work, and the difficulty in shifting personnel especially for cross-discipline development work. A significant weakness of organization by scientific discipline is that a strong discipline orientation in R&D could very well hamper technological innovation, where concentration should be on the project—not the discipline—organization.[2] This form of organization implies that innovation is most likely to result from pushing back the frontiers in a specific discipline, whereas innovation more frequently stems from a combination of advances in several often unrelated disciplines and technologies.

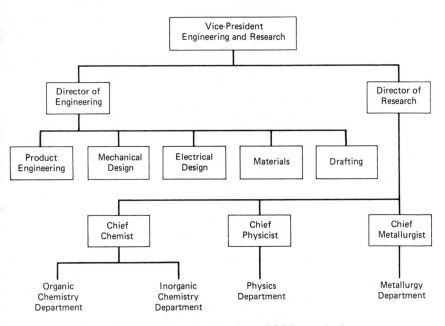

Figure 9-2. A functional engineering and R&D organization.

---

[2] Twiss, Brian C. "Managing Technological Innovation." London: Longman, 1974, p. 216.

Table 9-1. Advantages and Disadvantages of Different Types of
Engineering and R&D Organizations.

ORGANIZATIONAL PATTERN	ADVANTAGES	DISADVANTAGES
Functional Organization	1. Technical specialization.	1. Slower work flow.
	2. Fits well in homogeneous groups.	2. Less appropriate for cross discipline development w■
	3. Reduces overlapping and duplication.	3. Multiple supervision.
	4. Aids with individual career development (strong discipline orientation).	4. Difficulty in shifting perso■
		5. Complex liaison.
	5. Highly suitable for the acquisition of new knowledge.	
Product Organization	1. Clarity of authority and responsibility as each product line manager is in charge of all technical resources required for product development.	1. Possible duplication of act■ ties if individual laborator■ have strong discipline orie■ tation.
	2. Close work relationships with marketing and field liaison.	2. Reduced overall direction control by corporate R&D and engineering over divisi■ laboratories.
	3. Teamwork and close coordination by matching customer needs with technical projects and profit requirements (strong marketing orientation of R&D and engineering).	3. The strong marketing orie■ tation of R&D and engine■ that could create a serious■ balance between basic and■ plied research (in favor of applied research).
Project Organization	1. Assures fast decisions and tight control over technical performance, cost, and schedule.	1. High degree of uncertainty and ambiguity involved in project assignments, proje■ duration, and organization relationships.
	2. Ability to change staff abilities and size as needed; get best people on top-priority jobs.	2. Lack in many managers of usual skills to deal with hu■ and interpersonal problem■
	3. Provides for better interchange of ideas and communication among technical specialists with diverse qualifications.	3. Imbalance in authority an■ sponsibility of project ma■ gers.
	4. Better coordination of project activities and strong results orientation.	4. Natural grounds for poten■ conflict and strained relati■ with functional managers.
	5. Integrated planning, scheduling, and control of scarce resources.	5. The "two-bosses" problem for functional managers.
		6. The fact that many manag■ are ill-trained in negotiatic

Table 9-1. Continued

;ANIZATIONAL PATTERN	ADVANTAGES	DISADVANTAGES
	6. Early identification of problems that might hinder successful project completion. 7. Clear accountability and responsibility of the project manager for overall project performance. 8. Assures decision-making based on the overall good of the project rather than on the competing priorities of different functional departments. 9. Provides challenging opportunities for lower-level management, and serves as excellent vehicle for identifying and training of potential talent.	bargaining, games and politics, and conflict resolution techniques. 7. The temporary nature of the project, which might generate job insecurity problems for project members (no permanent home). 8. The "two-bosses" problems for project members. 9. The inability of the project manager to judge individual's capabilities. 10. Possible use of the project by functional managers as a dumping round for their "deadwood" employees.
ix Organization	1. High degree of coordination is provided by the program manager and his team without distraction by details of execution. 2. Technical support and expertise is provided through functional managers. 3. Attractive setup for highly skilled professionals who desire working on challenging projects without leaving their organizational home (functional units). 4. Flexibility and efficiency in using scarce resources and making the necessary adjustments in manpower requirements. 5. Conflict between project requirements and organization policies might be easier resolved through interference by general management.	1. The dual authority relationships which can cause problems for professional personnel reporting to a functional supervisor and a program manager (shared loyalties). 2. Biases of functional unit heads, which may subtly work against the priorities desired by general management. 3. The fact that authority for distributing rewards and recognition usually resides with the employee's functional supervisor, so the matrix manager is stripped of a valuable management tool. 4. Difficulty for the sponsor to identify clear lines of authority since it is shared between the program manager and several functional managers. 5. High degree of frustration and tension for the program manager and functional managers when roles and organizational relationships are vague and loosely defined.

Product Organization

In the case of diversified product lines, companies usually adopt a multidivisional organizational structure with a division for each product line. Each division has a high degree of autonomy. Engineering and R&D operations can be organized to match the divisional structure. One way to do this is to set up a line organization with central engineering and R&D laboratories. As shown in Figure 9-3, there is a division for each product line headed by a manager reporting to the chief engineer who, in turn, reports to the vice-president of research and engineering. Note that the departments within the central engineering and R&D laboratories simply correspond to each of the manufacturing divisions. Also, engineering and R&D activities, although separate units, are combined in this discussion to avoid redundancy.

Another way to approach organization by product line is to set up the engineering and R&D activities on a divisional basis, that is, to divisionalize the entire program so it is actually a part of each manufacturing division. Thus, instead of having a central laboratory, each division has its engineering and R&D department report to its own engineering manager who has final responsibility for all engineering and R&D activities on his division's product line. Departmental engineering managers report to each division's general manager. Figure 9-4 presents a divisionalized engineering and R&D organization by product-line.

Note that each divisional engineering and research product line can be further divided functionally according to electrical design, mechanical design, materials and insulation design, metallurgy, organic chemistry activities and so on. It is also important to note here that headquarters engineering and R&D has a staff relationship (dashed line) to division engineering plus an advisory relationship on general engineering. Needless to say, this organizational setup leaves the engineer-

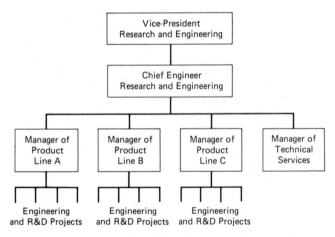

Figure 9-3. Centralized organization by product line.

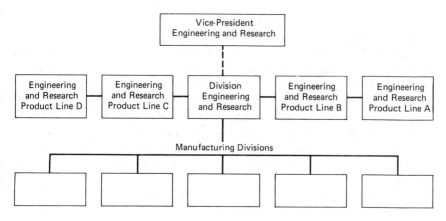

Figure 9-4. Divisionalized engineering and R&D organization by product line.

ing or R&D director in the group headquarters with much more limited staff than in a functional organization setup.

It is obvious from Table 9-1 that the product form of organization has a number of advantages and disadvantages. The strengths of this organizational model relate to the clarity of authority and responsibility of product line managers, and the strong marketing orientation of engineering and R&D acitivities. However, this organizational form can lead to duplication of R&D activities if individual laboratories have a strong discipline orientation, and to reduced overall direction and control by corporate engineering and R&D over individual laboratories. Perhaps the major weakness of the product form of organization is that the strong marketing orientation of R&D and engineering can create a serious imbalance between basic and applied research in favor of applied research and application.

Project Organization

Nature of Project Management. A project is a multitude of activities requiring the performance of certain tasks directed to the achievement of a set of objectives within a well-defined time span and with a specified budget. The project is dissolved once the objectives are achieved. The project team, then, is a task force or a temporary organization charged with a specific task under the direction of a project manager. Since every project is created for achieving a specific task, it follows that every project imposes a unique set of requirements on the organization. This is because the activities and objectives for which the project entity was created in the first place are not achievable through the normal functional organizational structure. A different set of policies, techniques, and procedures will be required to make project management work effectively.

But why would the traditional functional form of organization have difficulty handling the unusually complex or the distinctively different projects? Because it is designed to deal with systems of highly homogeneous tasks with continuous flow of products and services. Functional department executives are concerned only with doing specialized work activities within a well-defined budget.[3] They can also be guilty of "tunnel vision," that is, they are primarily concerned with their own portions of the task without regard for the impact of their actions on the company and on the project. More important is that the advantage of faster decision-making in a project context could be slowed down or even lost by passing interdepartmental problems to the top through all levels of the functional organization.

You can see from the above analysis why the project management approach can be used to counteract deficiencies of the functional organizational structure. It can be effectively applied to a one-time undertaking which often involves a new product, where emphasis is on research, development, testing, and initial production.

The project-type organization has been used extensively in high-technology organizations in industry, business, government, and academia, and is being increasingly introduced in nontechnical areas of private and public organizations. *Project management* and *program management* are usually used synonymously to describe the same organizational arrangement. While the term project management is more popular throughout the American business scene, the term program management is frequently used in the aerospace and electronics industries (following the Department of Defense, their major customer).

The project type of organization is an excellent management tool for dealing with situations and problems that cut across many departmental boundaries, are highly complex in nature, and require a great deal of coordination of a large number of separate functions and divisions, each with its unique disciplines, expertise, and practices.

How Project Management Works. In the project management arrangement, individuals are grouped by project teams under a project manager who is responsible for project performance. It is important to remember here that the project organization structure should not replace functional organizations since functional specialization in areas such as engineering, manufacturing, and procurement is essential for the preservation and perpetuation of industrial capabilities.[4] Rather, project organizations are temporary task forces and should complement or supplement functional departments. A typical project organization structure appears in Figure 9-5.

---

[3] Middleton, C. J. How to Set Up a Project Organization. In Heyel, Carl (Ed.). "Handbook of Industrial Research Management," Second Edition. New York: Van Nostrand Reinhold, 1968, p. 297.

[4] This section is partly based on Middleton, Ibid., pp. 297-304.

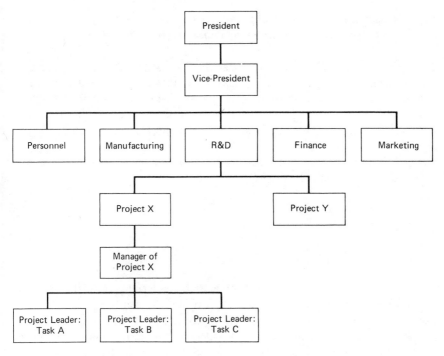

Figure 9-5. Typical organizational structure.

There are two basic types of project organizations: individual and staff. In an individual project organization, the project manager exercises control through the functional departments performing all of the work to be done. No activities or personnel other than clerical support report directly to him. So, this is a "one-man" show where the project manager relies on other organizational units to support and accomplish project objectives. The project manager, however, is responsible for the overall management and integration of the project.

In a staff project organization, most of the actual project work is still performed by the functional departments. These include the primary activities such as engineering, procurement, and manufacturing. The project manager exercises control over activities such as scheduling, funds allocation, and project financial control.

It is crucial to understand that in both types of project organization, the project manager may be totally responsible for his project, but may possess limited authority over the supporting functional areas. The project organization form may change radically during the project's lifetime. It may start out as an individual project organization supported by talent borrowed from functional departments. A more elaborate structure might emerge, including engineering and manufacturing for the development phase. The project might then be reduced to a staff type after the production phase has been started.

Steps for Establishing a Project Organization. You will recall that a distinguishing characteristic of the project organization is that it has a well-defined time span or a life cycle with start and end points. Figure 9-6 shows the life cycle phases of various types of projects as they advance from the point of inception to final termination. These phases are highly interrelated, and are rarely clearly separated.

The project life cycle can be described in terms of four successive phases or dimensions. As shown in Figure 9-7, these phases are:[5]

1. The concept phase.
2. The organization phase.
3. The operational phase.
4. The completion phase.

The concept phase comprises the initial activities leading up to the decision to organize and implement a project. This phase may begin as a special task-force study, as the resolution of a board meeting, or as a specific decision by a key executive. The end product or output of the concept phase is a directive charting the project (Figure 9-7). An outline for a project charter is shown in Figure 9-8.

In the organization phase, authorities and responsibilities should be clearly established. The project manager and key personnel should be appointed; direction for the assignment of other required personnel should be issued. This phase is crucial for project success.

The operational phase takes the longest part of the project activity. This phase covers the actual activities relating to the direction, execution, and control of the project. Measurement and evaluation of the performance of the project against previous plans and predetermined objectives is an integral part of this phase.

In the completion phase, project team members are finally reassigned to functional departments and other appropriate units. This phase concludes the project and is, hence, terminated.

It is important to emphasize here how project management "fits" within the more traditional management concepts. It is clear from the previous discussion that because of its unique features, the objectives of the project organization are not easily achievable through the functional form of organization. This, however, should not mean that the "normal" management processes of planning,

---

[5] This discussion is partly based on Martin, Charles C. "Project Management: How to Make It Work." New York: AMACOM (American Management Association), 1976, pp. 13-15.

TYPE OF PROJECT \ PROJECT PHASE	1 CONCEPT	2 DEFINITION	3 DESIGN	4 DEVELOPMENT	5 APPLICATION	6 POST COMPLETION
Telecommunication equipment contract	Preproposal: identification of opportunity; decision to bid	Prepare proposal; submit; receive award	Engineering design	Procure materials; fabricate, assemble, install, and test	Concentration and acceptance testing	Creation of new projects for follow-up on contracts; spares; field support, final evaluation report
New product or service development project	Identify opportunity or need; establish basic feasibility	Prepare new-product proposal, product plan, review and approval sheet, R&D case, project appropriation request	Design product or service; build and test prototype	Design production article; build and test tooling; produce initial production articles	Distribute and sell product; verify performance	Creation of new projects to further improve product; final evaluation report to compare results with product plan, project appropriation request, etc.
R&D case project for manufacturing development	Identify opportunity or need; establish basic feasibility	Prepare R&D case	Conduct studies, analysis, and design work	Conduct pilot tests; analyze and document results	Conduct full-scale tests; analyze and document results	Final evaluation report
Capital facilities project	Identify opportunity or need; establish basic feasibility	Investment analysis, budget preparation, preparation of project appropriation request	Process design, engineering for construction, equipment design and/or specification	Procure equipment, construct civil works, install and check out equipment	Start up and commission operating facility	Final evaluation report to compare results with project appropriation request
Systems project	Idenfity opportunity or need; establish basic feasibility	Investment analysis, budget preparation, preparation of project appropriation request	Systems analysis and detailed design	System coding, compiling, testing, and documentation	Install and test system under production conditions	Final evaluation report to compare results with project appropriation request

Figure 9-6. Life cycle phases of various types of projects. (Adapted from Archibald, Russel, D. "Managing High-Technology Programs and Projects." New York: Wiley, 1976, pp. 20-21.

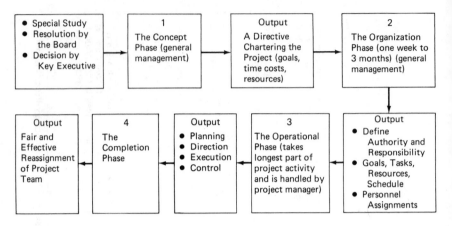

Figure 9-7. Steps for establishing a project.

organizing, directing, and controlling do not fit well with the requirements for the effective management of projects.

As you can see in Figure 9-9, the managerial processes are, in fact, the same. The four phases of any project are in line with the managerial functions performed within a different organizational setup. The major problems with the project management arrangement, then, revolve around the fact that many of the fundamental principles of organization discussed in Chapter 8 have been violated. These violations constitute some of the weaknesses of the project management form of organization, as will be discussed later in this chapter.

Role and Responsibilities of the Project Manager. The project manager's task is a complex one. This job requires someone with a high degree of flexibility and adaptibility, aggressiveness, persuasiveness, superb communication skills, an ability to deal with conflict and to function well within a highly ambiguous environment and ill-defined organizational relationships. No wonder that competent project managers are rare birds, indeed! This is why project management assignments are often used as testing ground for management candidates for high-level executive positions. The point is simple: It takes a delicate blend of solid interpersonal, administrative, and to a lesser degree, technical skills to succeed as a project manager. If appointed for such an assignment, you should very well know what you are getting yourself into. But also remember that a well-done project assignment could pay off very handsomely in terms of personal and career development rewards.

Now, what are the responsibilities of the project manager? These include:[6]

---

[6] Archibald, Russel D. "Managing High Technology Programs and Projects." New York: Wiley, 1976, pp. 35-36.

1. To produce the specific end prodcut or result within the technical, cost, and schedule specifications, and with the organizational resources available.
2. To meet the profit objectives of the project, when it is under contract with a customer.
3. To alert higher management at any time that it appears that the technical, cost, or schedule objectives will not be met.

Subject: Establishment of Project X

To: Key Executives

Copies to: Managers Affected

I. Charter for the project
   A. Project goals
   B. Name of the project
   C. Estimate of resources needed. (This may be omitted because it is sensitive; however, the estimate should be recorded somehow.)

II. Organization
   A. Management Responsibility
      1. Establishment of a project manager
      2. Directive authority
      3. Review authority
      4. The executive responsible for completing the organization phase
      5. Chartering authority. (This is implicit in the signature of the charter and may be omitted.)
   B. Organization affected (division, departments, etc., that will participate in the project)

III. Schedule
   A. General time frame of the project
   B. Schedule for completing the organization phase
   C. Interim reviews (if desired)

IV. Resources allocation. (This paragraph may be omitted if adequate resources are under the control of the given responsibility for the organization phase.)
   A. Resources assigned to the organization phase
   B. Method of cost charging by participating organizations

V. Statement of management support for the project

Signed

Chartering Authority

Figure 9-8. Outline for a project charter. (From Martin, Charles C. "Project Management: How to Make It Work." New York: AMACOM, 1976, p. 97.

PROJECT PHASE	MANAGERIAL FUNCTION	RESPONSIBILITY
A. Concept	Idea Generation and Project Chartering	General Management
B. Organization	Organizing	General Management
C. Operational	• Planning • Direction • Execution • Evaluation and Control	Project Manager
D. Completion		Project Manager and Functional Executives

Figure 9-9. The project management process.

4. To make or force the required decisions to assure that the project objectives will be met.
5. To recommend termination of the project or alternative solutions if the project objectives cannot be achieved and contractual obligations permit.
6. To serve as the prime point of contact for the project with the customer, top management, and functional managers.
7. To negotiate "contracts" (work orders) with the various functional departments for performance of work packages to specification and within time and cost limits.

Relationship Between Project Manager and Functional Managers. There are considerable variations in the supervisory limits imposed over the project manager's authority relationships with functional managers. In some companies, project managers are authorized to direct any department or division to take whatever action is needed to maintain good program performance, timely delivery, and follow-on business.[7] Dealing directly with the functional manager or with his representative, the project manager can prescribe to the functional departments what is required on the project and when, leaving the how to do it under the functional department's supervision.

Another common practice is for the project manager to define tasks and assign them to functional departments. Although he has no line authority, he monitors task performance. Tasks, then, are performed at the functional departments under project management control.

Experience and observation show that an effective practice is for top management to give the project manager full backing and support, including having him report to a high-level executive. This arrangement gives him enough "clout" and influence in his dealings with functional managers. If he also controls budgets,

---

[7] Middleton, op. cit., p. 299.

sets schedules, and defines performance criteria, he can adequately control a project even through none of the departments working on it report directly to him.

Authority, Power, and Influence in Project Management: How Project Managers Get It Done. If you look at the project manager's job from the standpoint of authority-power relationships, you will note several differences between his position and those of "traditional" managers like marketing, manufacturing, and so on. You should, however, realize that these differences are relative in nature—they are a matter of degree—and that they constitute major deviations from the traditional principles of organization discussed in Chapter 8. Through the following discussion of authority, power, and influence relationships in project management, the differences between the project manager's position and other management positions will become clear.[8]

First of all a major characteristic of the project manager's position is that he always has more responsibility than authority. This imbalance is much more significant in the case of the project manager than other management positions and is a clear violation of the parity of authority and responsibility organizational principle.

Authority, as you will recall from our discussion in Chapter 8, is always based on power which emanates from several sources. Of the two types of power, positional and personal, the project manager's authority is actually based on power which largely stems more from his personal abilities and less from his position. His positional power (the basis for his "legal" authority) is derived from:

- Organizational charter
- Organizational position
- Position or job specification
- Executive rank
- Policy documents
- Superior's right to command
- Delegated power
- The hierarchical flow
- Control of funds

His personal power (the basis for his "earned" or personal authority) is derived from:

- Technical and organizational knowledge
- Management experience
- Maintenance of rapport

[8] This section draws heavily from: Archibald, Russel D., op. cit., pp. 42-45; Wilemon, David, and Gimmill, Gary R. Interpersonal Power in Temporary Management Systems. *Journal of Management Studies* (October 1971): 319-320; Middleton, op. cit., p. 300; and Thamhain, Hans J., and Wilemon, David L. Conflict Management in Project Life Cycles. *Sloan Management Review* (Summer 1975).

- Negotiation with peers and associates
- Building and maintaining alliances
- Project manager's focal position
- The deliberate conflict
- The resolution of conflict
- Being right

Secondly, successful project managers typically have superb interpersonal and political skills. This is crucial since their authority is not commensurate with their responsibility. Building bridges with others, persuading, manipulating, and forming solid friendships and alliances are some of the prerequisite skills effective project managers must have. Three influence bases of major importance to project managers have been identified:

1. The first basis is reward and punishment power which may be either possessed (positional) or attributed (personal). Possessed reward and punishment power is derived from the sources indicated above. Attributed reward and punishment power, on the other hand, is derived from the other set of sources identified above. It refers to the power assigned to the project manager by those with whom he interacts. It is what they believe he can do directly or indirectly to them or block or facilitate their personal goals if they neglect his requests. Put differently, it is not the real but the perceived power that matters. If the project manager has a direct line to top management, project team members may perceive that he is capable of influencing their careers by comments on their performance, whether or not in fact he has this influence.

While possessed reward and punishment power is usually the basis for attributed reward and punishment power, it is not always present. Differently put, a project manager has as much reward and punishment power as others perceive him as possessing. If others believe he possesses it when he does not, for all intents and purposes, the effect is the same as if he actually had it. Such bluffing is often effective because the power world of an organization is unofficial and ambiguous and the reward and punishment power of a project manager is more often than not indirect. An interfacing functional manager simply does not ask a project manager how much power he has, or how much influence he has over a third party, or what he can do to him if he fails to do what is requested. In short, the point is that a project manager may have a great deal of indirect reward and punishment power (derived from earned or personal power sources), even if he lacks direct reward and punishment power (derived from positional or "legal" sources of power). Additional sources of indirect reward and punishment power include sharp negotiation skills, personality, persuasive ability, competence, and reciprocal favors.

2. Expert power stems from project members' perceptions of the project manager as a person who is a knowledgable and qualified to evaluate the consequences of certain project actions or decisions.

3. Referent power emanates from project members' admiration of and attraction to the project manager: They value both their relationship with him and his opinion of them. It follows that personal friendships and alliances can become an important source of influence for a project manager. If a project manager is personally disliked, he may have a negative referent power, which will make the task of influencing the project contributors even more difficult.

The third and final characteristic of the project manager's position is that the project management form, by nature, is a furtile ground for conflict. Conflict emanates from several sources including the "two-bosses" problem. That is, the functional manager (or his representative) receives direction from two persons: the project manager and the functional superior. This is a clear violation of another fundamental organizational principle—the concept of unity of command. This dual responsibility results in ambiguity, frustration, and tension when the priorities of the project manager and the senior functional head are frequently at odds.

While there might be a sound justification for the "two-bosses" in combining superior technical judgment and expertise while focusing on the tasks and goals of the project, this is a delicate situation and should be handled with tact. Functional unit managers often dislike the project concept because it superimposes the project manager and his organization upon a functional structure that has existed for many years. Most of the managerial know-how and experience are in functional departments, and these may have difficulty in adjusting to becoming service organizations for the project, relinquishing some of the authority previously exercised. In short, to many functional unit managers, the project manager is an unwelcome interloper.

Now, how can we deal with the "two-bosses" problem? A clear definition of the role and responsibilities of the project manager and his relationship with functional managers could certainly help. Responsibilities should be divided as clearly as possible in the following manner:

1. The project manager provides direction regarding *what* the project tasks are, *when* they should start and finish to meet the overall project goals, and *how much* money is available to perform the work.
2. The functional manager provides direction regarding *who* will perform the tasks, *how* the technical work will be accomplished, and *how much* money is required to perform the work.

While there is no guarantee that this arrangement will eliminate the conflict and tension in the project manager-functional manager relationship, it will certainly provide a framework of the responsibilities of each. However, demarcation lines can never be absolutely clear, and frequent bargaining and negotiations will still be necessary. While conflict situations can always be appealed to a higher authority, the intent is to minimize this practice and settle these differences as close to the firing line as possible.

In summary, the major differences between project managers and functional managers in terms of authority and power relationships can be summed up as follows:

1. Responsiblity of the project manager far exceeds his authority.
2. He must elicit performance from others not under his direct control.
3. His power is much more earned or attributed (personal power) than possessed (official power).
4. To get things done, he must rely on interpersonal and political influence bases (i.e., expert or referent power, friendships, alliances, and political maneuvers etc.).
5. He must realize that he is an unwelcome interloper to many functional unit managers.
6. He must get unusual backing and support from top management.

Project Organization: An Assessment. Table 9-1 provides you with a detailed account of the advantages and disadvantages of the project form of organization compared to other forms discussed earlier in this chapter.

For finite, well-defined, one-of-a-kind projects, the project management approach has several advantages over the functional form of organization. The two basic advantages of a project management approach are:

1. Project commitments are made only to achievable technical, cost, and schedule goals.
2. Every project is planned, scheduled, and controlled so that the commitments are in fact achieved.

On the other hand, project organization has its problems, which are also presented in Table 9-1. The point you should keep in mind is that the primary problems of project management are human, not technical. A well-seasoned project manager with sharp interpersonal skills and the ability to manage conflict and live with high amounts of uncertainty and ambiguity can do wonders. His success, however, will not come about without a clear definition—as clear as possible—of the dimensions of his authority and accountability, and the full support and backing of top management.

It is obvious from the above discussion that project management is a complex mechanism introduced into an organization for good reasons, but its success is flatly contingent on how well it is implemented.

Matrix Organization

So far in this section, I have discussed three types of organizational forms in engineering and R&D: the functional organization, the product organization, and the project organization. The fourth, and last, type is matrix organizational structure.[9]

In traditional forms of organization, organizational charts are developed, clear-cut hierarchies are defined, and orders are handed down while decisions are passed upward until the buck stops with the chief executive. But as businesses diversify and market environments grow more complex, top-level executives are discovering that the old functional and product-line hierarchies, despite their straightforewardness, are bugging down. Executives are swamped with data while the company languishes, awaiting orders.

The matrix organization is a relatively new organizational form developed to deal with these problems in an effort by upper management to get out from under the paper crush and speed up decision-making. The matrix management system helps to break down barriers to action in the traditional hierarchies, pushes decision-making down to more people, puts a premium on teamwork, and helps restore a measure of small-company flexibility to the large and complex high-technology organizations using it.

While the matrix system has been identifed and studied as a distinct organizational form only in recent years, its origins date to the beginning of the space program over 20 years ago. Aerospace companies formed project teams that included members from diverse functional units within the companies who were brought together to focus on one specific product or task. The teams were quickly disbanded once the project was completed. Among the several companies where the matrix management has been adopted are TRW Systems, General Electric, Equitable Life Insurance, Citicorp, Shell Oil, and Dow Corning. Let us now take a look at the matrix structure and how it works.

Nature of Matrix Organization. The matrix organization is an overlay of management system whereby the project managers and the functional departments share manpower and facilities resources. In this arrangement, the project manager works horizontally across the functional organization.

---

[9] This section is partly based on: How to Stop the Buck Short of the Top. *Business Week* (a McGraw-Hill publication), (January 16, 1978): 82-83; Galbraith, Jay R. Matrix Organization Designs: How to Combine Functional and Project Forms. *Business Horizons* (February 1971): 29-40; Twiss, Brian C. Managing Technological Innovation. op. cit., pp. 219-220; Francis, Philip H. "Principles of R&D Management." New York: AMACOM (American Management Associations), 1977, p. 257; Wolff, Michael. The Joy (and Woe) of Matrix. *Research Management*, **XXIII**, 2 (March 1980): 10-12; and Webber, Ross A. "Management: Basic Elements of Managing Organizations." Homewood: Irwin, 1975, Ch. 18.

Why matrix organization? The problem of designing organizations arises from the choices available among alternative bases of the authority structure. The most common alternatives are to group together activities which bear on a common product, common customer, common geographic area, common business function (marketing, engineering, manufacturing, and so on), or common process (forging, stamping, machinery, and so on). Each of these bases has various costs and economics associated with it. For example, the functional structure facilitates the acquisition of specialized inputs. It permits the hiring of an electromechanical and an electronics engineer rather than two electrical engineers. It minimizes the number necessary by pooling specialized resources and time-sharing them across products or projects. It provides career paths for specialists.

The problem, however, is that when one basis of organization is chosen, the benefits of the other are surrendered. If the functional structure is adopted, the technologies are developed but the projects fall behind schedule. If the project organization is chosen, there is better cost and schedule performance but the technologies are not developed as well. In the past, managers made a judgment as to whether technical development or schedule completion was more important and chose the appropriate form. However, the matrix design attempts to achieve the benefits of both forms.

How Matrix Organization Works. As you can see, the matrix organization is a development of project management designed to avoid the disadvantages of the simple project management organization by separating clearly the managerial and professional responsibilities for the project. As shown in Figure 9-10, in an R&D setting, for example, the R&D director has reporting to him the discipline heads, who are responsible for maintaining professional standards within their own disciplines and for the career development of their staff, as well as the project managers, who are responsible for the progress of their projects. The individual research worker is responsible to the project manager for the day-to-day progress of his work on the project, but is responsible to his discipline head, to whom he looks for career guidance and development, for the professional standard of his work.

Let us take another example from engineering. Figure 9-11 illustrates the organization of a nuclear engineering firm which in part demonstrates the matrix system. Across the top are the permanent functional departments into which specialists are hired, and down the left side are three projects currently being pursued. The development of a nuclear-powered rocket is the largest, so this project is composed of a person from each of the functional departments and the production manager. The other two projects are somewhat smaller: the development of more effective shielding for a nuclear reactor and preliminary investigation on the use of nuclear explosives for large excavations such as canals. These teams draw on only the most appropriate functional specialists.

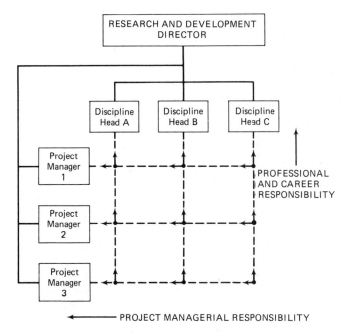

Figure 9-10. Matrix organization. (From Twiss, Brian. Managing Technological Innovation. London: Longman, 1974, p. 219.

For the duration of the project, the individual team members are under the direction of the project manager. However, their permanent corporate homes remain in the functional departments, which continue to handle routine administrative tasks such as keeping personnel files, maintaining office spaces, and administering supervisory employee fringe benefit programs.

The matrix organization is sometimes called the "multidimensional structure" because it combines the functional and project organizational forms. One dimension comprises the line or functional activities that provide the pool of support for the ongoing projects. Research, systems design, production, and business operations are but some of the functional activities that may be called upon to support project activities. The other dimension of the matrix organization is made up of the programs themselves. They may be great in number, and all have a relatively short life cycle; hence, this dimension, in contrast to the fixed dimension of functional structure, is constantly changing.

Two things characterize the role of the matrix or program manager. First, he is given authority and responsibility for his program just as in the conventional project management concept. In the matrix organization, the line or functional structure develops from the program it serves so that these functional activities play a supportive rather than a primary role. Second, the program manager receives from the supporting functional units a certain commitment of per-

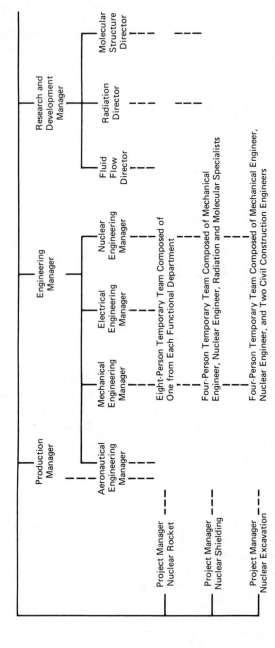

Figure 9-11. Matrix structure for nuclear engineering company. (From Webber, Ross A. "Management Basic Elements of Managing Organizations." Homewood: Irwin, 1975, p. 423.)

sonnel needed to accomplish his program requirements. Program personnel will, thus, be on temporary assignments from various functional groups. Along with responsibility and accountability for successful program completion, the program manager has the authority for work design, work assignments, and procedural relationships. He may also have the authority to reward personnel with promotions (very rarely), salary increases, or other forms of recognition while they are assigned to his program. On program completion, functional group personnel are returned to their departments for reassignment.

Matrix Management versus Other Organizational Forms. Figure 9-12 presents a typical matrix organizational structure. Two features distinguish the pure matrix organization from the functional and project structures: First, the pure matrix organization requires a dual authority relationship somewhere in the organization. Second, there exists a balance of power between program and functional managers. Dual authority and balance of power are difficult to achieve and maintain in practice. Indeed, to a certain extent these two concepts contradict the basic precepts of good functional management. However, through enforced collaboration on budgets, salaries, and promotions, and in conjunction with dual information and reporting systems, this balance of power can be approached.

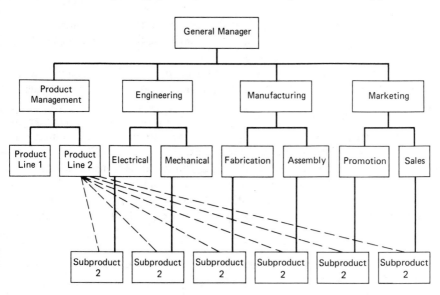

Figure 9-12. A typical matrix organization. (From Galbraith, Jay R. Matrix Organization Designs. *Business Horizons* (February, 1971): 36.)

At any rate, there are two major differences between project and matrix organizations. A significant difference is that while the project organization constitutes an autonomous self-contained unit, the matrix structure retains administrative relationships with the mother departments. The other difference concerns the fact that the project draws on its own internal resources, while the matrix actually borrows resources from the functional divisions. A detailed account of the advantages of the matrix organizational structure appears in Table 9-1.

Although the matrix form of organization has several advantages, it is not without its limitations. The matrix organization provides a high degree of coordination, technical support by functional units, and flexibility in using skilled technical resources efficiently and effectively. In a real sense, this organizational pattern combines the benefits of both the functional and project types of organization. However, the problems associated with matrix management revolve around the creation of a complex organizational environment, the dual authority relationships, the stimulation of conflict situations, and the exceptionally demanding role of the program manager (Table 9-1).

The Matrix Organization: How to Make It Work for You. The main problems relating to the matrix form of organization can be summarized as follows:

1. There can be a distinct culture shock (even to research scientists!) when any change disturbs the organization, and having more than one boss can be hard to accept, especially for older people.

2. Adjustments need to be made by many people including some middle managers who fear (often with justification) that their jobs will be superfluous in the matrix.

3. Matrix organizations require a team commitment. A project manager, in a matrix setting, must work to pull the best ideas from his group—contrary to the old days when the inventor was the key person.

4. Setting priorities can be a problem particularly in R&D management.

5. Matrix can be a fad. Do not go overboard and think it will solve everything. Remember, for example, that ideas only come from individuals, and consequently, the more oriented a project is toward research, the less need there is for a matrix.

In addition to the benefits of the matrix organization discussed in the previous section, two other major advantages can be added:

1. It helps minimize risk by unleashing an incredible amount of creativity that will quickly give you many more ideas than you can possibly use.

2. A matrix can be extraordinarily productive, telescoping the time to commercialization for major projects very significantly. It has been reported that,

in the matrix situation, 8 out of 10 laboratory projects could become commercially successful within 2 to 4 years, as opposed to the more usual 1 out of 20 within 7 to 10 years.

To achieve these benefits, here are some pointers:

1. Recognize as a myth the common criticism that a matrix requires one person to report to two different bosses. A matrix requires one person to report to different people for different things. The key is to define who is to be reported to for what, and when. It is essential that both the project manager and the leader of the technical skills group (chemical, mechanical, electronic, analytical, testing, and so on) clearly understand the limits of their respective roles and the circumstances under which they have 51% of the vote in those decisions which they must reach together.

2. Provide careful and considerable supervision to help people learn to define and limit their responsibilities in this way. Much individual counseling is necessary, and professionally led courses in developing personal skills and sensitivity can be a definite aid.

3. Insulate those people who cannot cope with a matrix despite this help and who are very valuable. Help others to find different jobs.

4. Establish a business guidance committee with marketing, legal, financial, production, and other representatives of the profit center toward which a project is targeted. This helps overcome the "not-invented-here" syndrome, and ensures that progress can be monitored effectively and schedules met.

5. Recognize that a matrix is a highly interrelated system requiring sensitive and considerate people to manage it. Such people must be good interpersonal communicators with low hostility quotients. And they must be persistent because the changeover to a matrix will not go smoothly at first, particularly when you are changing an existing organization rather than starting a brand new one.

For the effective organization of engineering and R&D operations with scarce resources, complex technology, diverse and constantly changing product lines, and highly sophisticated and specialized professional talent, the matrix organization structure seems to be a natural. The available data from companies such as Shell Oil, Dow Corning, and TRW clearly demonstrate that the matrix structure—in spite of the many problems associated with its implementation—is a success.

ALTERNATIVE ORGANIZATIONAL FORMS

So far, I have described the four major patterns of organization in engineering and R&D: the functional organization, the product organization, the project organization, and the matrix organization. There are other bases of organizational structure. These include:

- Organization by geographic area
- Organization by type of customer
- Organization by phase, stage, or process

Because of the conventional nature of these bases of departmentalization and the fact that they are frequently used in the organization of other traditional business activities such as marketing, finance, and manufacturing, they will not be discussed here. They are simply beyond the scope of this volume. For the reader desiring more detailed information on these organizational forms, several references are given below.[10]

HOW TO CHOOSE AN ORGANIZATIONAL PATTERN

Now that fundamental principles of organizational structure have been discussed (Chapter 8), and alternative forms of organization have been described and analyzed (Chapter 9), is there a "best" way to organize? Is there an "ideal" organizational structure? How do you go about choosing an organizational design? Just as with your other managerial functions (planning, decision-making, performance evaluation, etc.), there is not an "ideal" organizational design. The appropriate form of organization for your engineering and R&D units depends on a set of variables or factors that must be considered in building the structure. Changes in these factors require corresponding changes in the structural shape of the organization. The most important of these factors are:

1. Nature and characteristics of technical people.
2. Nature of organizational goals.
3. Task characteristics.
4. Product lines.
5. Level of technology.
6. Functional coupling.
7. Balanced arrangement of barriers and bonds.
8. Nature of organizational environment.

Nature and Characteristics of Technical People

Scientists and engineers are well-educated and creative professionals. Their personality styles, needs, value orientations, and backgrounds are quite different

---

[10] See, for example, Webber, Ross A. Management: "Basic Elements of Managing Organizations." Homewood: Irwin, 1975; Gannon, Martin J. "Management: An Organizational Perspective." Boston: Little, Brown, 1977; and Duncan, Jack W. "Essentials of Management," Second Edition. Hinsdale, Dryden, 1978.

from other segments of the labor force. There are also differences between scientists and engineers as two separate populations. It follows that engineering and scientific resources do have special characteristics that set them apart from those working in other traditional industrial activities (such as purchasing, personnel, and marketing) and, thus, they have different task orientations and role expectations.

An important factor in designing the structure of R&D and engineering organizations, then, is the nature, qualifications, and behavioral orientations of technical professional personnel. The importance of this point is further signified by the fact that R&D is inherently a future-oriented organization and a labor-intensive industry. Thus, the effective organization and management of R&D resources is crucial to its effectiveness.

Nature of Organizational Goals

The structure will be partly determined by the type of goals set by the organization and also those objectives established in engineering and R&D. It is important to remember here that the structure is usually the vehicle through which organizational objectives will be achieved. Short-range concrete objectives can be achieved best in a project or matrix type of organizational design, while multiple product lines (engineering) and heavy discipline orientation (R&D) call for the product or functional type of organization.

Task Characteristics

The proper form of organization will depend to a large degree on the characteristics of the task to be performed. There are, of course, differences between research and development, relating mostly to the uses to be made of the work and whether its aim is the expansion of knowledge or an immediate commercial goal.[11] To a lesser extent the differences reflect the degree of uncertainty inherent in a given problem and the length of time work can be expected to proceed without demonstratable payoff.

Furthermore, the differences between R&D activities on the one hand and other corporate functions (i.e., marketing, finance, and so on) on the other hand are even more apparent. At the risk of generalizing, these broad differences are summarized in Table 9-2.

It is clear from this table that R&D activities are generally unstructured and vague, with a high degree of uncertainty involved and creativity required for their effective performance. Because these tasks are integrative, complex, and creative, they are better handled through informal decentralized structures. Con-

---

[11] Kingsbury, Sherman. Organizing for Research. In Heyel, Carl (Ed.) "Handbook of Industrial Research Management, " Second Edition. New York: Van Nostrand Reinhold, 1968, p. 66.

Table 9-2. Differences Between R&D and Other Corporate Activities

	RESEARCH AND DEVELOPMENT	OTHER CORPORATE FUNCTIONS
1. Nature of task	Ambiguous, less programmed, less defined	More programmed, more defined
2. Central management focus	People (labor-intensive industry)	Structure
3. Most important managerial skills	Social and interpersonal skills	Administrative (structural aspects of the organization)
4. Key management priorities	The research director is the chief technologist of the business	Marketing, production, and finance are key functions with top priorities
5. Managerial leadership style	Participative	Directive

versely, repetitive, routinized, and simple tasks are best handled through formal centralized organizational structures. Perhaps a realistic approach would be to consider the two types of tasks as opposite ends of a continuum, with most work activities containing elements of both types. Differences in task orientations are thus, relative rather than absolute.

Product Lines

As you will note in Figure 9-13, you have a wide range of choices extending from the product to the functional organization, with the matrix halfway between. A major determining factor is the product lines involved. The greater the diversity among product lines, and the greater the rate of change of products in the line, the greater the pressure to move toward product structures.[12] When product lines become diverse, it becomes difficult for general managers and functional managers to maintain knowledge in all areas; the amount of information they must handle exceeds their capacity to absorb it.

Similarly, the faster the rate of new-product introduction, the more unfamiliar are the tasks being performed. Managers are, therefore, less able to make precise estimates concerning resource allocations, schedules, and priorities. Since trade-off decisions among engineering, manufacturing, and marketing have to be made, there must be greater product influence in the decision process and, hence, the product organization type (see Figure 9-13).

---

[12] Galbraith, op. cit.

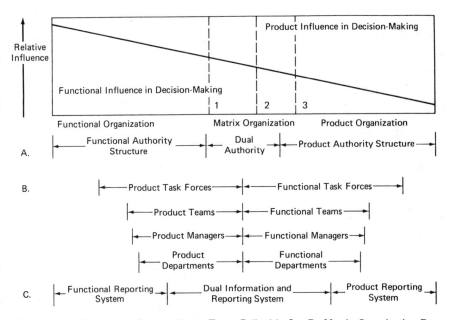

Figure 9-13. The range of alternatives. (From Galbraith, Jay R. Matrix Organization Designs. *Business Horizons* (February 1971): p. 37.)

Level of Technology

The type of technology the organization uses will be a major determinant of its structural design. Since different organizational units might utilize different technologies, their departmental structures should differ. Because of the unpredictable, ill-defined, and creative nature of R&D tasks, the problem-solving or "organic" structures will tend to be characteristic of R&D organizations. Furthermore, the more important new technology, expertise, and technological development are for organizational effectiveness and competitiveness, the greater is the need for the functional form of organization (i.e., organization by discipline). Under these circumstances, the tendency will be toward the functional authority structure—as shown in Figure 9-13—with an increased functional influence in decision-making.

Functional Coupling

While the degree of coupling (the amounts of interactions) between departments results from the organizational structure, the structure should also reflect the actual needs of the situation.[13] For example, a close coupling between R&D and marketing would certainly relate what can be done—the invention—to what is worth doing—what is potentially marketable—and would, thus, be perhaps the most important element in the process of innovation.

For effective functional coupling aimed at enhancing innovation, here are some recommendations:[14]

1. Recognize that innovation is a complex series of events taking place within the corporation as a whole. Failure to couple any of the functions in this series can make the whole system fail. Consistency of support is required by the long-time horizons of technology innovation. On/off support discourages risk taking or personal commitment at the technical innovative level.

2. Realize that there is no such thing as relying on an isolated function to be solely responsible for creativity. The whole corporation must share this responsibility.

3. Be aware that classical financial analysis rigidly applied to the early stages of the innovation process can seriously inhibit or even totally stifle the process. A sustained level of funding over long periods of time is a critical requirement.

4. Encourage the coexistence of technology development champions and the kind of top management that is supportive yet forceful. These two elements create the push-pull action needed to move innovation forward.

Appropriate functional coupling is, obviously, a critical factor in technological innovation and should thus be seriously considered in designing or modifying organizational structures of technical organizations.

Balanced Arrangement of Barriers and Bonds

The necessity of coupling R&D with other organizational functions has been established; without it, results will not be useful or practical. Another crucial determinant of the structure of R&D organizations—which also helps resolve the coupling dilemma—is to establish an appropriate set of barriers and bonds. This means that organizational and spatial bonds and barriers should be established in such a way as to ensure a balanced flow of information between basic research, applied research, development, and product engineering. A balanced arrangement of barriers and bonds is shown in Figure 9-14.

As you will note in Figure 9-14, basic and applied research can be coupled in one way with a space bond—people in applied and basic work in the same build-

---

[13] Twiss, op. cit., pp. 213-214.
[14] Kottcamp, E. H., and Rushton, Brian M. Stimulating Technological Innovation—Improving the Corporate Environment. *Research Management,* **XXII,** 6 (November 1979): 20-21.

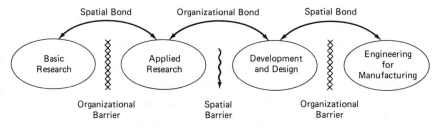

Figure 9-14. Balanced arrangement of barriers and bonds.

ing.[15] But at the same time, if applied people or engineering people can dictate what the basic research people do, they will kill the long-range basic research. To solve this problem, an organizational barrier is created by having basic and applied research people report to two different bosses. This process is repeated to create bonds and barriers, as appropriate, between applied research, development and design, and engineering for manufacturing.

You should remember, then, that a spatial bond enhances communication and feedback, while an organizational bond enhances planning and goal congruence. On the other hand, a spatial or organizational barrier detracts from these, but also prevents overdominance of current crises (e.g., a screaming emergency in manufacturing could cause all work in research to stop—the old story).

Another thing to keep in mind is that there should be one bond and one barrier; never zero and two. In other words, you must not have a space barrier (physical separation of two units) and an organizational barrier (separate reporting relationships). Organizational and spatial links must be used in complementary relations—wherever you have a space barrier, you also have an organizational bond and vice versa (see Figure 9-14). This gives an integrated design by allowing each function to perform its assigned role while linking it to the prior and the subsequent function in the chain.

Nature of Organizational Environment

The environment within which the organization operates will have significant bearing on its structure. The relationship between environment and structure is shown in Table 9-3.

It is clear from this table that the environment of the R&D organization is highly changing, ambiguious and uncertain. Indeed, it is usually turbulent. This suggests that more differentiation and flexibility should be built into the struc-

---

[15] Morton, Jack A. From Research to Technology. *International Science and Technology* (May 1964): 82-92.

Table 9-3. Common Relationships Between Environment and Structure.[a]

ENVIRONMENT	STRUCTURE
Stable	
High certainty	Very formalized
Unchanging products and services	Centralized structure
Few new competitors	Adherence to static principles of organiza-
Consistent government actions	tion
Little technological innovation	Mechanistic system
Mature labor relations	
Stable political and economic conditions	
Changing	
Moderate uncertainty	Moderately formalized
Moderately changing products or services	Functional staff and moderate decentrali-
Stable large competitors with other entering	zation
Predictable change in government actions	Adherence to mixture of static principles and dynamic guidelines
Incremental technological innovation	
Evolutionary external trends	
Turbulent	
Great uncertainty	Informal and ambiguous
Continually changing products or services	Fairly decentralized structure
Changing competitors	Flexible structure
Unpredictable government actions	Pursuit of dynamic guidelines
Major technological innovation	Organic problem-solving system
Rapid social change	
Sense of greater system	

[a]Adapted from Webber, Ross A. "Management: Basic Elements of Managing Organizations," Homewood: Irwin, 1975, pp. 431-439.

ture. In response to the need for differentiation, R&D organizations would have to develop their own mechanisms and organic problem solving structures for performing their tasks and dealing with other corporate divisions as well as external clients and agencies.

The net result would be that the standardized and differentiated structures would exist at different divisions within the same company. Manufacturing electric lamps, for example, is much different from designing community transportation systems, although both are activities at General Electric. Similarly, since manufacturing an automobile is different from designing an aircraft engine, these two units in General Motors should not be similarly structured, nor should they be held rigorously to the same organizational policies and procedures like other organizational units.

To sum up: Choosing an organizational pattern for your engineering or R&D division is, indeed, a complex undertaking. Several factors have been identified as criteria or independent variables that will shape the ultimate character of your organizational structure. While the list of factors is not inclusive, it certainly contains the major forces in shaping the organizational structure.

You must always remember that the structure only provides a framework, it cannot guarantee the achievement of corporate objectives in engineering and R&D. However, it is so important that a poorly structured organization could seriously hinder the achievement of the best defined objectives. Also please bear in mind that since there is no "ideal" organizational structure, the impact of the above determinants of an organizational pattern will vary between different structures. These variations—based on the above analysis—are summarized in Table 9-4.

PRACTICAL TIPS FOR SKILL DEVELOPMENT

As you can see from the discussion throughout this chapter, building (creating and modifying) a sound organizational structure will have a significant impact on the effectiveness of engineering and R&D operations. By way of helping you develop your skills in this area, I shall identify some causes of managerial failure (in addition to those discussed in Chapter 2) and follow with some practical tips for managerial success.

Twenty Easy Ways to Fail as a Manager

Causes of managerial failure are numerous. Here are 20 guaranteed ways to fail in management (fail to accomplish results or to advance in the organization):[16]

1. Have the wrong concept of the job (the good old days).
2. Do not pay the price for management (lonesomeness, fewer peers, self-restraint, etc.).
3. Strive to be liked instead of striving to be respected (opposite of firm but fair).
4. Try to be the good guy or caretaker or father confessor (do not tell subordinates when they are not cutting the mustard).
5. Overdepend on job descriptions for your job and subordinates (remember that the only important way to do the job is by doing what your boss wants and how he wants it done).

---

[16] Based partly on McCarthy, John J. "Why Managers Fail . . . and What to Do About It," Second Edition. New York: McGraw-Hill, 1978, pp. 1-34.

Table 9-4. How to Choose an Organizational Pattern.[a]

DETERMINANTS OF ORGANIZATIONAL STRUCTURES \ ALTERNATE ORGANIZATIONAL DESIGNS	FUNCTIONAL ORGANIZATION	PROJECT ORGANIZATION	PRODUCT ORGANIZATION	MATRIX ORGANIZATION
1. Development of technical people	High	Medium	Low to Medium	Medium
2. Organization goals (achievement of short-term goals)	Low	Medium	Medium to High	Medium to High
3. Task characteristics (extent the design better fits):				
a. scientists	High	Medium	Low	Low
b. engineers	Low	High	Low	High
4. Product lines	Low	Low	High	Low
5. Level of technology (new knowledge, processes, and product development)	High	Low	Medium	Low
6. Functional coupling	Low	Low	Medium	Medium to High
7. Balanced arrangement of barriers and bonds	High	Low	High	Low
8. Environment (degree of stability)	High	Low	Medium	Low

[a]Some information in this table is from Twiss, Brian C. "Managing Technological Innovation." London: Longman, 1974, p. 231.

6. Fail to understand what your boss expects from you.
7. Do not let your subordinates know what you expect from them (poor communication of managerial expectations, standards, etc.).
8. Do not continually upgrade your managerial competence (knowledge, skills, and attitudes).
9. Continue to operate as a technologist with management as part-time job (do not let go of the last job).
10. Do not delegate (do not give your subordinates the opportunity to grow and develop).
11. Make yourself indispensable (i.e., you cannot be promoted because there is no one else to take your place).
12. Fail to protect your most important investment: your career.
13. Fail to stay marketable.
14. Change jobs or careers looking for glamorous rewards (but not considering your ability to excell, your wife, frineds, etc.).
15. Have a tunnel vision (look only at job areas that interest you—jobs you used to handle—and forget the whole picture).
16. Emulate your predecessor blindly.
17. Do not apply management by exception.
18. Fail to maintain a balance between your job objectives, career objectives, and life-style (family, self-fulfillment, hobbies, etc.)
19. Adopt a "leave it to the sergeant" attitude (i.e., if you dislike details leave them to someone else to the point that you are not informed on details and become overdependent on "assistants to").
20. Think and present plans in the language of management (a good manager should think in the language of management—profit and income—but present plans to nonmanagerial people in the language of stimulation—added effort).

How to Develop your Organizational Design Skills—and Succeed

In order to avoid managerial failure in your capacity as organizer, you must develop your skills in this area. Here are some practical tips for building your competence and developing your organizational design skills.[17]

1. Have an organization chart.
2. See that the people concerned are permitted to express opinions and offer suggestions before it is made final.
3. Group similar tasks together.
4. Change the chart to reflect increased capabilities.
5. Have the chart indicate career paths and dual lines of progression.
6. Accompany the chart with a text that clearly defines responsibilities and authorities.

---

[17] Ibid., pp. 252-253.

7. When a chart is changed, make certain that reasons are given. Do not just "feed them the pill."
8. Be constantly aware that change is a threat. Show the benefits of the change.
9. Do not change the organization capriciously as a panacea for meeting new problems.
10. Avoid overlapping responsibilities.
11. Do not regard the chart as "wallpaper," to show observers you have met your responsibilities for "organizing."
12. While resisting the temptation to change frequently, do not regard the chart as static. Be sure it represents the best structuring to meet changing conditions.
13. Provide for meeting anticipated changes. Do not be forced to change the entire organization every time one of these changes takes place.
14. Do not keep the chart under lock and key. Have copies in the hands of everyone involved. It is a form of charter for the enterprise, a means of implementing, to a degree, your objectives. It provides the answer to the questions, "Where do I go for this information? Who has primary responsibility?" It should not be a dark secret, so do not let it become one!

Clarifying your Managerial Roles and Relationships: Develop the Management Responsibility Guide

A key factor for better management of technical organizations is the clear definition of managerial roles and relationships not only within engineering and R&D but also between these divisions and other organizational units. As discussed earlier, position descriptions, like organization charts, delineate the detailed task to be performed, but they cannot show how the organization really functions.[18] Position descriptions are far more concerned with defining an individual's tasks than with how, in carrying out his responsibilities, he interacts with his colleagues. As a result, there is no opportunity to build a framework that can be used to relate and integrate each manager and the work he does to the organization and its goals.

An effective tool that has evolved is called the *management responsibility guide*. Its development was sparked by a linear charting technique, developed by Ernest Hijams and Serge A. Bern, that is used to relate management positions, functions, and responsibility relationships to each other. This guide is a valuable tool used to describe managerial roles and relationships between different positions.

Figure 9-15 presents an example of the management responsibility guide for several functions, management positions, and relationships. You can use this

---

[18] Melcher, Robert D. Roles and Relationships: Clarifying the Manager's Job. *Personnel,* 44, 3 (May-June 1967): 33-41.

Management Position

Relationship Code

- A — General Responsibility
- B — Operating Responsibility
- C — Specific Responsibility
- D — Must be Consulted
- E — May be Consulted
- F — Must be Notified
- G — Must Approve

Number	Function	President	Vice-President Aerospace	Vice-President Manufacturing Director	Manager Engineering Industrial	Manager Technology Industrial	Manager Quality Assurance	Manager Marketing	Manager Contracts	Manager Master Scheduling	Manager Financial Services	Treasurer and Controller	Vice-President Earth Sciences	Vice-President Test Laboratories	Manager Industrial Relations
10.1	Coordinate division budgeting and financial planning activities and communicate financial information to division management.	A-F	A		E-F	E-F	E-F	E-F	D	D-F	Ⓑ				
10.2	Develop project and program schedule requirements, establish, coordinate, and control schedules, and report on status.	A	D-F	D	D-F	D-F	E-F	E-F	E-F	Ⓑ	E			E	
10.3	Direct contract activities and evaluate and approve contract provisions of all division sales proposals and contract documents.	A-F		E	E	E	D-F	D-F	Ⓑ	F	E-F	E-F	E	E	
10.4	Plan and coordinate divisional marketing activities in order to secure the business necessary to maximize the division's capabilities.	A-D	E-F	E-F	E-F	E	D-F	Ⓑ	D-F	F	E-F	E-F	E		
10.5	Develop and design new, and improve existing, electronic and electromechanical aerospace products and processes.	A	E-F	E	Ⓑ	D-F	D-F		D-F		E				
10.6	Secure materials and tools, coordinate personnel and manufacture products to specified quantity, quality, time, and cost requirements.	A		Ⓑ	E	D-F		E	E-F	E	E-F	E-F			
10.7	Establish quality assurance policies, procedures, and controls to insure that products meet applicable standards and specifications.	A	D-F	D-F	E	E	E	D-F	E-F	F	E	E-F			
10.8	Develop and design proprietary products and processes using proven technology specifically adapted to industrial automation.	A-F	E	E	E	Ⓑ	E-F	D-F	E-F	F	E	E-F			

Organization Identification		Number	Management Responsibility Guide	Date	Page
Aerospace		200			No. 1 of 1
Aerospace Division			Approval		

Figure 9-15. The management responsibility guide. (From Melcher, Robert D. Roles and Relationships: Clarifying the Manager's Job. *Personnel,* 44, 3 (May-June 1967): 39.)

valuable device to understand and clarify your managerial roles and relationships with managers on other levels and in other units.

Learn to Succeed in Spite of Top Management

While management is usually an orderly process, innovation can be a disorderly process. To be a good manager, you must find the means to manage a disorderly innovative program in an orderly way without inhibiting disorderly effectiveness. You must learn—and teach your people—to succeed in spite of top management! This attitude is illustrated in the following statement—a permanent part of the successful 3M Company mystique (by its chief executive officer).[19]

As our business grows it becomes increasingly necessary to delegate responsibility and to encourage men and women to exercise their initiative. This requires considerable tolerance. These men and women to whom we delegate authority and responsibility, if they are good people, are going to want to do their jobs in their own way. These are characteristics we want, and people should be encouraged as long as their way conforms to our general pattern of operation.

Mistakes will be made, but if a person is essentially right, the mistakes he or she makes are not as serious in the long run as the mistakes management will make if it is dictatorial and undertakes to tell those under its authority exactly how they must do their job.

Management that is destructively critical when mistakes are made kills initiative and it is essential that we have many people with initiative if we're to continue to grow.

SUMMARY

Chapters 8 and 9 have presented an operational framework of the manager's responsibility in the managerial function of organizing. Chapter 8 has provided a detailed account of fundamental principles of organization structure. Chapter 9 has complemented this discussion by focusing on alternative forms of organizing in engineering and R&D. It has also discussed the criteria or variables that essentially shape the structural design of your organization and shown you how to choose an organizational pattern.

Combined, both chapters have provided you with a practical framework that you can use in evaluating your current organization. Some mechanisms for developing your managerial skills in this area have also been identified. Now that your first managerial function—organizing—has been analyzed and completed, your second function is planning, problem-solving and decision-making. This function will be explored in Chapter 10.

---

[19] Lehr, Lewis W. Stimulating Technological Innovation: The Role of Top Management. *Research Management,* **XXII,** 6 (November 1979): 23-25.

VI
THE PLANNING AND DECISION-MAKING FUNCTION

10
Developing Your Planning and Decision-Making Skills

Now that you have initiated an organizational structure for your division or unit, or made modifications in an existing one, the resulting structure is only a mean toward an end—divisional objectives and organizational goals. Defining these objectives is an integral part of the planning and decision-making function. This activity is a significant dimension of every manager's task.

This chapter deals with the planning and decision-making aspects of your job. The discussion will focus not so much on the tools and techniques (since these vary depending on the types of situations and problems involved), but rather on the processes of planning, decision-making, and problem-solving as managerial activities. The intent is to develop a solid understanding of the concepts and principles involved and a practical framework within which these concepts can be integrated. The theme prevailing throughout the chapter is that effective planning and decision-making are crucial prerequisites for managerial competence, and some guidelines for building your skills in these areas are included.

A detailed statement of strategic planning techniques and decision theory is clearly beyond the scope of this chapter. However, the new concepts in both areas and their practical implications for engineering and R&D managers and supervisors will be explored. While a managerial approach—which is the essence of this book—rather than the specialist's approach is taken in this chapter, the discussion will be indicative of the type of specialist approaches that may apply.

PLANNING SKILLS

Nature and Importance of Managerial Planning

All managers must plan. Planning is an intellectual activity and a major component of the managerial task. It is a process by which managers anticipate future developments and identify courses of action necessary to achieve organizational and divisional objectives. Planning, thus, is a futuristic activity directed toward anticipating, predicting, and dealing with change. Because the only certain thing about the future is its uncertainty, anticipating and managing change—the essence of planning—is a vital managerial function. Indeed, it is the most crucial of all functions.

The output of the planning process is a statement of a recommended course of action to deal with certain future developments. This is the plan. It should be regarded as a blueprint that extends over a future period of time. While the scope and complexity of planning may vary from one organizational level to another, the planning process is essentially the same: a mental process resulting in making decisions about courses of action to be taken in the future. A plan is essentially a commitment to specific courses of action in terms of the what, who, how, when, where, and why of a certain situation.

Why is planning an important managerial task? There are several benefits you can acquire through sound planning. First, it enables you to anticipate problems rather than be surprised by them. It therefore reinforces management by anticipation or proaction rather than management by reaction. Pan American World Airways has a slogan that it would be profitable for us all to adopt: "We want pilots who fly out in front of our planes."[1] In other words, "We want managers who will anticipate the probability of problems and take appropriate actions so that those problems will never arise. Or, if they do arise, corrective actions will be available without the need to produce off-the-cuff, ill-considered actions, which may produce even more problems."

Second, sound planning helps you establish concrete objectives and, thus, creates a sense of mission. Working with these objectives helps you motivate and measure your subordinates' performance.

Third, planning is an absolute requisite for performing your other executive functions, namely, organizing, directing, and controlling. Designing the structure of an organization, directing subordinates, and evaluating progress and performance largely depends on a thorough understanding of divisional objectives and a sound planning of future directions of the organization.

Finally, sound planning is usually characteristic of good management. When management only responds to developments, the bell has begun to toll.[2] Excellent management predetermines developments and thereby controls its corporate future.

To sum up: Of all management functions, planning has a certain primacy. All your other managerial functions are dependent on the effectiveness of planning. Planning also bridges the gap between where an organization is at present and where it wants to be in the future. In this sense, planning is an invaluable managerial function.

---

[1] McCarthy, John J. "Why Managers Fail—and What to Do About It," Second Edition. New York: McGraw-Hill, 1978, p. 224.
[2] Sloma, Richard S. "No-Nonsense Management: A General Manager's Primer." New York: Macmillan, 1977, p. 73.

Who Does the Planning and When?

All managers need to plan regardless of their position in the hierarchy. However, the scope and complexity of planning will increase as you move up the organizational ladder. The same point holds for the degree of uncertainty and the number of variables considered in the planning process. While top managers are preoccupied with overall corporate strategy, rate of growth, and new products and markets, lower-level managers plan different things. Midlevel managers, for example, try to achieve a high degree of coordination, minimize overlapping, and enhance resource utilization between different divisions and organizational units. First-level managers and supervisors spend considerable time planning the actual implementation of policies and procedures, assigning work activities, and devising ways to enhance the efficiency and effectiveness of work operations.

It is clear from this discussion, then, that planning is not an individual or a one-man task; rather it is a team effort encompassing all levels of management. Effective planning is based on the availability of information flowing in all directions in the organization: up, down, and sideways.

Turning to the question of timing, tasks and projects may confront you at any time and may require preparation, organization, and scheduling. Other projects may need to be planned periodically as dictated by the calendar. Examples of planning schedules include launching new projects, annual forecasts and performance planning activities, and quarterly reviews and employee appraisal plans.

Types and Content of Plans

As shown in Table 10-1, a practical classification of plans managers use in terms of their type and content would be according to: duration of the plan, function or use, and breadth or scope.[3]

By Duration. Short-range plans, obviously, cover actions to be completed over short time periods, while long-range plans cover a longer time period. Long-range planning is usually done at upper management levels, while short-range planning takes place chiefly on the lower levels of the organizational structure. Generally speaking, short-range plans include single-use plans which are usually developed to deal with "one-shot" situations for a given purpose or a given period of time and then discarded. A popular form of single-use plans is the budget; once the period of time covered by the budget is completed, the budget is replaced by a new one.

---

[3] For other types of classifications, see Uris, Auren. "The Executive Deskbook," Second Edition. New York: Van Nostrand Reinhold, 1976, p. 82; Sisk, Henry L. "Principles of Management: A Systems Approach to the Management Process." Cincinnati: South Western, 1969, pp. 86-89; and Mosley, Donald C., and Pietri, Jr., Paul H. Management: "The Art of Working With and Through People." Encino (Calif.): Dickenson, 1975, pp. 27-44.

Table 10-1. Types of Plans.

BASIS OF CLASSIFICATION	TYPES OF PLANS
By duration of the plan	Single-use plans
	Standing Plans
By function or use	Operational plans for key organizational functions
By breadth or scope	Objectives
	Policies
	Procedures
	Methods
	Rules

Standing plans or repeat-use plans are usually long-range plans. Such plans are used over and over again to help guide the behavior of members of the organization. Several types of standing plans will be discussed below.

By Function. Another way to classify plans is in terms of the function or use to which they are applied. Plans may be developed for key organizational functions such as marketing, manufacturing, finance, engineering, and research and development. The functional grouping of plans would assist management in understanding the interactions between major areas of operations. This would, in turn, help in spotting potential conflicts and problem areas and help in dealing with them.

By Breadth or Scope. A third way of classifying plans is in respect to their breadth or scope. The major types that can be identified include: objectives, policies, procedures, methods, and rules (Table 10-1). These are also common examples of standing plans.

Objectives. Objectives are statements of company ends and goals to be accomplished. An objective is a general statement of the mission of the organization and of what it intends to do. This statement tells what the organization is after but does not identify how the objectives are to be achieved. Organizational objectives are filtered down to divisions and departments, where they are translated into specific plans to be implemented for achieving overall organizational ends. This process results in establishing a hierarchy of objectives for each kind of function at each level in an organization constituting a mean-end chain.

Defining organizational and divisional objectives is an integral part of the planning process. You should always have a clear and concise picture of your organizational and divisional objectives because without it you will not be able to perform your other managerial functions: organizing, directing, and controlling.

Policies. While objectives tell *what* is to be done, policies focus on *how* the objectives will be accomplished. A policy can be defined as a general guide to action. Policies, out of necessity, are broad statements directed to guide the behavior of organization members in making decisions and handling problem situations. Well-developed policies ensure a continuing focus on predetermined objectives, enhance consistency in action, and minimize randomness in decision-making situations. Policies are usually developed by high-level executives. Managers and department heads, however, may make policy recommendations subject to the approval of management at higher levels. Examples of policies include: "R&D projects will not be subcontracted unless the company does not have the necessary resources and expertise to perform the job," or "We encourage promotion from within of engineers with demonstrated managerial potential."

Procedures. Whereas policies are broad guides to accomplish the objectives, procedures are more specific steps describing how to accomplish policies. A "standard operating procedure" specifies the steps to be followed in handling intradepartmental or interdepartmental daily operations. Well-established procedures help reduce ambiguity and confusion in the manner in which divisions and departments operate and provide uniformity of action through a standardized sequence. For example, to implement the policy of promoting from within, a standard operating procedure will spell out how promising talent will be identified, developed and trained, and how managerial potential of candidates will be determined. Another example is the standard operating procedure identifying the steps to be followed by engineering, in its relation with other company divisions, in competitive bidding for internal and external operations.

Methods. Methods are detailed plans describing the manner and sequence of performing individual tasks necessary for completing a specific assignment within an operating division or department. Methods are developed to influence the behavior of an individual. Examples include a prescribed method for developing a prototype design or for the assembly of a given product.

It is important for you to remember here that the difference between policies, procedures, and methods in terms of their scope and depth is a matter of degree—it is a relative difference. Policies and methods can be perceived as falling at the opposite ends of a continuum with procedures somewhere between the two. Put differently, while policies are the broadest of all plans and originate at the highest levels of an organization, procedures are concerned with the operations of major functional departments and are interdepartmental in their effect; and methods are specifically stated steps to guide and direct the performance of individuals.[4]

Rules. Rules are prescribed standards of behavior directed to impose restrictions concerning the personal behavior of employees. They are inflexible and

---

[4] For more on this point, see Sisk, op. cit., p. 89.

spell out penalties for violations. Examples include rules concerning smoking regulations on company premises, dress codes, employee absences, and so on.

Implications. The discussion of type and content of managerial plans has at least three practical implications for you. First of all, while the components of plans (objectives, policies, procedures, methods, and rules) are necessary and have important functions, an overabundance of such plans can stifle initiative and result in overmanagement. A balance must be maintained between the organization's needs for planning and control, and the individual's need for autonomy and flexibility.

Second, the amount of discretion and freedom of choice the employee has will tend to decrease as the number of plans adopted by the organization increases. In other words, as the organization moves from setting objectives to policies, procedures, methods, and rules, the employee will increasingly have less discretion and choice in performing his responsibilities.

Finally, any organization can tolerate a truly enormous number of errors in detail—if the strategic direction is relevant and correct.[5] Therefore, it pays to invest proportionately more time in strategic rather than tactical planning.

How to Plan: An Action Planning Model

Since planning is a logical and systematic activity, it would be helpful to develop a sequence of planning steps that you can follow in "planning for planning." Steps of an action planning model along with the outcome of each phase appear in Table 10-2. The model consists of eight phases:

1. Objectives.
2. Tasks.
3. Human resources.
4. Facilities and resources.
5. Procedures for implementation.
6. Cost estimates.
7. Time schedule.
8. Follow-up and review.

Objectives. As shown in Table 10-2, the first step in the planning process is to identify the purpose of your planning. Stating your objectives in concrete form helps determine the direction of your plan. Good objectives should be achievable, measurable, and operational (not abstract). When it is difficult or impossible to state objectives quantitatively, qualitative objectives are better than no objectives at all. In setting up your planning objectives, it is also helpful to ask, "why

---

[5] Sloma, op. cit., pp. 83-84.

Table 10-2. An Action Planning Model.

PHASE	ACTION PLANNING	PLANNING OUTCOME
1	What is the objective of your plan? Why is it necessary? What are the most important priorities?	Objective definition and determining priorities (the why)
2	What is the task to be done?	Identification of the task to be done to achieve objectives of the plan (the what)
3	Who should be involved in furthering the plan?	Manning the plan (the who)
4	What are the resources available to achieve the objectives of the plan? What will it take to achieve these objectives?	Facilities and resources needed
5	How will the plan be put into action? What are the methods to be employed for executing the plan?	Mechanisms and procedures for plan implementation
6	How much would it cost to implement the plan?	Cost budget
7	When will the plan be completed? How long will it take to complete each phase?	Timetable
8	How can the plan be evaluated? What type of control mechanisms are needed for follow-up and control?	Follow-up, control, and review mechanisms

is this plan necessary?" This forces you to think of the general objectives of the plan, its relationship to other jobs and activities within your own division, and its overall link with the objectives of the organization. Therefore, establishing the objectives of your plan has a paramount importance for determining its general thrust and, ultimately, its success.

Tasks. After defining planning objectives, determine the task to be done: What do you need to do to achieve these objectives? Here you should get a clear understanding of what is expected of your division in order to achieve the objectives in question. It is critical at this point to see a close link between the "what" and the "why" of planning to ensure consistency between the objectives and the content of the plan.

Human Resources. Determine the people who should be involved in furthering the plan. Several questions need to be answered here including:[6]

---

[6] Some parts of this section are based on Uris, op. cit.; and Sartain, Aaron Q., and Baker, Alton W. "The Supervisor and the Job," Third Edition. New York: McGraw-Hill, 1978, p. 40.

- Who will authorize the plan?
- What people need to coordinate in the plan?
- Who will develop the plan?
- Who will approve the plan?

This phase in the planning process relates to the manning of the plan. Checking the capabilities and qualifications of your staff at this point would help you spot the areas needing to be strengthened, identify your training needs, and perhaps more important, determine the key people to be involved with the plan.

Facilities and Resources. In addition to the human resources necessary for manning your plan, review the other resources and facilities needed for implementing the plan. Given that these resources will vary depending on the nature of the project involved, you may list available resources for a production plan, for example, under the following headings:

Raw materials
Fittings and supplies
Production equipment
Auxiliary equipment
Standby equipment
Handling equipment
Packing materials

The combined outcome of the last two steps in the planning process then would enable you to identify the resources necessary for implementing the plan as well as the available resources of your department, and the company, to help achieve the objectives.

Procedures for Implementation. Determine the methods to be employed for putting the plan into action—for executing the plan. This phase of the model (Table 10-2) concerns the actual implementation of the plan and what it will take to get the plan moving. Here you will need to identify, among other things, the means you intend to use to achieve your goals. You should now see the strong interrelationship between different phases of the planning process: objectives, resources, and methods and means to be employed.

Cost Estimates. Determine a cost estimate or a budget for the plan. Cost considerations are prime factors in all projects and must, therefore, be explicitly stated and always kept in mind. In engineering and R&D projects—like all other projects—resources, schedule, and performance are of prime importance. In your planning activities, then, your utmost concern should be given to getting the job done most efficiently and effectively within the budget and resources you have and on time.

Time Schedule. Set up a timetable of the planned operation. Specific dates and deadlines should be drawn up for the various phases of the plan. These deadlines must be realistic. Setting up unrealistic deadlines regardless of the amount of work to be done and your staff capabilities will achieve nothing but sheer frustration. It is also important to take into account the nature of each phase of your plan and resources available.

Follow-up and Review. Finally, establish built-in control mechanisms for follow-up and control. Such mechanisms would ensure up-to-date information about the status of the plan and progress reports so the necessary adjustments can be made on time. Furthermore, appropriate review mechanisms should be developed using specific yardsticks based on the predetermined planning objectives. It would also be desirable in the case of large expensive projects to have a substitute or a contingency plan just in case the original plan fails.

Needless to say, the above action planning model does not necessarily have to be followed in this sequence, which was developed essentially to simplify the discussion. Different phases of the model can be implemented simultaneously. Two important points should be kept in mind: First, all phases of the model are necessary and integrating them would provide you with an effective tool for sound planning. Second, management planning is a two-step process: analysis—defining in detail the objectives and the tasks needed to achieve those objectives; and synthesis—ranking by priority the sequence of specific assignment of the defined tasks.[7]

Barriers to Planning and What To Do About Them

Now that the case for planning as a managerial activity has been made, it is important to recognize the fact that there are some obstacles and barriers to the planning process. The most common barriers relate to the following factors:

1. Tedium of planning.
2. Management ego and attitudes.
3. Time and cost.
4. Intellectual activity.
5. Clarity of objectives.
6. Inadequate information.
7. Management philosophy and external forces.

Tedium of Planning. Since planning is always a "staff" function, there is a strong tendency by some managers not to recognize its importance. To them managerial planning is not complicated, but it is tedious—that is why the temptation is strong to avoid it.[8]

---

[7] Sloma, op. cit., p. 149.
[8] Ibid., pp. 61-62.

Managers are hesitant to seek out and perform planning tasks because the most salient aspect of planning is that it is an iterative process. That is, one must examine all feasible alternatives and document possible scenarios so that, given any plausible eventuality, one has prepared a response that will lead to one's goal. This is a painstaking, desk-bound activity. Indeed, planning requires patience and perseverance beyond any "doing" action.

You must check and recheck to make sure that all feasible alternatives in a certain situation have been identified and that proper weights have been assigned to those alternatives. This could be a tedious process—and no one enjoys tedium.

Management Ego and Attitudes. Business failures and poor decisions are rarely the result of too much planning.[9] Almost universally they can be traced to management ego—the temptation to say, "I don't need a plan, I am sure I can handle what ever develops." This attitude—characterized as "shooting from the hip"— should be distinguished from paralysis by analysis, where the manager creates an illusion of insatiable desire for more information disguised as the "need for thorough planning." Relying on a collective well-developed and documented plan, though taking more effort and time, is usually far superior in managerial decision-making than one individual's experience and judgment.

Time and Cost. Another major barrier to planning is the time, money, and effort involved in it. What many managers fail to recognize, however, is that effective planning is a good investment and is less costly to an organization than no planning at all. Since planning is basically a tool of preventive action, the payoffs of good planning are far greater than the costs incurred.

Intellectual Activity. Planning is essentially a mental activity, but many managers are more comfortable—by habit—taking actions than thinking about problems. They find it difficult to deal with abstractions and think conceptually in terms of models and relationships between complex variables in hypothetical situations.

This barrier undoubtedly exists because managers, by nature, are doers not thinkers. In addition, managers are subject to constant pressures and demands on their time to the point that they do not have any time left for real, uninterrupted thinking, let alone planning.

In one of my recent management development seminars for middle-level technical managers, many of them agreed that they only had time to think and to plan different activities while driving back and forth from work or while in the bathroom. This point was supported by the findings of a study of British middle and top managers reporting that managers worked for a half hour or more without interruption only about once every two days![10]

---

[9] Ibid., pp. 71-72.
[10] Stewart, Rosemary. "Managers and Their Jobs." London: Macmillan, 1967.

Clarity of Objectives. Another obstacle to better planning is the lack of clear objectives and a sharp definition of the problems toward which planning is being directed. The situation is even worse when the problems and objectives may not only be unclear, they may also be wrong. For proper planning, the problem needs to be clearly defined, with the symptoms and real causes neatly identified and separated.

Inadequate Information. Having too much, too little, or the wrong information can be a major barrier to the planning process. Getting the right information, in the right amount, at the right time is a prerequisite for effective planning.

As discussed in Chapter 7, remember that one of the fundamental roles managers assume is the informational role. This is the manager's role as a monitor, scanning his environment for information; as disseminator, passing some of his privileged information directly to his subordinates; and as a spokesman, keeping his superiors informed and sending some of his information to people outside his unit.

Management Philosophy and External Forces. A major determinant of the effectiveness of the planning process is the values, philosophies, and attitudes of top management toward the planning activity. It is, therefore, beneficial to the manager to understand the orientations, biases, and value judgments of key managers and executives. This understanding enables hime to better deal with potential interdepartmental conflicts and to carefully identify directions for his planning efforts.

While the attitudes and psychological makeup of all managers within an organization affect the planning process, external forces are undoubtedly of equal importance. Although the manager might have little or no control over such forces, he must seriously consider them in planning. Examples include the political climate, social and economic trends, cultural values and customs, technology, changes in customers' tastes and preferences, labor philosophy, and so on.

This is, of course, why the manager need to think in "systems" terms, looking at the organization as an open system in constant interaction with its environment. Failure to do so can only result in a superficial understanding of the organization and an oversimplified image of the manager's job. Managerial failure will, then, be inescapable.

As you can see from the above discussion, there are several barriers to the planning process. It cannot be done in a vacuum or haphazardly. Recognizing the existence of barriers is an essential requirement for understanding and coping with them. Dealing with these barriers along the above guidelines is crucial for the effectiveness of your planning efforts.

Managerial Planning In Action

To what extent do managers really plan? As discussed in Chapter 7, there is considerable evidence that the view that the manager is a reflective and systematic planner is actually a myth and does not really hold up in practice (real-life situations). Research clearly shows that managers work at an unrelenting pace, and that their activities are characterized by brevity, variety, and discontinuity.[11] Managers are strongly oriented to action and dislike reflective activities. The point you need to remember, however, is that managerial planning is not unimportant activity, but rather the manner in which it is done is not as neat, intellectual, and systematic as management textbooks lead us to believe.

There is reason to believe, then, that the pressures of his job drive the manager to be superficial in his actions—to overload himself with work, encourage interruption, respond quickly to every stimulus, seek the tangible and avoid the abstract, make decisions in small increments, and do everything abruptly.[12] So planning, while still important, is apparently done unsystematically.

How to Develop your Planning Skills: Some Guidelines

Developing planning skills is very crucial. Here are some practical tips in order to help you in this respect.

Recognize Causes of Managerial Failure in Planning. Managerial failure in planning is caused by several factors. These include the following:[13]

1. Failure to consider each of the people whom the manager's plan will affect. Viewing the plan from these people's standpoint and seeing how it could affect their needs, objectives, and personal interests would facilitate getting their support in adopting the plan.
2. Failure of the manager to provide alternative options in case the original plan does not get adopted.
3. Failure of the manager to anticipate change. Just because a course of action produced satisfactory results in the past does not necessarily mean it will work again now or in the future. In this period of unprecendented rate of change, do not look at things the way they used to be—they always change. While we cannot always predict change, we can anticipate it, and effective planning should reflect such consideration.
4. Unwillingness of the manager to take calculated risks. Risk-taking is always associated with planning which is an integral part of management. Note that advancement to higher-level management positions is partly contingent on the manager's record of risk-taking in planning and decision-making.
5. The manager's failure to establish priorities makes him attracted to work on the short-range goals but overlooks the long-range objectives. The

---

[11] Mintzberg, Henry. The Manager's Job: Folklore and Fact. *Harvard Business Review* (July–August 1975).
[12] Ibid.
[13] This discussion is partly based on McCarthy, op. cit., pp. 240-244.

easy projects, therefore, get done first, while the hard ones may die in the top right-hand desk drawer!

6. The manager's failure to make plans known to those involved would result in poor planning and communication breakdown. Information withholding is a powerful game in many quarters. The manager holds the cards close to his chest because it makes him feel privy to information denied others.

7. Failure to establish appropriate measurements at the time a plan is prepared. This failure makes evaluation of the plan difficult, if not impossible.

From the above sample of possible causes of managerial failure in planning, it is clear that by recognizing these factors—and doing something about them—your planning efforts should be more effective and your skills should be improved.

Follow the Ten Commandments for Effective Planning.

1. Review and incorporate policy guidelines into the planning process. Policy determination should precede planning.
2. Marshall organizational resources—such as labor, capital, and equipment—specifically for planning.
3. Recognize budgeting as both a planning and a control process. A budget is one of the tangible expressions of the planning effort.
4. Consider the time element in planning. Time frames are important because planning is related to various time spans: short-range, intermediate, and long-range. Control addresses itself to the present, and evaluation reviews the impact and success of plans in the past.
5. Involve people who are affected in the planning process. Keep plans, budgets, and systems as simple as possible.
6. Define task assignments, authority delegations and responsibilities for individuals involved. Determine desired outcomes or results.
7. Develop priorities among the various plans put into action.
8. Be prepared to resolve conflicts arising during plan implementation. Deal directly with the attitudes and feelings of those who disagree with an adopted plan.
9. Put plans in writing as this will improve planning itself, facilitate communication, and creates a commitment to a specific action. Incorporate reasoning in every plan.
10. Maintain the plans through specific review and control processes. Provide for appropriate monitoring and evaluation by setting deadlines and making necessary changes.

Develop a Continuation Plan for Keeping Things Rolling in Your Absence. Naturally, the details of the continuation plan will vary from executive to executive depending on his job responsibilities, the length of time he will be away, who will be left in charge, and so on. The following tips will make your continuation plan work in your absence.[14]

1. Always keep your superior and subordinates reasonably well informed about what is going on.
2. Train one particular person to take over your job in emergency absences.
3. Make your assistant privy to as many of your current problems and concerns as possible.
4. Use short absences and your vacation as training periods for both plan and personnel.
5. Prepare a continuation folder to include key job descriptions, an outline of your own duties, whom you report to on what, who reports to you, where key items are located, who can answer questions, etc.
6. Have job descriptions written by key personnel, outlining their areas of responsibility and detailing their duties and the names of all subordinates.
7. Make sure your folder includes a plan of action for continuing present projects and for deciding about upcoming matters of major significance, plus a review of proposals for change, an outline of future projects, and any other helpful information.
8. Revise and update these reports as often as advisable, but at least semi-annually.
9. Keep your continuation folder constantly up to date by filing recent correspondence, memoranda dealing with current problems, etc., in it. Weed these out from time to time.
10. Go over this folder with the man you have picked to take over in your absence, and let him know where it is kept.
11. Since the typical executive's secretary becomes a key source of information and opinion ("I believe Mr. Jones would handle that situation this way . . ."), let your secretary know your expectations in this regard.
12. Be sure to give some thought to the question of whether you should leave word as to where you can be reached in case of emergency. This highly personal decision must be made and acted on.

So far in this chapter I have focused on the planning process as a significant aspect of your job. The nature, importance, and types of managerial plans have been identified. An action planning model has also been developed and the barriers to the planning effort discussed. Finally, some mechanisms for developing your managerial skills have been described. The balance of this chapter will deal with your decision-making and problem-solving skills.

---

[14] Uris, op. cit., p. 90.

DECISION-MAKING AND PROBLEM-SOLVING SKILLS

Nature and Importance of Decision-Making

Decision-making is what managers get paid for. Indeed, the manager's prime purpose in being is to make decisions. Whether he is building (or modifying) an organizational structure, developing a plan, evaluating subordinates' performance, or directing them, the manager is constantly making decisions. Making decisions, then, is a primary managerial task and—as discussed in Chapter 1—one of the major criteria an individual should meet in order to be considered a manager.

It is important for you to remember that the essence of managing is to take risks—to make decisions.[15] Sometimes, of course, the manager manages best by delaying a decision, or even by refusing to make one. But this still entails a risk, because delay may give a problem a chance to grow. Even then the manager has made a decision—he has decided not to decide.

It is a fundamental of managing that the person who is not willing to take the risk of deciding will never be a manager. However, you might be interested to know that some managers do not live—they simply exist. They stand in the stadium but rarely do they come down into the arena. They are watchers, not doers.

Your decision-making ability, then, is the factor that weighs most heavily in your success or failure as a manager. It requires a set of specific skills such as the ability to collect information, organize it, and synthesize it into a meaningful form so alternate options can be identified and evaluated.

As you can see, decision-making is an intellectual process which, in addition to the skills, must be based on sound knowledge of basic concepts, principles, and techniques. But knowledge by itself is passive—it must be put into action; it must be applied and used. In short, for effective decision-making you should require and develop sound intellectual abilities (analysis, conceptualization, synthesis, and so on) backed up with practical skills relating to information gathering, resource allocation, negotiation, and so on.

However, knowledge and skills by themselves are not sufficient ingredients for effective decision-making. There is a third element: attitude, that is, the manager's attitude toward risk taking. Indeed, a decision without risk is not even worth making. While your education, social and economic background, personality style, common sense, values, and experience have a lot to do with the type of decisions you make, both personal and professional, the single most important variable in the decision-making process, I believe, is your judgment.

Good judgment cannot be taught. It can probably be developed and sharpened through practice and experience. These combined factors, then, will shape your risk-taking attitude. Not only will they determine your attitude

---

[15] Mason, Joseph G. "How to Build Your Management Skills." New York: McGraw-Hill, 1965, p. 5.

toward the risk associated with decision-making, but they will also influence the amount of risk you will be willing to assume or undertake. To sum up: Making decisions is a way of life for managers. This activity encompasses the entire management spectrum and is an integral part of every function the manager performs. This includes the knowledge of when to stick by a decision, as well as when to reverse a decision that is proving to have been a bad one. Good judgment is the key to good decisions. Effective decision-making requires a solid knowledge of principles, concepts, and decision-making techniques; sharp skills in gathering, analyzing, and evaluating information and alternate options; and psychological readiness to live with the risk and uncertainty associated with managerial decisions.

Decision-Making as a Managerial Task

Decision-making, then, is a process requiring a specific set of skills using certain techniques. Specifically, what is decision-making? In operational terms, decision-making is the process of selecting a course of action from among all courses of action available to the decision-maker to solve a specific problem or set of problems. By its very nature, decision-making involves a choice, and decision-making situations are choice situations. The alternative selected is the decision. The process view of decision-making is a realistic approach because it is functional, practical, and conceptually sound. It also views decision-making as an intellectual process consisting of a sequence of steps involved in solving a problem or problems.

Remember that your managerial task can be perceived as a sequential process of planning and implementing activities and decision points. Because decision-making covers the entire spectrum of engineering and R&D management functions, making a decision usually involves the transformation of a requirement into an operational actuality. It follows that as a decision-maker, your task is to alter current activity states to attain an objective expeditiously by selecting from vague or conflicting alternatives.

An important point here is that if you are faced with a situation where there are no possible alternative choices of ways for solving a problem, a decision is not involved. Put differently, any situation where you do not have a choice is not a decision-making situation by definition. Examples include the instructions given by your boss as "orders" or situations where organizational policies must be followed rigidly to the point that the manager does not have any choice but to manage "by the book."

While these might still be problem situations, solving them does not involve choice. Indeed, in some instances you do not have choice at all, and thus going through the decision-making process is pointless. Those are the situations where the manager receives instructions from above, and he is simply expected to carry them out.

How, then, does decision-making differ (or relate to) from planning or problem-solving? If planning is one of the major subsystems of your managerial task, decision-making is part of that subsystem. The scope of planning is much broader than that of decision-making. Since decisions are made at every step in the planning process, as discussed above, they are closely interrelated with planning. Also note that while it is possible to use a plan to arrive at a decision, decisions and plans are not the same. Decision-making, therefore, should not be considered as an end in itself. Rather, the decision-making process is one of the critical steps in the broader—and more inclusive—process of planning.

In the course of planning, many decisions are made. These include selecting or rejecting certain types of information, allocating certain resources, pursuing selected objectives, and formulating strategies to achieve them. These activities involve choices or decisions. While decision-making is a mental activity encompassing the entire management process, it is probably a higher proportion of the content of the planning function of management than it is of any of the others.[16]

It is interesting to note here that the difference between an executive's decision and the decision of a planner is one of degree—not kind—since both are making choices.[17] The executive's decisions are overt in their nature and are recognized because they commit company resources, but the planner's decisions are covert and can be retracted and reevaluated at will.

So much for the relationship between decision-making and planning. What about decision-making and problem-solving? Some authorities tend to see both sets of activities as being different.[18] I do not share this view. Problem-solving situations are essentially decision-making situations as long as the manager has several options open to him—choice. In the absence of this choice, as discussed above, there still is a problem to be solved, but it is not a decision-making situation.

The processes that managers go through for decision-making or problem-solving (choice situations) are basically the same. In fact, decision-making is actually applied problem-solving.[19] However, there might be a difference in terms of the degree of risk.[20] In problem-solving situations, a proper, right solution to a problem is sure-fire—you are practically sure of getting the results desired. But in decision-making situations, there is always an uncertainty factor since you seldom have total information about the situation with which you are dealing.

---

[16] Emory, William, and Niland, Powell. "Making Management Decisions." New York: Houghton Mifflin, 1968, p. 282.
[17] Sisk, op. cit., p. 83.
[18] Fulmer, Robert M. "Supervision: Principles of Professional Management." Beverly Hills: Glencoe Press, 1976, p. 181.
[19] Duncan, W. Jack. Supervisory Decision-Making and Employee Participation. In Newport, M. Gene (Ed), op. cit., p. 37.
[20] Uris, op. cit., p. 68.

Types of Decision Situations

It is difficult to classify decision situations because there is no single satisfactory way to do a job. As discussed above, any problem involving a choice process is a decision situation. Two types of decision situations can generally be identified: programmed and nonprogrammed.

Programmed Decisions. Programmed decisions are recurring and predictable. When problems are of repetitive nature, well-defined search and choice procedures are developed and used to solve these problems each time they occur. Decisions of this type are programmed in contrast to nonprogrammed decisions, which occur in ill-defined, complex, and nonrepetitive problem situations.[21] Simple programmed problems are solved by the use of habits of response, standard operating procedures, and clerical routines. Examples include production scheduling, shift assignments, and reordering as inventory reaches a certain level.

Nonprogrammed Decisions. While programmed decisions can be planned for and anticipated, nonprogrammed decisions must be dealt with as they develop. The nonprogrammed problem does not lend itself to a response routine.[22] These problems are usually ill-defined and complex, with a large number of variables which are often less predictable or measurable. The manager has little specific experience to guide him. Many engineering and R&D decisions are highly nonprogrammed. Just like nonprogrammed decisions in other areas, they do not follow routinely from explicit decision rules.

Levels of Decisions

At what level should a decision be made? The level at which a decision should be made is based upon the nature of the decision. Five decision characteristics must be assessed.[23]

1. Futurity, how far into the future the decision commits the department or organization. The longer the commitment, the higher the level at which it should be made.
2. Reversibility, the speed with which a decision can be reversed and its major consequences resolved. The more difficult a decision is to reverse, the higher the level at which it should be made.
3. Impact, the extent to which other areas or activities within the department or organization will be affected by the decision. The more extensive the impact of the decision, the higher up it should be made.

---

[21] Simon, Herbert A. The New Science of Management Decision. New York: Harper & Row, 1960, p. 5.
[22] Emory and Niland, op. cit., p. 6.
[23] This discussion is partly based on Fuller, Don. Decision-Making: A Little Technique Goes a Long Way. *Machine Design* (July 22, 1976): 102–106.

4. Quality, the way the social, human, ethical, and other values go into making a decision. The more qualitative factors involved, the higher the level at which the decision should be made.
5. Periodicity, whether the decision is recurrent or rare. The rarer the decision, the higher up it should be made.

When the specific level at which a decision should be made is determined, two principles should be followed:

1. The decision should be made at the lowest level consistent with good operations, thereby placing it as close to the scene of action as possible.
2. The decision must be made at a level high enough to ensure full consideration of, though not necessarily full involvement in, all activities or objectives that affect it.

The first principle is a guide for determining how far down in the organization the decision *should* be made; the second indicates how far down it *can* be made. When these two points are too widely separated, or the number of persons involved seems excessive, close scrutiny is suggested, especially if it is suspected that personalities and their preferences are playing a major role.

The following quote spells out the above principles very well:

The best person to decide what research work shall be done is the man who is doing the research. The next best is the head of the department (within the research laboratory). After that you leave the field of best persons and meet increasingly worse groups. The first of these is the research director, who is probably wrong more than half the time. Then comes a committee which is wrong most of the time. Finally, there is a committee of company vice presidents, which is wrong all the time.[24]

The Decision-Making Process

How do managers make decisions? What are the steps in the decision-making process? Are there some guidelines that managers can follow for action in decision-making? Since these questions are very interrelated, let me answer them by discussing, first, an approach to how managerial decisions "should be" made; second, how managers actually make decisions in practice; and, finally, some of the barriers in the decision-making process.

In spite of the prime role decision-making plays in the management process, executives often find it difficult to describe and analyze the decision-making process. Consider the two following situations:

---

[24] VanTassel, Karl R. Managing Research and Development. *Research Management,* **VIII**, 3 (1965): 148.

"To what do you attribute your success?" asked a young man of a corporate president.

"Two words," responded the president, "good decisions!"

"But how did you learn to make good decisions?" the young man continued.

"One word," replied the president, "experience!"

"But how did you get the experience?" asked the young man.

"Two words," the president answered, "bad decisions!"[25]

Fortune magazine asked executives of some of the largest and most successful
corporations to describe how they make decisions. A few of their illuminating
answers were:

"I don't think businessmen know how they make decisions. I know I
don't."

"You don't know how you do it. You just do it."

"There are no rules."

"It is like asking a pro baseball player to define the swing that has always
come natural to him."

"Whenever I think, I make a mistake."

"If a vice-president asks me how I am able to choose the right course, I
have to say, I'm damned if I know."[26]

While the above comments show the difficulties encountered in undertaking
a systematic analysis of the decision-making process, there is a growing body of
knowledge in this area contributed by both practitioners and scholars. A starting point for understanding these contributions would be an analysis of how
managerial decisions should be made.

Steps in the Decision-Making Process. Decision-making is an affair of the mind,
an intellectual process. It consists of a sequence of steps starting with an input
(a problem) and ending with an output (action). In this sense, decision-making
is a system of inputs, processes, and outputs.

There are some clear rational steps to decision-making that compose a prescrip-
tive model of how decisions should be made. This model, implemented properly,
can improve the process and help the manager make better decisions. After a
description of this rational model of what should be, a discussion of how managers actually make decisions—what is—will follow.

As shown in Figure 10-1, the steps in the rational decision-making process
are:

1. Objective definition.
2. Problem diagnosis.

---

[25] Unknown source.
[26] McDonald, John. How Businessmen Make Decisions. *Fortune* (August 1955): p. 84.

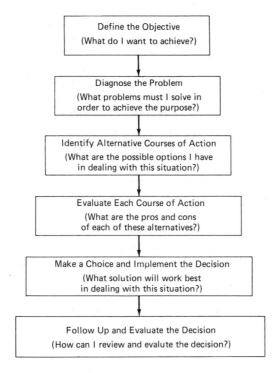

Figure 10-1. Steps in the decision-making process—the rational approach.

3. Identification of alternative courses of action.
4. Evaluation of each course of action.
5. Making of a choice and decision implementation.
6. Follow-up and decision evaluation.

Objective Definition. The first step in the decision-making process is to identify the objective of this activity. Since decision-making is a goal-directed effort, defining the basic end or ends which the manager seeks through his decision effort is of prime importance at this stage of the process. The end purpose of any decision, after all, should be to accomplish certain results. This phase is often implied, assumed, or taken as a "given." Whether stated explicitly or implicitly, the main question the decision-maker should answer at this point is, "What do I want to achieve?"

Why is it important to have a set of objectives in mind? Because these objectives or goals represent ends or states of affairs the organization seeks to reach (increasing market share, reducing inefficiency, increasing return on investment, and so on). Without having a set of objectives in mind, it is impossible to recognize the existence of a problem (the next step in the decision-making process).

It follows that for effective decision-making, the manager needs to recognize that something should be done differently or that something is being done differently that should not be.[27]

In other words, the decision-maker must be aware of the problem situation, and the key to this awareness is the concrete identification of objectives as desired states of affairs. An increase in sales by 5% in a certain year, for example, does not mean much until compared with the company's objectives in this area only to find out that it fell short of these objectives. By the same token, a student will be unhappy with his performance if his course grade is lower than he expected.

You should distinguish between "purpose" and "objective." While a purpose is usually a general statement that is long-term in nature, an objective (or a goal) is considered something more immediate, deriving from a purpose.[28] It is also important to illustrate the hierarchical relationship of goals through the means-end chain: The means at a higher level become an end for the next-lower level. In this sense, the objectives or goals of the engineering or R&D unit (just like any other unit) are actually means toward an end—they are means for achieving the ultimate purpose(s) of the organization.

In this stage of the decision-making process, the objectives to be defined should be operational, practical, attainable, and challenging. The statement of an objective should include an explicit statement of any necessary constraints.[29] Such contraints may exist in relation to how the objective is to be attained; or how resources are to be used; or how to avoid conflicts with other organizational goals.

Organizational units or departments frequently make decisions that are good for them individually but that are less than optimal for the larger organization. This is called *suboptimization.* It is a situation where there is a trade-off that increases the advantages to one unit or function but decreases the advantages to another unit or function. For example, the engineering manager might argue effectively for an increased product development budget to make the product "technically perfect" while the marketing manager wants to rush the product to the marketplace and thus buy valuable time (getting there before the competition), which might prove to be more beneficial to the organization in the long run.

It is important to emphasize the fact that you will run into many of these trade-offs characterizing suboptimization situations. This is because of the multiple objectives organizations want to achieve simultaneously, the varying degrees of importance attached to these objectives, different perceptions and value systems between departments and managers, and their tendency to take a segmental

[27] Huse, Edgar F. "The Modern Manager." St. Paul: West Publishing Company, 1979, p. 118.
[28] Emory and Niland, op. cit., p. 272.
[29] Ibid.

view of the organization (from their divisional perspective) rather than a holistic view of the total system.

There are two tips that can help you at this stage of the decision-making process.[30] First, answer the two following questions in a definitive, measurable way:

1. What is to be accomplished? What are the results expected to come from a decision?
2. What are the resource limits within which I must stay? What are the resources (people, space, equipment, budgets, and so on) available for expenditure in carrying out this decision?

The answer to both questions will provide you with the objectives to be accomplished and their constraints. Remember that without a well-defined objective, any route will get you there!

The other practical tip is to classify objectives according to importance. As discussed above, since objectives do vary in importance, you should list them under two headings: MUSTS and WANTS. The MUSTS set the limits that cannot be violated by any alternatives. Objectives that are WANTS do not set absolute limits but express relative desirability. By distinguishing between MUSTS and WANTS in setting objectives, you will avoid the mistake of settling for an alternative action, only to find later that it is not satisfactory because some essential requirement in making the decision was forgotten.

To sum up: Objective definition is an integral part of the decision-making process. Concrete objectives must be identified which should be consistent with the general purposes and the stated prime objectives of the organization. Well-defined operational objectives would be quite helpful in detecting and identifying problems to be solved by the decision-maker.

Problem Diagnosis. As shown in Figure 10-1, the second step in the decision-making process is to diagnose the problem: to recognize and analyze it. This is the most important step in the decision-making process—and also the most difficult. It is the most important because your task here is quite similar to that of the doctor—to come up with the right diagnosis. What differentiates a good from a poor doctor is not, in fact, the ability to prescribe (anyone can prescribe). Rather, it is the ability to diagnose.

An excellent prescription for the wrong disease will not do the patient any good—it might, in fact, kill him! In short, your job as a manager is to identify the right problem, but if you fail to do so, your solution either fails completely or succeeds only temporarily. In a very fundamental sense, then, the diagnostic

---

[30] This discussion is partly based on Sartain and Baker, op. cit., p. 42.

phase of decision-making sets the tone for the remaining steps in the problem-solving process and largely determines the extent of its effectiveness.

In addition to the prime importance of this phase, problem diagnosis is also the most difficult out of all the steps in the decision-making process. This is because, in practice, problems do not really present themselves to managers on silver platters. They have to be found. The challenge, then, is not in problem-solving; rather it is in problem finding. And this is no easy task. Not only do managers get bombarded with mountains of bits and pieces of relevant or irrelevant information, they also find it difficult to differentiate between symptoms and problems.

It follows that the difficulty of this phase of the decision-making process emanates from the common error in the diagnosis of problem situations of confusing obvious symptoms with the problem itself. Poor decisions are many times correct solutions to the wrong problem and are considered poor because they do not contribute to stated goals. In short, no amount of care and effort in the subsequent steps of the decision-making process will yield a decision capable of reaching desired objectives unless the problem is properly diagnosed and defined.

Now, how do you go about diagnosing the problem? The following steps will greatly help you in this respect. Bear in mind that these steps are separated for purposes of analysis, but they are closely interrelated. In their thinking patterns, managers frequently combine more than one step and go about them simultaneously. These steps are:

1. Determine whether there is a problem.
2. Determine what is wrong.
3. Gather available information.
4. Identify the real problem and its possible causes.

1. Determine whether there is a problem. For purposes of diagnosis, the first question you should ask yourself is: Is there a problem? You will recall that the output of the first phase of the decision-making process is a concrete definition of the objectives you want to achieve and their relationship to the purpose of the organization. Keeping this in mind, a very effective way to determine whether there is a problem is through a comparison of one's existing condition with the condition that would exist if one had achieved one's purposes.

Unless the existing position is inferior to the desired-purpose condition, the executive has no problem for solution. Only when the actual state (what you end up with) is lesser (or lower) than the ideal state (what you wanted to achieve) is there an indication of a problem. This condition will require proceeding through the rest of the model; otherwise this step is the end of the decision-making process.

This step is so crucial that you must give it serious consideration as it is senseless to go through the decision-making process (considering the time and effort involved) with the assumption that there is a problem while, in fact, there is not any. My experience clearly demonstrates that managers frequently find themselves in this unfortunate situation, where the problems are definitiely more perceived than real. So, watch out!

2. Determine what is wrong. Now that you have decided that there is a problem, your next task in the diagnostic phase of the decision-making process is problem identification. A problem, by definition, is something that is wrong. The question, then, is, what is wrong? No problem can be correctly solved unless its real causes are found out. It follows that problem identification is a matter of locating deviations from objectives and then looking for the reasons behind them. Like a competent doctor, the manager must come up with a concrete definition of the problem which is a statement of the things that must be changed if he is to achieve his objective. Indeed, diagnosis requires a clear definition of the problem. Therefore, the question you should address yourself to at this point is, "What problems must I solve in order to achieve my objective?"

How do you go about determining what is wrong? Here are some pointers:

a. Develop your problem-finding skills. Decision-making is largely an art. The ability to discover an existing or a potential problem is a personal skill. It takes a clear vision, foresight, and a high degree of sensitivity. It also takes a superior ability to gather information, sort out the relevant pieces, and synthesize them into a meaningful pattern.

Problem situations are never clear-cut, and the "problem" may be only a hunch that something is not quite right. Problem-finding skills can be developed through experience, education, trial and error, and personal development efforts.

b. Take an analytical, realistic approach to the problem. Taking an analytical approach to the problem helps substantially with problem identification efforts. For example, the purpose may be to capture a major segment of a new market through the development of a new product or by making major technical changes in existing products. A realistic analysis of this problem would require determining:

1. How far the company is from achieving this purpose.
2. The major factors that account for the deficiency or the problem.
3. The barriers that stand in the way of success.
4. The requirements of a satisfactory solution which will ensure sharpening the direction of the problem-solving effort and enhancing objectivity in the development and analysis of alternative courses of action (later stages of the decision-making process).

c. Identify constraints. As noted above, it does not pay to explore and extensively probe into solutions that, although feasible, cannot be implemented. Determining restrictions or limits on solutions—cost, information, personnel and so on—beforehand would simplify the decision-making process and enable the manager to identify the critical boundaries within which the decision must fall.

d. Concentrate on causal problems rather than deviations from defined standards. Many managers never get beyond basic deviations in their decision-making. In fact, they end up making decisions but they do not solve problems. This is because they are continually dealing with effect rather than causal problems.

For example, the manager may be blamed for a turnover problem (an effect) when the real issue may be traced to inadequate recruiting and selection practices by the personnel department (a real cause). Not until the real problem and its causes are identified can an effective solution be devised.

e. Do not deal with symptoms. Closely related to the basic deviation from defined standards (item "d" above) is the situation that is a symptom of a larger problem. If the symptom is defined as the problem, the devised solution will achieve nothing but will create more problems.

For example, when the marketing department continually criticizes the ideas coming out of the R&D unit, without judicial evaluation, this is a symptom of a deeper problem relating to a fundamental difference in the values and cultures of both divisions. Getting the heads of both units to interact and communicate freely (dealing with a symptom) will do little toward solving the basic problem, namely learning to coexist and appreciate each other's orientation, values, and role in the organization.

The point is that problems seldom appear in a form in which meaningful decisions can be made. What you see on the surface may be a reflection, or symptom, of a more basic problem, with which you must deal. For effective diagnosis of the situation, the true problem must be identified; causes on the one hand must be separated from effects and symptoms on the other.

A good method for getting behind the symptom and to the problem itself is to ask: Why are research expenditures too high? Why is the project success ratio too low? This approach requires listing all possible causes and thus takes considerable time and effort; nonetheless, it is better than solving the wrong problem.

f. Recognize the barriers to effective problem identification. Several barriers can hinder effective problem identification on the part of managers. These include managers' reluctance to recognize that a problem exists, their feeling that the cure may be worse than the disease, their tendency to rationalize and to postpone decisions, and their reluctance to make unpopular decisions.[31] Furthermore, managers tend to stick to the "tried and true" rather than to collect and analyze information to really identify a problem.

Since a problem identified is half solved, it is crucial that you understand the above barriers to effective problem identification so you can deal with them. Through effective diagnosis, sifting out relevant information and separating real

---

[31] Huse, op, cit., p. 119.

causes from symptoms and effects, you will be able to properly define and identify problems.

3. Gather available information. Having determined what is wrong, you should begin getting the facts and gathering available information.

A major point you should keep in mind is that throughout the decision-making process, you will need to continually collect and analyze information. Does a problem really exist? Why is it a problem? Has the problem occurred before? Is the problem really a symptom of another problem? What are its possible causes? What are the possible options? Which option appears to best contribute to the goals and objectives of the organization?

Gathering information and collecting facts is a rather time-consuming activity. However, this is also an extremely crucial activity in order to come up with an accurate diagnosis of the problem. Indeed, there is nothing more tragic and wasteful than making decisions to solve the wrong problem. A comedian once boasted that he discovered a cure for a disease that did not even exist.[32] It happens in executive suites everyday—we solve problems that do not exist, because we have not properly identified them.

4. Identify the real problem and its possible causes. The net outcome of the diagnostic phase of decision-making is accurate problem identification. Through the proper determination of objectives, identification of constraints and the separation of symptoms from real causes, you should be able to pinpoint the real problem and explore its causes. This phase is really an outgrowth of the three previous steps in the problem diagnosis process.

Identification of Alternative Courses of Action. So far you have defined the objectives to be achieved and identified the problem to be solved and its possible causes. The next step in the decision-making process is to identify alternative courses of action to solve the problem (Figure 10-1).

As noted in an earlier section of this chapter, decision-making situations are problem situations that involve choice. Your task here is to begin searching for those choices (alternatives) which represent feasible courses of action for dealing with the problem. In order to ensure that those courses of action are feasible, you must keep in mind the solution constraints you have identified in the previous step of the decision-making process—problem diagnosis.

Also, keep in mind the MUSTS and WANTS objectives identified in the first step of the decision-making process (objective definition). These objectives become a set of specifications by which to develop alternative courses of action.[33] The objectives spelled out are individual statements of functions to be performed or fulfilled by the course of action.

You should make a thorough and comprehensive effort to identify all logical alternatives to the problem at hand, but never underestimate the importance of

---

[32] Uris, op, cit., p. 76.
[33] Sartain and Baker, op. cit., p. 42.

intuition, hunch, chance, and luck in finding alternatives. Creative and original solutions to problems should be encouraged. Group participation, brain-storming sessions, and an atmosphere conducive to the free flow of ideas are crucial elements in generating a variety of alternative courses of action. This type of environment will further enhance creativity in problem-solving when decision-makers have creative personal qualities including problem sensitivity, flexibility of thought, fluency of thinking, and originality.[34]

Here are some practical tips to help you in this phase of the decision-making process: First, do not stick to the tried and true. Managers have a tendency to do that, but this is very restricting since they never look for newer, more creative ways of doing things.

Second, consider the possible solution of taking no action at all. In generating alternative courses of action, one should not overlook this option. Remember that to decide on no action involves a decision in the same sense as does the generation of other alternatives. A "no action" option would be quite appropriate when the problem is more perceived than real, or when this alternative would be much more desirable under a particular set of circumstances. In short, the attitude that some action must always be taken is a dysfunctional assumption in spite of the common bias toward action characteristic of managerial practices in many corporations.[35]

Third, recognize the importance of one's personal values and experience in the decision process. Our values reflect our own physical, social, and psychological needs, as well as our own interpretation of what is rewarded and what is punished in our society. These values, along with a memory bank of experience, play a crucial role in our judgment—a central determinant of the decisions we make. Be sure to compare notes with others to see how they are handling similar problems and what ideas they might have. Supplementing our own experiences in this way can contribute significantly to both the quantity and quality of alternatives developed to deal with problem situations.

Finally, recognize the barriers that can sabotage the alternative identification process. These barriers include the tendency for decision-makers to originate replicative solutions, that is, to propose solutions that have worked on similar occasions in the past (analogy). There is also a tendency to limit proposals to those which involve variables that the decision-maker personally controls (control). Finally, there is a tendency to deal with immediate rather than long-run effects (time).[36] It is important to stress the need for an orientation of "open-end" thinking at this stage of the decision-making process. This calls for avoid-

[34] Guilford, J. P. Creativity: Its Measurement and Development. In Parnes, Sidney J., and Harding, Harold F. "A Source Book for Creative Thinking." New York: Scribner's, 1962, pp. 157–158.
[35] "Putting Excellence into Management," *Business Week* (McGraw-Hill), (July 21, 1980): 196–205.
[36] For more elaboration on this point, see Emory and Niland, op. cit., pp. 67–73.

ing the tendency to use a "narrow scan" in searching and generating alternative courses of action.

Evaluation of Each Course of Action. The fourth step in the decision-making process is to evaluate each course of action (Figure 10-1). The process of assessing alternative courses of action requires screening alternatives, exploring the advantages and disadvantages of each course of action, and analyzing each alternative. Here are some practical recommendations for guiding you through this phase of the decision-making process.

First, develop a set of decision rules as prescribed guides or tests for judgment. These rules are the yardsticks by which you will judge the worth of proposed solutions to problems. A simple rule might be "choose the least expensive product design." These rules must, of course, be consistent with the objectives or goals the decision-maker wishes to attain.

Second, determine how realistic each alternative is in terms of the goals, objectives, and resources of the organization. This will help you determine the restrictions on acceptable solutions. In order to do this, you will, obviously, need to review each activity in the first two steps in the decision-making process (objective definition and problem diagnosis).

Third, determine how well each alternative will help solve the identified problem. If an alternative is logical, but not feasible, it is not a useful alternative. An excellent solution, for instance, might be too expensive to implement and, thus, not feasible.

Fourth, evaluate the consequences resulting from adopting each alternative course of action. This requires devising a system to deal with two problems:[37]

1. How to value the outcomes of each course of action.
2. How to treat the degree of uncertainty attached to each predicted outcome.

In order to deal with the first problem, the decision-maker should employ a value system such as a monetary value system, an utility scale, or a rank order scale. Furthermore, the value system may have two or more dimensions, such as weight and appearance, as well as cost. If there is more than one dimension to the value system, there is the further problem of how to weight each in reaching a decision. One may simply explore all of the consequences only in monetary terms and attempt to weight the several elements intuitively in reaching a decision.

Alternatively, the decision-maker may eliminate any alternatives that do not meet minimum standards with respect to one or more nonmonetary value scales

---

[37] This discussion is based on Emory and Niland, op. cit., pp. 274-275; Sartain and Baker, op. cit., pp. 42-43; and Eckles, R. W., Carmichael, R. L., and Sarchet, B. R. "Supervisory Management." New York: Wiley, 1975, p. 69.

and decide among the remaining options only on the basis of monetary value. In evaluating alternative courses of action, a payoff table helps to present the consequences of each alternative in an orderly fashion. Another useful technique is the decision tree, which enables the decision-maker to analyze more easily a complex series of consequences involved in evaluating the outcomes of a single alternative.[38]

The other problem you need to deal with, as mentioned above, is how to treat the degree of uncertainty attached to each predicted outcome. Bear in mind that this process would have to be based upon a combination of objective facts and intuition. Certain probability factors must be considered in evaluating each alternative. The possibility of risk, uncertainty, and ignorance must be considered. Since there is no single best criterion for decision-making where a perfect knowledge of all the facts is present, a set of criteria must be used as determined by the manager for the problem at hand.

Risk is a state of imperfect knowledge in which the decision-maker judges the different possible outcomes of each alternative and determines the probabilities of success for each. Uncertainty is a state in which the decision-maker judges the different possible outcomes of each alternative but lacks any feelings for their probabilities of success. Ignorance is a state in which the decision-maker cannot judge the different possible outcomes of each alternative, let alone their probabilities.

The fifth, and last, recommendation is to evaluate each alternative against the stated objectives to see how good a job it will do. Each alternative should first be assessed against the MUST objectives on a go/no-go basis. If an alternative fails to perform what a MUST objective requires, it must be immediately discarded.

Alternatives that satisfy all the MUST objectives can then be evaluated further against the WANT objectives; each of them should be scored against one of the objectives separately. You can use a scoring scale for this, say 1 to 10, with the best alternative receiving the top score. To get an overall judgment of the relative worth of each alternative, you must multiply the score of each alternative by the weight assigned to each objective. The weighted scores can now be added up to give totals for each of the alternatives. These total figures give the relative positions of each of the alternatives on those items of performance considered in the specific objectives.

To sum up: The above discussion outlines a systematic approach to the evaluation and analysis of alternative courses of action. This evaluation clearly requires a concrete definition of the results expected or the objectives to be achieved, a statement of the restrictions (constraints) on acceptable solutions, and an as-

---

[38] For more information on this technique, see Churchman, C. West, Ackoff, Russel, and Arnoff, Leonard E. "Introduction to Operations Research." New York: Wiley, 1957; Miller, David W. "Executive Decisions and Operations Research." Englewood Cliffs: Prentice-Hall, 1960; and Magee, John F. Decision Trees for Decision-Making. *Harvard Business Review* (July-August, 1964): 126-138.

sessment of the advantages and disadvantages of each alternative. Figures 10-2 and 10-3 provide you with two worksheets that can be used in conducting a systematic analysis of alternative courses of action.

Making of a Choice and Implementing the Decision. After evaluating alternative courses of action, the manager must make a choice—this is the fifth step in the decision-making process (Figure 10-1). The question you must ask at this point is: What solution will work best in dealing with the present situation? There are several considerations you should keep in mind in attempting to select the "best" solution to the problem:

First, regardless of the highly sophisticated tools and techniques you have used throughout the decison-making process, there will always be a certain degree of risk in your attempt to pinpoint the best move. As discussed above, the uncertainty element can only be minimized but can never be eliminated. Therefore, there will always be room for hunch, intuition, and luck to be combined with facts, logic, and systematic analysis in the decision-making process.

Second, in selecting a course of action, do not strive for the best course, because it does not exist. In other words, reaching an optimum solution is impossible and, therefore, making satisfactory decisions (satisficing rather than optimizing) is all you can hope for, as will be discussed below. There are several reasons why optimization in decision-making is impossible. These include the following:

1. Seldom is there one correct choice with all others classified as incorrect. Instead, decisions are neither black nor white; for the most part they are gray.

List Objectives in Order of
Importance and Results Expected

Constraints on Acceptable Solutions

1.

1.

2.

2.

3.

3.

4.

4.

List Each Course of Action	Major Advantages of Each Alternative (by degree of importance)	Major Disadvantages of Each Alternative (by degree of importance)	Problems Concerning Implementation	Required Mechanisms to Deal With These Problems
1.				
2.				
3.				
4.				

Figure 10-2. Worksheet: analysis of alternative courses of action.

Alternative Courses of Action	Objective 1			Objective 2			Objective 3			Constraints Violated
	Highly Acceptable	Moderately Acceptable	Unacceptable	Highly Acceptable	Moderately Acceptable	Unacceptable	Highly Acceptable	Moderately Acceptable	Unacceptable	
1st Course of Action										
2nd Course of Action										
3rd Course of Action										
4th Course of Action										

Figure 10-3. Worksheet: analysis of alternative courses of action.

2. The dynamic nature of the environment of the firm (states of nature) makes it difficult to realistically assess the probable success or failure of any action (the degree of risk).

3. Incomplete and unavilable data limit the number and quality of courses of action developed to deal with the problem. Since not all alternatives may have been either identified or analyzed, the solution may not be the best.

4. An ideal solution today might not be so tomorrow because of the continually changing environment and the decision-maker's limited ability to forecast the future.

5. The solution chosen at any time is "best" only in the sense that it appears to make the greatest contribution to objectives while working within the framework of known resources. What if the objectives or resources happen to change? Is this solution still necessarily the best?

6. Decisions are frequently made on the basis of incomplete information, and they often require a compromise among a number of different factors each with its own trade-offs. It would, therefore, be impossible to make "optimum" decisions.

7. There are limits to the rational decision-making process.[39] These include "satisficing" and bounded rationality. *Satisficing* refers to the practice of striving for a satisfactory rather than an optimum decision. It is a deliberate choice to limit the alternatives considered to reach a satisfactory solution. *Bounded rationality* is the practice of reducing the complexity of a problem to the level at which a manager can handle the possible alternatives. Note that while satisficing is purposefully selected, bounded rationality is naturally imposed (because of the natural limit on the human ability to handle complex situations).[40]

8. Managers are always working under pressure; they simply do not have the luxury of time. Since they are always rushed, they cannot look for "optimum" decisions which take considerably longer time and more information than what is typically available.

In short, maximization in decision-making is a luxury managers can not afford. Therefore, they end up striving to make satisfactory or "good enough" decisions—not optimal decisions.

A third consideration in making a choice among courses of action is to remember that there are other possiblities that must be kept in mind. These include:[41]

1. No alternative is desirable. It might be appropriate not to take any action because of the riskiness of all alternatives available at this time.

---

[39] Huse, op. cit., p. 117.
[40] For more on these concepts, see Simon, Herbert. "Administrative Behavior." New York: Macmillan, 1957; and Lindblom, C. The Science of Muddling Through. *Public Administration Review,* 19 (Spring 1959): 79–88.
[41] Uris, op. cit., p. 68.

2. You might be able to merge two or more alternatives, combining the elements that will provide you with the most likely plan.
3. The "resources factor" might lead you to adopt less than what you consider to be the best decision. This happens when alternative B, for instance, although inferior to alternative A would result in some cost or time savings.

Once a choice is made, decision implementation will follow. The way the decision is implemented will have significant bearing on its success. You should develop a plan of action concerning announcement of the decision, communication of it (the what, when, who and how of communication), the resources involved in decision implementation, and the assignment of responsibility to the appropriate individuals charged with this implementation.

An important point you should keep in mind is that acceptance of the decision by other people is very crucial to getting their commitment and backing for decision implementation. A good decision can fail if it does not have the sound and active support of everyone involved. People tend to support the decisions they have had a voice in shaping and making. It follows that seeking inputs from the people who will be affected by the decision, obtaining their active participation, and keeping them informed throughout the decision-making process will certainly simplify your future job of implementing the decision.

To sum up: Selecting a solution is a major step in the decision-making process—indeed, it is the ultimate outcome. Since rationality is bounded, you should not strive for optimum decisions, but for satisfactory decisions. Satisficing, rather than maximizing, is a sound decision-making strategy since it is irrational to be excessively rational. For implementing the decision, a sound action plan should be developed. Remember that it is not what you do, but the way you do it that is going to make the difference in terms of the success of your decision-making efforts.

Follow-up and Decision Evaluation. The last step in the decision-making process is to follow up, control, and evaluate the results of a decision. As you will note in Figure 10-1, the question here is: How can I review and evaluate the decision?

This evaluation, of course, depends on many factors such as the type of the decision, its importance, and the availability of information for purposes of feedback and review. The time element is also crucial as instant feedback might be possible in the case of simple decisions while it takes years (sometimes never!) to evaluate complex decisions regarding R&D project expenditures. Worse yet, by the time the data are available, a cause-effect relationship will be impossible to construct since many organizational units have already contributed to the project development, progress, and completion.

However, although not frequently included as a step in the decision-making process, control and evaluation plays a significant role in determining the success and failure of a decision. Also, if you do not get some feedback on the degree of accuracy of the decision, how else are you going to find out about the quality of your decision-making skills? And how else can you learn, improve, and develop these skills?

Control and decision evaluation is not an easy task since decisions are seldom completely right or wrong. Some criteria for judging the potential effectiveness of a decision can, however, be established. These include:

1. To what extent has the decision enabled the manager to deal with the problem at hand? Has it achieved the objective for which it was made?
2. How well did the manager carry out the steps of the decision-making process discussed above?
3. How well was the decision accepted by those involved?

In short, while these are not easy questions to answer, the decisions you make must be continually reviewed. On the basis of control and feedback data, other decisions have to be made to continue, refine, or totally modify previous decisions. This is a never-ending process and in a very real sense, decision-making is the essence of managing.

So far, I have described the rational decision-making process in considerable detail. The various steps in the decision-making process have been analyzed. Various tips and practical guidelines about each step have also been given in an effort to help you acquire and develop the ingredients necessary for effective decision-making. A summary of the major points made in this section appear in Table 10-3.

You must remember here that no method, no matter how elegant it is, will guarantee making good decisions. Indeed, it is not the method, it is how it is used that makes the difference. In other words, the process starts with you, and ends up with you. Now it is your responsibility to put what you have learned into action—to implement it.

How Managers make Decisions: Decision-Making In Action

Having discussed the rational decision-making process in the previous section, let us now look at how managers actually make decisions in practice.

Do Managers Really Make Rational Decisions? Unfortunately, the model of rational decision-making (Table 10-3) is frequently not followed in practice. Why? Because it is too neat, too elegant, too theoretical, and too unrealistic for dealing with everyday management decisions.

Table 10-3. Summary of Steps in the Rational Decision-Making Process.

I. Objective Definition

II. Problem Diagnosis
    A. Determine whether there is a problem.
    B. Determine what is wrong.
        1. Develop your problem-finding skills.
        2. Take an analytical, realistic approach to the problem.
        3. Identify constraints.
        4. Concentrate on causal problems rather than deviations from defined standards.
        5. Do not deal with symptoms.
        6. Recognize the barriers to effective problem identification.
    C. Gather available information.
    D. Identify the real problem and its possible causes.

III. Identification of Alternative Courses of Action
    A. Do not stick to the tried and true.
    B. Consider the possible solution of taking no action at all.
    C. Recognize the importance of one's personal values and experience in the decision process.
    D. Recognize the barriers that can sabotage the alternative identification process.

IV. Evaluation of Each Course of Action
    A. Develop a set of decision rules as prescribed guides or tests for judgment.
    B. Determine how realistic each alternative is in terms of the goals, objectives, and resources of the organization.
    C. Determine how well each alternative will help solve the identified problem.
    D. Evaluate the consequences resulting from adopting each alternative course of action.
        1. Evaluate the outcome of each course of action.
        2. Treat the degree of uncertainty attached to each predicted outcome.
    E. Evaluate each alternative against the stated objectives to see how good a job it will do.

V. Making of a Choice and Decision Implementation
    A. Remember that there will always be a certain degree of risk in your attempt to pinpoint the best move.
    B. Do not strive for the best course, because it does not exist. Optimization in decision-making is impossible because:
        1. Decisions are neither black nor white; for the most part they are gray.
        2. The environment of the firm is continually changing.
        3. Not all alternatives may have been either identified or analyzed.
        4. Human ability to forecast the future is limited.
        5. Changes in objectives or resources may render the solution less than the "best."
        6. Decisions often require compromises and trade-offs.
        7. The decision-making process is limited by satisficing and bounded rationality.
        8. Working under varied pressures, managers do not have the luxury of time.
    C. Consider other possibilities including:
        1. No alternative is desirable.
        2. Merge two or more alternatives.
        3. The "resources factor."

VI. Follow-up and Decision Evaluation
    A. To what extent has the decision enabled the manager to deal with the problems at hand?
    B. How well did the manager carry out the steps of the decision-making process?
    C. How well was the decision accepted by those involved?

As discussed in Chapter 7, the world of the manager is too disorderly for this orderly systematic model to apply.[42] It would be a mistake, then, to think of managers as emotionless machines who can function like computers in an entirely rational manner with their emotions, values, and feelings having no impact on the type of decisions they make. This is a glaring example of the failure of the classical rational model of decision-making as it does not, in fact, describe reality. Does this mean that this model is totally useless? No! It is a good stereotype of an ideal by which managers can measure their decision-making efforts. It can serve as a standard in the same way that other models and theories serve in the natural and social sciences.[43]

The key point is that managers, before anything else, are human beings. Like all of us, they are neither so orderly nor so rational in the way they made decisions. Managers often fail to set explicit objectives; they fail to diagnose effectively; they neglect to seek out course of action possibilities; they select a course of action on an intuitive basis; and they fail to specify strategies by which to achieve goals. The rational approach does, however, provide a standard toward which to strive.

How Are Managerial Decisions Made in Practice? It is clear that managers face several problems in trying to make decisions rationally. Managers have little or no control over factors that are critical to the decisions.[44] Managers also vary in their personal abilities, and some have more native decision-making talent and skills than do others. In addition, a decision-maker's success is heavily influenced by a variety of personal factors such as his mental set, the degree of his action orientation, and his ability to overcome fallacies in thought patterns.

Experience and observation show that there is no single decision-making style that all managers use in practice, nor is there a single style adopted by the same manager in all decision-making situations. There are, however, some common characteristics that form a profile of the manager as a decision-maker. This profile is presented in Table 10-4. Remember that this is a stereotype and does not necessarily describe all managers.

As shown in Table 10-4, managers' efforts, by and large, are continually focused not on decision-making that involves getting down to the root of problems and dealing with them rationally, but on putting out the day-to-day pressing fires—which usually represent symptoms of problems—and troubleshooting. They are short-range oriented, looking for quick results required by the way the "system" is set up: a strong financial orientation (profit and loss) and a bottom line that looks good at all cost.

---

[42] Mintzberg, Henry. The Manager's Job: Folklore and Fact. *Harvard Business Review* (July–August 1975).
[43] Emory and Niland, op. cit., pp. 15 and 21.
[44] Ibid., p. 21.

Table 10-4. A Profile of the Manager as a Decision-Maker:
A Practical Stereotype.

1. Crisis management, putting out fires, managing by the seat of his pants.
2. Short-range orientation and quick results.
3. Paralysis by analysis.
4. Decision not to decide.
5. Decisionless decisions.
6. Tendency to minimize personal risk.
7. Failure to act when he sees a problem; tendency to procrastinate.
8. Emotions, feeling, politics, and value judgment playing a large part in the decision-making process.
9. Satisficing rather than maximizing as the common decision-making strategy.
10. Bounded rationality characteristic of decision-making situations.
11. Steps of the rational decision-making model being more of an ideal than reality.

This orientation simply reinforces crisis management and management by intuition or the seat of the pants. It follows that managers, in effect, do not make decisions in the scientific sense the rational model describes (Table 10-3). Rather, they react by dealing with one problem or crisis after another. Their style, then, is reactive rather than proactive.

Another characteristic of managerial decision-making behavior is that managers tend to satisfice, not optimize. Aside from the several reasons discussed above concerning the difficulty of optimization as a decision-making goal, this tendency to satisfice is caused by two psychological reasons:[45]

1. The tendency to make decisions that minimize personal risks. Managers are sometimes more concerned about avoiding risks of losses than about making gains, more concerned about the personal consequences of the decision than about the organization's goals.
2. The common tendency of managers to procrastinate, hoping that the problem will go away.

A third common characteristic, experience shows, is that managers employ what can be called "decision-avoidance tactics." As noted in Table 10-4, these tactics include such things as paralysis by analysis, the never-satiated desire for more information before making the decision; decision not to decide, letting somebody else make the decision; and the decisionless decision—when the manager takes decisive action under the pressure of the moment without necessarily

---

[45] Huse, op. cit., pp. 124 and 128.

thinking of the move as a decision (e.g., firing a subordinate on the spur of the moment in anger or irritation).

Finally, because of the pressures involved in the managerial task and the disorderly nature of managerial activities, the decision-making process defies scientific analysis and systematic exploration. Both objective and subjective factors—value judgment, intuition, politics, and so on—are considered in making choices. The manager usually reduces the complexity of the problem through bounded rationality, as discussed above.

Furthermore, the decision-making process usually is not a single sequence of "decide, plan, and execute"; instead, it is a series of sequences of "decide, plan, select, implement, evaluate, compare, revise decisions, revise plans," and so forth. The descriptive model of decision-making—what happens in practice—is shown in Figure 10-4.

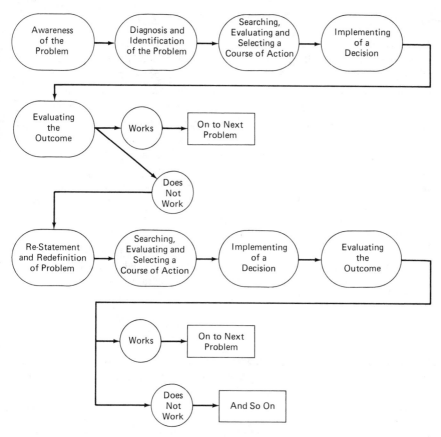

Figure 10-4. How managers make decisions: decision-making in action
(the descriptive approach).

To sum up: There is a world of difference between how managers should make decisions—the rational approach—and how they really make decisions—the descriptive approach. While both approaches are important, the rational model makes unrealistic assumptions about the world and about how managers should strive to maximize goal accomplishment. This model, usually advocated by economicians and other pure academicians, is an oversimplification of what takes place in organizations and does not really pass the test of reality.

The descriptive model, on the other hand, recognizes the complexity of real-world situations, admits that maximization is impossible, and favors satisficing and bounded rationality as legitimate decision-making strategies. This model, usually advocated by behavioral scientists, is far more realistic and offers a set of concepts and techniques the practicing manager can easily use.

Techniques and Analytical Aids to Decision-Making

The manager has at his disposal a set of techniques that are special aids to help him in the decision-making process. These decision techniques comprise a body of details or methods of procedure essential to expertness of execution in the decision-making process.[46] Thus, there are diagnostic techniques, brainstorming techniques, linear programming techniques, simulation techniques, and the like.[47] They range in scope and sophistication from simply intuitive actions to complex mathematic designs.

A thorough analysis of these techniques is beyond the scope of this volume.[48] Because of this and the vast literature already available on this subject, an extensive list of references will be found in Chapter 13.

As you can see from the above discussion, decision-making is an involved and complex managerial task. Developing your problem-solving and decision-making skills is crucial for managerial competence and effectiveness. The balance of this chapter will provide you with guidelines and practical tips on how to develop your skills in this area. As discussed above, while decision-making is viewed in this book as applied problem-solving, separate guidelines will be provided in each area only for discussion purposes.

How to Develop your Problem-Solving Skills: Some Guidelines

The following three sets of guidelines will provide you with several practical tips that will enable you to develop your problem-solving skills:

---

[46] Emory and Niland, op. cit., p. 2.

[47] Ibid., pp. 275–280.

[48] Another volume in this book series deals exclusively with these techniques: "Modern Management Techniques for Engineers and Scientists." New York: Van Nostrand Reinhold (in press).

1. Understanding the working rules for effective problem-solving.
2. Keep management "laws" in mind for effective problem-solving.
3. Follow the ten commandments of effective problem-solving.

Understand the Working Rules for Effective Problem-Solving. There are two sets of precepts that may help you in the problem-solving process. These rules are based on psychological research, and their usefulness depends on the manner in which they are applied.[49] Preventive rules are intended to keep the problem solver from getting stuck on an incorrect line of attack. Remedial rules are intended to help him get free when he is stuck.

Preventive Precepts

1. Run over the elements of the problem in rapid succession several times, until a pattern emerges that encompasses all these elements.
2. Suspend judgment. Do not jump to conclusions.
3. Explore the environment. Vary the temporal and spatial arrangement of the materials.

Remedial Precepts

1. Produce a second solution after the first.
2. Critically evaluate your own ideas. Constructively evaluate those of others.
3. When stuck, change your representational system. If a concrete representation is not working, try an abstract one, and vice versa (e.g., if you have been dealing with a problem in verbal terms, and if you are stuck, then try to switch to a picture, a model, a graph, numbers, or even to other words).
4. Take a break when you are stuck.
5. Talk about your problems with someone.

These eight precepts can be reduced to two:

1. Look before you leap.
2. After you have leaped, if you become bogged down, find out what you are doing and then do something else.

Keep Management "Laws" in Mind for Effective Problem-Solving. Because of its nature, there are not any laws in management. However, there are several

---

[49] This discussion is partly based on Hyman, Ray, and Anderson, Barry. Solving Problems. In Allison, David (Ed.). "The R&D Game." Cambridge: The MIT Press, 1969, pp. 92-105.

principles that can be considered laws. None can stand up to scientific analysis, yet each has a ring of truth.[50] Here are five major "laws":

1. Parkinson's Law. "Work expands so as to fill the time available for its completion."

Frequently, the same amount of work could have been done in a one-hour meeting that, in fact, took two hours! If you want a meeting to be short, start it just before lunch, or just before quitting time (this latter ploy works especially well when the attendees are in different car pools).

Another aspect of Parkinson's law can be summarized as follows: There need be little or no relationship between the work to be done and the size of the staff to which it may be assigned. This is especially true when the work is mostly paperwork.

Also, in time, a staff organization tends to increase in size regardless of the size of the organization that it is serving. In general, in large organizations, this rate of increase is between 5% and 10% per year unless some specific management action is taken to reduce it.

2. Murphy's Law. Murphy's three laws are:

a. Nothing is as easy as it looks.
b. Everything takes longer than you think it will.
c. If anything can go wrong, it will.

A fourth element in Murphy's law that should have a special interest to you is:

d. There is no way at all to please everybody any of the time.

3. Weber's Law. "In any given kind of perceiving, equal relative (not absolute) differences are perceptible."

This law can be applied to length, weight, brightness of light, intensity of sound, products and packages, and even individual or group performance evaluations.

Weber's law can be expressed as $\Delta I = KI$ where K is a constant ratio, I is the stimulus, and ΔI is the "just noticeable difference."

This law indicates that psychophysical experiments can be run to establish the constant (K) for different stimuli. Typical applications would be to use Weber's law to determine just how much difference there would have to be between two products to be perceived by someone in terms of one being lighter, milder, sweeter, larger, cheaper, safer, heavier, louder, softer, etc., than the other.

4. Peter/Paul's Law. Lawrence J. Peter formulated the Peter principle: In a hierarchy every employee tends to rise to his level of incompetence.

---

[50] Gautschi, T. F. Five Laws for the Manager, *Design News* (November 22, 1976): 129-130.

Healey proposed the Paul principle.[51] For every employee who rises above his level of competence, there are several whose full talents are not utilized.

He supports this contention with four factors:

a. People get locked into particular pyramids (organizational structures), and promotions or transfers are often difficult because of the requirement for high technical specialization.
b. Managers tend to recognize only the immediate and observable talents that a person has, and do not appreciate total capability.
c. A person often does not commit his total capabilities to the organization because he cannot identify with its goals or objectives.
d. Poor supervisory practice can submerge much of the talent that a subordinate possesses.

5. Pareto's Law. "Significant items in a given group normally constitute a small portion of the total items in the group and the majority of items in the total will, in the aggregate, be of minor significance. Roughly this works out to be an 80/20 pattern." For example:

a. 20% of a salesperson's customers usually account for 80% of the sales.
b. 80% of complaints will come from 20% of the customers.
c. 20% of the items in an inventory will account for 80% of the total cost.
d. 80% of a manager's problems will be associated with 20% of his subordinates.
e. 20% of the people in a volunteer organization do 80% of the work.
f. 80% of the contributions come from 20% of the contributors, etc.

As a manager, you can make better use of your most limited resource—time—by using Pareto's law as a guide when you select your priorities.

Follow the Ten Commandments of Effective Problem-Solving[52]

1. Ask yourself, Is there a solution to this problem? Not all problems can be solved.
2. Say it or write it down: Lay it out so you can analyze its complications.
3. Define the problem positively: The optimistic outlook inspires a positive solution in both yourself and others.
4. Have you forgotten anything? Do not let the omission of important data fog your focus on the problem.

---

[51] Healey, James, Why Not a Paul Principle? *Business Horizons* (December 1973).
[52] Uris, op. cit., pp. 76-77.

5. Get additional information: Research may bring out facts you have over-looked or simply do not know about.
6. Look for more than one solution: Are there alternative solutions, and if so, which is best? Can you combine?
7. Welcome new ideas, and give a new idea the opportunity to prove itself.
8. Check your solution and check yourself: Evaluate your answers. Since you cannot foresee precisely how a solution will work, changes and corrections may be necessary.
9. Do not look for a perfect solution. Aim for the best you can get under the circumstances.
10. Rest your ego: Insistence on being right all the time only alienates others. If your problem involves other people, give them the chance to be right once in a while.

How to Develop your Decision-Making Skills: Some Guidelines

Decision-making is an applied science. It is also a complex art requiring a combination of knowledge and skills that can be developed through study and training. In this sense, decision-making is, to a large degree, learnable. The ability to plan and make decisions is one that can be taught and learned and constantly improved. We cannot eliminate unpredictability and risk, but we surely can improve our ability to lessen them.

Your decision-making capacity can, actually, be developed in two interrelated ways:

1. By enhancing your knowledge of decision-making concepts and techniques.
2. By putting this knowledge into action through practice and the development of your skills.

To help you develop your decision-making knowledge and skills, Table 10-5 provides nine practical tips and guidelines. A discussion of these guidelines will follow.

Adapt Your Decision-Making Style to the Situation. As noted earlier in this chapter, there is no single decision-making style that will work in all situations. In fact, the decision-maker should adapt different styles to different situations. The appropriate style will depend on several factors including the type of decision, the nature of information needed to make the decision, the desirable amount of participation by subordinates and peers in making the decision, the amount of time available to the manager, and the type of relationship the manager has with his superior.

Table 10-5. Guidelines for Developing Your Decision-Making Skills.

1. Adapt your decision-making style to the situation.
2. Recognize the mental blocks to decision-making.
3. Understand barriers to effective decision-making.
4. Diagnose your personal decision-making shortcomings—and deal with them.
5. Learn how to handle wrong decisions.
6. Never make decisions unless you really have to.
7. Time your decisions wisely.
8. Elude the traps to sound decision-making.
9. When nothing else works. . . .

As shown in Figure 10-5, there is a variety of decision-making styles that can be conceived as a continuum but none of these is really suited to fit all situations. Therefore, the appropriateness of any style is situation-bound—it is contingent on the situation.

Recognize the Mental Blocks to Decision-Making. You should recognize and deal with the psychological hurdles to decision-making. While some of these hurdles have already been noted in this chapter, it is beneficial to group them into four major mental blocks.[53]

1. *Hamlet's disease.* Some managers are simply men of thought rather than action, and taking action of a decisive kind is difficult for them.
2. *Compulsion.* This is the opposite of the Hamlet syndrome. Some individuals feel compelled to make decisions, to take action that is often premature and, just as often, ill-considered.
3. *Consequence anxiety.* For some, the decision-making situation is fraught with mental discomfort. They have an excessive fear of "guessing wrong" and tend to distort the consequences of a less-than-perfect decision.

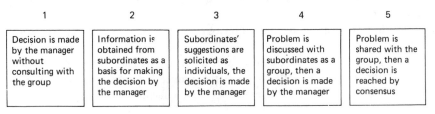

1	2	3	4	5
Decision is made by the manager without consulting with the group	Information is obtained from subordinates as a basis for making the decision by the manager	Subordinates' suggestions are solicited as individuals, the decision is made by the manager	Problem is discussed with subordinates as a group, then a decision is made by the manager	Problem is shared with the group, then a decision is reached by consensus

Figure 10-5. Decision-making styles continuum.

---

[53] Ibid., pp. 66–67.

4. *Do-nothingism.* This shows up as a disinclination to act, a tendency to procrastinate. But unlike consequence anxiety, the individual who suffers from this difficulty does not seem excessively anxiety-ridden. And unlike Hamlet's disease, the deterrent to action seems to be unawareness, rather than a personal antipathy to action.

Understand Barriers to Effective Decision-Making. There are several barriers that hinder the effectiveness of the decision-making process. You should understand and beware of the following barriers:[54]

1. Make sure you are not just dealing with a symptom. Unless the real problem is identified and dealt with, it will arise again.
2. Watch for the individual in a group who will not allow investigation. He has a problem to solve *now*, not later. He does not need any more facts. It is a clear-cut situation! He is a good-decision maker already.
3. Consider the time barrier: When the pressures are so intense, and you are rushed for time, mistakes are bound to increase. There certainly is a lot to be said in support of the statement, "Why is there never time to do it right the first time and always time to do it over?" Taking more time doing it right the first time could actually save you the time spent on fighting the crises in the long run!
4. Check the common attitude that the area in question is someone else's responsibility even though it affects your own ability to get results, makes your job hectic, and results in the job running you instead of your running the job.

Diagnose Your Personal Decision-Making Shortcomings—and Deal with Them. We all have our personal weaknesses. This is only part of being human. Recognizing our shortcomings, through self-awareness, and devising appropriate mechanisms to deal with them will certainly work to our advantage. You, therefore, should identify your own decision-making style, diagnose the difficulties you may have in this area, and deal with them. Remember that facing up to a problem and trying to solve it is much better than running away from it or even denying its existence.

The human decision-making problems emanate from the following sources.[55]

1. The lack of effective control over the decision-making environment forces the manager to settle for something much less than perfect knowledge. This frequently creates an uncomfortable feeling.

---

[54] Scanlan, Burt K. "Management 18: A Short Course for Managers." New York: Wiley, 1974, pp. 48–49.
[55] For a detailed statement of these problems, see Emory and Niland, op. cit., pp. 15–21.

2. The maldistribution of decision ability among the human population creates major variations in individual decision-making capacities and the quality of decisions made. This condition is compounded by some research findings suggesting that:

   a. Decision-making ability is probably not a single factor but a complex array of abilities in which the individual may be strong in some and weak in others.

   b. Individuals, in fact, do very widely in their basic abilities to solve administrative problems.

   c. While one may have a limited potential for problem-solving, most people use only a fraction of the ability that they do have.

3. Careless or faulty personal reasoning practices contribute to poor decision-making. An example of these practices is the individual's mental set. Our view of a problem is a function of what we want to see and expect to see. We see many aspects of any problem facing us in view of our past frame of reference—experience. We then move mentally to the conclusion that the answer to today's problem is the same as the answer to yesterday's problem.

In order to deal with problem-solving barriers, it is very important, therefore, to question and challenge the assumptions that have become part of your mental outlook. Abandoning preconceived notions and assumptions could open the door for new ideas and fresh thoughts.

Other examples of causes of faulty reasoning—as noted above—are the executive's strong action orientation, inertia (caused by legion and fear of making a decision), and crooked thinking (faulty logic).

It can be concluded, then, that your success in decision-making is heavily influenced by a number of personal factors. Through your awareness of your own strengths and weaknesses, and through your personal development efforts, you can alleviate some of these problems and enhance your decision-making skills.

Learn How to Handle Wrong Decisions. Few managers know how to proceed when a decision goes wrong. Five positive moves may save the day.[56]

1. Recognizing. You must accept full responsibility by honest recognition of the fact that, on this particular decision, you have come up with a clinker. You must accept the losses, analyze the causes, and try to recoup what you can.

---

[56] Uris, op. cit., pp. 71–73.

2. Reversing. Since decision-making is a multistep process, you should back up and follow through to determine exactly where you might have tripped.

3. Replacing. There will be times when you have a decision that looks great—on paper. If you have had problems in executing it, it does not necessarily mean that the idea is not workable. By discovering the weak link and replacing it, you can make the decision look good again—on paper and in execution.

4. Revising. If a bad decision cannot be remedied by simply replacing or retracing, a complete revision of the original plan might be in order. Considering other alternatives and other means of achieving your objectives would help you come up with a workable plan.

5. Reviewing. Results are the proof of the decision-making pudding. When they go wrong, analyzing when, why, and how can teach you a great deal about your own decision-making ability, the techniques that need sharpening, and the pitfalls to be avoided. Failure often triggers more knowledge than success.

Never Make Decisions Unless You Really Have To. The buck does indeed stop at your desk. Each decision that you make represents a time at bat and will affect your batting average.[57] Making unnecessary decisions only increases the risk of losing your control, your leadership position, and your effectiveness. Unnecessary decisions are always premature decisions in the sense that insufficient time was invested in determining the need to make the decision. This, of course, increases the likelihood of making erroneous decisions. Moreover, do not make decisions others can or should make. Subordinates, actually, like to put the monkey on their boss's back.[58]

Time Your Decisions Wisely. Remember that the right answer at the wrong time is a bad decision. In French cooking, the sauce is everything. In business management, timing is everything.[59] Taking action to introduce a new product or to abandon one may clearly be the right thing, in principle, to do, but unless your timing is right, the action might turn out to be regrettable.

Keep in mind that the logic of success in any endeavor is to get there first and to exploit the opportunity first. Furthermore, when we are low and feeling blue, our decisions tend to be aggressive and destructive. But when we are feeling good, our behavior becomes more tolerant and balanced. Understanding your own moods and behavior is crucial for timing decision-making.

---

[57] Sloma, op. cit., p. 136.
[58] Oncken, Jr., William, and Wass, Donald L. Management Time: Who's Got the Monkey. *Harvard Business Reveiw* (November–December 1974): 75-80.
[59] Sloma, op. cit., p. 151.

It is noteworthy here that one of the most difficult problems for engineering and R&D managers is the general problem of timing—both business and technical. You will do well to keep the following pointers in mind.[60]

1. Identify the key or pivotal problems early.
2. Concentrate on these problems and determine whether they can be solved now—often their solutions are so far beyond the present state of the art that it would be impossible or impractical to try to solve them now. A massive attack now would not result in a positive payoff; in fact it would likely also result in a technical failure. The moral of this point is that you should not beat your head against a stone wall unless you find a few loose stones.
3. If the overall project is important, review the pivotal problems from time to time—keep to the fore that the solution may come from developments in fields not directly related to the problem. Again, the moral of this point is that you should not bury your head in the sand. If you cannot do it today, and the problem is still important, do not forget it.

Elude the Traps to Sound Decision-Making.   In accumulating data for decision-making, you must recognize and learn to avoid some of the traps for the unwary.[61] These include the following:

1. Misdirection. You should be careful not to get the right answer to the wrong question. Not only should you make sure to ask the right question, but you should also ask it of the right people and get the right information.

2. Bias. You should get your information from the right people and not from those who may have an axe to grind. Also, where bias is involved, some estimate should be made of the degree to which it will affect answers.

3. The ubiquitous average. Averages bury extremes. A person can drown in a river that averages 2 inches deep if he falls into the one spot in its entire length that just happens to be 50 feet deep. A practical guide for checking the validity of an average is: If more than 50% of the instances depart from the derived average by more than 25%, or more than 25% of the instances depart from the derived average by more than 50%, the validity of the figure should be questioned.

4. Selection of only the favorable. Selectivity is the rejection of unfavorable results and the acceptance of favorable ones, or the selection of a method that will be certain to give favorable results rather than unfavorable or mixed ones. Selectivity can be guarded against only by demanding all the facts, including the figures swept under the rug as being contrary or antagonistic to the thesis.

---

[60] Karger, Delmar W., and Murdic,, Robert G.   "Managing Engineering and Research," Second Edition. New York: Industrial Press, 1969, pp. 187–188.
[61] Fuller, op. cit.,

5. Interpretation. The same set of facts or the information may be open to more than one interpretation. While the interpretations of qualified experts must be respected, blind faith is never a good policy. Whenever possible, you should determine whether, given the expert's data, you would have arrived at the same conclusions. The person providing you with information for decision-making has an obligation to present it in such a fashion that you will understand it in the same sense in which he does.

6. The jumped-at conclusion. This is a trap that no one really sets for the decision-maker. Others provide the building materials, but the decision-maker builds the trap, walks into it, and springs it all by himself. Just because more airplane accidents occur in clear weather than in foggy weather, it is not necessarily safer to fly in foggy weather.

7. Connotation. Connotation is the suggested emotional content or implication that is added to an explicit literal meaning. While it is natural to draw out all the meaning there is in a remark, do not draw out meanings that are not there. Your boss says, "If it does not work as you expect, we'll have to make some changes." This may mean nothing more than a change of approach to the secure engineer, but it may imply a change of personnel to the insecure one.

8. The meaningless difference. The meaningless difference, and its twin, the meaningless similarity, are cases where a lot is hoped to be done with practically nothing. You cannot create a difference where none exists, nor can you make the insignificant seem significant. Do not inflate minor differences to increase their importance or the validity of your decision.

9. The status syndrome. The status barrier between a superior and a subordinate limits communication in either direction, due to fear of disapproval on the one hand or of loss of prestige on the other. The boss may fear to ask a question if to do so may suggest that he does not know his business. So, as a cover-up for his ignorance, he acts as though he already knew the answer. Also, a subordinate may fear to ask the boss a question. "Maybe I should know the answer," he thinks, "and if he finds out I don't, I may be in trouble."

10. Sweeping failures under the rug. It is human nature to want to forget about past failures, but they have a great value—as a warning. Keep records of past failures—just as you do with successes—so if similar circumstances arise in the future, you can use your past experience as a guide.

11. Tolerating walking filing cases. Far too much reliance is placed on the memories of fallible individuals in engineering and R&D departments. Individuals are not only fallible, they are mortal and movable. They can drop dead or change jobs—and take valuable unrecorded experience with them. This practice should be avoided at all cost.

12. Treating other departments like foreign powers. Some engineering departments seem to be more concerned with keeping a secret from Production than from Russia. They give the impression that they are working strictly for the department and not for the company. Someone in every department should

have total access to the records and experience of every other department in all matters of mutual concern. This responsibility may be divided, but it should be known. Liaison is vital. Otherwise the growing attitude will be, "Well, thank God the leak isn't at my end of the lifeboat!"

13. Tolerating private files of company data. Some insecure persons, even in high places, seek to make themselves indispensable by hoarding information that should be generally available. Such persons hope to increase their importance by forcing others to come to them or to be dependent upon them. This may reach the stage where an individual can distort whole functions and organization plans by compelling his inclusion on the team because it is "his baseball bat." There has to be some reasonable limits on what constitutes "private" data. Experience that cannot be easily located simply does not exist for the person who needs it.

When Nothing Else Works. . . . There will be moments, when, despite all the training and experience you have acquired, despite the knowledge and tips you have gained from this book and others, you will need help. This may not be technical or quantitative help, but inspirational help.[62] It is really not a bad idea to start each business day by renewing your awareness of your need of these qualities.

Please, God, grant me:

- The spark to imagine
- The daring to innovate
- The discipline to plan
- The skill to do
- The will to achieve
- The commitment to be responsible
- The leadership to motivate

and do not forget (to expand on Sloma's words):

- The courage to decide!

SUMMARY

This chapter has dealt in considerable detail with the planning and decision-making functions of management. The processes, techniques, and skills necessary for effective planning, problem-solving, and decision-making have been analyzed and several mechanisms have been presented for developing and sharpening your capabilities in these areas. A practical framework of the concepts,

---

[62] Sloma, op. cit., p. 157.

principles, and techniques of planning and decision-making has been developed as a handy tool you can use in handling this aspect of your job.

This chapter concludes our discussion of the first two administrative skills necessary for effective managerial performance: building a viable organizational structure (Chapters 8 and 9), and planning, problem-solving, and decision-making (Chapter 10). The third, and last, administrative skill required for managerial competency is controlling and evaluating the engineering and R&D efforts. This will be the subject of Chapter 11. As you know, these three functions—planning, organizing, and controlling—are your primary administrative tasks.

VII
THE CONTROLLING
FUNCTION

11
Developing Your Control and Evaluation Skills

Achieving is the essence of managing. Measuring progress and evaluating what has been achieved is at the heart of the manager's task. Indeed, controlling is an enormously valuable managerial function as it enables the manager to measure progress toward objectives and take the necessary, if any, corrective action. Thus, the capacity to control, evaluate, and measure performance achievement is the last administrative skill you would have to acquire or develop as an executive.

Helping you understand and develop your skills in the managerial function of control is the aim of this chapter. The nature, importance, and types of control systems will first be discussed. The responsibility for control, timing, and characteristics of effective control systems will then be explored. This will be followed by a discussion of the various steps involved in devising an effective control system. The application of control systems in engineering and R&D will then be dealt with, followed by a discussion of the barriers and practical problems relating to establishing controls. The chapter will be concluded with a discussion of some guidelines to develop your skills in managerial evaluation and control.

NATURE OF MEASUREMENT, EVALUATION, AND CONTROL

There would be no need for control if plans, policies, and procedures would be flawlessly implemented and followed. As you know, this takes place only under static conditions. But since change is the law of the age, then there are always changes in management policies, goals, strategies, and tactics in a continuing effort to both control the environment and cope with it. The conditions inside and outside your organization are not static — they are dynamic. There is a strong need, therefore, for control. Taking a corrective action to assure the fulfillment of departmental and organizational objectives is the primary purpose of control. In this sense, your managerial task in the controlling function is very similar to that of a ship's captain — to bring the ship back on the right course once it has deviated.

While there is no question about the profound importance of the control function within the total scope of your managerial job, controls should be placed in the right perspective. They should not be overemphasized. In other words, control is a mean towards an end — not an end in itself.

The purpose of the control system is simply to help the organization meet its objectives — not to find wrongdoers.[1] In handling negative response to control, the positive approach of emphasizing the goals and objectives to be met should be taken, rather than catching the culprit and punishing him. "What seems to be the problem?" is the question, not "Who did something wrong or whom can we blame?" A manager should control in order to achieve organizational objectives, not to feed his ego.

I have clearly noticed the negative overtones the word *control* has for man work groups, especially for professionals in organizations. It is obvious that no organization can really function effectively without some sort of control system. Granted the special orientation of engineering and scientific personnel, their education, expectations, and task characteristics, they have — to varying degrees — a need for autonomy, freedom, and a colleagual type of control in organizations. It is also obvious that the professional requirements for a colleagual control system are not in tune with the bureaucratic requirements for a traditional authoritarian control system. This results in an intensive case of conflict for professionals in organizations, especially for scientists in R&D.[2]

Given the organization's need for some sort of controls and the professional's need for autonomy and colleagual control, both needs can be fulfilled through the design of appropriate organizational climates and control mechanisms directly tuned to the special needs of the professional.[3] It would appear that most engineers and scientists are cognizant of the fact that their efforts must be measured and evaluated if the company is to survive, grow, and stay profitable.

Perhaps the resentment and the negative sentiment witnessed against controls in many engineering and R&D laboratories are not so much directed toward controls as such but toward the manner in which they are enforced. In short, excessive bureaucratic controls applied rigidly can create resentment and hostility among engineers and scientists. In order to deal with this situation effectively, appropriate criteria to measure and evaluate their progress in terms of cost, time, and technical performance should be established.

Experience shows that many managers do not really understand the meaning of control as a managerial function. They also fail to differentiate between control and other managerial activities. To clarify this situation, let us now turn to a discussion of the differences between control and measurement and evaluation, planning, and performance appraisal.

---

[1] Webber, Ross A. Management: "Basic Elements in Managing Organizations." Homewood: Irwin, 1975, p. 341.

[2] For a review of this evidence see Badawy, M. K. Bureaucracy in Research: A Study of Role Conflict of Scientists. *Human Organization* (Summer 1973): 123-133.

[3] Ibid., pp. 130-131.

Control is a much broader concept than measurement and evaluation. It is the process of correcting the deviations from established values or limits of standards for performance.[4] Actually, controlling is a three-step process of measuring progress toward an objective, evaluating what remains to be done, and taking the necessary corrective actions to achieve or exceed the objectives.[5]

These steps can be defined as follows:

1. Measuring: Determining through formal and informal reports the degree to which progress toward objectives is being made.
2. Evaluating: Determining the cause of, and possible ways to act upon, significant deviations from planned performance.
3. Correcting: Taking control action to correct an unfavorable trend or to take advantage of an unusually favorable trend.

As you can see, measurement is but one aspect of the control process and precedes the actual correction of deviations from preestablished standards. Measuring is certainly a part of the manager's job and consists of:[6]

1. Devising and establishing measuring systems and media.
2. Recording and reporting performances of people and components.
3. Analyzing, appraising, and interpreting measured results.
4. Making known the measuring systems, media, and results.
5. Using results of measuring to readjust continually the work of measuring.
6. Exercising judgment and making reasoned, objective, and timely decisions to effect the measuring work and progress.

The other aspect of the control process is evaluation. Evaluation is the process of determining the value or amount of a specific entity, such as the causes of significant deviations from planned performance. Obviously, evaluation involves measurement and should be related to pertinent objectives and standards.[7] Determining objectives is possible in research and development, for example, but establishing standards is extremely difficult because the work is usually nonrepetitive and lacks precedent.

In the case of research and development, evaluation is the appraising, qualitatively and quantitatively, of the value or worth of scientific productivity and its

---

[4] Karger, Delmar W., and Murdick, Robert G. "Managing Engineering and Research," Second Edition. New York: Industrial Press, 1969, p. 366.
[5] Kerzner, Harold. "Project Management: A Systems Approach to Planning, Scheduling, and Controlling." New York: Van Nostrand Reinhold, 1979, p. 168.
[6] Karger and Murdick, op. cit., p. 367.
[7] Roman, Daniel D. "Science, Technology and Innovation: A Systems Approach." Columbus: Grid Publishing, Inc., 1980, p. 441.

administration.[8]   In R&D, evaluation tells how well the R&D is done, how much is accomplished by it, and how it is adjusted by feedback. The "how well" means how satisfactorily, how expertly, how appropriately — the degree of excellence of the results. "How much" refers to extent of the R&D. Evaluation means that a small or large amount of research and development can be done well or poorly.

Now that the difference and interrelationships between control and both measurement and evaluation-are clear, how does control differ from planning? Planning? and control are twin managerial functions. They are absolutely necessary for getting things done with and through people — for managing. Planning and control are so closely related that at times it is difficult to determine where the one ends and the other begins.[9]   However, they are not the same. A plan represents anticipated action; it is a passive concept until activity is actually initiated. At this point, control starts.

Control comprises the instigation of action, the determination of the activity required to meet objectives, and the evaluation of actual compared with planned performance. Control is an active process. The purpose of control, then, is to enable management to accomplish plans. It would be impossible to evaluate and control R&D activities, for example, without prior objective definition and planning. This is why research evaluation has been defined as the "process of judging past performance for the purpose of guiding future action."[10]

What about the difference between control and performance appraisal? Control is concerned, as we have seen, with measuring progress toward unit objectives through comparing actual versus planned performance. Performance appraisal, on the other hand, is concerned with individual employee performance. While many of the same factors will be measured, the approach is quite different, and the two activities are not to be confused.[11]

Another approach to differentiating between the activities is that the management activity of measuring and evaluating unit performance constitutes the controlling function. This is one of the administrative skills a manager must acquire. Measuring the individual employee performance, on the other hand, constitutes the performance appraisal activity which is part of the management function of direction. It is also one of the interpersonal — not administrative — skills of the manager.

To sum up: Since this book is intended to help you acquire and develop administrative skills, the focus of this chapter is on the managerial function of control. Developing your performance appraisal skills is, therefore, beyond the scope

[8] Walters, J. E. "Research Management: Principles and Practice." Washington, D.C.: Macmillan and Co., 1965, p. 250.
[9] Roman, op. cit., p. 369.
[10] Blood, Jerome (ed.). "The Management of Scientific Talent." New York: American Management Association, 1963, p. 215.
[11] Morrisey, George L. "Management by Objectives and Results for Business and Industry," Second Edition. Reading, Mass.: Addison-Wesley, 1977, p. 160.

of the present volume and will be mentioned only to clarify the discussion.[12] In the sense used here, controlling is measuring the progress toward the accomplishment of objectives and taking the necessary corrective actions. In this sense, control is different from the managerial activities of evaluation and measurement, planning, and performance appraisal.

IMPORTANCE OF CONTROLLING AS A MANAGERIAL FUNCTION

Control is a process by which managers measure and evaluate current performance against preestablished standards and take the necessary corrective action to ensure that objectives will be achieved. As discussed above, the three steps in the control process can be described as: measuring, evaluating, and correcting. These steps can also be stretched into five steps (the essense of the process, however, remains the same) as follows:[13]

1. Establishing goals and standards (planning).
2. Measuring performance.
3. Comparing performance with standards.
4. Analyzing deviations or variances.
5. Taking remedial action, if necessary (even modifying the orginal standards).

The view adopted here is that establishing standards, measuring performance, and taking corrective action comprise the basic steps in the control process. These steps will be discussed in further detail in a later section.

Why is controlling important? One reason for the importance of control is that in many respects, controlling is the essence of management. As you know, the manager's job is to get things done through other people, and he remains ultimately responsible and accountable for their achievements. It is only natural for him, then, to enforce a control system that will continually keep him informed of their performance and their progress toward preestablished objectives.

In fact, the concept of control is squarely founded and has strong premises in the other managerial functions. Consider the following:

Planning
1. A business exists only for accomplishment.
2. People work for a business only for accomplishment.
3. Resources are employed only for accomplishment.

---

[12] Developing the interpersonal skills of the manager — including performance appraisal — is the subject of another volume by the author in this series.
[13] Mosley, Donald C., and Pietri, Paul H., Jr. "Management: The Art of Working With and Through People." Encino, Calif.: Dickenson, 1975, p. 39.

Organization
   4. The right combination and balance of resources are needed for accomplishment.

Direction, Coordination, and Execution
   5. These resources must be properly directed through effective motivation, communication, leadership, coaching, and counseling for accomplishment.
   6. These resources must work in consonance with each other for accomplishment.

   Therefore,

Control
   7. The effectiveness of these foregoing steps is measured only for accomplishment.

It is obvious that controlling is closely interrelated with other managerial functions. Without effective controls, the manager will simply be operating in a vacuum without appropriate measures, feedback and accomplishments! (And at a prohibitive cost, I am afraid!)

Another reason why controlling is important is that the prime purpose of control is to determine not where we have been but where we are going. Since controls are concerned with the present and future, they enable the manager to continually detect whether events conform to plans.

Related to the second reason is a third: the fact that the only justification for managerial controlling to exist is to alert us when we are about to get into trouble, in sufficient time to take the necessary corrective action.[14] If we never needed to take corrective action, we would not need controlling as a management function. Corrective action in this respect is considered as a positive and anticipated part of the management process and not as evidence that someone has botched up.

A fourth reason is that since controls are means to an end, properly established controls can be very effective tools for ensuring a uniform understanding of organizational policy. On the other hand, if controls become objectives in themselves, they can turn the organization into a paper mill producing useless information without being cost-effective.

Finally, controlling complements planning.[15] Actually, planning sets a plane's course and controlling keeps the plane on it. You may lay out careful and elaborate plans, but unless you employ effective control, accomplishing the plans becomes largely a matter of luck.

---

[14] Morrisey, op. cit., p. 147.
[15] Mosley and Pietri, Jr., op. cit., p. 39.

Consider Murphy's law: If anything goes wrong, it will (this was discussed in Chapter 10). You might want to think of good control as trying to combat Murphy's law. Some variations of this law include the following:

- If several things can go wrong, the one that will go wrong is the one that will do the worst damage.
- There is never time to do it right, but always time to do it over.
- Once a job is fouled up, anything done to improve it only makes it worse.
- Left to themselves, things always go from bad to worse.

Having this short list on your bulletin board side by side with departmental controls might not be a bad idea!

In summary, in a very fundamental sense, controlling is the essence of managing. It is future-oriented; gives the manager advance warning signals when he is about to get into trouble; enables him to take necessary corrective action in time; ensures a proper understanding of policy; and serves as an attempt to combat Murphy's law. Properly installed and implemented controls can be enormously valuable means for achieving desired ends.

TYPES OF CONTROL SYSTEMS

There are several classifications of control systems. As shown in Table 11-1, three of the most common types are:

1. By type of input.
2. By dimension of control.
3. By time element.

By Type Of Input

Control mechanisms exist for different types of inputs or resources. These resources include human resources, financial resources (money), materials, time, space, machinery, hardware, and management (e.g., quality of management decisions).

By Dimension Of Control

The critical dimensions depend on the nature of the operation, the type of resources involved, and the purpose of controls. There are four common dimensions of control: quality, quantity, cost, and time. These are analogues to the three criteria common in evaluating engineering and R&D operations: performance (quality and quantity), schedule, and budget.

As you will note, Table 11-1 (pp. 296-297) presents control mechanisms for these four dimensions (criteria) employed by most organizations for controlling several types of organizational inputs or resources. Note that some of these control devices are used to fulfill more than one dimension in any of these areas. For example, performance appraisal is employed to assure both quality and quantity of performance. Also bear in mind that Table 11-1 is hardly exhaustive, and many other types of control devices can be employed.

By Time Element

There are four common types of control depending on the time when controls are enforced:

1. Pre-Controls. These controls are preliminary in nature and usually take place before the activity starts. Examples of such controls are market research and feasibility studies. They enable the manager to analyze market conditions, formulate sales forecasts and study consumer preferences before implementing manufacturing and production plans.
2. Steering Controls. These are concurrent controls where corrective action, if needed, is taken while the task or operation is being performed. Steering controls, therefore, offer the manager an excellent opportunity to deal with deviations in actual from desired results as they take place while the activity is still in progress.
3. Yes-No Controls. Because steering controls may be too expensive or not fully reliable, so yes-no controls are frequently needed. They indicate that the work is either acceptable or unacceptable. Examples of such controls include safety devices such as quality inspection and legal approval of contracts.
4. Post-action Controls. These controls come "after the fact" as they provide feedback comparing results to a standard when the action or task is completed. Examples of such controls include budgetary controls and final inspections. They can be an effective means for rewarding subordinates for good performance and for providing planning data for pre-controls and steering controls.

It is important to note here that all four types of controls are necessary for an effective control system; each has purpose and reason. The interrelationships among the different types of controls are shown in Figure 11-1.

To sum up: There are many classifications of control systems. Three major types have been introduced in this section: by type of input or resources used, by dimension of control, and by the time when controls are enforced. Needless to say, other classifications exist including functional control (marketing, engineering, R&D, and so on), project control, and information control.

RESPONSIBILITY FOR CONTROL AND USES OF CONTROL INFORMATION

Who should have the responsibility for controlling? The act of taking a corrective action is a function of the line manager. Every manager charged with the responsibility of functional performance in a certain area or division is ultimately accountable for results of that division or unit. The manager, therefore, is responsible for requesting information, measuring progress toward objectives, evaluating causes of deviations, and taking corrective actions. Bear in mind that control by the line organization is not limited to any level of management; effective control, in fact, requires that all management levels exercise control over those functions assigned to them.

It is interesting to note that whereas planning is usually done topside and communicated downward to the various organizational levels, control has generally been decentralized, except for company budgets, with information flowing from the bottom up.[16] Sine control should be formulated to achieve objectives, and since plans support objectives, the top-down planning and bottom-up controlling that most organizations practice might represent a contradiction. To deal with this problem, an integrated system of planning and control can be established in which an operation audit department or function is allied to planning so that management may get a complete picture of operations.

Who should get control information and how should it be used? Control information can be given to the manager or employees of the division whose performance is being measured. This information can also be given to managers at higher levels and to staff units. Remember that there are no specific formulas or prescriptions as to who should get what control information; and every organization should develop its own policies and procedures in this area.

However, an important guideline to keep in mind is that control information should be fed directly to the division or unit that can make the most meaningful use of the data.[17] This is in line with the concept that immediate feedback is a powerful learning tool. The sad fact, however, is that the departments or groups who should get and know first about control data end up being the last to find out! This frequently causes motivational and communication problems, especially for engineers and scientists who would like to be kept informed of what is going on and receive immediate feedback about their job performance.

---

[16] Roman, op. cit., pp. 387-388.
[17] Cammann, C., and Nadler, D. Fit Control Systems to Your Managerial Style. *Harvard Business Review*, 54 (January-February 1976): 65-72; and Lawler Edward E., III, and Rhode, John. "Information and Control in Organizations." Pacific Palisades, Calif.: Good Year Publishing Company, 1976, Chapter 8.

Table 11-1. Some Types of Control Systems.

DIMENSION OF CONTROL	TYPE OF RESOURCES (INPUTS)	HUMAN RESOURCES	MONEY	MATERIALS	TIME	SPACE
Quality		Performance appraisal Psychological tests Performance requirements reports Memoranda Manpower inventories Accountability	Audits Work measurement Reports Memoranda	Statistical quality control Visual inspection Inspection instruments Work measurement Inventory control Blueprints Reports Memoranda	Work measurement Reports Memoranda	Reports Memoranda
Quantity		Time study Work measurement Performance appraisal Accountability reports Memoranda	Budgets Profit planning Audits Work measurement Reports Memoranda	Operations manual Work measurement Inventory control Blueprints Reports Memoranda	Time study Deadlines Commitments Schedules Work measurement Reports Memoranda Ratios	Productivity per square foot Reports Memoranda Ratios

Table 11-1. Some Types of Control Systems. (Continued)

DIMENSION OF CONTROL	TYPE OF RESOURCES (INPUTS)	HUMAN RESOURCES	MONEY	MATERIALS	TIME	SPACE
Time		Committees Staff meetings Standard procedure Reports Memoranda Policy manuals Organization manuals	Forecasts Policy manuals Standard procedure Reports Memoranda	Operations manual Standard procedure Reports Memoranda	Forecasts Reports Memoranda Standard procedure	Standard procedure Reports Memoranda
Cost		Standard procedure Ratios Charts Performance requirements Policy manuals Organization manuals	Profitability accounting Return on investment Standard costs Policy manuals Standard procedure Ratios Charts	Operations manuals Estimates Standard procedure Charts Ratios	Standard procedures Charts	Cost per square foot Standard procedures Estimates Charts

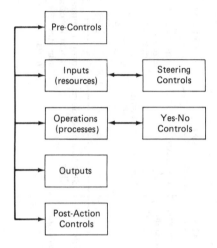

Figure 11-1. The interrelationships among the different types of controls.

The manner in which the control information will be used will have a bearing on its degree of accuracy. The data fed into the system by different divisions will generally tend to be more valid if they will be used for problem-solving, that is, if the control system is problem-oriented. However, the more the system is blame-oriented, the stronger the tendency of individuals to fudge the figures and play the numbers game. Because people do not like to be blamed or punished, the control system should have a low degree of policing orientation and a high degree of correcting thrust.

In short, line managers have the responsibility for measuring and evaluating their divisional performance. Control information should be given directly to the unit that can make the most useful use of the data. Such practice will minimize the hostility and resentment generated when data are first made available to higher-level executives. Control information should largely be used for correcting and not for catching people making mistakes or for punishing them. This latter practice will create distrust and reinforce employees' attempts to beat the system.

FUNDAMENTAL PRINCIPLES OF CONTROL

As you might have gathered by now, there is no cookbook or cure-all system of controls that will apply effectively to all situations and in all organizations. However, there are some important principles of control widely accepted by managers. These general principles constitute alternative possibilities that you might want

Table 11-2. Fundamental Principles of Control.

1. Principle of strategic control points.
2. Fail-safe principle of control.
3. Principle of random sampling.
4. Principle of subordinate's psychology of learning.
5. Principle of control choices.
6. Accountability principle of control.
7. Gresham's law of controls.
8. Principle of accuracy and timeliness.

to consider in solving control problems.[18] As shown in Table 11-2, there are eight principles of control.

Principle Of Strategic Control Points

Since an exhaustive control over all operations is seldom possible or justified, one approach to achieving optimum controls is to establish major control efforts at only the key, or limiting, points in a process. These are the points where important changes occur and are sometimes termed strategic control points.

A useful assumption in some situations is that people will concentrate their efforts on the parts of their job that they know will be inspected. This provides you with a very important tool for control. If you concentrate on the key-result area of their jobs (or if you are concerned with trivia), they may do the same. If the points selected for control are in fact the most strategic to the operation – either in the sense that they are the limiting factors or that they, better than others, show whether activities are occurring as projected – you may be able to exercise your talents over a larger group of subordinates and thereby possibly increase your span of management, with resulting benefits in cost savings and improvement of communication.

There are no universal rules for the actual selection of such points because of the diversity in organizational and departmental functions, the variety of products and services to be measured, and the infinite number of policies and plans. There are, of course, many rules of thumb. For example, strategic control points should be located at points in a process or operation where the cost of a failure is significantly greater than the cost of the control. Thus, in aircraft production, a critical control point is inspection of internal riveting in an outer-wing panel at that point in assembly prior to installation of the metal skin covering.

---

[18] This section is based on Sartain, Aaron Q., and Baker, Alton W. "The Supervisor and the Job." New York: McGraw-Hill, 1972, pp. 78-82.

Fail-safe Principle Of Control

If there is a danger that any part of an important plan might fail, then it should be assumed, for control purposes, that the failure will occur. Consequently, one or more duplicate or alternative ways of performing that part of the plan should be built into the plan.

Put more simply, some points are sufficiently vulnerable that they should be checked twice or more. In case of a failure, an alternative plan should (sometimes instantly) be available. You might recall that attempting to combat Murphy's law is one of the reasons for establishing managerial controls.

Principle Of Random Sampling

The principle of random sampling is really a supplement to the principle of strategic control points. Along with periodic inspections, you should pay random personal attention to what is going on in your department. Otherwise, as stated above, employees may spend a disproportionate amount of time and effort in work designated as strategic control points.

Presuming you have an understanding with subordinates as to exactly what is expected, this kind of random checking can consist in a large number of short conversations with each individual. This approach may be as simple as asking questions such as, Is everything OK? Any problems? Are you going to finish on time? Of course at other times it may have to be carried out formally.

Principle Of Subordinate's Psychology Of Learning

Your subordinates are continually trying to understand your personality, habits, and what makes you tick. They may even try to take advantage of (and capitalize on) your weaknesses and bad habits. In the course of an organization development (OD) consulting assignment, one engineer observed to me that his boss was always checking the slightest details in a project and was not satisfied until he came up with some mistakes, however trivial. Having learned about his boss's bad habit, the engineer, besides feeling resentful, decided to let the boss catch the errors instead of assuming personal responsibility for them.

Principle Of Control Choices

The principle of control choices relates to the corrective-action phase of control. The essence of this principle is that an effort should be made to consider several alternative kinds of correction before action is taken. It also stresses a critical point, that one of the choices is better administration of the existing ways in which things are being done. For example, before expensive replanning or reorganizing or establishing a new control system, an analysis may reveal that present plans, organization, and control systems are quite adequate if properly administered.

It is commonly cited that we as individuals, whether managers or subordinates, may frequently perform at no more than 35% to 60% of our actual capacity. If such a situation exists, the most promising alternative action might be better administration of present management systems (e.g., better employee motivation) rather than development and installation of an expensive new control system, or an attempt to find new employees. The rationale of this strategy is to try to "make do with what you've got" through better administration and utilization before you look for another expensive control system.

Accountability Principle Of Control

When corrective action is taken, many deviations from standards may very well not be the fault of a specific employee involved in the deviation. According to the accountability principle of control, an individual can be held responsible for deviations from standards only provided the following conditions are met: First, he must know what he is supposed to do. Second, he must know how to accomplish what he is assigned to do. Third, it must be within his personal control to regulate what he is doing.

To illustrate, employees can be held responsible for costs only if they know what their costs should be, according to a budget or some cost standard. Further, they must know what their costs are; there must be available a means of informing them of the costs as they are actually incurred. Finally, they must be able to regulate costs, for example, they alone should have the authority to requisition materials, or utilize services and facilities if they have the sole cost responsibility for such factors.

If all these conditions are present simultaneously, then a manager might be warranted in holding subordinates responsible. If any one of them is absent, the subordinates cannot be held fully responsible.

Gresham's Law Of Controls

Gresham's law of controls is derived from Gresham's law of money: bad money drives out good money. The point to be made here is that bad controls tend to drive out good controls. If managers establish employee controls that are unrealistic or unethical or are not being enforced, the result can be the abandonment of all reality in meeting standards. Unless such "bad" controls are corrected, they may drive out all controls, including the "good" ones.

It is especially important that a control be established in such a manner that if the activity it monitors ceases, the control becomes inoperative. Obviously, if a control continues to function beyond the life of the activity, costs increase, the accuracy of total input data is sometimes questionable, and confusion may arise.

Principle Of Accuracy And Timeliness

An obvious but frequently neglected principle is that critical control information must be gathered by the manager and relayed upward with optimum accuracy and timeliness. A properly devised control system filters out unimportant information and reports only significant items. This reporting or feedback must accurately report deviations. Of course, in an attempt to attain a high degree of accuracy, more time may be necessary to get adequate data. On the other hand, unless controls provide data on a timely basis, results may be nothing more than an historical record of events.

If time and accuracy come into conflict, the manager is, of course, faced with the important responsibility of determining which is more critical. This decision will depend upon such factors as the magnitude of the decision, the time pressure involved, and the amount of additional information necessary to make a better decision.

CHARACTERISTICS OF EFFECTIVE CONTROLS

While a well-designed control system can be of enormous help to the manager in enhancing efficiency and effectiveness, a poorly designed system can be dysfunctional, costly, and inoperative. It can also cause a lot of negative sentiment and resentment among employees. It would be important, then, to understand the criteria good control systems must meet and the characteristics of effective controls.

Table 11-3 presents 14 characteristics of effective controls. In going over this list, keep in mind that while these characteristics are quite desirable in designing (or modifying) any control system, you might have to make some trade-offs to maintain appropriate balance in the system.[19] Please be sure, as noted in the previous section, to use good judgment.

Controls Must Be Tied To The Needs And Nature Of The Activity

The control system must be based on the area in which results are expected and on the job they are expected to perform. A marketing department, for example, may use precontrols for product introduction and yes-no controls for specific advertisements. A vice-president in charge of manufacturing may generally use more sophisticated and broad-ranging controls than a shop floor supervisor.

---

[19] This section is based on Koontz, Harold, O'Donnell, Cyril, and Weihrich, Heinz. "Management," Seventh Edition. New York: McGraw-Hill, 1980, pp. 720-739; Huse, op. cit., pp. 189-191; Sartain and Baker, op. cit., pp. 78-80; Fulmer, Robert. "The New Management." New York: Macmillan, 1974, p. 259; Caplan, E. "Management Accounting and Behavioral Science." Reading, Mass.: Addison-Wesley, 1971, pp. 68-69; Morrisey, op. cit., pp. 147-148; and Scanlan, Burt K. "Management 18: A Short Course For Managers. New York: Wiley, 1974, pp. 89-90.

Table 11-3. Characteristics of Effective Controls.

1. Controls must be tied to the needs and nature of the activity.
2. The system must be current.
3. The system must develop records on all objectives.
4. Controls must indicate deviations promptly.
5. The system must report deviations directly to the employee responsible.
6. Controls must be forward looking.
7. Controls must point out critical exceptions at important points.
8. Controls must be reliable.
9. Controls must be valid.
10. Controls must be flexible.
11. Controls must be understandable.
12. Controls must indicate corrective action.
13. The system must reflect individual responsibilities as well as overall results.
14. Controls must be economical.

The closer controls are designed to reflect the specific nature of plans and expected results, the more effective they are.

The System Must Be Current

Control, as stated earlier, is concerned with the present. If its purpose is to be achieved, then the system must be current.

The System Must Develop Records On All Objectives

The achievement of the total organization's overall goals and objectives is possible only if individual departments and functional areas accomplish their objectives. Therefore, to ensure success, the control system must develop records on all objectives for all units of the organization. Assuming that corrective action is taken wherever and whenever it is needed, there will then be a coordinated thrust throughout the entire organization.

Controls Must Indicate Deviations Promptly

The ideal control system detects potential deviations before they become actual ones. Although it is important to know when things are going wrong, it is even more important to know beforehand that they are likely to go wrong.

The System Must Report Deviations Directly To The Employee Responsible

Although an employee's superior should also receive feedback on the status of an operation, if the employee is to direct and control his own performance, he must know on a periodic basis where he stands.

When progress reports are made available to those who are actually doing the work, a climate is created in which they can adjust their own performance as opposed to being told to do so. Also, there is less need for the manager to be acting in a policing capacity. Rather, he can function as a coach. The only time he needs to step in is when adjustments are not being made or if the performance gap is such that he wants to make sure that it has been spotted and something is being done.

Controls Must Be Forward Looking

Since there is usually a time lag between a deviation and a corrective action, forecasting should be used as a method of control. For example, although accounting reports are usually accurate, they occur after the fact. The manager may, however, want to forecast the future (with all its potential for error) rather than wait for an accurate report about which little can be done.

Controls Must Point Out Critical Exceptions At Important Points

The manager is almost constantly faced with varying degrees of pressure of one kind or another. A properly designed and administered control system can go a long way toward simplifying the manager's task. The control system should focus on deviations from objectives so that problem areas can be quickly spotted.

The idea behind focusing on deviations is not, of course, to chastize but rather to help to quickly pinpoint where some type of corrective action needs to be taken. If control system does not specifically pinpoint deviations, the manager must spend a considerable amount of time analyzing and trying to interpret the reports with which he is being furnished. Also there is the danger that some potential problem areas will be overlooked.

The exception principle specifically holds that at least major controls over quality, quantity, time, and cost should be restricted to the relatively few, exceptionally important work tasks or things. Put differently, in any series of elements to be controlled, a selected small fraction, in terms of numbers of elements, always accounts for a large fraction, in terms of effect (obviously this does not mean the "trivial many" should be ignored).

This principle applies to the control of both people and things. It recognizes that controls are always expensive to some degree, and if not carefully developed and installed, can quickly mushroom to the point where the cost in maintaining them far exceeds their value to the organization.

For example, as applied to people the principle holds that a small percentage of the total employees on the payroll usually account for the bulk of the personnel headaches, accidents, and so on. Also relatively few of a large number of workers are accident prone, generally speaking. Similarly, on the positive side, relatively few are highly creative or are the informal leaders. The manager's attention to these out-of-the-ordinary people is likely to pay large dividends.

An example relating to the control of things is the concept that a relatively few exceptional items out of an inventory of thousands of items can justify having the most concentrated controls. In an assembly plant a great many items such as bolts, nuts, and rivets may receive only minimal control. They may be placed at the point of use; and even though a considerable amount of pilferage or destruction may be predicted, this may be less expensive in terms of total cost than extensive control of such items would be.

On the other hand, exceptional items of inventory, such as metal hardness testers and expensive tools and dies, may justify extensive controls. However, these controls may be expensive, involving perhaps floor space, an enclosed structure, storage shelves and other equipment, a requisition clerk, and requisition paperwork. Not least among other costs is the time of staff personnel who must process such paperwork and the time of workers who must requisition such inventory and return it after use. Thus, the exception principle is to be applied carefully and exceptional things controlled no more than necessary.

Controls Must Be Reliable

Accuracy in reporting results is essential. As computers are used more widely in organizations, information transferral becomes less of a problem and good data more of one. One way of ensuring the reliability of data is to make certain that those reporting it do not perceive the ultimate use as being punitive to them. We all hate to testify against ourselves!

Controls Must Be Valid

The validity of a measurement is the degree to which it actually measures what it is supposed to measure. Counting the number of different clubs used by a golfer gives no idea of the person's score. One of the best examples of deliberate mismeasurement occurred a few years ago. Two cars were entered in an international road trial. One was from Russia, and the other was from the United States. The U.S. car won, but the Russian press reported that "while the Russian car had finished second, the American car came in next to last." Although the figures were accurate and the reporting reliable, the conclusion was not valid.

Controls Must Be Flexible

Because we live in an uncertain world, it is dangerous to make controls too objective and inflexible. There are always going to be changes in plans and unforeseen circumstances to alter any situation. One way of maintaining flexibility is to have alternative plans (and controls) for various possible situations. A sure sign of an organization that has inflexible controls is the failure to remove obsolete ones. This could, in fact, encourage people to ignore controls.

Controls Must Be Understandable

In the age of complex mathematical formulas, charts, and computer printouts, a tendency has arisen to develop controls that are not understandable by those who use them or by those who are controlled by them.

An often told story goes this way: A man was told by his superior to dig a hole. As soon as the hole was dug he was told to fill it up. Then he was instructed to dig a second hole and to fill it up, too. After his third hole, he declared, "I quit—this is silly." The manager finally explained that he was trying to locate an old pipeline. "Why didn't you tell me?" demanded the employee. "I was stationed here during the war when this was a fort, and I helped lay that pipeline." He promply took the boss to the exact spot in question.

Ridiculous? One in a million? Not at all! This kind of thing happens quite often in your organization and mine with infinite variations. Remember that objectives must be clear to subordinates, and that if the control system cannot be understood and easily used by those involved, it is a liability rather than an asset.

Controls Must Indicate Corrective Action

An effective control system must do more than just flash a red light. It must indicate not only that deviations are occurring but also what corrective action should be taken. A control is of value only if it allows decisions to be made before a crisis develops. This means that the control system must show where failures are occurring, who is responsible for them, and what should be done about them.

The System Must Reflect Individual Responsibilities As Well As Overall Results

Overall results are the sum total of the efforts of individuals. Therefore, the control system must be complete in that it produces records for individuals as well as in the total. If the system does not deal with individual responsibilities, there is not only the danger that overall results will not be achieved but also the danger that attention will focus on identifying, after the fact, who made a mistake. This, of course, is not congruent with the purpose of control.

Controls Must Be Economical

Controls are means to an end, not an end in themselves. A control process that costs more than the results it controls is not worth having. The effective manager carefully reviews control systems to ensure that they are cost-effective, and one way of doing this is to control only critical and important areas. A constantly increasing expenditure of people and money is often a lazy manager's way of trying to counterbalance an inherent inefficiency. In one company, an executive vice-president spent many hours a week reviewing expense accounts of sales engineers and other employees. In two years, he changed not a single expense account, but he continued the reviews anyway. From the viewpoint of the total organization, his time could have been more profitably spent in other activities.

The point that should be kept in mind here is that controlling is a cost item. It does not produce any unit output. While it is a very crucial process, controlling represents time and effort that the manager and his subordinates could otherwise be devoting to productive activities. Therefore, it must be clearly recognized that effective controlling provides for adequate visibility in a timely fashion with the least expenditure of time and effort.

It is also important to note that the degree of controlling exercised by individual managers tends to be one of extremes. Either there is little or no systematic method of controlling the work, or at the other extreme, there is far more control than is necessary to reasonably ensure effective performance.

Furthermore, what is even more of a problem is the tendency of many managers to continually vacillate between the two extremes, while rarely stopping at some point in the middle. For example, an organization whose employees spent a substantial amount of time in travel required three approval signatures on detailed travel expense vouchers, yet no advance authorization for the trip itself.

In short, just as there is no reason for an employee to be on a payroll if he fails to pay his way, so it is with controls. They must pay for themselves. Since controlling is a nonproducing cost item, managerial judgment must be exercised to make certain that it is used in a consistent manner and in proportion to the value of the data derived. In other words, a cost-benefit analysis must be applied to the function of controlling. Although there is a risk in this approach, the effective manager must take risks—which means that on occasions his judgment will be wrong. However, the cost of being certain that he is always right is prohibitive.

HOW TO DESIGN AN EFFECTIVE CONTROL SYSTEM

Designing an effective control system, like many facets of management, is an art. It takes imagination, creativity, judgment, and experience. In developing such a system, you should address yourself to four major questions the system you devise must answer:

1. What should be controlled?
2. Where should controls be concentrated?
3. How do we control? What are the steps in the control process?
4. What are the major tools and techniques for control?

These questions will be discussed in the balance of this section. While these questions will be answered separately, they are closely interrelated. Throughout the discussion, please bear in mind that these four aspects constitute the primary phases of a control system, and that managers, in designing the system, go through these phases simultaneously.

What Should Be Controlled?

As noted above, it would not be economically feasible to establish control measures on all factors affecting departmental and organizational objectives. How, then, can we determine where our control emphasis should be placed? In deciding where to place control emphasis, two things need to be done.[20]

First, you must identify the relatively small number of critical factors that will have the greatest impact on the achievement or lack of achievement of objectives. Control efforts can then be concentrated in those areas where the risk is greatest. This concept is known in economics as Pareto's law or the *principle of the critical few*. A variation on the concept of cost-benefit analysis, this principle shows the relationship between the cost of the input and the value of the output as we set priorities on where our efforts should be directed. For control purposes, you also need to examine your departmental objectives in terms of the four basic elements discussed above: quantity, quality, time, and cost. Anything that will require corrective action will relate to one or more of these basic elements.

As discussed above, in applying the principle of the critical few to the function of controlling, you will recognize such things as:

- A small group of employees that can be counted on to produce the greatest amount of acceptable work.
- A small group of employees that can be counted on to produce the largest number of errors.
- A small group of employees that will consistently have the highest rates of accidents, absenteeism, or tardiness.
- A small group of employees that can be counted on to produce the largest number of creative new ideas.
- Certain operations or units that will regularly cause the biggest and most frequent bottlenecks.
- Certain equipment that will have the heaviest breakdown rate.
- A few products or services that will generate the greatest sales return.
- A few products or services that will create the most customer dissatisfaction.
- A limited number of customers or markets that will produce the greatest profit.
- A limited number of customers or markets that will produce the greatest number of sales problems.

---

[20]Morrisey, op. cit., pp. 148-150.

- A limited number of customers who will present serious collection problems.
- Certain times of the day that are most likely to present opportunities or problems.
- Certain times of the year that are most likely to present opportunities or problems.

The second consideration in determining what should be controlled is to place controls where they have the greatest potential—at the point where action takes place. This is called the *principle of point of control.* As discussed above, this principle drives home the point that control data must be made available to the manager and/or the employee directly accountable for the action at least simultaneously with, if not prior to, its availability to higher-level management.

This becomes increasingly critical with the use of computers to supply control data. One of the most frustrating and demoralizing things that can happen to a first-line supervisor is to learn about a production problem in his unit as a result of a report first issued to upper management and then fed downward. Aside from being a poor management practice, the problem might have been solved sooner if the supervisor had not had to wait for the data to filter down.

Where Should Controls Be Concentrated?

This phase of the design of control systems concerns the functional areas that should be controlled. Controls should be established in areas relating to the inputs, processes, and outputs of the organization. Examples of areas of control include organizational resources such as people, financial resources, materials, time, and space. There are several forms of control including production control, quality control, inventory control, and budgetary control. Dimensions of control include cost, time, quantity, and quality of the output. Since these items were already discussed earlier in this chapter in the section on types of control systems, they will not be further elaborated here.

How Do We Control? What Are The Steps In The Control Process?

As discussed earlier in this chapter, the basic control process includes three steps. (Figure 11-2):

1. Establishing performance standards.
2. Measuring performance against standards.
3. Taking corrective action.

Establishing Performance Standards. Standards are units of measurement serving as criteria against which actual performance will be compared. As you know, the essence of the control process is to take corrective action and deal with deviations

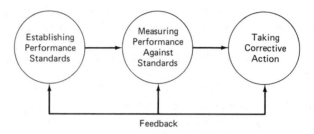

Feedback

Figure 11-2. Steps in the control process.

in such a way that objectives will be achieved. In order to evaluate current performance, we need to have some measures against which this performance will be evaluated. These measures are the standards without which controlling will be impossible. These standards are, of course, based on the goals predetermined in the managerial planning function. It follows that establishing standards is a crucial step in the controlling process.

How do we go about establishing performance standards? There is no easy rule. Standards can be objective (quantitative) or subjective (nonquantitative). Appropriate standards depend, among other things, on the nature of the task to be evaluated, the manager's experience and background, organizational policy, management philosophy and constraints, and subordinates' orientation and expectations.

It is important to keep in mind here that managers are, understandably, much more comfortable with quantitative measurements and standards than with subjective qualitative criteria for evaluating performance. However, you should also understand that there are no such things as perfect units of measurement. In no other field is this point more accurate than in the field of management, because of the nature of the activity, the complex world of the manager, the subjective nature of the managerial task itself, and the complexity of the human factor. It would be much easier to control and measure the behavior of things than the behavior of people.

As a former scientist or engineer, you have to learn and get used to living with subjective measuring units in management which are far less elegant and much fuzzier than those in engineering and science. Perhaps you can understand by now that the managerial control problems in engineering and R&D management are less related to establishing goals and objectives than to establishing standards for measurement and control. There is no substitute, I am afraid, for deciding on the best indicators of successful performance toward the achievement of your unit's objectives—however subjective those might be.

What type of standards can you use? Some of the possible control standards you can use are shown in Table 11-4. Remember that the main purpose of a standard is to serve as an effective indicator of successful performance. When the standard is not met, it is a warning signal that something is wrong, and some sort of corrective action is needed. The degree of appropriateness of a set of perfor-

Table 11-4. Some Types of Performance Standards.[a]

TYPE OF STANDARD	PERFORMANCE INDICATORS
1. Physical standards	Materials used, labor employed, services rendered, and goods produced or sold.
2. Cost standards	Monetary measurement, costs of operation in dollars, and indirect costs per unit produced or sold.
3. Capital standards	Asset usage, return on investment, current assets to current liabilities, and judgment of how well present resources are being used.
4. Revenue standards	Sales in dollars, dollars per ton, average revenue per customer, and per capita (population) sales in a given market.
5. Program standards	Subjective, experimental timing, appraisal of programs, and performance reports.
6. Intangible standards	Competence, loyalty, alertness, and employee morale.

[a]Adapted from Eckles, R. W., Carmichael, R. L., and Sarchet, B. R. "Supervisory Management: A Short Course in Supervision." New York: Wiley, 1975, p. 48.

mance standards depends on the nature of the activities to be measured along with the extent to which these standards meet the characteristics of effective control systems discussed earlier in this chapter.

It is very difficult to establish realistic performance standards in engineering and R&D because of the creative nature of these activities. These are "think" types of work which, in may ways, defy objective quantitative measurement.

However, here are some examples of standards that might be used as indicators of successful performance in engineering and R&D operations.[21]

- Number of new ideas generated.
- Number of new applications generated for current products or services.
- Approval/implementation of engineering and R&D plans.
- Anticipated dollar value of new ideas generated.
- Anticipated cost savings from innovations.
- Cost of engineering and R&D investment as related to total organization budget.
- Successful testing of prototypes.
- Quality of R&D effort—evaluated by accepted professional standards.
- Professional recognition of R&D efforts.
- Interest/response from customers.
- Interest/response from public/media.
- Interest/response from other organizations in similar fields.

[21] Ibid., pp. 155-156.

To sum up: The basic purpose of control is to make sure that plans and goals are achieved. Developing performance standards is an integral part of the control process and a fundamental prerequisite for implementing the two remaining steps in the control function. It goes without saying that providing the opportunity for your subordinates to participate in the design and development of performance standards will enhance their motivation, commitment, and support of these standards.

Measuring Performance Against Standards. The identification of variances is the prime purpose of applying standards to controlling performance toward objectives. This brings us to the second step in the control process: measuring performance. Rather than locking the barn door before or after the horse is stolen, a good control system will catch the thief in the act.[22] As discussed earlier, intermediate performance should be monitored to detect departure from expected performance when it first occurs rather than waiting until undesirable results have piled up. In this way corrective action can be initiated early.

It is important to note here that measuring results against performance standards actually requires two different activities—collecting the data and then comparing them with control standards. You should employ appropriate methods of data collection including status reports, various computer runs, statistical analyses, and so on—keeping in mind the fact that controlling, as noted above, is a nonproducing cost item. Once the data have been collected, appropriate measuring devices should be employed to compare actual results to performance standards. Examples of feedback mechanisms frequently used in the control process include visual aids (charts, graphs, etc.) computer printouts, written reports, staff meetings, periodic progress reviews, and "management by exception" technique.

In measuring current performance, please keep in mind that clear measurements are not always possible, especially in the case of R&D activities, as discussed above. This condition can be attributed to several factors including the nature of the activity itself, data availability, cost considerations compared to the potential use of the data, and the difficulty inherent in establishing performance standards in this area. The variety and the number of performance factors for which standards may be set make it virtually impossible to discuss problems of measurement applicable to all engineering and R&D operations. However, the characteristics of effective control systems discussed in a previous section of this chapter should be quite helpful in assessing the worth of different measuring devices you may consider.

Furthermore, management control systems are cybernetic systems, *cybernetics* being the processing and the interpretation of information. Control systems, therefore, are essentially information systems. Remember that the appropriateness of the corrective action (the next and final step in the control process) depends almost

---

[22] Webber, op. cit., p. 317.

entirely upon the kind of information received. This includes things such as timeliness of information, measurement units used, validity, reliability, and source—all of these criteria have been discussed in the section Characteristics of Effective Controls.

Now, how can you evaluate the control measures you have selected? As shown in Table 11-5 there are several questions you and your associates should ask; and the answers to these questions will assist you in this evaluation. This table also provides you with some practical tips for evaluating control measures.

Taking Corrective Action. The third, and last, step of the control process is taking corrective action. This is the moment of truth, since without action there is no control. Remember that the payoff of the control process is not the setting of standards, nor is it the measurement of performance against standards. It is taking the corrective action necessary to bring performance in line with the standards. This is a key part of your executive responsibilities.

Table 11-5. Key Questions for Evaluating Control Measures.[a]

1. What specific variances will these controls identify?
   Tip: Good controls should accentuate the occurrence of variances that have the greatest impact on the achievement of your objectives.
2. What significant variances may not be effectively identified?
   Tip: If you find that visibility on some significant variance is missing, you must either find another means of gaining this visibility or modify the proposed control measure so as to include it.
3. How much lead time is required to take effective corrective action? Does this control measure allow sufficient lead time?
   Tip: Finding out that something is wrong when it is too late to do anything about it is as bad as not finding out about it at all. A mechanism must be established to notify you when something is going off target (verbal notification by subordinates, progress reports, etc.).
4. How much time and effort will be required to apply this control measure?
   Tip: Before implementing a control measuring method, take a good look at what it will cost to get this information and then ask yourself:
   a. Does the value received justify this cost?
   b. Is there another, less costly measurement method available?
5. What is the danger of overcontrolling? How can this be minimized?
   Tip: It may be better to run the risk of too little control rather than too much. Spending an excessive amount of time looking over subordinates' shoulders could have two serious reactions:
   a. Natural resentment on the part of subordinates.
   b. Subordinates' tendency to let the boss catch the errors instead of assuming personal responsibility for catching them.

[a]Adapted from Morrisey, George L. "Management by Objectives and Results for Business and Industry." Reading, Mass.: Addison-Wesley, 1977, pp. 165-167.

This stage of the control process includes both a decision-making and an action-taking phase.[23] If there are deviations, there must first be an analysis and a decision about what is wrong and what corrective action should be taken. The second phase of correcting for deviations is initiating the corrective action, which may involve redrawing plans, modifying the goal or objective, or changing the general situation.

The point you should keep in mind here is that failure to meet expected levels of performance is sometimes unavoidable and calls for the development of new plans with the possibility of revised standards of performance. While it would be impossible to formulate a list of actions available to you (as each situation is unique and calls for its own solution), the frame of reference most valuable to you in evaluating the proposed action is the management process cycle. This means replanning, reorganizing, redirecting, and continued control since in a going organization all these functions have been performed in one way or another. In short, the management cycle is not composed of the four discrete steps of planning, organizing, directing, and controlling; instead it is a continuous process with control functioning as a catalyst to produce an integrated, continuous process.

Frequently, taking corrective action has a negative connotation. It automatically implies that the manager or someone else has done a bad job. This connotation should somehow be removed. One way to do this is by viewing the corrective action as a positive management activity and a normal part of the manager's job. Without action, there would be no control, and without control, the value of the entire activity of managing will be in serious question.

Now, assuming that performance standards are realistic, and that measuring devices are reasonably accurate, what kind of corrective action can you take? There are three types:

1. *Self-correcting action:* Acceptable tolerances in performance within which deviations tend to balance out over a period of time exist in certain situation. A deviation of 5% of the average daily output, for example, might not cause undue concern under certain conditions. Allowing for self-correcting performance without strong direction from above might also have considerable motivational value for the employee. Furthermore, this might contribute to the employee's self-development and reduce his need for such direction or correction in the future.

2. *Operating action:* Once it becomes clear that some corrective action needs to be taken, you should perform or have someone else perform specific operating work. You might, for instance, put another engineer in charge of a certain project or direct a production supervisor to revise operations schedules or to have one of his workers use a different machine.

---

[23] This discussion is based on Huse, op. cit., p. 188; Morrisey, op. cit., pp. 167-170; and Sisk, Henry L. "Principles of Management." Cincinnati: South Western, 1969, pp. 580-583.

Two crucial considerations must be kept in mind whenever such specific operating action is used: First, you might be dealing with just the symptoms and overlooking the actual cause of the variance. Sending a special courier out with a late dispatch may satisfy the immediate requirement, but it does not determine why the dispatch was late in the first place, so that future such occurrences can be prevented. Also, it is almost axiomatic that the more often we solve our subordinates' problems for them, the more often they will let us. The lesson to be learned is simple: Look for the real cause—not the symptom—of a problem, and coach the subordinate on how to deal with it.

The other consideration is to remember to resist the natural temptation "to get your hands back in the grease." After all, most of us probably became managers partially as a result of our technical competence and, deep donw, we still get our kicks out of solving technical rather than managerial problems. When we do this, though, we should recognize that we are not only performing work that a person in a lesser position (and, presumably, at a lower pay rate) should be performing, we may also be denying the subordinate a vital learning opportunity. The lesson to be learned from this is, again, a simple one: stick to managing and let the subordinate do what he was hired to do.

3. *Management action:* This type of corrective action requires the manager to review the management process that led up to the variance. It may have come as a result of poor planning, or an unexpected event may have made the variance inevitable. Corrective action, under the circumstances, might require changing the original objectives, plans, or policies to offset the variance. Management action in this situation would be directed toward adjusting performance to conform to objectives, and ensuring that the same problem will not occur again in the future.

So far I have described the three steps in the control process as if they were independent of each other. The fact of the matter, however, is that they are not. They are highly interrelated through the principle of feedback. As noted above, control is a cybernetic process. In a furnace system, the principle of feedback is used to "inform" the thermostat when the furnace should be turned on or off. In many respects, managerial control follows the same process—as shown in Figure 11-3.

What Are The Major Tools And Techniques For Control?

Control tools and techniques are numerous. Obviously, appropriate techniques depend on several factors such as the nature of the activity to be controlled, the technical know-how of the manager, subordinates' skills and backgrounds, policy requirements, corporate and departmental constraints (e.g., manpower requirements), and the cost of controls.

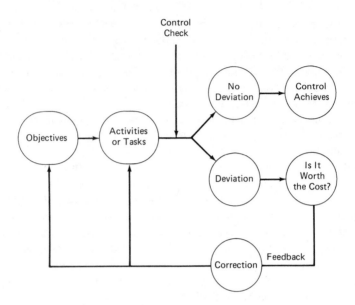

Figure 11-3. Control as a cybernetic process.

A detailed discussion of control techniques in engineering and R&D is beyond the scope of this book and would probably take another volume.[24] However, a brief treatment of some of the control tools used frequently by engineering and R&D managers will be discussed later in this chapter.

This concludes our discussion of how to design an effective control system. The focus has been on four major phases: the type of activities that should be controlled, the concentrations (locations) of control points, the steps in the control process, and the major tools and techniques for control.

BEHAVIORAL ASPECTS OF MANAGERIAL CONTROLS

It is probably true that there is nothing wrong with most organizations, it is only when you put people in them that they get fouled up. This observation applies most assuredly to managerial control.[25] It is people and their performance that become the subjects of control, and when this human element is introduced, problems invariably result. If people feel, for whatever reasons, that the control system

---

[24] These techniques are treated in Balderston, J., Birnbaum, P., Goodman, R., and Stahl, M. "Modern Management Techniques for Engineers and Scientists." New York: Van Nostrand Reinhold (forthcoming).
[25] This discussion is partly based on Scanlan, op. cit., pp. 92-93.

represents a threat to their overall security, they will adopt a pattern of behavior that in their estimation will, to a degree, defeat the system and thereby eliminate or at least temper the threat.

As shown in Table 11-6, there are several behavioral problems with controls. Eight major problems are discussed below.

Natural Resistance To Controls

In most situations, there is a natural resistance to controls. If the control system is administered in such a way that it is perceived as a threat, then people will react negatively to it. Examples include instances where the system focuses on mistakes rather than causes and corrections; where punishment is emphasized; where trust is lacking in the relationships involved; and where negative feedback affects the individual in terms of his employment relationships and career expectations.

Failure To Accept Organizational Goals

Since organizational goals are actually compromises between conflicting individual and group interests, then controls could be resisted by some organizational members. If the individual does not believe in what the organization stands for, he will not be motivated to conform to these goals. This, combined with group pressures and group norms will motivate the individual to seek the fulfillment of his needs via other routes possibly harmful to the organization.

Feeling That Standards Are Too High, Unattainable, Or Unclear

When the standards for evaluating performance are contradictory, unpredictable, or unattainable, people will object to these controls. For controls to be effective and to be accepted, standards must be consistent, predictable, and attainable. If the standards are too high, they will generate frustrations and disappointments among employees. If they are too low, the challenge and the incentive to meet or surpass these standards will be weakened. By the same token, when con-

Table 11-6. Behavioral Problems with Controls.

1. Natural resistance to controls.
2. Failure to accept organizational goals.
3. Feeling that standards are too high, unattainable, or unclear.
4. Excessive and mechanical controls.
5. Subjective and inaccurate data for controls.
6. Management's attitude.
7. Imbalanced controls.
8. Cost.

trols are vague, unclear, or not based on key factors affecting results, they are bound to be dysfunctional.

Excessive And Mechanical Controls

When plans and controls become ends to be followed blindly without assessment of their real contribution to the achievement of organizational or unit goals, they become ends in themselves. This is dangerous as it kills initiative and spontaneity. In this situation, people will object to controls because they are too restrictive, and this can generate frustration and apathy.

Subjective And Inaccurate Data For Controls

For controls to be effective, they must be impersonal and based on accurate and objective data. When controls are perceived to be biased, or based on inaccurate information, there will be a natural tendency to resist them.

Management's Attitude

Establishing an elaborate control system takes considerable effort and time. But if the system is not rigorously enforced, not only has this effort been wasted, but the resulting indifference will set an operational pattern throughout the entire organization. Both the control system and the manner in which it is implemented will largely determine its success.

Imbalanced Controls

Undercontrol and overcontrol are two undesirable extremes. Undercontrol produces confusion, discomfort on the part of subordinates, and indifference on the part of the superior. Overcontrol, on the other hand, creates excessive paperwork, robs the manager of valuable time, does not permit subordinates to do what they were hired to do, and fosters a feeling of distrust in them. Controls must be kept in balance: created for a good reason and implemented diligently.

Cost

As noted above, controls are expensive. Problems are created when people see the control system as not being cost-effective. If the system becomes a drain on company resources without corresponding tangible benefits, then management must consider whether doing away with control might be less troublesome than maintaining it.

TECHNIQUES FOR MEASURING AND EVALUATING ENGINEERING AND R&D

Problems In Measuring Productivity Of Technical Personnel

Several techniques have been used for measuring, evaluating, and controlling engineering and R&D operations. In the case of R&D, the word *control* is looked upon as a misnomer by scientists and engineers. Because of researchers' preoccupation with the quality of technical and scientific work, they believe that R&D cannot be controlled in the managerial sense. It can only be monitored, measured, and evaluated. Furthermore, researchers believe that the task of monitoring, measuring, and evaluating R&D performance can only be done by other scientists.

The reasoning is that managers frequently do not know enough to judge technical performance. Besides, they are naturally preoccupied with other business considerations such as cost, efficiency, and more importantly, the bottom line: profits. In short, research demonstrates that managerial controls are frequently perceived as major source of conflict or scientists and that they would much rather have colleagual controls than traditional bureaucratic controls.[26]

Several problems will face you in measuring the productivity of R&D and technical personnel. These include the following:

1. Difficulty in establishing goals in R&D.
2. Difficulty in establishing standards of performance because of the creative nature of the activity and the fact that it usually lacks precedent.
3. Labor-intensive character of R&D since a substantial part of R&D outlays are for labor.

As noted in this and previous chapters, the R&D activity, by nature, is quite different from other traditional corporate activities such as marketing or manufacturing. Evaluating R&D and its contribution to the company's well-being is, indeed, quite difficult since R&D activities are indirectly or distantly related to the final output of products and/or services.

It follows that traditional standard measures of performance (such as profit to sales, cash flow, or return on investment) are inappropriate in the case of R&D because:

1. R&D is only part of the overall innovation system of the company. In the chain of a company's activities, research stands at one end, followed in order by

---

[26] Badawy, op. cit.

advanced development, product or process design and development, pilot planting, production engineering, and finally, production.[27]

At the appropriate point a parallel set of activities is added in the form of marketing research, market development, and finally, sales. The key point is that it is quite difficult to evaluate the economic impact of an operation that is but one element near the beginning of a complex chain leading to the sale of products.

2. Significant time lags occur between research initiation and profitable results. This factor leads to complications introduced by the time required for passage along this long chain of activities, which may frequently be as long as 5 to 10 years, and in any case, at least a year.[28] Top management can and must be brought to appreciate this dilemma, and to accept evaluation standards that are applicable to the output of research and that convey some sense of relationship to income in accordance with the nature of the industry and the specific nature of the research program under scrutiny.

Internal And External Measures

There are two types of approaches to measuring engineering and R&D: internal and external. Internal measurement consists of comparing accomplishments against plans, standards, or goals.[29] Some direct criteria for measurement include evaluating the engineering and R&D inputs (money, personnel, facilities, time, and so on), processes (performance efficiency of individual activities), and output (type of contribution made to the organization). As discussed earlier in this chapter, the indirect approaches require using some indicators to measure the quality of engineering and R&D efforts such as number of patents, publications, citations of staff's work in literature, breakthroughs, firsts, discoveries, inventions, and developments.

External measurement evaluates R&D and engineering performance in comparison to selected competitors, companies in the same industry, and industry in general. Given the availability of the necessary data, this comparative analysis would provide R&D management and top executives with a useful indicator of how the company fares relative to others.

Regardless of the type of criteria used, the R&D and engineering measurement may be either in quantitative or qualitative terms. Quantitative measures, in spite of their weaknesses, are frequently used. These include financial ratios such as sales and earnings growth, net to sales, research and development to sales, and so

---

[27] Badawy, op. cit. Bracco, D. J. Top Management Reports and Controls. In Heyel, Carl (ed.). "Handbook of Industrial Research Management." New York: Van Nostrand Reinhold, p. 412.
[28] Ibid., p. 412.
[29] Karger and Murdick, op. cit., p. 367.

on. Qualitative measures evaluate the quality of judgment and decision-making, the degree of R&D and engineering integration into the objectives of the organization, and the quality of offensive and defensive R&D.

Table 11-7 present examples of both types of measures used in evaluating the efficiency and effectiveness of R&D operations. Both types of quantitative and qualitative measurements are necessary and should be used in evaluating engineering and R&D efforts. Generally speaking, the evaluation schemes should focus on such things as efficiency, quality, technical aspects, economics, cost reduction, product developments, basic and applied research, management evaluations, and overall contributions of engineering and R&D to the organization.

MEASUREMENT AND EVALUATION OF ENGINEERING AND R&D EFFORTS: EVALUATION IN ACTION

There are several levels or types of measurement in engineering and R&D. A brief discussion of the dimensions of evaluation and measurement techniques at six different levels will follow. These levels are:

- The individual.
- The group.
- The project.
- The product.

Table 11-7. Quantitative and Qualitative Measures of R&D.[a]

QUANTITATIVE	QUALITATIVE
1. Costs.	1. The prestige and image of the organization.
2. The percent of activity (sales) in new projects or products.	a. Professional.
	b. Public.
3. The number of new products or projects initiated within a given time period, as a percent of total product or project mix.	2. The technical caliber and reputation of the organization's work.
	3. The internal morale in the organization.
4. Profit.	4. The ultimate benefit to be derived from knowledge in related work.
5. Personnel turnover.	5. The retention of personnel.
6. The company's or organization's market position.	6. The ability, based on technical reputation, to attract capable new people to the organization.
7. The rate of growth.	
8. Patents granted.	7. The nature of work in process or contemplated as a means of maintaining technical competence and minimizing professional obsolescence.
9. Research reports.	

[a]Adapted from Roman, Daniel D. "Science, Technology and Innovation." Columbus: Grid Publishing, Inc., 1980, pp. 466-467.

- The engineering or R&D unit as a whole.
- The management of engineering and R&D functions.

The Individual. In general, measuring the performance of professionals has been a major challenge to management students and practitioners. This is partly because of the nature and diversity of what they do, and partly for the lack of appropriate measuring devices. It would appear, however, that measuring the performance of individuals engaged in development engineering is somewhat easier and more feasible than measuring the performance of those engaged in research. Goals and schedules are more specific and shadings of quality are easier to detect for engineers. The measurement of the creativity of scientists engaged in research has been based upon indexes such as quality and quantity of publications and estimates of potential value of discoveries to the company.

How can we measure the performance of researchers? There has been little agreement on operational definitions of scientific performance, let alone on what components to include or who should measure it.[30] Scientific output consists mostly of the discovery of new facts, the invention of new methods of doing things, and the combining of known concepts to create new devices.[31] In measuring the individual's scientific performance, the research available utilizes one or more of the following types of measures:

1. Overall performance.
2. Quantity of written output.
3. Quality of output.
4. Creativity of output.

Table 11-8 (pp. 324-325) presents various types of measures of individuals' research performance, along with the rationale behind each type as well as its weaknesses.[32]

In terms of measuring the scientist's overall performance, there is very little agreement as to what constitutes scientific output or what measures should be used to reflect the output. The instruments used to obtain performance scores range from very gross overall performance ratings to rather complex indicators of the quantity of written output and the quality and creativity of the scientist's output.

Even in what seem to be the most straightforward aspect of scientific performance, a scientist's written output, there is wide variability in the measuring methods. There is very little consistency with respect to what is included or left out of this measure, which makes it difficult to compare the results of different studies when written output is the dependent variable.

---

[30] Edwards, Shirley A., and McCarrey, Michael W. Measuring the Performance of Researchers. *Research Management* (January 1973): 34.
[31] Hirsch, I., Milwitt, W., and Oakes, T. W. Increasing the Productivity of Scientists. *Harvard Business Review,* **36** (1958): 66-76.
[32] This discussion is based on Edwards and McCarrey, op. cit., pp. 34-40.

Measuring the quality and creativity of output has raised numerous methodological problems relating to the type of criteria to be used in evaluation. Research has clearly revealed that scientific output is multidimensional and cannot be satisfactorily measured by any one criterion alone. Single criteria are, therefore, misleading.

In short, measuring the performance of researchers is a complex task. In addition to the problems spelled out above, measurement criteria must be both valid and reliable. They must also not be contaminated by other factors. Put differently, when an instrument is used to measure some aspect of scientific performance, it should not be sensitive to other variables.

Some of the criteria used in studies on measurement of scientific performance include productivity in written work, recent reports, originality of written work, professional society membership, judgment of actual work output, creativity ratings by high-level supervisors, overall quality ratings by immediate supervisors, likableness as a member of the research team, visibility, recognition for organizational contributions, status-seeking tendencies, current organizational status, and contract-monitoring load.

The Group. Measuring the performance of individual engineers and scientists means measuring one of the major inputs to the engineering and R&D functions. On the other hand, measuring the engineering and R&D process means measuring the group and its activities. The ultimate factor to be evaluated is how great a contribution this group makes in achieving the engineering and research objectives. Some criteria related to this aspect are:[33]

1. Actual development time for a project compared with a projected time based on standards established for the class of product involved.
2. Percentage or dollar change (plus or minus) in average yearly development cost per project by class.
3. Number of new improved products per year (or month).
4. Number of new products completed per year (or month).
5. Change (plus or minus) in the average yearly payoff per project for a class of products.
6. Change (plus or minus) in total payoff or profit earned on products designed by the group.
7. Square feet of new design drawings per month for a section.
8. Estimated or actual payoff for all products the section has developed.
9. Actual total payoff for all products developed and put in use on the market.
10. Development cost per person.
11. Development project cost per engineer or scientist.
12. Trend of the ratio of the cost of the engineering and R&D unit's cost to the sales volume of its product line, providing this is applicable.

---

[33] Karger and Murdick, op. cit., p. 374.

Table 11-8. Measuring the Performance of Researchers: The Individual Level.

TYPE OF MEASURE	RATIONALE	WEAKNESSES
1. Overall Performance	Scientific performance is defined in terms of the ranking or rating given a scientist (by superior, subordinate, and peers) on a dimension of overall performance.	1. This is a rough measure, and if used, should be in conjunction with other measures. 2. There is a halo effect (the tendency to rate the individual as either high on everything or low on everything). 3. Contribution to scientific knowledge and contribution to the organization are not necessarily the same.
2. Quantity of Written Output	It is reasonable to assume a high correlation between a scientist's value to an organization and the frequency with which he communicates his ideas.	1. Number of publications only measures a scientist's written output, not productivity. 2. It is not acceptable to operationally define scientific performance in terms of bibliographic counts alone. 3. No empirical basis for using particular weighting system for evaluating the scientist's written output or the quality of his papers. 4. Inconsistent measures are used for evaluating books vs journal articles.

Table 11-8. (Continued)

TYPE OF MEASURE	RATIONALE	WEAKNESSES
3. Quality of Output	Senior scientists evaluate works of others in terms of relevance, significance, originality, etc.; usually science citation index is used.	1. The different approaches used in the measurement of quality of output could generate conflicting evaluations of scientists. 2. What exactly do citations signify? 3. Significant work soon becomes common knowledge—referred to in papers but not cited. 4. Citations may be critical rather than positive. 5. Fewer "citers" are available for some papers. 6. Significance of scientific work is not always recognized by contemporaries. 7. Only the senior author is credited. 8. What is important to the scientist might not be to the organization.
4. Creativity of Output	Creativity can be rated on a graphic scale to measure such things as magnitude, originality, and usefulness.	1. There has been little agreement with respect to definitions of creativity or creative output. 2. There is no agreement on specific measures. 3. Demonstrated creativity vs creative ability or potential.

In the case of R&D, several studies were conducted for measuring performance. As noted above, there is sharp disagreement among researchers on the most appropriate criteria for evaluating scientific performance. Several performance measures were employed to evaluate both individual and group performance. Objective and subjective criteria were used in measuring the productivity of both basic and applied research. A classification of performance measures for individuals and research groups is presented in Table 11-9.

It is clear from Table 11-9 that whether we are talking about university or industrial scientists, multiple indicators should be used in a systematic fashion and the precise sense in which the term *performance* is used should be identified.[34] Internal measures of performance based on analysis of a scientist's publications should similarly be tested for validity and take account of the knowledge and the structure within which the scientist works.

It is particularly important in applied research to take account of the organizational context in which the work is carried out, just as it is important in assessing a scientist's contribution to basic science to be aware of the cognitive and technical norms in the discipline. The use of multiple indicators in measuring performance or social recognition is desirable in both types of research, preferably combined with an understanding of the process underlying the award of social recognition.

The Project. Technical projects and performance measurement is required to enable overall evaluation of the project. Project control ensures that task plans, schedules, and budgets are in order and that the objectives of the project will be achieved within time and cost constraints.

The project and functional managers achieve cooperative control by the following:[35]

1. Jointly understanding the project objectives and goals.
2. Jointly defining, planning, scheduling, and budgeting the tasks to be performed.
3. Using established procedures to authorize the work, to control changes and the scope of the work, and to control schedules and costs.
4. Measuring the evaluating performance in cost, schedule, and technical terms on a joint basis to identify current or future variances from the plan and to initiate appropriate corrective actions.

---

[34] Whitley, Richard, and Frost, Penelope. The Measurement of Performance in Research. *Human Relations,* **24,** 2 (April 1971): 161-178.
[35] Archibald, Russel D. "Managing High Technology Programs and Projects." New York: Wiley, 1976, p. 180.

Table 11-9. A Classification of Performance Measures.[a]

AREA OF RESEARCH:	BASIC		APPLIED	
TYPE OF MEASURE:	OBJECTIVE	SUBJECTIVE	OBJECTIVE	SUBJECTIVE
For individuals	Number of papers Number of books Number of citations Number of professional awards Number of powerful positions held	Prestige ranking by peers	Number of papers Number of patents Number of reports	Supervisor evaluation Colleague evaluation
For groups or organizations	Individual members' output Library facilities Number of graduate students Number of outside visitors	Prestige ranking by members of other groups	Individual members' output Cost and schedule overruns Number of adopted innovations "Parallel projects"	Executive evaluation Members' evaluation of organization relative to "top 10" University evaluation Professional society evaluation

[a]Adapted from Whitley, Richard, and Frost, Penelope A. The Measurement of Performance in Research. *Human Relations*, **24**, 2 (April 1971): 164.

Extensive literature is available explaining project control techniques—a subject too extensive to be further explored here.[36] However, to give you some examples a brief discussion of two of these techniques will follow. It should be emphasized that the use of both techniques is not, of course, limited to project planning and control. These techniques are: value engineering and analysis, and network analysis.

Value Engineering and Analysis. Value engineering and value analysis are closely allied techniques which identify unnecessary costs, that is, costs that do not provide high quality, greater usefulness, longer life, better appearance, or customer-desired features in a product.[37] Value engineering (VE) is concerned with the design aspects of a product, that is, the steps that take place before production is begun. Value analysis (VA) is concerned with the production materials and procedures, after completion of the design.

In practice, the terms value engineering and value analysis are sometimes used interchangeably. They are combined as *value management.* Value management is a control method that aims to find ways to get equal or superior performance from a product, a process, a function, or an activity at lower cost while retaining quality, performance, and reliability.[38] The broad objective, in other words, is to eliminate cost factors without jeopardizing the performance, salability, or usability of a product or the effectiveness of a function or activity.

To use VE and VA effectively you must seek and obtain valid and complete answers to these five questions:

1. What is the item?
2. What does the item cost?
3. What does the item do?
4. What else would do the job?
5. What would that alternative cost?

Effective use of value analysis requires developing a planned approach to each value problem. This, in turn, requires using a value analysis job plan consisting of the following seven steps:[39]

1. Orientation: Determine what is to be accomplished; what the customer really needs or wants; what size, weight, appearance, durability, and other characteristics are desirable.

---

[36] See, for example, Archibald, op. cit.; Martin, Charles C. "Project Management: How to Make It Work." New York: AMACOM (American Management Association, 1976; and Kerzner, Harold. "Project Management: A Systems Approach to Planning, Scheduling and Controlling." New York: Van Nostrand Reinhold, 1979.
[37] Hicks, Tyler A. "Successful Engineering Management." New York: McGraw-Hill, p. 161.
[38] Roman, op. cit., p. 378.
[39] Miles, Larry. "Techniques of Value Analysis and Engineering." New York: McGraw-Hill, 1961.

2. Information: Secure all pertinent information available—costs, quantities, drawings, specifications, manufacturing methods, vendors' names, etc. Examine the basic engineering and manufacturing. Determine the amount of effort that reasonably should be expanded on the important elements of cost.

3. Speculation: Generate every possible solution to the overall problems involved by free use of the imagination; brainstorming; exploration of materials, processes, parts, arrangements; etc.

4. Analysis: Estimate the dollar value of each idea; develop all ideas, emphasizing value and accomplishment; thoroughly investigate ideas having large dollar values; select the ideas and approaches having the most promise.

5. Program planning: Subdivide the job into a progression of functional areas, for example, a fastening job, and electrical-contact job, a support job, etc. Apply the applicable VA techniques. Select the best specialists and vendors for consultation. Investigate newest approaches; obtain the latest information on effective techniques. Supply all needed information to specialists and vendors to stimulate the best solutions.

6. Execution of program: Pursue constantly, regularly, thoroughly, and intensively each suggestion until it is completely appraised and evaluated. Provide more information and encouragement to specialists and vendors. Seek alternatives; use men who really want the different solution to work.

7. Summarization: Prepare a VA suggestion sheet. Use concise, meaningful, and readable language. Limit the suggestions to one page. Show a before-and-after sketch. Have the design or manufacturing engineer take action, once the suggestion is approved.

Network Analysis. The planning approach that stresses an awareness of every step in the production path is known as network analysis, a technique that makes full use of computers to attain maximum efficiency in planning and control.[40] Network analysis systems simplify project planning and control because the manager is forced to concentrate on only four main ingredients in establishing the critical path for production—the shortest route to a project goal:

1. A clearly recognizable end point or objective.
2. A list of separate, clearly defined, interrelated events.
3. The time required to complete each activity.
4. A starting point.

The two most common network analysis approaches are PERT (program evaluation review technique) and CPM (critical path method). PERT is a technique for defining, scheduling, costing, controlling, evaluating, and replanning activities

---

[40] Fulmer, Robert. "Supervision: Principles of Professional Management." Beverly Hills: Glencoe Press, 1976, pp. 245-246.

having sequential and concurrent steps.[41] CPM is a technique for planning a sequence of related and concurrent steps in a project so that the various steps are coordinated to ensure completion of the tasks as scheduled. The shortest and longest times for completion of the project can be determined by the CPM technique. The longest time interval is called the critical path. A major advantage of the CPM method is its ability to indicate which tasks can be done concurrently and which follow in sequence.

The basic elements of a network plan are events and activities.[42] Events indicate the start or completion of one or more activities, shown graphically as a circle, square, or other symbol. Activities indicate time-consuming tasks or actions without tasks shown as a line with an arrowhead representing the logical flow from start to finish.

The PERT user figures out three timetables for the completion of an entire operation: the most optimistic time (if everything goes right), the most likely time (if an average number of things go wrong), and the most pessimistic time (if everything goes wrong).[43] Although PERT's great strength lies in saving time, budget controls have been added to the approach by inclusion of a cost comparison factor.

While PERT is used primarily for first-time projects requiring complicated research and development, CPM can be used only with projects of a repetitive nature. The main advantage of the latter approach is its accurate computations of time and cost factors. CPM takes numerical information from previous projects and calculates how much time and money was spent in each step of these earlier operations. CPM works well in complex projects involving construction and maintainance, in which time limits are definite and cost is a significant factor. If three CPM activities are happening at the same time, each requiring different amounts of time, the control path follows the method expected to take the longest. Shortening the most time-consuming steps can shorten the overall project length. Figure 11-4 shows a typical operating-level PERT network from the electronics industry.

To sum up: The PERT/CPM networks, if used properly, can produce significant benefits, including:

1. Integration of all tasks with interface and milestone events.
2. Reduction in total project duration through improved overlapping of tasks and activities, where feasible and necessary.
3. Identification of the chain of events and activities leading to project completion, which forms the critical path. These are the activities and events that, if delayed, will delay the project completion, and that, if accelerated, will enable earlier project completion.
4. More effective integrated evaluation of actual progress by all contributors.[44]

[41] Hicks, op. cit., pp. 179-180.
[42] Archibald, op. cit., p. 159.
[43] Fulmer, op. cit., p. 248.
[44] Archibald, op. cit., p. 159.

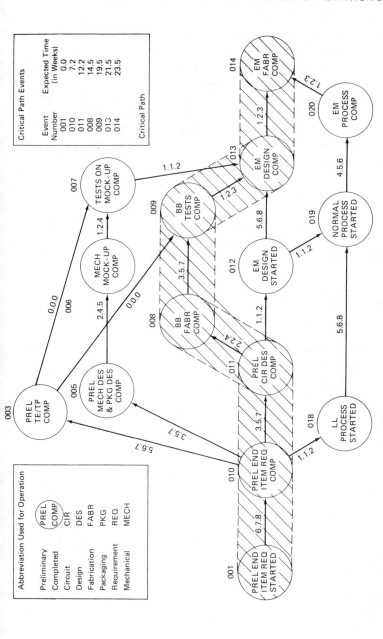

Figure 11-4. Typical operating-level PERT network. Numbers above circles identify events taking place. Numbers on arrows represent the three estimates of the time (in weeks) that the activity will require. (Adapted from Miller, Robert W. Project Control Techniques: "PERT" and "CPM" Networks. In Heyel, Carl [ed.]. "Handbook of Industrial Research Management," Second Edition. New York: Van Nostrand Reinhold, 1968, p. 264.)

The Product. Evaluation of the products created by the engineering and R&D functions can provide some insights into their contribution. While a material product can be measured and subjected to comparison and its approximate value in the commercial market can be assessed, products that have little or no direct commercial application is difficult to evaluate (as in the case of R&D).[45] For lack of a basis for direct comparison, the value of noncommercial hardware and knowledge must be measured in terms of mission requirements and accomplishment.

If common criteria for product evaluation can be established, R&D, engineering, management, marketing, finance, production, and the customer will probably place substantially different emphasis on them.[46] The product can be graded by the scientist or engineer according to how well it exemplifies the scientific principles involved. The financial people can evaluate it according to its profitability. The marketing division can judge its salability, share of the market, and potential as a means to sell other products. A product may not be analyzed by management for operational characteristics, but it can probably be evaluated for its contribution to the organization's objectives.

Several criteria can be employed for product evaluation. Examples of these criteria, which are closely interrelated, are presented in Table 11-10.

The Engineering or R&D Unit as a Whole. Imprecise as it might be, an evaluation of the efficiency and effectiveness of the engineering and R&D organization is crucial. It provides management with some indication of how both activities are contributing to the achievement of organizational objectives. While several criteria can be applied universally to both engineering and R&D, there are some specific measurement in each case. The following questions would be helpful in evaluating the effectiveness of the engineering organization.

1. How well is engineering doing in relation to competitors regarding the improvement of products and the finding of new ideas?
2. Are the products reliable, easily produced, and maintainable?
3. Do the products fit the market needs as interpreted by Marketing?
4. Does the engineering organization always have a backlog of potentially profitable projects that it was proposed?
5. Is the engineering organization building a reservoir of knowledge and attracting talented new people?
6. Are good technical reports of progress issued periodically?
7. Are costs of engineering controlled reasonably well?
8. Is there a steady flow of patents being issued?

---

[45] Roman, op. cit., p. 461.
[46] Ibid., p. 462.

9. Is the engineering group "lucky" enough to come up with a valuable discovery or innovation from time to time (jointly with the research group)?[47]

In evaluating the performance of the R&D organization or unit, the questions presented in Table 11-11 will provide management with several useful insights and guidelines.

Table 11-10. Criteria for Product Evaluation.[a]

1. Technical criteria
   a. Feasibility
   b. Reliability
   c. Performance–operating characteristics
   d. Structure
   e. Design
2. Production criteria
   a. Reasonable specifications
   b. Material
   c. Producibility
   d. Standardization
3. Financial criteria
   a. Production and development costs
   b. Growth potential
   c. Related capital investment
   d. Profitability
4. Marketing criteria
   a. Unique product characteristics
   b. Price
   c. Performance
   d. Potential market
5. Management criteria
   a. Product life expectancy
   b. Contribution to objectives
   c. Profit
   d. Prestige
   e. Relationship to other product activity
   f. Resource requirements
6. Customer criteria
   a. Price
   b. Quality
   c. Performance
   d. Safety features
   e. Repairability
   f. Operating costs

[a]Adapted from Roman, Daniel D. "Science, Technology and Innovation: A Systems Approach." Columbus: Grid Publishing, 1980, pp. 462-463.

[47]Karger and Murdick, op. cit., p. 377.

Table 11-11. Criteria for Evaluating the Performance of R&D Organizations.[a]

1. Is there a comprehensive long-range research plan that is aligned with corporate goals?
   a. Is it formalized, written, and updated at least annually on an organized basis?
   b. Does it give separate treatment to the profit and other corporate objectives that can be served by basic research, applied research, and development within the exististing businesses, and R&D as applied to new business, manufacturing technical service, and sales technical service—with appropriate balance among these activities?
   c. Does it break down the research plan by appropriate broad product areas?
   d. Do all the policymaking people in the research group understand the long-range plan and its foundations in corporate objectives?
2. Is the long-range research plan backed up with tangible, specific, and periodically updated programs to meet the research objectives?
3. What percentage of our earnings is derived from new products developed by research within the last 5 (or last 10) years?
4. To what extent were our products, and subsequent improvements, first introduced by us rather than by competitors?
5. What does market research show as to the quality standards of our products for the applications to which they are directed?
6. To what extent are the sources of our new products based upon our own research (vs licenses, purchase of patents, etc.)?
7. What has been happening to our share of the market? (This, of course, can also be strongly affected by marketing and manufacturing considerations.)
8. How does our ratio of patent grants and the use or value of granted patents compare with competition? (This, of course, is not an end in itself; it can be an indicator, but must be treated with caution.)
9. To what extent has research been instrumental in cost reduction programs? In increases of productivity?
10. How do our research expenditures, in proportion to our size, compare with those of individual competitors?
11. How do individual competitors score on the above pragmatic tests?
12. What is the quality and extent of our advance product-planning program?
13. Are the external groups with which Research deals effectively served (making allowances for normal gripes and complaints)? Criteria:
    a. Breadth of the line as measured by Marketing.
    b. Innovations in the line as measured by Marketing.
    c. Process quality as measured by operating units.
    d. Process economy as measured by operating units.
    e. Competitive sales technical service as measured by customer reaction.
14. Is there a stamp of innovation and creativity within the organization?
    a. Is there sufficient daring to depart from orthodox approaches?
    b. Does it adjust well to new challenges and changed conditions? (See also the pragmatic tests, 3 through 9, above.)
15. Are the key people within the organization possessed of strong motivations, as manifested by degree and sustenance of drive?
16. Are effective techniques in use to get the most value from the whole research organization?
    a. Organized system for idea feedback at all levels.
    b. Effective communications both up and down the line.
    c. Good level of internal cooperation and morale.
    d. Leadership ability to inspire incentives and rewards.
17. Is there a depth of personnel behind the key positions and an organized personnel development program?
18. Do we, personally, have confidence in the individual who is heading our research activities?

[a]Adapted from Hill, William E. Management of R&D Through Long-Range Strategic Planning. In Heyel, Carl (ed.). "Handbook of Industrial Research Management," Second Edition. New York: Van Nostrand Reinhold, 1968, pp. 58-59.

The Management of Engineering and R&D Functions. An important aspect of measuring and evaluating engineering and R&D operations is to assess the activities and quality of the management of both functions. An audit is an independent evaluation of an activity against specific requirements or criteria.[48] Examples of these are applicable codes and standards, contract requirements, and local management policies and directives.

A management audit of engineering and R&D is a systematic examination, critical analysis, verification, and reporting of results of the quality and quantity of management and its effects, by an investigation or survey of how well the elements of management are being carried on, accomplished, and developed.[49] In other words, it is the breaking down of engineering and R&D management into its elements and subelements; the analysis of each by finding the quantitative and qualitative factors that show how well R&D or engineering is being managed; the nature, proportions, function, and the relationships of those factors.

How would you go about performing an audit? There are four major steps in conducting effective audits:

1. Planning and preparation.
2. Performance of the audit.
3. Reporting of the results.
4. Follow-up and closing out.

These steps and the techniques that should be employed in each step are presented in Table 11-12.

In an engineering department, for example, there are a number of areas that should be audited periodically. These areas include the following:[50]

1. Basis for design (customer contract, marketing specification, sample of final products).
2. Specifications and drawings (requirements as proper approval, authorizations for use in specific applications, and control of required changes).
3. Design analysis (structural, thermal, fluid flow, etc. Check relevant methods and records as well as computer programs used in design analysis).
4. Test programs (prototype designs. Compare tested designs with the design that is being delivered to the customer).
5. Engineering changes (documentations, supporting analysis, test efforts, instruction manuals, spare parts data, etc.).
6. Control of deviations (check how well the deviation from the design requirements is controlled).

---

[48] Burgess, J. A. Auditing an Engineering Operation. *Mechanical Engineering* (September 1979): 22-25.
[49] Walters, J. E. op. cit.
[50] Burgess, op. cit., pp. 24-25.

Table 11-12. Steps in Conducting Effective Audits.[a]

BASIC STEPS FOR AUDITING	TECHNIQUES
1. Planning and preparation	a. Name of group to be audited. b. Date of audit. c. Brief statement of the scope of the audit. d. Names of audit team members. e. List of applicable requirements (standards, regulations, procedures, etc.).
2. Performance of the audit	a. Request local management to explain what work is performed in group and how it is done; then review actual activities and records to determine if group actually works that way. b. Compare the performance of work and review existing documents and files against existing written policies and procedures. c. Select a contract or project and follow it through all phases to determine if it is being accomplished as required. d. Examine complaints, returned products, or failure data against expected performance norms.
3. Reporting of the results	a. Give purpose and scope of audit. b. Date audit. c. Give names of persons contacted during audit and identify their department or group. d. Give names of audit team members. e. List governing requirements that were investigated during audit (policies, procedures, regulations, etc.) f. Summarily describe results and findings from audit (depending on the complexity or importance of the findings, it may also be appropriate to provide recommendations or suggestions on how the deficiencies noted should be corrected).
4. Follow-up and closing out	a. Group audited should investigate findings and conclusions and develop appropriate plans for corrective action. b. Written response to audit report should be prepared and submitted to engineering or R&D manager (or vice-president) within about 30 days. c. Audit team leader should review the response and verify that corrective action is planned or has been taken on all deficient conditions reported. d. Audit team leader should issue an evaluation report, documenting the acceptability of each proposed corrective action, the timeliness of planned actions, and the items requiring future follow-up.

[a]Adapted from Burgess, J. A. Auditing an Engineering Organization. *Mechanical Engineering* (September 1979): 22-25.

As you can see, measuring and evaluating engineering and R&D efforts is an involved and complex activity. The above discussion has focused on six major types or dimensions of the measurement and evaluation process: The individual the group, the project, the product, the engineering or R&D organization as a whole, and the engineering and R&D management functions. The complexity of the measurement, evaluation, and control function calls for considerable skills in understanding this task. How to develop your skills in this area will be discussed in the balance of this chapter.

GUIDELINES FOR DEVELOPING YOUR CONTROL AND EVALUATION SKILLS

Building an effective control system is a crucial aspect of your management task. The importance of developing your skills in this area is, therefore, profound. While there is no cookbook or universally applicable formula for doing this, several guidelines are presented in Table 11-13 and should be enormously useful for developing your skills in this area.

Understand The Causes Of Managerial Failure In Measurement And Control

An understanding of the causes of managerial failure in measuring results can help you identify the ingredients of success in this endeavor. Causes for failure in measurement and control include the following:[51]

1. Failure to establish measurable goals and objectives in advance.
2. Establishment of complicated measuring and rating systems. Standards of measurement must have an organizationwide commonality of application that must be enforced. There is no such thing as an "average" employee

Table 11-13. Guidelines for Developing Your Control and Evaluation Skills.

1. Understand the causes of managerial failure in measurement and control.
2. Learn and apply the characteristics of effective control systems.
3. Avoid overcontrol.
4. Control "by exception."
5. Understand the human aspects of managerial controls.
6. Learn how to deal with resistance to change.
7. Follow effective guidelines for administering control systems.
8. Design control systems to fit professionals.
9. Use tested techniques for evaluating group performance.
10. Use the five golden rules on how to make controls work for you.

[51] McCarthy, John J. "Why Managers Fail—and What To Do About It." New York: McGraw-Hill, 1978, pp. 257-265.

or an "average" group. Individuals should be rated against the position requirements, not against other people.

3. Rigidity in measuring. Rigidity can cause hard feelings and make the control and evaluation program flounder and fail to produce results.

4. A negative attitude toward control and performance appraisal. Although managers know that they get results only through the efforts of the individuals working for them, many managers dread that time of the year when they must sit down with each employee and discuss the employee's performance. If you do not like something, you will not be good at it.

5. "Let the training experts handle it." This describes the reaction of managers who do not take responsibility for training subordinates and, conveniently, pass the buck to the training department.

6. Inappropriate feedback. Some managers hate to keep records and regard them as more paperwork. Therefore, they fail to feed back the results of their measurements into revised planning, organizing, and integrating activities. While we can only speculate on the future, we can learn from the past. We will learn little, however, if we rely only on memory.

Learn And Apply The Characteristics Of Effective Control Systems

Since the characteristics of effective control systems have already been discussed in detail earlier in this chapter, they will not be repeated here. It is crucial for developing your control and evaluation skills to review these characteristics and take them into account while designing control systems.

Avoid Overcontrol

Excessive controls create resentment on the part of subordinates, who feel they are being checked on too frequently. This might have dysfunctional consequences in terms of satisfaction and morale.

Control "By Exception"

Management by exception is a system of identification and communication that signals the manager when his attention is needed; conversely, it remains silent when his attention is not required. It allows the manager to concentrate his time and efforts on important problems or opportunities that require his attention. In a sense, it involves delegation of authority as well as controlling. It is a valuable concept that you should understand and apply.

Understand The Human Aspects Of Managerial Controls

People are motivated to satisfy their needs. Individuals or groups can respond to a particular set of controls in three basic ways. They might respond positively if they feel that the goals and plans are appropriate, relevant, or that they may bring rewards. A passive response can be elicited if the individual recognizes the objective of controls but is personally indifferent about the actual or desired results. The third possible response can be a negative one; the individual or group actively resists the control process.

To avoid misusing controls or designing ineffective controls, you must keep in mind these behavioral aspects of control systems. Remember, it is most frequently people whose behavior will be subjected to controls, and managerial controls, in such situations, will be a waste of effort unless they cause people to alter their behavior.

Learn How To Deal With Resistance To Change

It is paradoxical that individuals desire controls but also seek to avoid them. While employees generally like to know where they stand and what they are expected to do, it is also human nature to resist, in varying degrees, guidelines that act as constraints on behavior. In this sense, employees respond negatively to control systems. The negative responses to control can be reduced in such ways as allowing employees' participation in setting up controls, relating controls to accepted and meaningful goals, and employing constructive ways to deal with conflict.

Follow Effective Guidelines For Administering Control Systems

It is not enough for the control system to be technically sound; it must be properly administered. Keep in mind the following four guidelines for effective control administration:[52]

1. *Communicate:* Communicate and discuss with your subordinates the goals and objectives of the unit or department and their individual goals, and gain the highest possible degree of commitment from them to those goals.

2. *Educate:* Educate your subordinates with respect to the purpose of control in terms of how it helps to accomplish overall departmental goals, and also in terms of how it affects the individual. The control system should not be viewed as a tool for catching and disciplining a subordinate who made a mistake, but rather as a tool to help the individual perform at his full level of capability.

3. *Support:* Establish a climate of help and support in which your subordinates are convinced that you are truly concerned about helping them to do the best job possible. Remember, your actions, in this respect, speak louder than your words!

4. *Review:* Review continually with the individual and the total group the status of achievement and progress toward objectives. This includes getting their

---

[52] Scanlan, op. cit., pp. 39-44.

ideas as to the problems and difficulties being encountered, and jointly developing plans for action.

Design Control Systems To Fit Professionals

There is considerable research evidence suggesting that the professional pattern of colleagual control is inconsistent or incompatible with the bureaucratic pattern of hierarchical control. Given the difference between engineers and scientists as professionals, as noted earlier in this chapter, their role expectations, orientations, and need systems must be kept in mind in designing control systems.[53]

For example, procedures, as viewed by scientists, are merely means to an end which when proven ineffective are ignored or discarded. The bureaucracy, however, superimposes its own rules on the professional scientist which constrain his behavior in various ways and, specifically, constrain his choice of means. This can lead to conflicts and tensions in the scientist-organization relationship.

It follows that there is a need for a professional type of control which is an accommodation between the scientist's need for the colleagual pattern of control and the organization's need for the pattern of subordinate control.[54] Control mechanisms (project evaluations, research proposals, etc.), for example, should be designed in such a way that decisions are made on the basis of both professional as well as administrative considerations. Long-range planning, encouraging scientists' participation in the choice and evaluation of professional work, and providing overall direction and coordination with the primary goals of the organization are all appropriate mechanisms for controlling scientists' activities and performance in organizations.

Use Tested Techniques For Evaluating Group Performance

Several techniques for effective evaluation and measurement of engineering and research performance are already scattered throughout this chapter. Here are some more practical techniques:

1. Develop useful measures of individual and group performance based on the principlal "product" of the group—as discussed earlier.
2. Be persistent in measuring group performance—on schedule.
3. Rate the performance of your staff as frequently as possible (at least once a year). Make your expectations known to them; tell them when they excel, where they can improve.
4. Have your assistants rate themselves and their subordinates.

---

[53] Badawy, M. K. Understanding the Role Orientations of Scientists and Engineers. *Personnel Journal*, 50, 6 (June 1971): 449-455.
[54] Badawy, Bureaucracy in Research, op. cit., p. 131.

5. Keep accurate records of group and individual performance. Put someone in the group in charge of these records, and have these records available for use by your superiors should they want a quick review of your group's accomplishments.

6. Never compromise your standards for requiring outstanding performance from your group. Reasonably high standards will increase the opportunities for greater achievements by your group, and enhance your own chances for outstanding success as a technical manager.

7. Choose a control system that fits your managerial style. The style will be effective when you are most comfortable with it (it also should fit the nature of your subordinates' backgrounds and qualifications, your superior's managerial style, and the task to be accomplished). In short, if you do not believe in a participative management style (subordinates' participation in decision-making), for example, do not go around preaching it!

Use The Five Golden Rules On How To Make Controls Work For You

A few hints are still left. Here are some more pointers that actually work[55]

1. It is better to impose slight overcontrol than to lose control.

Remember: The ultimate penalty for failure to install and consistently enforce controls is failure to achieve objectives—and, consequently, failure to achieve tenure!

2. It is easier to remove controls (or ease them) than it is to install them.

Remember: Strong initial control will assert your management prerogatives, and you will be respected for it. Subsequent loosening will be interpreted as a gesture of faith in and respect for your subordinates. "After all," they will say, "we are capable and he recognized it."

3. The shorter the control cycle, the more effective the results.

The way to do this is through segmenting the control cycle, using program phase control, "milestones," network analysis, and other useful tools for monitoring program progress. Make sure that individuals, not departments, are identified and accountable.

4. The closer that accountability approaches the doer, the better (i.e., the more effective) will be overall performance.

Remember also that inspection of one's performance by one's peers is one of the most effective prods to productivity that there is. In fact, it is the only effective guarantee of peer surveillance than a firmwide reporting system which strips away the possibility of concealment of one's performance. An awareness that your performance will be visible to your peers and superiors ensures either and acceptable level of performance or the individual's termination.

---

[55] Sloma, op. cit., pp. 29, 31, 33, 39, 40, and 75.

5. Management control is like vitamins: You need a fresh dose every day to stay healthy; they are not supplied automatically.

Every individual is subject to the principle of diminishing response to a constant stimulus. Inescapably, in the absence of new stimuli, whether from external or internal (self-starting) sources, each individual becomes a little more lax, a little less disciplined, a little more out of control. You, as a manager, are the inevitable source of organization (your unit) stimuli. The pace you set, the example you show, the communication you transmit will reveal the level of control your subordinates can anticipate. Indeed, they will indicate whether any level of effective control will be sustained. The organization can no more store up a "supply" of management control than a human being can store up a supply of vitamins.

The vigor of management control is lessened with each and every one of the hundreds of assaults made on it daily, on the order of: "Can't we skip filling out this form just this once?" Or, "Aw, nobody's looked at these weight receipts for months. Let's skip it. I know you're in a hurry." As a manager, only you can replenish the supply of management control, and the only way you can do it is by your actions.

SUMMARY

Many managers do not understand the meaning of control as a managerial function. They fail to differentiate between control and other managerial activities such as measurement, evaluation, planning, and performance appraisal. Control is a process by which managers measure and evaluate current performance against preestablished standards and take the necessary corrective action to ensure that objectives will be achieved. Controlling is a significant aspect of your managerial task and is closely interrelated with the other managerial functions: planning, organizing, and directing.

In this chapter, principles and techniques of installing an operationally functioning control system have been discussed. The unique problems of designing effective systems for measuring and evaluating engineering and R&D operations have been analyzed. Since developing your control and evaluation skills is crucial for effective managerial performance, several mechanisms to help you in this respect have been presented.

This chapter concludes our discussion of the three functional administrative skills you must develop for managerial competency: organizational design skills, planning and decision-making skills, and control and evaluation skills. Some final thoughts along with practical tips for succeeding in management are presented in Chapter 12.

VIII
WHERE TO GO
FROM HERE

12
Managerial Skills: Some Final Words

In this concluding part of the book, we have two chapters. This chapter gives an overview of the entire book and presents practical tips for success in management. Chapter 13 will provide you with an extensive collection of references and bibliographical material to guide you through the vastly scattered literature and help you build and expand on the foundation developed in this book.

So, here it is! That magic formula that will "guarantee" you success in management! Despite the absurdity of that claim, there is no doubt in my mind that following the approach described in this book and using the techniques presented — tempered with good judgment and the practice of effective self and job management — will result in superior managerial competence and greater overall organizational performance.

Remember, it is one thing to make it in management, but it is quite another to achieve real success. One of the chief reasons is that few of us can even define the word in the only way that matters — in terms of ourselves. In this sense, no universally acceptable definition is possible because we are not a mass or even a category. We are individuals! So what constitutes success for you may be failure for another individual. The point remains, however, that in order to succeed in management, you must demonstrate some competence based on solid knowledge, sharp skills, and appropriate attitudes. This is where this book can help you.

As noted in Chapter 1, this book is based on five major premises: managers are made; there are no poor engineers or scientists — only poor managers; management is both an applied social science and an art; the only way to learn is by practicing; and, finally, the primary problems of engineering and R&D management are not technical — they are human.

I trust you have, by now, been able to understand, relate to, and appreciate these premises whose accuracy has been demonstrated throughout the book. We should conclude with the same theme we started with — that is, that the process of managing requires the performance of several functions through the possession of a set of professional skills acquired through the demonstration of an integrated set of ingredients of managerial competency. Helping you understand this process and develop or improve your functional management skills has been the prime purpose of this volume.

Another theme that has been dominant in my discussion is the fact that styles of management are as diverse as the individuals who apply them. You should never lose sight of the simple fact that you, as a manager, should perform your role in the style that is most comfortable for you, so long as it proves effective.

There is no "best" style. Not for everyone. Best for one manager may not even be possible for another. But selection of the style that is most comfortable is no snap; it requires a preliminary step on the part of the individual manager. A difficult — even painful — step: You must know yourself! This is precisely why three levels or types of managerial skill development were presented in Chapter 7: self-management, job management, and career management.

With all this in mind, the inescapable conclusion is that the routes to the executive suite are individual — they are not universally applicable. In this book, I have identified a number of these routes. This is the reason a major section of most chapters was addressed to a discussion of how to develop your managerial skills in each functional management area. As a starting point — and based on a keen understanding of the concepts, foundations, and techniques discussed throughout the volume — why not try some of these mechanisms on for size? They might give you a head start along the route to making it in management.

To put all the pieces together, whether you are a technical manager or manager-to-be or a student of technical management, here is a summary of what you will need to succeed in management:

1. Learn and understand the skills of management and the ingredients necessary for managerial competence (Chapter 1).
2. Find out the causes of managerial failure and how to deal with them (Chapter 2).
3. As a technologist, know yourself and know whether you really want to switch to management, and understand the "real" reasons for this move (Chapter 3).
4. As a manager, understand what management can do to help technologists make a smooth transition to management and what adjustments are necessary during career transition (Chapter 4).
5. As a technologist, learn the processes of career planning, life planning, and life-style management (Chapter 5).
6. Learn the alternate paths for developing your management knowledge and skills, including whether going for a graduate degree in management is feasible. Then make an informed decision in selecting the routes that fit you (Chapter 6).
7. Develop a solid understanding of what technical managers really do and of the nature of their diverse roles, tasks, and responsibilities (Chapter 7).

8. Acquire (or develop) the functional skills of management:
   a. Building (or modifying) a viable organizational structure (Chapters 8 and 9).
   b. Managerial planning, problem-solving and decision-making (Chapter 10).
   c. Measuring, evaluating, and controlling engineering and R&D activities (Chapter 11).
9. Follow up with your reading and self-development activities. Keep up with the dynamic and diverse literature on technical management (Chapter 13).

As discussed in the practical framework developed in Chapter 1 and again throughout this book, effective managers perform two types of activities:

1. Functional activities (planning, organizing, and controlling) whose performance requires administrative and technical skills.
2. Direction of people (motivation, communication, leadership, performance appraisal, conflict management, and handling of corporate power, games, and politics). For effective performance of these activities, the manager must develop his behavioral and interpersonal skills.

The scope of this book, as you know, has focused primarily on the functional and administrative aspects of management. Development of the behavioral and interpersonal skills necessary for success in management — the managerial function of handling people — will, therefore, be the subject of a forthcoming volume within this book series.

You now have a primer of principles, foundations, and techniques to get you on the road to management or to help you improve and upgrade your management knowledge and skills. I trust this primer is in good hands. The responsibility for intelligent use of these foundations and techniques is only yours. You will want to add a few of your own — and maybe strike a few of mine — as you go along. In short, as a manager, you must do what you are paid to do — manage. And this volume I trust, will show you how!

13
The Technical Manager's Bookshelf

Now that you have finished reading this book, I hope you do not think that you know all there is to know about technical management. As with any other field, learning about new management concepts and techniques is virtually limitless. In terms of developing your management knowledge and skills, this book, in fact, is simply a beginning. You must dig deeply into the vast literature in this area, and this chapter will provide you with a handy tool to do just that.

Basically, this chapter is an extensive bibliography on the subject areas covered in this book — the functional and administrative aspects of your job. In view of the tons of scattered material available on the subject, compiling a good selected list would be impossible without employing some criteria for selection. The criteria used here include the following:

1. Quality in terms of content, importance, and relevance of material cited.
2. Quantity: for practical purposes, an average of about 25 citations per chapter was considered reasonable (a total of 335 references).
3. Currency: This list reflects the latest material available to the author at the time of this writing. Most references were published within the last 5 years.
4. A balance was maintained between academic (theoretical) and nonacademic (practical) contributions with a tendency to lean strongly toward the latter type. This, of course, is in line with the basic orientation of the book.
5. A reasonable mix between books and articles in professional journals was maintained.

This chapter is organized into two parts. First is a list of books that, for the most part, deal with several of the topics discussed in this volume. Because the material in these books normally deals with more than one chapter in this volume, including them into a separate part was feasible to avoid confusing multiple references. The second part is an extensive list of articles appearing in relevant periodicals and professional journals. For your convenience, these items are grouped together for each chapter.

This bibliography does not duplicate the references in the foregoing chapters. While those references show sources of some of the material in this book, bibliographical citations are simply for your own future reading.

REFERENCES

BOOKS

Allison, David, "The R&D Game: Technical Men, Technical Managers and Research Productivity." Cambridge: MIT Press, 1969.

Archibald, Russell D. "Managing High-Technology Programs and Projects." New York: Wiley, 1976.

Blanchard, Benjamin S. "Engineering Organization and Management." Englewood Cliffs: Prentice-Hall, 1976.

Bolles, Richard N. "What Color is Your Parachute? A Practical Manual For Job Hunters and Career Changes," Revised Edition. Berkeley: Ten Speed Press, 1975.

Bright, James R. "Research, Development and Technological Innovation." Homewood: Irwin, 1964.

Cetron, Marvin J., and Goldbar, J. "The Science and Managing Organized Technology." New York: Gordon & Breach, 1970.

Cronstdedt, Val. "Engineering Management and Administration." New York: McGraw-Hill, 1961.

Dean, Burton V. "Operations Research for R&D." New York: Wiley, 1963.

Dean, Burton V. "Evaluating, Selecting and Controlling R&D Projects." New York: American Management Association (Research Study #89), 1968.

Drucker, Peter F. "The Practice of Management." New York: Harper & Row, 1954.

Drucker, Peter F. "Management Tasks, Responsibilities, Practices." New York: Harper & Row, 1973.

Farkas, Lucien L. "Management of Technical Field Operations." New York: McGraw-Hill, 1970.

Francis, Philip H. "Principles of R&D Management." New York: AMACOM, 1977.

Fuller, Dan. "Organizing, Planning, and Scheduling of Engineering and Other Operations." Boston: Industrial Education Institute, 1969.

Gee, Edwin A., and Tyler, Chaplin. "Managing Innovation." New York: Wiley, 1976.

Gerstenfeld, Arthur. "Effective Management of Research and Development." Reading: Addison-Wesley, 1970.

Hall, Douglas T. "Careers in Organizations." Pacific Palisades: Goodyear Publishing, 1976.

Heyel, Carl (Ed.). "Handbook of Industrial Research Management," Second Edition. New York: Van Nostrand Reinhold, 1968.

Hicks, Tyler Gregory. "Successful Engineering Management." New York: McGraw-Hill, 1965.

Homer, R. M., and Orth, D. C. "Managers and Scientists." Cambridge: Harvard University Press, 1963.

Jennings, Eugene E. "Routes to the Executive Suite." New York: McGraw-Hill, 1971.

Karger, Delmar, and Murdick, Robert A. "Managing Engineering and Research." New York: Industrial Press, 1969.

Kast, Fremont, and Rossenzuner'y, James. "Science Technology and Management." New York: McGraw-Hill, 1963.

Kaufman, Harold G. (Ed.). "Career Management: A Guide to Combating Obsolescense." New York: IEEE Press, 1975.

Kerzner, Harold. "Project Management: A Systems Approach to Planning, Scheduling, and Controlling." New York: Van Nostrand Reinhold, 1979.

Koontz, Harold, O'Donnell, Cyril, and Weihrich, Neinz. "Management," Seventh Edition. New York: McGraw-Hill, 1980.

Martin, Charles C. "Project Management: How to Make It Work." New York: AMACOM, 1976.

McCarthy, John J. "Why Managers Fail . . . and What To Do About It," Second Edition. New York: McGraw-Hill, 1978.

Morton, Jack A. "Organizing for Innovation: A Systems Approach to Technical Management." New York: McGraw-Hill, 1971.

Odiorne, George S. "Management by Objectives — A System of Managerial Leadership." New York: Pitman, 1965.

Orth, C. D., Bailey, J. C., and Wolek, F. W. "Administering Research and Development: The Behavior of Scientists and Engineers in Organizations." Homewood: Irwin, 1964.

Pascarella, Perry. "Industry Week's Guide to Tomorrow's Executive: Humanagement in the Future Corporation." New York: Van Nostrand Reinhold, 1981.

Pelz, D. C., and Andrews, F. M. "Scientists in Organizations." Ann Arbor: Institute for Social Research, University of Michigan, 1976.

Popper, Herbert. "Modern Technical Management Techniques for Engineers in Management and for Those Who Want to Get There." New York: McGraw-Hill, 1971.

Reeves, E. Duer. "Management of Industrial Research." New York: Van Nostrand Reinhold, 1967.

Roman, Daniel E. "Science, Technology and Innovation: A Systems Approach." Columbus: Grid Publishing, 1980.

Silverman, Melvin. "The Technical Program: Manager's Guide to Survival." New York: Wiley, 1967.

Steele, Lowell D. "Innovation in Big Business." New York: Elsevier, 1975.

Twiss, Bryan C. "Managing Technological Innovation." London: Longman, 1974.

Walters, J. E. "Research Management: Principles and Practice." Washington, D.C.: Macmillan, 1965.

Webber, Ross A. "Management: Basic Elements of Managing Organizations." Homewood: Irwin, 1975.

ARTICLES

Chapter 1

Baillie, Allan S. Management of Risk and Uncertainty. *Research Management,* **XXIII,** 2 (March 1980): 20-25.

Bartholome, Fernando, and Evans, Paul A. Lee, Must Success Cost So Much? *Harvard Business Review,* 58 2 (March-April 1980): 137-149.

Boettinger, Henry M. Is Management Really an Out? *Harvard Business Review,* 53 (January-February 1975): 54-64.

Burnet, Don. Inner Management — Swamp Style. *Journal of the Society of Research Administrators,* 11, 3 (Winter 1980): 47-53.

Carroll, Archie B., Paving the Rocky Road to Managerial Success. *Supervisory Management,* 24, 3 (March 1979): 9-13.

Drucker, Peter F. New Templates for Today's Organization. *Harvard Business Review,* 52 (January-February, 1974): 45-53.

Gordon, Paul J. Management Territory: By Their Buzz Words Shall Ye Know Them. *Business Horizons,* 22, 1 (February 1979): 57-59.

Hunsicker, Frank R. What Successful Managers Say About Their Skills. *Personnel Journal,* 57, 11 (November 1978): 618-621.

Likert, Rensis. Management Styles and the Human Component. *Management Review,* 66, 10 (October 1977): 23-28.

McCaskey, Michael B. The Management of Ambiguity. *Organizational Dynamics,* 7, 4 (Spring 1979): 30-48.

Odiorne, George S. Executives Under Siege: Strategy for Survival. *Management Reivew,* 67, 4 (April 1978): 7-12.

Pinto, J. J. The Evolution of Engineering Management. *IEEE Transactions on Engineering Management,* EM-17, 1, (February 1970): 48-50.

Putting Excellence into Management. *Business Week* (July 21, 1980): 196-205.

Steiner, G. A., and Vance, J. A. Managing the Commercial-Technical Enterprise. *IEEE Transactions on Engineering Management,* EM-18 (August 1971): 109-114.

This, Leslie E. Critical Issues Confronting Managers in the '80's. *Training and Development Journal,* 34, 1 (January 1980): 14-18.

Zemke, Ron. Is There One Best Way to Manage? Yes, No, and Maybe, Say 30 Years of Research. *Training,* 15, 4 (April 1978): 25-27.

Zemke, Ron. What Are High-Achieving Managers Really Like? *Training,* 16, 2 (February 1979): 35-36.

Chapter 2

Fraenkel, Stephen J. How Not to Succeed as an R&D Manager. *Research Management,* 23, 3 (May 1980): 35-37.

Jewkes, Gary, Thompson, Paul, and Dalton, Gene. How to Stifle a Technical Organization in Ten Easy Steps. *Research Management,* 22, 1 (January 1979): 12-16.

Madison, Dan L., Allen, Robert W, Porter, Lyman W., Renwick, Patricia, and Mays, Bronston, W. Organizational Politics: An Exploration of Managers' Perceptions. *Human Relations,* 33, 2 (February 1980): 79-101.

Niremberg, John. Managing Failure. *Supervisory Management,* 24, 6 (June 1979): 17-22.

Peters, T. J. Leadership: Sad Facts and Silver Linings. *Harvard Business Review,* 57 (November 1979): 164-172.

Skinner, Wickham, and Sasser, W. Earl. Managers with Impact: Versatile and Inconsistent. *Harvard Business Review,* 55, 6 (November-December 1977): 140-148.

Turmail, Richard L. What Ails Electronics Management. *Electronic Design* (July 19, 1973): 58-62.

Webber, Ross A. Managers and Heroes: How Maturity Levels Influence Managerial Values. *Management Review,* 69, 5 (May 1980): 43-46.

Chapter 3

Badawy, M. K. The Myth of the Professional Employee. *Personnel Journal,* 52, 1 (January 1973): 41-45.

Badawy, M.K. Bureaucracy in Research: A Study of Role Conflict of Scientists. *Human Organization,* 32, 3 (Summer 1973): 123-133.

Balderston, Jack. Do You Really Want to Be a Manager? *Journal of the Society of Research Administrators*, 9, 4 (Spring 1978).

Begosh, Donald G. So You Want to Be a Supervisor. *Supervisory Management*, 23, 2 (February 1978): 2-10.

Bronikowski, Ray J. Down-to-Earth Advice for the New Manager. *Machine Design*, 51, 10 (May 10, 1979): 56-59.

D'Onbeloff, Alexander. Let the Engineers Run the Company. *Electronic Design* (May 10, 1974): 102-106.

Gautshi, T. G. Who Should Switch to Management. *Design News* (July 18, 1977): 131-132.

Gergen, K. Multiple Identity. *Psychology Today* (May 1972): 31-35, 64-66.

Greenwald, Howard P. Scientists and the Need to Manage. *Industrial Relations*, 17, 2 (May 1978): 156-167.

Hall, Douglas T., and Lawler, Edward E., III. Unused Potential in Research and Development Organizations. *Research Management*, 12 (1969): 339-354.

Harrison, Frank. Goal Orientations of Managers and Scientists: An Illusory Dichotomy. *IEEE Transactions on Engineering Management*, EM-27, 3 (August 1980): 74-78.

Kacaoglu, Dundar, F. Engineering Management: An Emerging Discipline. *Professional Engineering*, 49, 4 (April 1979): 30-31.

Kanter, R. Power Games in the Corporation. *Psychology Today* (July 1977): 48-53, 92.

Korda, Michael. The Psychology of Power: How to Play the Corporate Power Game. *MBA* (September 1975): 23-28, 42.

Lewis, Robert. New Dimensions for Staff Talents Turning Engineers into Managers. *Personnel*, 49, 2 (March-April 1972): 53-59.

McClelland, David, and Bernhaion, D. Power-Driven Managers: Good Guys Make Bum Bosses. *Psychology Today* (December 1975): 69-70.

Menzies, Hugh D. The Ten Toughest Bosses. *Fortune* (April 21, 1980): 62-72.

Munson, J. M., and Posner, B. Z. The Values of Engineers and Managing Engineers. *IEEE Transactions on Engineering Management*, EM-26, 4 (November 1979): 94-100.

Storey, Walter D. Which Way: Manager-Directed or Person-Centered Career Pathing. *Training and Development Journal*, 32, 1 (January 1978): 10-14.

Thompson, Harvey A., and Walters, James A. Taking Over the New Job: Breaking Through Versus Breaking In. *SAM Advance Management Journal*, 44, 2 (Spring 1979): 4-16.

Chapter 4

Alpander, Guvenc G. Training First-Line Supervisors to Criticize Constructively. *Personnel Journal*, 59, 3 (March 1980): 216-221.

Badawy, M. K. Industrial Scientists and Engineers: Motivational Style Differences. *California Management Review*, 14, 1 (Fall 1971): 11-16.

Badawy, M. K. Easing the Switch from Engineer to Manager. *Machine Design*, (May 15, 1975): 66-68.

Bray, Douglas W., and Grant, Donald L. The Assessment Center in the Measurement of Potential for Business Management. *Psychological Monographs*, 80, 17 (1966) (Whole No. 625): 2.

Cohen, S. L. Bottom Line on Assessment Center Techology. *Personnel Administrator*, 25 (February 1980): 50-55.

Dalton, Gene W., and Thompson, Paul H. Accelerating Obsolescense of Older Engineers. *Harvard Business Review*, 49, 8 (September-October 1971): 57-67.

Fitzgerald, T. H., and Carlson, H. C. Management Potential: Early Recognition and Development. *California Management Review*, IV, 2 (Winter 1971): 18-23.

Gorb, Peter. Management Development for the Small Firm. *Personnel Management*, 10, 1 (January 1978): 24-27.

Guay, C. G., and Waers, J. A. Start with Results: A Bottom-Line Strategy for Management Development. *Management Review*, 69 (February 1980): 25-28.

Hart, G. L. Workshop Approach to Improving Managerial Performance. *Research Management*, 20, 5 (September 1977): 16-20.

Krondrasuk, J. Best Method to Train Managers. *Training and Development Journal*, 33 (August 1979): 46-48.

McNamara, C. P. Management Productivity: How to Uncover a Hidden Corporate Asset. *Management Review*, 68 (December 1979): 20-23.

Moody, D. R. Responsibility of Management in the World of Creativity. ASME Paper No. 79-WA/Mgt-5, December 1979.

Parker, T. C. Assessment Centers: A Statistical Study. *Personnel Administrator*, 25 (February 1980): 65-67.

Phare, G. R. Planning for Management Continuity. *Managerial Planning*, 218 (Spring 1979): 39-40.

Phillips, Jack. Promote Yourself. *Manage*, 32, 2 (April 1980): 2-6.

Reid, J. N. The Managerial Growth Selector. *Training and Development Journal*, 32, 4 (April 1979): 22-27.

Rosen, Ned, Billings, Robert, and Turney, John. The Emergence and Allocation of Leadership Resources Over Time in a Technical Organization. *Academy of Management Journal*, 19, 2 (March 1976): 165-183.

Sacco, Joseph J. Giving Engineers the Business. *Electronic Design* (November 23, 1973): 121-124.

Sanders, Bruce D. Fine-Tuning Team Spirit. *Supervisory Management*, 25, 6 (June 1980): 26-31.

Sasser, W. Earl, Jr., and Leonard, Frank A. Let First-Level Supervisors Do Their Job. *Harvard Business Review*, 58, 2 (March-April 1980): 113-122.

Smith, Judson. Selecting and Developing Only Your Best Employees. *Training*, 15, 9 (September 1978): 21*ff.*

Stewart, V., and Stewart, A. How to Spot the High Flyers. *Personnel Management*, 11 (Spring 1979): 28-31.

Symons, Anne. Management Succession – A Systematic Approach. *Work and People*, 3, 3/4 (Spring-Summer 1978): 26-30.

Teplitz, Charles J. How the Right Example Can Help the New Recruit Make the Team. *Supervisory Management*, 25, 5 (May 1980): 30-37.

Thompson, Charles W. N. Administrative Experiments: The Experience of Fifty-Eight Engineers and Engineering Managers. *IEEE Transactions on Engineering Management*, EM-21 (May 1974): 42-51.

Turecamo, Dorrine A. Maybe You Don't Want That Promotion. *Manage*, 32, 2 (April 1980): 11-13.

Turner, Carl. Don't Spoon-Feed Your Engineers. *Electronic Design* (October 11, 1973): 108-111.

Wohlking, Wallace. Attitude Change, Behavior Change; The Role of the Training Department. *California Management Review*, 13, 2 (Winter, 1970): 45-50.

Wolff, Michael F. Companies and Careers. *Research Management*, 23, 4 (July 1980): 8-9.

Zerra, Yoram. Sequential Evaluation of Managerial Development. *Business Horizons*, 17, 2 (April 1974): 87-93.

Chapter 5

Archer, Earnest R. Delegation and the "Dirty Hands" Syndrome. *Supervisory Management,* **22,** 11 (November 1977): 31-34.

Badawy, M. K. Should You Take That Promotion to Manager? *Chemical Engineering* (January 1979): 107-108.

Blake, R. R., and Mouton, J. S. Principles of Behavior for Sound Management. *Training and Development Journal,* **33** (October 1979): 26-28.

Brown and Hall. Career Planning for Employee Development: A Primer for Managers. *California Management Review,* **20,** 2 (Winter 1977).

Burack, Elmer H. Why All of the Confusion About Career Planning. *Human Resource Management* (Summer 1977): 21-23.

Burstiner, Irving. Moving Up: Guidelines for the Aspiring Executive. *Personnel Journal* (December 1974): 876-880.

Flowers, Vincent S., and Hughes, Charles L. Choosing a Leadership Style. *Personnel,* **55,** 1 (January-February): 48-59.

Gabarro, John J., and Kotter, John P. Managing Your Boss. *Harvard Business Review,* **58,** 1 (January-February): 92-101.

Gibson, J. E. How to Get Along with Your New Boss. *Machine Design* (August 11, 1977): 108-109.

Hall, Douglas. Relationship of Age and Seniority with Career Variables of Engineers and Scientists. *Journal of Applied Psychology,* **60** (1975): 201-210.

Hanson, M. C. Career Development Responsibilities of Manager. *Personnel Journal,* **56,** 9 (September 1977).

Haynes, Marion, E. Delegation: There's More to It Than Letting Someone Else Do It. *Supervisory Management,* **25,** 1 (January 1980): 9-16.

Hoh, Andrew K. Interpreting Employee Needs: Assuming vs Understanding. *Supervisory Management,* **25,** 4 (April 1980): 29-35.

Iverstine, J., and Kinard, J. A. Technical Manager's Guide to Success. *Chemical Engineering* (July 8, 1974): 65-68.

Jira, Wayne. The Paperwork Problem—How to Control It. *Manage,* **32,** 2 (April 1980): 31-32.

Kleiner, Brian, H. How to Give and Receive Criticism Effectively. *Supervisory Management,* **24,** 3 (March 1979): 37-41.

Kleiner, Brian H. Managing Your Career. *Supervisory Management,* **25,** 3 (March 1980): 17-24.

LeBoeuf, Michael. Managing Time Means Managing Yourself. *Business Horizons,* **23,** 1 (February 1980): 41-47.

Levinson, Harry. On Being a Middle-Aged Manager. *Harvard Business Review,* **47** (1969): 51-60.

McAlindon, Harold R. Toward a More Creative You: Developing the Whole Person. *Supervisory Management,* **25,** 3 (March 1980): 31-37.

McConnell, Charles. How to Form the Delegation Habit. *Supervision,* **XLII,** 5 (May 1980): 3-6.

McFarland, Dalton E. Your Domain and Others. *Supervisory Management,* **25,** 2 (February 1980): 14-22.

Oncken, William, and Wass, Donald. Management Time: Who's Got the Monkey. *Harvard Business Review* (November-December 1974): 75-80.

Pascarella, Perry. What Makes a Good Manager. *Industry Week* (September 1, 1975): 33-42.

Potter, Beverly A. Speaking with Authority: How to Give Directions. *Supervisory Management,* **25,** 3 (March 1980): 2-12.

Schein, Edgar H. The Individual, the Organization and the Career: A Conceptual Scheme. *Journal of Applied Behavioral Science,* 7 (1971): 401-426.

Schleh, Edward C. Handing Off the Subordinates: Delegating for Gain. *Management Review,* 67, 5 (May 1978): 43-47.

Tactzsch, Lyn, and Benson, Eileen. Taking Charge of Yourself and Your Job. *Supervisory Management,* 23, 10 (October 1978): 2-11.

Thompson, Neil H. Career Planning, or "How Do I Get Ahead Around Here?" *Journal of the Research Administration,* 11, 2 (Fall 1979): 13-23.

Tresmer, David. Fear of Success: Popular but Unproven. *Psychology Today* (March 1974): 82-85.

Weber, Ross. The Three Dilemmas of Career Growth. *Master of Business Administration,* 9, 5 (May 1975): 41-44, 48.

Weiss, Alan Jay. How to Influence People Outside Your Control. *Supervisory Management,* 22, 12 (December 1977): 2-9.

Weiss, W. H. Are You Promotable? *Supervision,* XLII, 1: 3-6.

Yeager, Joseph C., and Randsepp, Eugene. Participation: The Crucial Element in Managing Change. *Machine Design,* 50, 14 (June 22, 1978): 66-69.

Chapter 6

Babcock, Daniel L. Engineering Management Education-Status and Goals of University Degree Programs. *IEEE Transactions on Engineering Management,* EM-21, 3 (August 1974): 101-104.

Chrusana, Michael. Engineering Education: Changing to Meet Changing Times. *Design News* (September 9, 1974): 33-37.

Gilmore, Alexander S., Jr. Engineering Investments – An Approach to Management Education for Undergraduate Engineers. *IEEE Transactions on Engineering Management,* EM-23, 4 (November 1976): 157-162.

Goldberg, Edward D., and Gray, Irwin. Management Development for the Practicing Engineer. *Engineering Education* (November 1973): 105-107.

Knowles, Malcolm. Adult Learning: New Strategies Needed. *Engineering Education* (May 1978): 823-825.

Levitt, Theodore. The Managerial Merry-Go-Round. *Harvard Business Review,* 52 (July-August 1974): 120-128.

More Firms Avoid Hiring M.B.A.s Due to High Pay, Other Problems. *The Wall Street Journal* (September 12, 1980): 19.

Mosher, H. A., and Ackoff, A. E. Engineering Education: The Interdependent Roles of University and Industry. *Journal of Engineering Education,* 59, 9 (May 1969): 1022-1024.

Moskal, Brian S. The Great M.B.A. Talent Hunt. *Industry Week* (October 16, 1978): 91-96.

Chapter 7

Fraedel, Steven J. How Not to Succeed as R&D Manager. *Research Management,* XXIII, 3 (May 1980): 35-38.

Frohman, Alan L. The Performance of Innovation: Managerial Roles. *California Management Review,* XXX, 3 (Spring 1978): 5-12.

Holden, G. Fredric. So You're Going to be a Supervisor. *Chemical Engineering* (August 20, 1973): 146-152.

Jackson, Dale. Allocation of Time and Effort for Engineering Managers. SAE Paper No. 790514, April 1979.

Manners, G. E., Jr., and Steger, J. A. Behavioral Specifications of the R&D Management Role. *IEEE Transactions on Engineering Management,* EM-23, 3 (August 1976).

Martin, Jon A. Managing Small R&D Projects – A Learning Model Approach. *Research Management,* XXIII, 3 (May 1980): 15-22.

McKenney, James L., and Keen, Peter G. W. How Managers' Minds Work. *Harvard Business Review,* 52, 3 (May-June 1974): 79-80.

Pfeffer, Jeffrey, and Salancik, Gerald R. Determinants of Supervisory Behavior: A Role Set Analysis. *Human Relations,* 28, 2 (February 1975).

Posner, B. Z., and Munsun, J. M. Importance of Values in Understanding Organizational Behavior. *Human Resource Management,* 18 (Fall 1979): 9-14.

Roberts, Edward B. What Do We Really Know About Managing R&D? *Research Management,* 21, 6 (November 1978): 6-11.

Schrage, Harry. The R&D Entrepreneur: Profile of Success. *Harvard Business Review,* 43 (1965): 56-69.

Slusher, Allen, Van Dyke, Jon, and Rose, Gerald. Technical Competence of Group Leaders, Managerial Role, and Productivity in Engineering Design Groups. *Academy of Management Journal,* 15, 2 (June 1977): 197-204.

Stumpe, Warren R. No Ivory Tower. *Industrial Research Development,* 20, 3 (March 1978): 106-109.

Tohde, Edward F., and Costley, Dan L. Engineering Manager and Organizational Interfaces. *Professional Engineering,* 49, 2 (February 1979): 23-24.

Chapter 8

Bobbitt, H. Randolph, Jr., and Ford, Jeffrey D. Decision-Maker Choice as a Determinant of Organizational Structure. *Academy of Management Review,* 5, 1 (January 1980): 13-25.

Conrath, D. W. The Role of the Informal Organization in Decision-Making on Research and Development. *IEEE Transactions on Engineering Management,* EM-15, 3 (September 1968): 109-119.

Dalton, Dan R., Todor, William D., Spendolini, Michael J., Fielding, Gordon J., Whoelse, Christ, and Porter, Lyman W. Organizational Structure and Performance: A Critical Review. *Academy of Management Review,* 5, 1 (January 1980): 49-65.

Farris, George F. Organizing Your Informal Organization. *Innovation,* 4, 1 (January 1972): 1-10.

Gerwin, D. Relationships Between Structure and Technology at the Organizational and Job Levels. *Journal of Management Studies,* 16 (February 1979): 70-79.

Lovland, Paul. Discussion on Principles of Organizing Applied Research and Development. *Research Policy,* 2, 4 (January 1974): 322-334.

Shepard, H. A. Patterns of Organization for Applied Research and Development. *Journal of Business,* 29, 1 (January 1956): 52-59.

Wallmark, J. T., and Sellerberg, B. Efficiency Vs. Size of Research Teams. *IEEE Transactions on Engineering Management,* EM-13, 3 (September 1966): 137-142.

Chapter 9

Allen, T. J., Lee, D. M. S., and Tushman, M. C. R&D Performance as a Function of Internal Communication, Project Management and Nature of the Work. *IEEE Transactions on Engineering Management,* EM-27, 1 (February 1980): 2-12.

Badawy, M. K. Understanding the Role Orientations of Scientists and Engineers. *Personnel Journal,* 50, 6 (June 1971): 449-455.

Badawy, M. K. Organizational Design for Scientists and Engineers: Some Research Findings and Their Implications for Managers. *IEEE Transactions on Engineering Management,* **EM-22,** 4 (November 1975): 134-138.

Barks, J. V. Keeping Them in Line After You Realign. *Iron Age,* **221** (December 18, 1978): 32-36.

Duncan, R. What Is the Right Organization Structure? Decision Tree Analysis Provides the Answer. *Organizational Dynamics,* **7** (Winter 1979): 59-80.

Flaks, Marion, and Archibald, Russell. The E.E.'s Guide to Project Management — Part III. Network Systems. *The Electronic Engineer* (June 1968).

Gennill, G. A., and Thamain, H. J. The Effectiveness of Different Power Styles of Project Managers in Gaining Project Support. *IEEE Transactions on Engineering Management,* **EM-20,** 2 (May 1973): 38-43.

Gillespie, David F., and Birnbaum, Philip H. Status Concordance, Coordination and Success in Interdisciplinary Research Teams. *Human Relations,* **33,** 1 (January 1980): 41-57.

Grinnell, Sherman K., and Apple, Howard P. When Two Bosses Are Better Than One. *Machine Design* (January 9, 1975).

Gunz, Hugh P. How to Manage/Control Conflicts in Project-Based Organizations. *Research Management,* **22,** 2 (March 1979): 23-29.

Harrison, Frank. The Management of Organizational Conflict. *Michigan Business Review,* **XXXI,** 3 (May 1979): 18-23.

Hines, Willian W., III. Increasing Team Effectiveness. *Training and Development Journal,* **34,** 2 (February 1980): 78-83.

Jermakowicz, W. Organizational Structures in the R&D Sphere. *R&D Management,* **8** (1978, Special Issue): 107-113.

Joyce, W. B. Organizations of Unsuccessful R&D Projects. *IEEE Transactions on Engineering Management,* **EM-18** (May 1971): 57-65.

Kegan, Daniel L., and Rubenstein, Albert H. Trust, Effectiveness and Organizational Development: A Field Study in R&D. *Journal of Applied Behavioral Science,* **12,** 4 (October-December 1976): 498-513.

Leech, D. J., and Smart, P. M. Investing Ideas in an R&D Department. *Mechanical Engineering Science,* **21,** 3 (June 1979): 167-178.

Martindale, Colin. What Makes Creative People Different. *Psychology Today* (July 1975): 45-50.

Martino, Joseph P. Managing Interdisciplinary Research Teams. *IEEE Proceedings of National Aerospace Electronics Conference;* NAECON ' 78. (1978): 280-285.

Mayer, Richard J. Organization Development — The Engineering Side of Behavioral Science. *Management of Personnel Quarterly,* **10,** 3 (Fall 1971): 26-32.

McAlindon, Harold R. Toward a More Creative You: Creating the Ideal Organization. *Supervisory Management,* **25,** 1 (January 1980): 26-34.

Miller, W. B. Fundamentals of Project Management. *Journal of Systems Management,* **29** (November 1978): 22-29.

Owen, Robert P. Charting a Course to Project Success. *Machine Design,* **50,** 27 (November 23, 1978): 74-77.

Pywell, H. E. Engineering Management in a Multiple (Second and Third Level) Matrix Operation. *IEEE Transactions on Engineering Management,* **EM-26,** 3 (August 1979): 51-55.

Rickards, T., and Freedman, B. L. Procedures for Managers in Idea-Deficient Situations: An Examination of Brainstorming Approaches. *Journal of Management Studies,* **15,** 1 (February 1978): 43-55.

Sheridan, J. H. Matrix Maze: Are Two Bosses Better Than One? *Industry Week,* **201** (June 11, 1979): 76-79.

Slocum, John W., Jr., and Sims, Henry P., Jr. A Typology for Integrating Technology, Organization and Job Design. *Human Relations, 33,* 3 (March 1980): 193-212.

Stephenson, R. W., Gantz, B. S., and Erickson, C. E. Development of Organizational Climate Inventories for Use in R&D Organizations. *IEEE Transactions on Engineering Management,* EM-18 (May 1971): 38-50.

Thamhain, Hans J., and Wileman, David L. Diagnosing Conflict Determinants in Project Management. *IEEE Transactions on Engineering Management,* EM-22 (February 1975): 53-64.

Thompson, P. H., and Dalton, A. W. Are R&D Organizations Obsolete? *Harvard Business Review* (November-December 1976): 105-116.

Vasconcellos, E. A Model for Better Understanding of the Matrix Structure. *IEEE Transactions on Engineering Management,* EM-26, 3 (August 1979): 56-64.

Wolff, Michael. Managers at Work — The Joy (and Woe) of Matrix. *Research Management,* XXIII, 2 (March 1980): 10-13.

Wright, N. H., Jr. Matrix Management: A Primer for the Administrative Manager. *Management Review,* 68 (April 1979): 58-61; (May 1979): 59-62; (June 1979): 57-58.

Wymant, Larry. Essential Elements of Project Financing. *Harvard Business Review,* 58, 3 (May-June 1980): 165-174.

Youker, Robert. Organizational Alternatives for Project Managers. *Management Review,* 66, 11 (November 1977): 46-53.

Chapter 10

Baker, N. R. R&D Project Selection Models: An Assessment. *IEEE Transactions on Engineering Management,* EM-21, 4 (November 1974): 165-171.

Balthasar, H. U., Boschi, R. A. A., and Menke, M. M. Calling the Shots in R&D. *Harvard Business Review,* 56, 3 (May-June 1978): 151-160.

Bramson, Robert, and Parlette, Nicholas. Methods of Data Collection for Decision Making. *Personnel Journal,* 57, 5 (May 1978): 243-246.

Brown, Arnold. When the Planner Speaks, Does Management Really Listen? *Management Review,* 67, 11 (November 1978): 58-61.

Burt, John M. Planning and Dynamic Control of Projects Under Uncertainty. *Management Science,* 24, 3 (November 1977): 249-258.

Cecil, Earl A., and Lundgren, Earl F. An Analysis of Individual Decision Making Behavior Using a Laboratory. *Academy of Management Journal,* 18, 3 (September 1975): 600-604.

Clarke, T. E. Decision Making in a Technologically Based Organization: A Literature Survey of Present Practice. *IEEE Transactions on Engineering Management,* EM-21, 1 (February 1974): 9-23.

Cozzolino, John M. A New Method for Risk Analysis. *Sloan Management Review,* 20, 3 (Spring 1979): 53-66.

Dohrmann, R. J. Matching Company R&D Expenditures to Technology Needs. *Research Management,* 21, 6 (November 1978): 17-21.

Duckat, W. Check Your Decision Making Skills. *Supervision,* 41 (February 1979): 3.

English, Joh, and Marchione, Anthony R. It's Not Just the Plan but the Process that Counts. *Pittsburgh Business Review,* 46, 4 (December 1977): 6-11.

Ford, C. H. Manage by Decisions, Not by Objectives. *Business Horizons,* 23 (February 1980): 7-18.

Ford, Charles H. The "Elite" Decision-Makers. Whst Makes Them Tick? *Human Resource Management,* 16, 4 (Winter 1977): 14-20.

Ford, Charles H. Time to Redesign the Decision-Making Process. *Management Review,* 67, 7 (July 1978): 50-53.

Gallagher, Gerald R. Materials Requirements Planning: How to Develop a Realistic Master Schedule. *Management Review,* 69, 4 (April 1980): 18-26.

Grayson, C. J. Management Science and Business Practice. *Harvard Business Review,* 51 (July-August 1973): 41-48.

Greenblatt, B. J., and Hung, J. C. A Structure for Management Decision-Making. *IEEE Transactions on Engineering Management.* EM-17 (November 1970): 145-158.

Hakala, Neil V. Administration of Industrial Technology. *Business Horizons,* 20, 5 (October 1977): 4-10.

Hall, Robert W., and Vollmann, Thomas E. Planning Your Material Requirements. *Harvard Business Review,* 56, 5 (September-October 1978): 105-112.

Hazeltine, B. Decision-Making in the Management of Research and Advanced Development Activities. *IEEE Transactions on Engineering Management,* EM-17, 2 (May 1970): 61-68.

Hershey, Robert. Executive Miscalculation. *Michigan Business Review,* XXXI, 5 (September 1979): 1-7.

Hughes, R. Y. Realistic Look at Decision-Making. *Supervisory Management,* 25 (January 1980): 2-8.

Hunsicker, J. Quincy. The Malaise of Strategic Planning. *Management Review,* 69, 3 (March 1980): 8-14.

Ivancevich, J. M. Analysis of Participation in Decision-Making Among Project Engineers. *Academy of Management Journal,* 22 (June 1979): 253-269.

Kastens, Merritt L. The Why and How of Planning. *Managerial Planning,* 28, 1 (July-August 1979): 33-35.

King, Dennis C., and Beevor, Walter G. Long-Range Thinking. *Personnel Journal,* 57, 9 (September 1978): 504-509.

Knutson, J., and Scotto, M. Developing a Project Plan. *Journal of Systems Management,* 29 (November 1978): 22-29.

Kristy, James E. Managing Risk and Uncertainty. *Management Review,* 67, 9 (September 1978): 15-22.

Lazer, Robert I. The Pros and Cons of Flexible Working Hours in R&D Labs. *Research Management,* XXIII, 1 (January 1980): 19-23.

Lederer, V. Decision Making: Should Employees Get Into the Act? *Administrative Management,* 39 (September 1978): 51-52.

Lenz, R. T. Strategic Capability: A Concept and Framework for Analysis. *Academy of Management Review,* 5, 2 (April 1980): 225-235.

Lewis, A. C., Sadosky, T. J., and Connolly, T. The Effectiveness of Group Brainstorming in Engineering Problem-Solving. *IEEE Transactions on Engineering Management,* EM-22, 3 (August 1975): 119-124.

Lorange, Peter, and Vancil, Richard F. How to Design a Strategic Planning System. *Harvard Business Review,* 54 (September-October 1976): 75-81.

Maher, Michael P., and Rubenstein, Albert H. Factors Affecting Adoption of a Quantitative Method for R&D Project Selections. *Management Science* (Application Series), 21, 2 (October 1974): 119-140.

Malcolm, D., Roseham, J., Clark, C., and Fazan, W. Applications on Technique for Research and Development Program Evaluation. *Operations Research,* 7 (September-October 1959): 646-699.

McCreary, E. How to Grow a Decision Tree. *Think Magazine* (March-April 1967).

Michael, S. R. Control, Contingency and Delegation in Decision-Making. *Training and Development Journal,* 33 (February 1979): 36-42.

Naylor, Thomas H., and Neva, Kristin. The Planning Audit. *Managerial Planning*, **28**, 2 (September-October 1979): 31-37.

Olson, P. D. Overburdened Manager and Decision Making. *Business Horizons*, **22** (October 1979): 28-32.

Oxenfeld, Alfred R. Effective Decision Making for the Business Executive. *Management Review*, **67**, 2 (February 1978): 25-32.

Rosen, Nancy J., and Paperman, Jacob B. How to Use Material Requirements Planning. *Management Review*, **67**, 8 (August 1978): 17-23.

Saunders, George B., and Stanton, John L. Personality as Influencing Factor in Decision Making. *Organizational Behavior and Human Performance*, **15**, 1 (October 1975): 241-257.

Tagiuri, Renato. Planning: Desirable and Undesirable. *Human Resource Management*, **19**, 1 (Spring 1980): 11-14.

Von Bergen, Clarence W., Jr., and Kirk, Raymond J. Groupthink: When Too Many Heads Spoil the Decision. *Management Review*, **67**, 3 (March 1978): 44-49.

White, George R., and Graham, Margaret, B. W. How to Spot a Technological Winner. *Harvard Business Review*, **56**, 2 (March-April 1978): 146-152.

Chapter 11

Aldrich, Carole, and Morton, Thomas E. Optimal Funding Paths for a Class of Risky R&D Projects. *Management Science* (Application Series), **21**, 5 (January 1975): 491-500.

Allan, J., and Rosenberg, R. Formulating Usable Objectives for Manager Performance Appraisal. *Personnel Journal*, **57** (November 1978): 626-629.

Allen, Derek H. Project Evaluation. *ChemTec* (July 1979): 412-417.

Appraising the Performance Appraisal. *Business Week* (May 19, 1980): 153-154.

Augood, D. R. A Review of R&D Evaluation Methods. *IEEE Transactions on Engineering Management*, **EM-20**, 4 (November 1973): 114-120.

Augood, D. R. A New Approach to R&D Evaluation. *IEEE Transactions on Engineering Management*, **EM-22**, 1 (February 1975): 2-9.

Balderston, Jack. Performance Appraisal System. *Journal of the Society of Research Administrators*, **4**, 3 (Winter 1973).

Beer, M., et al. Performance Management System: Research, Design, Introduction and Evaluation. *Personnel Psychology*, **31** (Autumn 1978): 505-535.

Bell, R. R. Evaluating Subordinates: How Subjective Are You? *SAM Advanced Management Journal*, **44** (Winter 1979): 36-44.

Bennett, R., and Langford, V. How to Measure Managers. *Management Today* (December 1979): 62-65.

Berry, S. J. Performance Review: Key to Effective Planning. *Long Range Planning*, **12** (December 1979): 17-21.

Burgess, J. A. Auditing an Engineering Organization. ASME Paper No. 78-WA/Mgt.-7, December 1978.

Burgess, J. A. Auditing an Engineering Organization. *Mechanical Engineering* (September 1979): 22-25.

Caplan, Robert H., and Kinner, Raymond M. The Domain of Management Control. *Michigan Business Review*, **XXX**, 3 (May 1978): 1-9.

Carter, Eugene, E. Project Evaluations and Firm Decisions. *Journal of Management Studies*, **8**, 3 (October 1970): 253-277.

Collier, Arnold. Measuring the Performance of R&D Departments. *Research Management* (March 1977): 30-34.

Cook, D. R. Improving Productivity Through Efficient Engineering Management. *Mechanical Engineering*, **101**, 6 (June 1979): 27-31.

Dailey, R. C. Antecedents of Performance for Scientists and Engineers: A Path Analytic Study. *Review of Business and Economic Research,* 14 (Winter 1978-1979): 37-46.

Danzig, Selig M. What We Need to Know About Performance Appraisals. *Management Review,* 69, 2 (February 1980): 20-25.

Edwards, Shirley A., and McCarrey, Michael W. Measuring the Performance of Researchers. *Research Management* (January 1973): 34-41.

Eilon, S. Some Useful Ratios in Evaluating Performance. *Omega,* 7, 2 (1979): 166-168.

Ewers, Jack. Taking Management's Measure. *Datamation,* 26, 5 (May 1980): 184-195.

Fuller, Don. Rating Engineer Performance. *Machine Design* (August 24, 1978): 88-97.

Gilbert, Tom. Measuring the Potential for Performance Improvement. *Training,* 15, 12 (December 1978): 25-28.

Glass, E. M. Methods of Evaluating R&D Organization. *IEEE Transactions on Engineering Management,* EM-19, 1 (February 1972): 2-11.

Hanks, Nelson L. Employee Performance Appraisal. *Mechanical Engineering* (July 1979) 32-34.

Hensey, Melville D., and Gibble, Kenneth. Improving the Effectiveness of Engineering Organizations. *Issues Engineering Journal* (January 1980): 21-26.

Hoffman, R. R. MJS: Management by Job Standards. *Personnel Journal,* 58 (August 1979): 536-540.

Kerzner, H. Evaluation Techniques in Project Management. *Journal of System Management,* 31 (February 1980): 10-19.

Kushell, R. E. Identifying the Good, the Bad, and the Indifferent. *Supervisory Management,* 24 (April 1979): 2-7.

Litras, T. S. A Practical Application of Peer Evaluation. *Research Management,* XXIII, 2 (March 1980): 13-20.

Lyman, D., et al. For Managers in New Jobs: An Accountability and Appraisal System. *Management Review,* 69 (January 1980): 46-51.

Mason, Richard O., and Swanson, E. Burton. Measurement for Management Decision: A Perspective. *California Management Review,* XXI, 3 (Spring 1979): 70-81.

McFillen, J. M., and Decker, P. G. Building Meaning into Appraisal. *Personnel Administrator,* 23 (June 1978): 75-76.

Mollenhoff, David V. How to Measure Work by Professionals. *Management Review,* 66, 11 (November 1977): 39-45.

Rosenau, Milton D., Jr. Assessing Project Value. *Industrial Research Development,* 20, 5 (May 1978): 129-133.

Sanser, W. I., Jr. Evaluating Employee Performance: Needs, Problems, and Possible Solutions. *Public Personnel Management,* 9 (January 1980): 11-18.

Souder, William E. System for Using R&D Project Evaluation Methods. *Research Management,* 21, 5 (September 1978): 29-37.

Teel, K. S. Self-Appraisal Revisited. *Personnel Journal,* 57 (July 1978): 364-367.

Thompson, Paul H., and Dalton, Gene W. Performance Appraisal: Managers Beware. *Harvard Business Review,* 48, 1 (January-February 1970): 149-157.

Training Managers to Rate Their Employees. *Business Week* (March 17, 1980): 178-183.

Whitley, Richard, and Frost, Penelope. The Measurement of Performance in Research. *Human Relations,* 24, 2 (April 1971): 161-178.

Williamson, D. Primer on Performance Appraisals. *Supervisory Management,* 24 (June 1979): 35-37.

Index